The Market for Retirement Financial Advice

The Market for Retirement Financial Advice

EDITED BY

Olivia S. Mitchell
and Kent Smetters

OXFORD
UNIVERSITY PRESS

OXFORD
UNIVERSITY PRESS

Great Clarendon Street, Oxford OX2 6DP
United Kingdom

Oxford University Press is a department of the University of Oxford.
It furthers the University's objective of excellence in research, scholarship,
and education by publishing worldwide.

Oxford is a registered trade mark of Oxford University Press in the UK
and in certain other countries

© Pension Research Council, The Wharton School, University of Pennsylvania 2013

The moral rights of the author have been asserted

Reprinted 2015

All rights reserved. No part of this publication may be reproduced, stored in
a retrieval system, or transmitted, in any form or by any means, without the
prior permission in writing of Oxford University Press, or as expressly permitted
by law, by licence or under terms agreed with the appropriate reprographics
rights organization. Enquiries concerning reproduction outside the scope of the
above should be sent to the Rights Department, Oxford University Press, at the
address above

You must not circulate this book in any other binding or cover
And you must impose this same condition on any acquirer

British Library Cataloguing in Publication Data
Data available

Library of Congress Cataloging in Publication Data
Data available

ISBN 978-0-19-968377-2

Preface

The long-term shift away from traditional defined benefit pensions toward defined contribution personal accounts requires that people saving for retirement must become more sophisticated than ever before. Yet the landscape for financial advice is changing, with new rules and regulations transforming the financial advice profession. This volume offers new insights into the marketplace for retirement financial advice, seeking to illuminate market and regulatory challenges so as to enhance consumer, plan sponsor, and regulator outcomes. We inform this discussion by exploring what financial advisors do, how they are compensated, how one might measure performance and impact, and how clients can be protected from bad advice and steered toward good advice.

The volume, an invaluable addition to the Pension Research Council/ Oxford University Press series, should interest a wide range of readers including consumers, researchers, and employers seeking to design better retirement plan offerings, and policymakers charged with oversight and enhancement of the financial system.

In the process of preparing this book, many people and institutions played essential roles. My co-editor and Wharton School colleague, Kent Smetters, contributed ideas and suggestions. We thank him, along with our Advisory Board, Senior Partners, and Institutional Members of the Pension Research Council for intellectual and financial sustenance. Additional support was received from the Pension Research Council, the Boettner Center for Pensions and Retirement Research, and the Ralph H. Blanchard Memorial Endowment at the Wharton School of the University of Pennsylvania. We also offer our appreciation to Oxford University Press which hosts the Pension Research Council series of books on retirement security. This manuscript was expertly prepared and carefully edited by Andrew Gallagher and Donna St. Louis.

Our work at the Pension Research Council and the Boettner Center for Pensions and Retirement Security of the Wharton School of the University of Pennsylvania has focused on aspects of pensions and retirement well-being for over half a century. This volume contributes to the fulfillment of our mission, which is to generate research and debate on policy issues affecting pensions and retirement security.

Olivia S. Mitchell
Executive Director, Pension Research Council
Director, Boettner Center for Pensions and Retirement Research
The Wharton School, University of Pennsylvania

Contents

List of Figures ix
List of Tables x
List of Abbreviations xiii
Notes on Contributors xv

1. The Market for Retirement Financial Advice: An Introduction   1
   Olivia S. Mitchell and Kent Smetters

Part I. What Do Financial Advisers Do?

2. The Market for Financial Advisers   13
   John A. Turner and Dana M. Muir

3. Explaining Risk to Clients: An Advisory Perspective   46
   Paula H. Hogan and Frederick H. Miller

4. How Financial Advisers and Defined Contribution Plan Providers Educate Clients and Participants about Social Security   70
   Mathew Greenwald, Andrew G. Biggs, and Lisa Schneider

5. How Important is Asset Allocation to Americans' Financial Retirement Security?   89
   Alicia H. Munnell, Natalia Orlova, and Anthony Webb

6. The Evolution of Workplace Advice   107
   Christopher L. Jones and Jason S. Scott

7. The Role of Guidance in the Annuity Decision-Making Process   125
   Kelli Hueler and Anna Rappaport

Part II. Measuring Performance and Impact

8. Evaluating the Impact of Financial Planners   153
   Cathleen D. Zick and Robert N. Mayer

9. Asking for Help: Survey and Experimental Evidence on
    Financial Advice and Behavior Change   182
    Angela A. Hung and Joanne K. Yoong

10. How to Make the Market for Financial Advice Work   213
    Andreas Hackethal and Roman Inderst

11. Financial Advice: Does It Make a Difference?   229
    Michael Finke

12. When, Why, and How Do Mutual Fund Investors Use
    Financial Advisers?   249
    Sarah A. Holden

Part III. Market and Regulatory Considerations

13. Harmonizing the Regulation of Financial Advisers   275
    Arthur B. Laby

14. Regulating Financial Planners: Assessing the Current System
    and Some Alternatives   305
    Jason Bromberg and Alicia P. Cackley

End Pages   321
Index   325

List of Figures

6.1	Online advice usage	113
6.2	Aggregate usage (online and management)	118
6.3	Net new managed account members	120
6.4	Aggregate usage with defaults	121
7.1	Annuity quotes for a $100,000 deposit over one year	140
8.1	Randomized field experiment to assess the impact of consulting a professional financial planner	159
8.2	Estimated incremental effect of consulting a financial planner on total financial wealth	174
8.3	Estimated incremental effect of consulting a financial planner on proportion of total financial wealth held in stocks	175
8.4	Estimated incremental effect of consulting a financial planner on the number of different types of financial assets held	176
9.1	Survey questions of ALP modules: Panel A. Screen shot of task description: high returns + affirmative decision advice treatment; Panel B. Screen shot of task: rules treatment. Panel C. Screen shot of task: portfolio checkup treatment	196
9.2	Experimental design schematic	199
10.1	Comparison of stated risk preferences and average actual portfolio risk. Panel A: Risk categories for target portfolio risk (Financial Institution 1); Panel B: Risk categories for target portfolio risk (Financial Institution 2)	223
12.1	Majority of mutual fund investors initially seek professional investment advice during their peak earning and saving years	251
12.2	Mutual fund investors and help with asset allocation	254
12.3	Mutual fund investors and help with financial planning	255
12.4	Sources used by mutual fund investors to purchase mutual funds	259
12.5	Nearly half of mutual fund-owning households held shares through multiple sources	260
13.1	Broker-dealers' profit margins from 1975 to 2005	280
14.1	Summary of key statutes and regulations that can apply to financial planners	309
14.2	Differences in the standards of care required of financial planners	311

List of Tables

3.1	The current financial planning mosaic	48
3.2	How it all plays out	64
4.1	Financial advisers' role in advising clients on Social Security	75
4.2	Adviser input on the timing of claiming Social Security benefits	77
4.3	Adviser framing of the decision of when to claim Social Security benefits	79
4.4	Adviser evaluation of Break-Even Analysis	80
4.5	Adviser recommendations on when to claim benefits in different scenarios	81
5.1	Percent of pre-retirement salary required to maintain living standards, 2008	90
5.2	Current law Social Security replacement rates, 2030 and later	91
5.3	Saving rates required for a medium earner to attain an 80 percent replacement rate with a 4 percent rate of return	92
5.4	Saving rate required for a medium earner to attain an 80 percent replacement rate with a starting age for saving of 35, by rate of return	92
5.5	Households falling short of target	96
5.6	Wealth levels by wealth deciles	96
5.7	Amount required as compensation for retaining typical portfolio allocation	98
5.8	Typical and optimal portfolio allocations	99
5.A1	Comparison of workers with all HRS households under age 65	102
6.1	Demographic comparison of online advice users	114
6.2	Demographic comparison of managed account users	117
7.1	Types of retirement guidance or education provided by companies to their employees	129
7.2	Comparison of structural and active guidance in institutional platform delivery models through different channels	132

7.3	Obtaining annuity income through retail purchase, institutional purchase, and/or DB payout	134
7.4	Characteristics of annuity purchasers and what they purchased through different channels	135
7.5	Characteristics of single premium immediate annuities purchased: amounts of income purchased and annuity features chosen	138
8.1	Weighted means and *t*-tests for financial outcome variables	166
8A.1	Weighted means for ordinary least squares regression covariates	167
8.2	Ordinary least squares parameter estimates of total financial wealth	168
8.3	Ordinary least squares parameter estimates of proportion stock equity	169
8.4	Ordinary least squares parameter estimates of the number of asset categories	170
8A.2	Logistic regression parameter estimates of the first stage of the propensity score analysis: dependent variable is 'consults a financial planner'	172
9.1	Summary statistics: American Life Panel (ALP) data	186
9.2	Ordinary least squares estimates of the determinants of the propensity to seek advice	187
9.3	Portfolio allocation patterns of current defined contribution (DC) planholders	188
	Panel A. Portfolio characteristics	188
	Panel B. 'Mistakes' in reported portfolio allocations	188
9.4	Ordinary least squares parameter estimates	190
	Panel A. Empirical determinants of portfolio allocations by DC planholders	190
	Panel B. 'Mistakes' in reported portfolio allocations	190
9.5	Portfolio allocations and financial literacy: ordinary least squares estimates for current DC planholders	192
	Panel A. Reported portfolio allocations and financial literacy (current DC planholders)	192
	Panel B. 'Mistakes' in reported portfolio allocations and financial literacy	192
9.6	Summary statistics on the ALP experimental sample	198
9.7	Determinants of the propensity to seek advice: affirmative decision treatment	200
9.8	Experimental results: comparisons of means	201

9.9	Intent-to-treat effects on portfolio quality: all choice treatments	202
9.10	Portfolio quality, advice, and financial literacy: affirmative decision treatment	205
9.11	Estimates of the average effect of treatment on those treated on portfolio quality and financial literacy: affirmative decision treatment vs. controls	206
10.1	Four possible configurations in the market for financial advice	218
11.1	Household characteristics and retirement planning	232
11.2	Financial planner regressions	236
12.1	Achieving specific financial goals often prompts mutual fund investors to seek professional investment advice	252
12.2	Mutual fund investors and research and investment advice	256
12.3	Investor/adviser split of decision-making	257
12.4	Mutual fund investor head of household characteristics	262
12.5	Variables used in probit regression model	264
12.6	Probability mutual fund investor has ongoing advisory relationship	265
13.1	Financial information for broker-dealers (1969–2010)	297

List of Abbreviations

AICPA	American Institute of Certified Public Accountants
AIME	Average Indexed Monthly Earnings
ALP	American Life Panel
AUM	Assets Under Management
BLP	best linear predictors
BLS	Bureau of Labor Statistics
BMELV	German Ministry of Consumer Affairs
CE	Continuing Education
CFA	Chartered Financial Analyst
CFP	Certified Financial Planner
CFS	Certified Fund Specialist
ChFC	Chartered Financial Consultant
CIC	Chartered Investment Counselor
CIMA	Certified Investment Management Analyst
CLU	Chartered Life Underwriter
CPA	Certified Public Accountant
CRRA	coefficient of relative risk aversion
DB	defined benefit
DC	defined contribution
DOL	Department of Labor
EBRI	Employee Benefit Research Institute
EBSA	Employee Benefits Security Administration
EC	European Commission
ERISA	Employee Retirement Income Security Act
ESOP	Employee Stock Ownership Plan
FINRA	Financial Industry Regulation Authority
FPA	Financial Planning Association
FSA	Financial Services Authority
FSA	Fellow of the Society of Actuaries

FSB	Financial Stability Board
FTC	Federal Trade Commission
GAO	Government Accountability Office
HRS	Health and Retirement Survey
IAA	Investment Adviser Association
ICI	Investment Company Institute
IFIC	Investment Funds Institute of Canada
IPO	Initial Public Offering
IRA	Individual Retirement Account
IRS	Internal Revenue Service
LP	linear probability
MiFID II	markets in financial instruments directive II
NAIFA	National Association of Insurance and Financial Advisors
NASD	National Association of Securities Dealers
NIA	National Institute on Aging
NLSY	National Longitudinal Survey of Youth
NYSE	New York Stock Exchange
OLS	ordinary least squares
OMO	open market option
PACFL	President's Advisory Council on Financial Literacy
PFS	Personal Financial Specialist
PPA	Pension Protection Act
QDIAs	qualified default investment alternatives
RFE	randomized field experiment
RIA	Registered Investment Adviser
RMD	required minimum distribution
SANCO	European Commission Directorate—General Health and Consumers
SCF	Survey of Consumer Finances
SEC	US Securities and Exchange Commission
SRO	self-regulatory organization
SSA	Social Security Administration
TPAS	Pensions Advisory Service
US	United States

Notes on Contributors

Andrew G. Biggs is Resident Scholar at the American Enterprise Institute, where he focuses on Social Security reform, fiscal consolidation, state and local government pensions, public/private compensation comparisons, and financial literacy. Previously, he was the Principal Deputy Commissioner of the Social Security Administration; he also worked on Social Security reform at the National Economic Council and staffed the President's Commission to Strengthen Social Security. He holds a Bachelor's degree from the Queen's University of Belfast, Northern Ireland; Master's degrees from Cambridge University and the University of London; and a Ph.D. from the London School of Economics and Political Science.

Jason Bromberg is Assistant Director of Financial Markets and Community Investment with the U.S. Government Accountability Office (GAO). He has overseen several GAO studies on financial literacy and education, consumer protection, financial regulation, bankruptcy reform, identity theft, and consumer privacy. He received his Bachelor's degree in Philosophy from Vassar College and the Master's degree in Public Policy from Harvard University.

Alicia P. Cackley is Director in the Financial Markets and Community Investment team at the U.S. Government Accountability Office. She manages projects on program evaluation and policy research in consumer protection, housing, and finance issues; her areas include financial literacy, consumer product safety, bankruptcy, and homelessness. She earned her Ph.D. in Economics from the University of Michigan.

Michael Finke is Associate Professor and Director of Ph.D. studies in Personal Financial Planning at Texas Tech University. His research interests focus on financial planning, including household financial decision-making, individual investment performance, the value of financial planning advice, and the importance of contracts among financial service agents. He earned his Ph.D. in Family Resource Management from The Ohio State University and in Finance from the University of Missouri.

Mathew Greenwald is President of Mathew Greenwald & Associates, Inc., a market research company that focuses on retirement matters. He previously worked at the American Council of Life Insurance. He is an elected member of the Market Research Council, and he was nominated by Congress to serve on two National Summits on Retirement Saving. He received his Bachelor's degree from Binghamton University and his M.A., M.Phil., and Ph.D. degrees in Sociology from Rutgers University.

Andreas Hackethal is Professor of Finance at Goethe University Frankfurt, where he is also Dean of the Faculty of Economics and Business Administration. He is a member of the advisory council to the German Financial Supervisory Authority and of the Exchange Experts Commission advising the German Ministry of Finance. He earned his degrees in Business Administration from Goethe University and the University of Iowa.

Paula H. Hogan is the founder of Paula Hogan, a fee-only financial advisory firm (formerly known as Hogan Financial Management) in Milwaukee, Wisconsin. She is a nationally recognized leader in the financial advisory field and her firm has been selected as one of the nation's top advisory firms. She also serves on the advisory boards for Money Quotient and Veritat. She earned her B.A. degree in Economics from Princeton University and an M.S. degree from the Harvard School of Public Health.

Sarah A. Holden is Senior Director of Retirement and Investor Research at the Investment Company Institute (ICI), where she researches the US retirement market, retirement and tax policy, and investor demographics and behavior. She has conducted analysis of 401(k) plan participant activity using data collected in a collaborative effort with the Employee Benefit Research Institute (EBRI), and she also oversees The IRA Investor Database™. Previously, she was a staff economist in the Flow of Funds Section of the Research Division at the Federal Reserve Board. She graduated from Smith College and earned her Ph.D. in Economics from the University of Michigan.

Kelli Hueler is CEO and founder of Hueler Companies, an independent data and research firm providing reporting and systems designed for the annuity and stable value marketplace. Her work focuses on stable value investments and guaranteed investment contracts. She received her Bachelor's degree from St. Olaf College.

Angela A. Hung is Senior Economist at RAND, where she is Director of the Center for Financial and Economic Decision Making, and Associate Director for the RAND Roybal Center on Financial Decisionmaking. Her research examines on how people collect and use financial information; how they match their financial decisions to their interests and goals; conflicts of interest in financial advising; and testing materials for financial statements. Previously, she taught at the H. John Heinz III School of Public Policy and Management at Carnegie Mellon University. She received her Ph.D. in Social Science from the California Institute of Technology.

Roman Inderst is Finance Professor at Goethe University Frankfurt, where his work focuses on corporate finance, banking, competition policy, and information economics. He is a member of the academic advisory board to the German Federal Ministry of Economics and Technology. He received a B.A. in Business Administration from Reutlingen University, a Magister Artium in Sociology from Fernuniversität Hagen, and a Diploma in Economics from Humboldt University of Berlin. His Ph.D. in Economics was earned at the Free University of Berlin, and his Habilitation was conducted under the supervision of Benny Moldovanu at the University of Mannheim.

Christopher L. Jones is Chief Investment Officer and Executive Vice President of investment management for Financial Engines. He leads a team responsible for investment analysis, financial research and development, and portfolio management. Additionally, his group has pioneered the technology for online advice and professional management services. He earned his Master's degrees in Business Technology and Engineering Economic Systems, and his Bachelor's degree in Quantitative Economics, from Stanford University.

Arthur B. Laby is Professor of Law at Rutgers University School of Law in Camden, New Jersey, and former Assistant General Counsel of the US Securities and Exchange Commission in Washington, DC. His interests are securities regulation, business organizations, investment management regulation, and fiduciary law, as well as the regulation of investment advisers and broker-dealers, conflicts of interest, and the fiduciary relationship. He earned his Law degree from Boston University School of Law.

Robert N. Mayer is Professor in the Department of Family and Consumer Studies at the University of Utah, where he focuses on consumer problems and policy, global consumer movements, and currently, retirement planning in the aftermath of the Great Recession and the role of consumer advocates in creating the Consumer Financial Protection Bureau. He received his Bachelor's degree from Columbia University and the Ph.D. in Sociology from the University of California-Berkeley.

Frederick H. Miller has worked in financial services as Management Consultant—in product and business development at Scudder Investments, and now at Sensible Financial, which he founded. His firm is one of the fastest growing registered independent advisory firms. He is a CFPR Certificant and a member of both the National Association of Personal Financial Advisors and the Financial Planning Association. He recently served on the Trends in Financial Planning and Job Analysis Task Forces of the CFPR Board. He earned his A.B., A.M., and Ph.D. degrees in Economics from the University of Chicago.

Olivia S. Mitchell is the International Foundation of Employee Benefit Plans Professor of Insurance/Risk Management and Business Economics/Public Policy at the Wharton School of the University of Pennsylvania. Her main areas of interest are private and public insurance, risk management, public finance, labor markets, compensation, and pensions with both a US and an international focus. She is also the Executive Director of the Pension Research Council and the Director of the Boettner Center on Pensions and Retirement Research at Wharton, Faculty Research Fellow at the National Bureau of Economic Research, and Associate Director of the Financial Literacy Center. She received her B.A. in Economics from Harvard University, and her M.S. and Ph.D. degrees in Economics from the University of Wisconsin-Madison.

Dana M. Muir is Arthur F. Thurnau Professor of Business Law at the Stephen M. Ross School of Business at the University of Michigan. Her research interests focus on fiduciary, remedial, and international issues pertinent to investments, pension plans, and retirement saving plans. She earned her M.B.A. at the University of Detroit and her J.D. from the University of Michigan.

Alicia H. Munnell is the Peter F. Drucker Professor of Management Sciences at Boston College's Carroll School of Management. She also serves as the Director of the Center for Retirement Research at Boston College. Previously, she served on the President's Council of Economic Advisers, was Assistant Secretary of the Treasury for Economic Policy, and co-founded the National Academy of Social Insurance. She earned her B.A. at Wellesley College, she received her M.A. from Boston University, and Ph.D. from Harvard University.

Natalia Orlova is a Research Associate at the Center for Retirement Research at Boston College, where she conducts research on retirement issues. She earned her BA in Mathematics and Economics from Boston University and her M.A. in Economics from the University of San Francisco.

Anna Rappaport is an actuary, consultant, author, and speaker with Anna Rappaport Consulting; her interests focus on the impact of change on retirement systems and workforce issues. Previously, she was at Mercer Consulting. She is an FSA and MAAA, she also chairs the Society of Actuaries Committee on Post-Retirement Needs and Risks, and she has served as President of the Society of Actuaries. She is on the ERISA Advisory Council and serves on the Board of the Women's Institute for a Secure Retirement (WISER), and the Advisory Board of Wharton's Pension Research Council. She received her M.B.A. from the University of Chicago.

Lisa Schneider is Research Director at Greenwald & Associates, where her work focuses on financial services and opinion research. Previously, she was Marketing Coordinator for the American Council of Life Insurers' Membership and Development Department. She received her Bachelor's degree in Sociology from George Washington University.

Jason S. Scott is Managing Director of the Financial Engines Retiree Research Center, where he works on projects to help retirees maximize their standards of living given uncertain investment performance, uncertain longevity, and uncertain health care costs. His research has focused on longevity annuities, efficient retirement spending, investment strategies, and investor behavior. Previously, he directed the research and development group at Financial Engines. He earned his Bachelor's degree in Economics from Texas A&M University and his Ph.D. in Economics from Stanford University.

Kent Smetters is the Boettner Chair Professor at the University of Pennsylvania's Wharton School and Faculty Research Fellow at the National Bureau of Economic Research. His research examines incomplete markets, investment risk management, and the interaction of risk management and public policy. Previously, he worked at the Congressional Budget Office and served as Economics Policy Coordinator for the US Treasury. He received his Bachelor's degrees in Economics and Computer Science from The Ohio State University and his Ph.D. in Economics from Harvard University.

John A. Turner is Director of the Pension Policy Center, where he provides pension policy analysis for various US and international organizations. Previously, he conducted research at the US Social Security Administration, the US Department of Labor, the AARP Public Policy Institute, and the International Labor Office. He has also taught economics at the George Washington University and Georgetown University, and he was a Fulbright Scholar in France at the Institut de Recherches Economiques et Sociales. He earned his Ph.D. in Economics from the University of Chicago.

Anthony Webb is Research Economist at the Center for Retirement Research at Boston College. His research examines the impact of pensions on retirement ages, the financing of long-term care, the process of asset decumulation, and the impact of bargaining within the household on asset allocation and drawdown. Previously, he worked at the International Longevity Center—USA and served as economic adviser to the British government. His Bachelor's degree in Industrial Economics is from the University of Nottingham, he also earned a Master's degree in Economics from the University of Manchester, and a Ph.D. in Economics from the University of California, San Diego.

Joanne K. Yoong is Economist at RAND and Professor at the Pardee RAND Graduate School. Her work explores individual decision-making with an emphasis on finance and health in vulnerable populations. Previously, she was a credit derivatives research analyst in the Fixed Income, Commodities and Currencies Division of Goldman Sachs. She earned her Bachelor's degree in Economics at Princeton University and her Ph.D. in Economics from Stanford University.

Cathleen D. Zick is Professor in the Department of Family and Consumer Studies, and Director of the Master of Public Policy program, at the University of Utah. Her research examines how public policies alter the choices that families make about allocating their money and time resources, as well as the role of familial health histories and retirement planning. She has served as President and on the Board of Directors for the American Council on Consumer Interests. She earned her Bachelor's degree from the University of California, Davis, and her Master's and Ph.D. degrees in Consumer Economics and Housing from Cornell University.

Chapter 1
The Market for Retirement Financial Advice: An Introduction

Olivia S. Mitchell and Kent Smetters

The market for retirement financial advice has never been more important and yet more in flux. The long-term shift away from traditional defined benefit (DB) pensions toward defined contribution (DC) personal accounts requires all of us to become more financially sophisticated today than ever before. But the landscape for financial advice is changing, with new rules and regulations transforming the financial marketplace as well as the financial advice profession. In the United States, more than 46 million Baby Boomers are fast approaching retirement; and many are unprepared to handle a range of concerns including when to stop working, when to claim Social Security and DB pensions, how much to withdraw from retirement saving and DC accounts, how to manage retiree medical expenditures, and whether (and when) to annuitize some of their assets. Younger people confront a menu of additional decisions including managing multiple goals that compete for resources, such as whether to pay down loans while targeting saving for homes and retirement, determining the appropriate level of precautionary saving, purchasing insurance, evaluating bequest needs, and, of course, how to invest assets consistent with their risk preferences.

The complexity of choices is enormous and in most cases daunting, and many people are unable to make informed decisions without the help of professional financial advisers. Financial decisions are very personal, and, when queried, most people say they would like to speak one-on-one with trusted professionals about their own situations (Charles Schwab, 2010; Doyle et al., 2010) rather than seek advice from online tools or general seminars. But who are these professionals and what standards must they abide by? How do they make money and what are their incentives? How can one protect clients from bad advice, and what is good advice? Does advice alone effect changes in personal habits?

Answers to these questions, along with new technology that will decrease the delivery costs of advice, will play a transformative role in helping more households receive the quality financial advice that they need. But the

2 The Market for Retirement Financial Advice

job is a big one. In the United States alone, between 15 and 32 million households are willing to pay to receive financial advice—but most do not, often regarding advisers as unaffordable, conflicted, or offering an unclear value proposition (Doyle et al., 2007; Janowski, 2012). For instance, Mangla (2010: n.p.) recently wrote:

> Unfortunately, finding objective, affordable, individual advice from a live person can be a challenge. Many 'financial advisers' are simply brokers who get paid to push products. And while fee-only planners, who don't earn any commission, may have fewer conflicts, they typically prefer to work on contract with people who are already quite wealthy. Then too, the cost can go well into the thousands per year.

And as Lieber (2011: n.p.), of the *New York Times*, recently put it:

> Advice from a human being is sorely lacking when we sign up for workplace retirement plans, and there is a severe shortage of moderately priced financial advisers who will help non millionaires and put customers' interests ahead of their own.

For their part, regulators are not sitting idle. Instead, around the world there is intense debate about how to structure the marketplace for retirement financial advice, along with a regulatory renaissance generating many new rules to address these problems. The United Kingdom and Australia have recently passed laws that essentially ban the commission-based selling of investment advice due to conflicts of interest. Germany appears to be making strides in that direction as well. In the United States, the movement toward less-conflicted advice has several fronts. But reform is moving more slowly in America than in Europe, partly due to regulatory fragmentation, industry resistance, and lack of consumer understanding.

Tax-deferred retirement plans in the United States are regulated by the Department of Labor (DOL) under the Employee Retirement Income Security Act (ERISA) of 1974. This legislation, along with subsequent rulings, has conventionally deemed workplace financial advice to be a 'prohibited transaction,' meaning that pension plan sponsors take on fiduciary liability if they provide investment guidance.[1] But the 2006 Pension Protection Act and clarifications in 2007 did open the way for investment advice at the workplace under rules that sought to reduce conflicts of interest between plan participants (employees) and investment advisers (those giving advice). The DOL continues to examine a range of related issues, including whether general 'education' (a topic which usually escapes its review) constitutes 'advice' that it should regulate.

Outside of ERISA-covered retirement accounts, investment advice in the United States is regulated by a multitude of different entities. Large Registered Investment Adviser (RIA) firms—generally, firms with $100 million or more in assets under management—are supervised by the Securities and Exchange Commission (SEC). Smaller RIA firms are regulated by individual states, typically under the guidance of the Uniform Securities Act (along with modifications that differ between states).[2] All human advisers (known as Investment Adviser Representatives, or IARs) operating under a RIA entity must serve as legal fiduciaries that are bound to put client interests first. As a result, RIA firms are generally paid by fees coming directly from clients, either in the form of planning fees and/or as a percentage of assets under management. By contrast, broker-dealer representatives who tend to work at larger national firms do not have to put client interests first. Rather they must only make sure that the investment advice is 'suitable' for the client. Broker-dealers are typically compensated with commissions they receive from the investment companies, a fact that is often not clear to the clients. Brokers-dealers are regulated by a 'self-regulatory organization' known as the Financial Industry Regulatory Authority (FINRA).

If these distinctions were not already confusing enough, many financial advisers are so-called dual-registered: they operate as both RIAs and broker-dealers. Dual registration produces a problem that the US Government Accountability Office (GAO, 2011) refers to as 'hat switching,' where advisers alternate seamlessly between their roles as fiduciary-level advice givers and conflicted salesperson, typically without the client understanding the distinctions.[3]

More recently, the US Dodd-Frank Law which was passed in response to the 2008 financial crisis mandated that the SEC explore and propose a consistent uniform fiduciary standard. In apparent retaliation, recent legislation introduced by some members of Congress attempted to shift much of the SEC's investment advice oversight to FINRA for practical purposes. This counterproposal, though, has confronted stiff resistance from advisers concerned that the FINRA will fail to enforce a true fiduciary standard and increase compliance costs. In response, FINRA has sought to reposition itself as more accommodating to higher advice standards, by redefining the 'suitability' standard to a level of care that incorporates elements of the fiduciary standard. Whether this new standard will be chipped away if FINRA obtains a fuller set of regulatory responsibilities vis-à-vis the SEC is an open question.

While regulators, policymakers, business interests, and consumer groups carry on the long and intense battle over this important legal landscape, many people need practical help in the meantime. Boomers, in particular, cannot wait, and their children and grandchildren also require advice in an ever-changing financial arena. Plan sponsors designing benefit plans, along with the consultants guiding them, must also move ahead to do what they can from a practical viewpoint. This volume seeks to contribute to a greater understanding of how the market for financial advice works, what the pitfalls are, and what consumers, plan sponsors, advisers, and regulators can do to better manage the risks.

What do financial advisers do?

In what follows, we begin with a discussion of the practices of financial advisers, how they actually operate, and the advice they provide. The chapters offer perspectives from an interesting blend of academics and practitioners, who have considerable 'street' experience giving advice to real clients. To set the stage, Turner and Muir (2013) explore the financial adviser space and address the question of what is meant by the term 'financial adviser.' Surprisingly, the answer is not straightforward, as many different sorts of individuals call themselves financial advisers. A practical viewpoint is provided by Hogan and Miller (2013), who are independent advisers taking a holistic perspective when assessing client needs and explaining risks. Their work examines several common pitfalls in explaining risks to clients, as well as how to do a better job. They show how different approaches to discussing risk can lead to very different client perceptions and choices.

The chapter by Greenwald et al. (2013) examines how advice helps shape when people claim their Social Security benefits in the United States. Most workers are discouragingly poorly informed about how Social Security works, and most claim benefits currently at age 62, far earlier than many experts believe is optimal. Building on a survey and in-depth interviews, the authors examine information about how advisers and plan sponsors counsel clients and participants on Social Security. Their results point to ways to increase the effectiveness of education and advice on Social Security and claiming.

Pension asset allocation is examined by Munnell et al. (2013), focusing on how this can help influence retirement security. In the US context, they conclude that most workers save relatively little, so they suggest that advisers should emphasize boosting saving rates instead of concentrating on asset allocation. Jones and Scott (2013) describe the factors encouraging employees to enroll in the workplace-based asset management program that their firm, Financial Engines, provides to plan sponsors. The company derives most of its revenue from managing DC account assets on behalf of workers.

In addition to saving and investment, stakeholders also need help in deciding how to manage their money so as not to run out in retirement. Accordingly, Hueler and Rappaport (2013) note that financial advice can strongly shape employees' decisions to annuitize part of their pension assets. Hueler's innovative lifetime annuity platform is offered by some plan sponsors as a means to help retirees generate income protection over their entire lifetimes. While life annuities currently represent only a small fraction of total annuity sales, this chapter explores how financial advice can play a key role in adoption.

Measuring the performance and impact of financial advice

Next, the volume turns to an in-depth evaluation of the impact of financial advisers asking: do they matter; do they do a good job; and do they have an impact on client choices and behavior? Zick and Mayer's careful analysis (2013) points out that many prior studies fail to identify the clear impact of financial advisers in effecting change because they have not used a scientific randomized approach in the analysis. Moreover, the few studies that do are limited in their delivery of financial advice. The authors offer a useful roadmap guiding serious evaluation efforts if one is to clearly identify the impact of advisers on outcomes.

In an interesting experimental study, Hung and Yoong (2013) use the RAND American Life Panel to explore whether enhanced behavior can be attributed to actual investment advice. They come to two interesting findings. First, unsolicited general advice has a limited effect on investment behavior. Second, people who actively solicit advice do improve their performance, but they are not a randomly selected group. As a result, their results suggest that general advice might not be a 'silver bullet.' That is, plan sponsors and policymakers may need to consider additional mechanisms (including how to make advice more personalized), and to allow participants receive more help with actual implementation of advice.

The related chapter by Hackethal and Inderst (2013) notes that financial advice can benefit consumers by bridging gaps in knowledge and facilitating transactions, but in practice, it is often used to exploit consumers' lack of financial literacy and inexperience. In an effort to correct this problem, regulators have sought to enact policies that mandate more disclosure regarding products and conflicts of interest. But the authors argue that these measures often fall short of creating tools and policies to enhance transparency. For instance, the financial products could be much simpler and more uniform, making them easier to compare. Additionally, policies could ensure that the quality of advice improves, perhaps by having advisers meet higher standards of qualification, or giving them appropriate incentives to gather information and provide unbiased advice.

In his chapter on adviser services, Finke (2013) proposes that advisers can substitute for costly investments in specific finance-related human capital that may not be efficient for households or society to engage in as a whole. Nevertheless, even when financial advisers improve financial outcomes, and when the adviser's and households' interests are aligned, professional advice can still harm consumers if conflicts of interest create high agency costs. Fee compensation may reduce agency costs associated with commission compensation, such as the incentive to increase portfolio turnover and recommend low-performing investments. Fees may also reduce the focus on short-term advising services by creating an incentive to establish a long-run advising relationship. One way to reduce possible agency costs under commission compensation might be to eliminate commissions and apply a uniform fiduciary standard among financial advisers.

Using several different surveys, Holden (2013) explores when, why, and how mutual fund investors use financial advisers. Among other issues, she looks at whether certain 'trigger' events prompt fund investors to seek professional financial advice, and she analyzes whether some investors are more likely to work with advisers than others. The level of assets appears to be a key marker, with households that have an advisory relationship reporting a median of $170,000 of household assets, compared to a median $85,000 of among households that do not have an advisory relationship.

Market and regulatory considerations

The third section of this volume takes up regulatory and market considerations. Laby (2013) deals with the way that brokers and advisers may perform similar functions yet are regulated differently under US laws dating back to the Great Depression. The labels used by financial services providers tend to confound investors; federal securities laws contain separate regulatory schemes for brokers and for advisers; and the duties and obligations differ under each. Regulators are currently pondering how to harmonize these regulations, but the process is fraught with difficulties. Furthermore, although brokers and advisers historically provided distinct services, today their roles are often similar or nearly identical. Yet since regulation has not kept pace with changes in the industry, brokers and advisers remain subject to separate regulatory regimes. The US Securities and Exchange Commission (SEC) is considering whether to harmonize the regulation of broker-dealers and investment advisers and place a fiduciary duty on brokers that give advice to retail customers, subjecting them to a higher duty of care.

The US Government Accountability Office (GAO) is also exploring a regulatory gap, as explained by Bromberg and Cackley (2013). Currently, no single law governs providers of financial planning services. Many investors find the standards of care confusing, and they do not appear to appreciate the differences between investment advisers and broker-dealers or the standards of care that apply to them. Consumers generally do not understand the distinction between a suitability and fiduciary standard of care, nor when financial professionals are (or are not) required to put their client's interest ahead of their own. The authors outline several different approaches to create a more unified approach.

A look ahead

In the wake of the financial crisis, numerous analysts and policymakers have expressed deep concern about the extent and consequences of consumer financial ignorance. For instance, the US President's Advisory Council on Financial Literacy (PACFL, 2008: n.p.) has expressed concern that 'far too many Americans do not have the basic financial skills necessary to develop and maintain a budget, to understand credit, to understand investment vehicles, or to take advantage of our banking system. It is essential to provide basic financial education that allows people to better navigate an economic crisis such as this one.' In a similar vein, Federal Reserve Board Chairman Bernanke (2011: 2) argued: 'In our dynamic and complex financial marketplace, financial education must be a life-long pursuit that enables consumers of all ages and economic positions to stay attuned to changes in their financial needs and circumstances and to take advantage of products and services that best meet their goals. Well-informed consumers, who can serve as their own advocates, are one of the best lines of defense against the proliferation of financial products and services that are unsuitable, unnecessarily costly, or abusive.' And the US DOL has estimated that pension participants could save billions of dollars a year in financial mistakes, if they were better versed with regard to financial advice (Turner and Muir, 2013).

While we focus here on ways to make markets work better for saving, investing, and decumulating retirement assets, there is one topic we do not address in detail as it deserves a separate and lengthy treatment on its own: how to plan for and manage retiree medical care expenditures. In the future, these costs will inevitably rise due to extending longevity and healthcare cost inflation. Additionally, in the United States, many employers have terminated their retiree medical insurance programs over the last decade, and the few still providing plans have imposed higher contribution rates, rising copayments, and higher deductibles.[4] The Affordable Health Care Act will interact with the projected solvency problems confronting the Medicare program, implying that future retirees will surely be need to pay more for medical costs than in the past.[5] Yet few employees are well-versed about their employer's retiree medical insurance offerings or what benefits are available through Medicare,[6] implying a large and growing role for financial advice in this arena as well.

Looking to the future, regulatory efforts are underway in many nations to address informational issues and to rationalize the application of fiduciary standards, in the hopes of increasing the quality and quantity of investment advice to support retirement security. But in the long run, better-educated and informed stakeholders will need to bear a larger role in managing their retirement accumulation, investment, and decumulation processes. Accordingly, there seems little choice but to bring to market more appropriate products, explain them better, and price them fairly, so participants in the retirement advice marketplace do a better job managing retirement risk. To this topic we turn next.

Endnotes

1. Some exceptions existed, most notably the DOL December 14, 2001, Advisory Opinion to SunAmerica Retirement Markets which allowed certain asset allocation services to participants in ERISA-covered plans. See <http://www.dol.gov/ebsa/regs/AOs/ao2001-09a.html>.
2. Most states require legal registration of the RIA, mandate that each adviser pass a Series 65 or similar exam (although some states exempt individuals holding the CFP® designation), and submit a U4 background application. The state of Florida and a few others require advisers to also submit fingerprints.
3. This might be akin to medical doctor having a financial interest in the companies producing medications that he prescribes to his patients.
4. As Fronstin (2010) notes, the Financial Accounting Statement No. 106 (FAS 106) of 1990 requiring private sector employers to account for the liabilities associated with post-retirement healthcare insurance prompted many firms to cut back and even terminate these plans.
5. The Employee Benefit Research Institute (2009) estimated that the present discounted value of an average couples' out-of-pocket expenditures (exclusive of employer subsidy) would total $268,000. At the 90th percentile, the estimated cost was $414,000 and inclusive of Medigap/Part D premiums, $807,000.
6. See, e.g., Schur et al. (2004) and Kaiser Public Opinion (2011).

References

Bernanke, B. S. (2011). Statement of the Chairman of the Board of Governors of the Federal Reserve System at a Hearing conducted by the Subcommittee on Oversight of Government Management, the Federal Workforce, and the District of Columbia of the Committee on Homeland Security and Governmental Affairs, U.S. Senate, Washington, DC (April 12).

Bromberg, J., and A. P. Cackley (2013). 'Regulating Financial Planners: Assessing the Current System and Some Alternatives,' in O. S. Mitchell and K. Smetters, eds., *The Market for Retirement Financial Advice*. Oxford, UK: Oxford University Press, pp. 305–20.

Charles Schwab (2010). *The New Rules of Engagement for 401(k) Plans*. San Francisco, CA: The Charles Schwab Corporation. <http://www.aboutschwab.com/images/uploads/schwab_engagement_study_slides.pdf>.

Doyle, B., E. Dolan, B. Tesch, and C. Johnson (2007). *Who's Willing to Pay the Most for a Financial Plan?* Cambridge, MA: Forrester Research, Inc.

——P. Wannemacher, B. McGowan, and B. Ensor (2010). *Segmenting US Investors.* Cambridge, MA: Forrester Research, Inc.

Employee Benefit Research Institute (EBRI) (2009). *EBRI Note.* Washington, DC: EBRI (June).

Finke, M. (2013). 'Financial Advice: Does It Make a Difference?' in O. S. Mitchell and K. Smetters, eds., *The Market for Retirement Financial Advice.* Oxford, UK: Oxford University Press, pp. 229–48.

Fronstin, P. (2010). 'Implications of Health Reform for Retiree Health Benefits.' Employee Benefit Research Institute Issue Brief No. 338 (January).

Greenwald, M., L. Schneider, and A. G. Biggs (2013). 'How Financial Advisers and Defined Contribution Plan Providers Educate Clients and Participants about Social Security,' in O. S. Mitchell and K. Smetters, eds., *The Market for Retirement Financial Advice.* Oxford, UK: Oxford University Press, pp. 70–88.

Hackethal, A., and R. Inderst (2013). 'How to Make the Market for Financial Advice Work,' in O. S. Mitchell and K. Smetters, eds., *The Market for Retirement Financial Advice.* Oxford, UK: Oxford University Press, pp. 213–28.

Hogan, P. H., and F. H. Miller (2013). 'Explaining Risk to Clients: The View from Two Advisers,' in O. S. Mitchell and K. Smetters, eds., *The Market for Retirement Financial Advice.* Oxford, UK: Oxford University Press, pp. 46–69.

Holden, S. A. (2013). 'When, Why, and How Do Mutual Fund Investors Use Financial Advisers?' in O. S. Mitchell and K. Smetters, eds., *The Market for Retirement Financial Advice.* Oxford, UK: Oxford University Press, pp. 249–72.

Hueler, K., and A. Rappaport (2013). 'The Role of Guidance in the Annuity Decision-making Process,' in O. S. Mitchell and K. Smetters, eds., *The Market for Retirement Financial Advice.* Oxford, UK: Oxford University Press, pp. 125–49.

Hung, A. A., and J. K. Yoong (2013). 'Asking for Help: Survey and Experimental Evidence on Financial Advice and Behavior Change,' in O. S. Mitchell and K. Smetters, eds., *The Market for Retirement Financial Advice.* Oxford, UK: Oxford University Press, pp. 182–212.

Janowski, D. (2012). 'Behind LPL's Acquisition of Veritat,' *InvestmentNews* (July 10).

Jones, C., and J. Scott (2013). 'Choice and Defined Contribution Retirement Income,' in O. S. Mitchell and K. Smetters, eds., *The Market for Retirement Financial Advice.* Oxford, UK: Oxford University Press, pp. 107–24.

Kaiser Public Opinion (2011). 'Pop Quiz: Assessing Americans' Familiarity with the Health Care Law.' Kaiser Family Foundation Data Note (February).

Laby, A. B. (2013). 'Harmonizing the Regulation of Financial Advisers,' in O. S. Mitchell and K. Smetters, eds., *The Market for Retirement Financial Advice.* Oxford, UK: Oxford University Press, pp. 275–304.

Lieber, R. (2011). 'Investment Advice for Small Fry,' *New York Times*, May 27.

Mangla, I. S. (2010). 'Good Financial Advice on a Budget,' *Money Magazine*, 39(1).

Munnell, A. H., N. Orlova, and A. Webb (2013). 'How Important is Asset Allocation to Financial Security in Retirement?' in O. S. Mitchell and K. Smetters, eds., *The Market for Retirement Financial Advice.* Oxford, UK: Oxford University Press, pp. 89–108.

President's Advisory Committee on Financial Literacy (PACFL) (2008). *Annual Report to the President: Executive Summary.* Washington, DC: PACFL.

Schur, C. L., M. L. Berk, G. R. Wilensky, and J. P. Gagnon (2004). 'Paying For HealthCare in Retirement: Workers' Knowledge Of Benefits And Expenses,' *Health Affairs* 4: 385–95.

Turner, J. A., and D. M. Muir (2013). 'The Market for Financial Advisers,' in O. S. Mitchell and K. Smetters, eds., *The Market for Retirement Financial Advice*. Oxford, UK: Oxford University Press, pp. 13–45.

United States Department of Labor (DOL) (2001). *Advisory Opinion.* 2001-09A. Washington, DC: DOL. <http://www.dol.gov/ebsa/regs/AOs/ao2001-09a.html>.

United States Government Accountability Office (GAO) (2011). *Improved Regulation Could Better Protect Participants from Conflicts of Interest.* GAO-11-119. Washington, DC: GAO.

Zick, C. D., and R. N. Mayer (2013). 'Evaluating the Impact of Financial Planners,' in O. S. Mitchell and K. Smetters, eds., *The Market for Retirement Financial Advice*. Oxford, UK: Oxford University Press, pp. 153–81.

Part I
What Do Financial Advisers Do?

Chapter 2

The Market for Financial Advisers

John A. Turner and Dana M. Muir

Many individuals lack basic financial knowledge (e.g., McCarthy and Turner, 2000; Lusardi and Mitchell, 2006), and hence they would likely benefit from financial advice. Pension plan sponsors also need financial advice when choosing what types of plans to offer, setting up pension plans, choosing investment options for 401(k) plans (by far the most common type of employer-provided plan), managing the investments of defined benefit (DB) plans, establishing pension plans for executives, and hiring service providers. This chapter focuses on financial advice related to preparing for retirement, considering advice provided to both individuals and pension plan sponsors.

We begin by providing background on ways that advisers interact with their clients, and on the scope of their investment advice. Second, we discuss the types of firms providing advice and requirements for some of the certifications that financial advisers use. These certifications provide individuals and plan sponsors a way to assess adviser qualifications. Third, we investigate issues related to the level and disclosure of fees financial advisers charge. Next, we explain how the structure and level of advisory fees may result in conflicts of interest that can affect the quality of advice provided. Then we outline how the US legal and regulatory environments are evolving in response to conflicts of interest and investor confusion about standards of care identified in several studies as being potentially problematic. Finally, conclusions appear in the final section.[1]

Financial advice for individuals

First we discuss the ways in which financial advice can be provided and topics covered in financial advice.

How financial advice can be provided for managing investments

Financial advisers can provide clients assistance with their investments by offering education, decision support, advice, or marketing information;

alternatively, they can manage the individual's investments themselves. Decision support is education targeted to help a client reach a decision. Marketing information may appear to the client to be unbiased advice, but it is designed to sell a product.

Many advisers also assist their clients in carrying out their advice. If an adviser provides financial management, he makes investment decisions and carries them out without involving the individual investor in the decision. Some 401(k) plans offer employees managed accounts, where the individual's assets are professionally managed. This option is also available for non-pension accounts. Advice and marketing materials of some service providers encourage clients to have professionally managed accounts, which tend to generate higher ongoing fees. We focus in this study on investment advice, and not asset management.

An alternative to a financial adviser is advice generated by financial planning software, some of which is available for free over the Internet (Turner and Witte, 2009). A further alternative to a financial adviser, at least for investment advice, is a target date investment fund, in which the asset mix of a diversified portfolio is automatically adjusted to take into account a shortening investment horizon as the client's expected retirement date approaches.

We focus here on advice that includes interaction with a financial adviser. The financial adviser provides advice as to financial decisions, and the individual decides whether to follow the advice. An adviser can provide advice through a variety of methods, including online, by telephone, at call centers or help desks, at company offices, at group seminars, or in one-on-one sessions.

Topics covered and topics often overlooked

The retirement-related topics on which individuals may need financial advice are far broader than investments. They can include when to leave work, when to claim Social Security benefits; and for those with a pension or personal savings, whether to roll over a 401(k) plan to an Individual Retirement Account (IRA), how to liquidate assets in retirement, and whether to purchase an annuity.

Some advisers focus only on investments, and do not provide advice on some of the other decisions individuals must make concerning retirement. For example, some advisory companies focusing on investments note that they do not provide tax or legal advice (e.g., T. Rowe Price, 2011*a*, 2011*b*). Nevertheless, despite the disclaimer provided for legal reasons, some do discuss tax considerations related to selecting investments and deciding in what order to sell investments in retirement.

A survey of free financial planning software available online found that most programs do not provide advice as to purchasing an annuity, even when confronted with a scenario rigged to make purchasing an annuity desirable (Turner, 2010). One mutual fund company we contacted indicated that few of its clients sought advice as to how to take pension payouts. For that reason, the firm's decision to not provide advice concerning annuities was partly demand-driven. Another reason it cited is that financial experts do not have a standard methodology for determining how much a client should annuitize. By contrast, life insurance companies are expected to advise concerning purchase of an annuity.

One reason some financial advisers have not recommended annuities in the past is that annuitization would reduce their assets under management, and thus their fees. More recently, insurers have introduced variable annuities that allow the adviser to still manage the asset base and capture management fees. For instance, in some variable annuities, the account is typically invested in mutual funds chosen by the client during the accumulation phase. During the payout phase, generally the client has the choice of receiving a fixed payout, or having a payout that varies depending on the investment performance of the underlying assets.

Advisers' employers and credentials

Financial advisers differ in the types of companies they work for and in the certifications they obtain.

Companies providing financial advice

Companies providing financial advice include banks and trust companies (e.g., UBS), mutual fund companies (e.g., Vanguard), financial advisory companies (e.g., Veritat), brokerage companies (e.g., TD Ameritrade), and insurance companies (e.g., MetLife). Accounting and law firms also provide financial advice. With financial companies acquiring each other, facilitated by more permissive regulation, the distinctions as to the nature of companies are increasingly blurred (e.g., Bank of America Merrill Lynch, 2011). In 2010, 19 percent of investment advisory firms that provided financial planning services also provided brokerage services, while 27 percent also sold insurance (GAO, 2011*b*).

Some financial services companies provide only advice, while others only investment management. Some advisers offer the option of advice only or investment management (TD Ameritrade, 2011). Financial Engines is a company that began by providing financial advice to 401(k) plan participants through employers sponsoring 401(k) plans. From its early experience it observed that often its clients did not take the steps necessary to follow its advice, so it now primarily manages 401(k) accounts, for which it accepts fiduciary responsibility (Financial Engines, 2011). By contrast, many companies that provide financial advice to plan sponsors do not accept fiduciary responsibility (Simon, 2004). Guided Choice (2011) and Bank of America Merrill Lynch (2011) provide advice to 401(k) participants through arrangements with plan sponsors. Using a different business model, Smart401(k) (2011) provides investment advice directly to individual 401(k) plan participants. On the websites of these three companies, there is no indication that they accept fiduciary responsibility.

Insurance companies may also provide financial advice relating to the marketing of various insurance products, including variable annuities and other payout products. The advice they provide can also go beyond these traditional areas: for example, MetLife Securities, Inc., a subsidiary of MetLife (the holding company for Metropolitan Life Insurance Company), offers traditional financial planning assistance, including fee-based financial planning (MetLife, 2011). An insurance agent who works for an insurance company is referred to as a 'captive agent.' Independent agents who sell the products of multiple companies are called insurance brokers. In both cases, compensation is often based on commissions (Kolakowski, 2011).

As a general matter, advisory firms must register as investment advisers with the Securities and Exchange Commission (SEC), which is an agency of the federal government, or with a state government, depending on the amount of assets receiving continuous and regular supervisory or management services (Assets Under Management, or AUM). The minimum amount for required SEC registration as of 2011 is $100 million (SEC, 2011*d*). Firms with AUM of below $100 million must register with state government regulators.

An advisory firm that does not meet the minimum AUM test for SEC purposes may still register with the SEC instead of state regulators if it is a 'pension consultant' that provides investment advice to employee benefit plans or a plan fiduciary on a minimum aggregate asset value. That minimum increased in 2011 to $200 million. The SEC's rationale is that pension consultants who provide various services regarding large amounts of plan assets may have an effect on national markets, even if they do not technically have AUM (SEC, 2011*e*: 42,959).

Professional certifications of financial advisers

BrightScope, Inc. (2011), a company started in 2009 that analyzes 401(k) plans, argues that 401(k) plan sponsors need more information about investment advisers than they currently have. Its website provides information on about 450,000 investment advisers, including their experience and employment history. The database is slated to over a million names, once advisers registered with individual states are included (Bliman, 2011).

In addition, the Financial Industry Regulatory Authority (FINRA) maintains a database on 1.3 million current and former stock brokers registered with FINRA, and 17,000 current and former brokerage firms registered with FINRA (FINRA, 2011b). FINRA is a private-sector self-regulatory organization for broker-dealers. Private-sector self-regulation of brokerage firms is generally not found in other countries, with the government having sole regulatory responsibility.

The term 'financial adviser' is not regulated by law, and financial advisers have a wide range of professional backgrounds. They can be accountants, attorneys, estate planners, insurance agents, stock brokers, and investment advisers (Certified Financial Planner Board, 2011c). FINRA (2011a) warns consumers that the terms *financial analyst, financial adviser, financial consultant, financial planner, investment consultant*, and *wealth manager* are generic job titles that are generally not regulated. That is, these titles do not necessarily indicate any given level of expertise or credential.

The requirements for certifications used by financial advisers vary considerably. FINRA (2011a) lists over 100 professional designations for financial advisers. While some designations require examinations and continuing education, others merely signify that the certificate holder has paid membership dues (GAO, 2011b).[2] Certifications that financial advisers use include Certified Financial Planner, Chartered Financial Analyst, Chartered Investment Counselor, Personal Financial Specialist, Chartered Financial Consultant, Chartered Life Underwriter, and Certified Employee Benefit Specialist. Some financial planners obtain none of these certifications but instead have educational backgrounds as attorneys, accountants, economists, or MBAs.

Certified Financial Planner

The Certified Financial Planner (CFP) certification is administered by a private-sector organization, the CFP Board. In dealing with clients, CFPs agree to follow the principles of confidentiality, integrity, objectivity, competence, fairness, professionalism, and diligence (Certified Financial Planner Board, 2011a). CFPs must have at least a Bachelor's degree and have taken specific courses, either at an academic institution or proprietary courses approved by the CFP Board that cover topics on the CFP certification examination. Having a Ph.D. in Economics automatically meets the education requirement, but it would generally not adequately prepare someone to take the examination. Beginning in 2012, the education requirement includes completion of a financial plan development course approved by the CFP Board.

Once the education requirement is met, a candidate can sit for the CFP certification examination, which takes 10 hours over two days; the exam fee is $595. Topics covered include insurance planning and risk management, employee benefits planning, investment planning, income tax planning, retirement planning, and estate planning. Having passed the examination, the candidate must satisfy ethics requirements concerning past illegal activity and agree to adhere to ethical standards in the future. The candidate must also have at least three years of qualifying work experience. Once certified, the CFP must take 30 hours of continuing education every two years, including 2 hours on professional conduct.

Chartered Financial Analyst

The Chartered Financial Analyst Institute has more than 100,000 members worldwide, making it the world's largest association of investment professionals (Chartered Financial Analyst Institute, 2011). The Chartered Financial Analyst (CFA) educational program requires passing three examinations for which candidates spend on average 300 hours preparing for each. Candidates can complete the program in eighteen months, but, on average, take four years. To enter the education program, an individual must have a Bachelor's degree or be in the final year of earning that degree, or have four years of qualified professional work experience.

The CFA program focuses on corporate finance and investments, including derivatives and alternative investments such as real estate, commodities, and hedge funds. By comparison, the CFP program includes those issues and also covers financial planning issues more broadly. For example, the CFP educational program has a section on Social Security benefits not covered in the CFA program (Certified Financial Planner Board, 2011*b*). Similarly, annuities are discussed in the CFP program, but they are not covered in the syllabus for the CFA program.

Chartered Investment Counselor

The Investment Adviser Association (IAA) has established the Chartered Investment Counselor (CIC) program (IAA, 2011). A CIC must be a CFA and meet additional requirements established by the IAA, including being employed by an IAA member firm and having five years of qualifying experience.

Personal Financial Specialist

The Personal Financial Specialist (PFS) program enables Certified Public Accountants (CPAs) to receive professional recognition for their expertise in personal financial planning (American Institute of CPAs, 2011). CPA is the title for accountants who have passed a qualifying examination and have met state requirements concerning education and experience. A PFS must be a member of the American Institute of Certified Public Accountants (AICPA). More than 3,000 CPAs have the PFS certification, or about 1 percent of the membership of the AICPA (Drucker, 2005). According to the AICPA, the PFS's knowledge about tax issues distinguishes this credential from others. Nonetheless, many CPAs who do not have the designation engage in aspects of providing financial advice (Drucker, 2005).

The PFS examination takes over 7 hours. The PFS must have at least two years of full-time business or teaching experience related to financial planning, and must complete at least 80 hours of personal financial education. The PFS must pass the PFS examination. The cost of the examination is $400 for AICPA members.

Chartered Financial Consultant

The certifications discussed thus far are awarded by industry or professional groups, but some certifications are awarded by academic institutions. One example is the Chartered Financial Consultant (ChFC) program is offered through the American College in Bryn Mawr, Pennsylvania (The American College, 2011a). The ChFC is trained to meet the financial planning needs of individuals, professionals, and small business owners. The ChFC must complete nine courses—seven required and two elective. The seven required courses include Fundamentals of Insurance Planning and Fundamentals of Estate Planning. The cost of admission to the program is $135, and the cost per course is $599. According to the American College, the ChFC program has more extensive education requirements than any other financial planning credential. The education program can be done through self-study or through attending live webinars.

Chartered Life Underwriter

The Chartered Life Underwriter (CLU) certification is also offered by the American College (The American College, 2011b). The CLU program participant must take five required courses and three elective courses, some of which overlap with the ChFC courses. The cost of each course is approximately $600. Topics include life insurance law, insurance and estate planning, insurance for business owners and professionals, and retirement planning. Both the ChFC and CLU programs require three years of full-time professional experience within the past five years. Both require adherence to an ethical code.

20 The Market for Retirement Financial Advice

Other professional designations include the Certified Fund Specialist (CFS), Certified Investment Management Analyst (CIMA), and actuarial designations such as Fellow of the Society of Actuaries (FSA).

Fees for financial advice

This section discusses the types of fees charged, issues related to the clarity and usefulness of the disclosure of fees to individuals, fees charged to individuals, fees charged to plan sponsors, and the compensation received by financial advisers.

Types of fees

Financial advisers charge fees in various ways (Anspach, 2011a; Maxey, 2011).

1. They charge a fee as a percent of the client's account balance or the amount of assets they help manage. The larger the minimum account balance and the larger the account, the lower fee percentages tend to be, due to economies of scale. This is the traditional and most common approach, accounting for 85 percent of the revenues of advisory firms in 2010 (Maxey, 2011).

This approach not only provides incentives for the adviser to attempt to increase the individual's asset base, but it may also encourage too much risk taking. In addition, the adviser may have an incentive to not let money exit the asset under management, such as purchasing an annuity or insurance, paying down a mortgage, or drawing down assets to postpone taking Social Security benefits (Maxey, 2011). The adviser may also have an incentive to make moves that bring money into the asset base, such as rolling over a 401(k) plan into an IRA.

Finally, fees based on AUM may give rise to what are known as 'reverse churning' claims. In churning claims, clients accuse brokers of changing their investments in order to increase commissions payable to the broker. Reverse churning claims occur when advisers allegedly ignore accounts by failing to properly monitor or reallocate investments, because the adviser's compensation is based on AUM.

2. Advisers may receive commissions on insurance or financial products they sell to their clients. This compensation may be entirely based on sales commissions, or partly on referral fees paid by third parties. To the client, the advice may appear to be free, but in actuality the client is paying through the fees that third parties charge for managing the investments, conducting trades, etc. This approach has the problem that advisers may have an incentive to buy and sell products when they get a commission for trades (Maxey, 2011).

3. Many advisers collect both fees and commissions, acting under the descriptor of fee-based adviser versus the fee-only adviser. An adviser receiving both fees from the client and commissions from third parties may rebate some or all of the commissions received to the client through a reduction in fees. This arrangement is called a fee offset.

4. Advisers may charge an hourly rate for their time spent advising clients, or a flat fee for a specific project.

5. Advisers may charge a quarterly or annual retainer fee if the client has an ongoing need for advice, or they may charge a fixed annual maintenance fee.

6. Advisers may charge a fee based on the client's income, or based on the client's net worth (not just their portfolio holdings).

The SEC also lists two other ways financial advisers might charge fees: (*a*) subscription fees for a newsletter or periodical; and (*b*) performance-based fees tied to the rate of return the client receives on his investments. Performance-based fees can only be charged to wealthy clients.

Advisers who charge fees as a percentage of account balances generally establish minimum fee levels by requiring that their clients have a minimum amount of assets to invest; such asset minimums range from $20,000 to $500,000. For example, Merrill Lynch has a minimum of $250,000 in investable assets for one class of advice, while its Merrill Edge Advisory Center is for people with $20,000 to $250,000 in assets to invest and for whom a lower level of service is provided (Merrill Edge, 2011). Vanguard's financial advisers use a minimum of $500,000 (Vanguard, 2011*a*). The minimum asset requirements for clients of a number of companies are high compared to the average households' stock holdings. The median holdings of stock outside retirement plans by households aged 45–54 with stock was $45,000 in 2007 (Bucks et al., 2009).

Different fee structures may be preferable to different types of investors. For example, an hourly fee or a flat fee would presumably be preferable to individuals with insufficient assets to meet the minimums set by advisers charging asset-based fees (Maxey, 2011).

Disclosure of advisory fees to individuals

Fee levels charged by financial advisers vary widely, but few companies compete based on fees when marketing their services. Financial advisers, even low-cost ones, generally do not highlight fee information on their websites. Generally, websites do not contain information on fees, or if they do, that information can only be obtained with effort. For example, the main pages at the Vanguard (2011*b*) financial advice website do not report information as to asset management. This information for asset management can be obtained with sufficient diligence by following links, but fees for advice are apparently not disclosed on the website. (Vanguard does mention on the first webpage for advice that it provides advice at low cost.) GuidedChoice (2011) indicates on its website that it favors transparency in fees, but it does not provide fee information. Merrill Lynch (2010) never mentions fees on its Global Wealth & Investment Management website. While it might be expected that footnotes would contain technical information of interest only to specialists, TD Ameritrade discloses its fee structure for account management in small print in the third paragraph of a footnote on its website (TD Ameritrade, 2011).

Individuals can obtain information about fees by going to the website of the SEC and examining disclosure forms, called ADV forms, for different advisory companies. Yet few individuals are likely to be aware of this source of information, and even fewer use it. As part of the requirement that advisory firms file an ADV form, the SEC requires that registered investment advisers provide a written disclosure statement (called a brochure) to clients and prospective clients. Disclosure includes information concerning fees. It also requires advisers to make disclosures as fiduciaries, including material facts about the advisory relationship and any conflicts of interest.

Fees for investment advice to individual investors are tax deductible, but fees for investment management are not deductible. Tax deductible financial advisory fees are disclosed on the Internal Revenue Service (taxing authority) IRS Form 1099 provided to clients by their financial services companies after the calendar year has ended; that disclosure does not include management fees and transaction costs. Transaction costs resulting from financial advice involving active management, which are fees the participant pays, are rarely, if ever, disclosed to clients (Turner and Witte, 2008). Advisers acting as brokers are not required to disclose commissions at the point of sale (Maxey, 2011). That information is disclosed later, when the individual receives the confirmation of the transaction.

An issue related to the disclosure of fees is whether such disclosure is used by pension participants, or whether the added cost of disclosure fails to benefit participants. The effects of the disclosure may depend for some investors on the format of the disclosure. Hastings and Mitchell (2011) show that people with low levels of financial literacy are more affected by the formats in which fee information is disclosed, compared to people with high levels of financial literacy who are more likely to understand the information whatever the format used.

Level of advisory fees charged to individuals

In practice, the level of advisory fees varies widely. For example, T. Rowe Price (2011a) offered financial advice in 2011 to its clients at a flat fee of $250, with the fee waived for clients with $500,000 or more invested, or who made a one-time purchase of $100,000 or more.

Motley Fool (2011) has an innovative way of providing low-cost financial advice that involves greater participation by the client than is generally true. This program, called the TMF Money Advisor, charged a flat annual fee of $195 in 2011. Part of the cost of providing individual financial advice is the cost of gathering information from the individual and inputting that information into a computer model. Motley Fool's clients input their own financial information into an online computer model, taking about an hour to do so (not including the time required to gather the information). Subsequently, a financial adviser at a call center can look at the information provided online and discuss a computer-generated financial plan with the clients.

One company charges fees at the rate of 1 percent of the individual's Adjusted Gross Income plus 0.5 percent of their net worth (excluding closely held businesses), with the second fee declining to 0.25 percent and then 0.1 percent as net worth grows (Maxey, 2011).

Hourly rates charged by advisers vary widely (Anspach, 2011a), with the average hourly fee starting at around $175 an hour in 2011 (Motley Fool, 2011). In practice, we found that company websites rarely reported hourly rates; instead, companies generally require clients to call to find out their hourly rates.

New Means Financial Planning (2011) is a fee-only service in New Hampshire that does provide detailed information about its fees. A financial consultation for clients in their 20s and early 30s costs $800 to $1,000. A typical fee to assess how much life insurance and other insurance a person needs ranges from $600 to $1,000. Advice on investments in a 401(k) plan ranges between $400 and $800 per plan. An assessment of the person's entire portfolio ranges from $1,000 to $2,200. Advice on retirement planning ranges from $1,000 to $2,000. A comprehensive financial plan costs between $2,200 and $4,400. Alternatively, a client can receive advisory services at an hourly rate of $200 (in 2011 dollars).

Advisers who charge fees as a percentage of assets may have formulas that take several factors into account. For example, as well as the amount of assets, they may take into account the complexity of the client's investment strategy, the frequency of meetings or investment reviews, and the extent of trading activity.

Some financial advisers charge insurance companies for recommending purchase of an annuity. For example, Schwab (2011a) could recommend purchase of an annuity, but only from insurance companies that compensate Schwab for its role as agent for the sale and servicing of annuity contracts. Generally, Schwab's compensation is based on the amount to be annuitized and the type of annuity. A fixed deferred annuity in 2011 had a 1.50 percent commission paid at the time of purchase, with a 0.65 percent trail commission, paid annually. A trail commission offsets the disincentive to Schwab of removing assets from the base of AUM. A fixed immediate annuity has a 3.50 percent commission paid at time of purchase. These costs are in addition to the charges of the insurance company, and they presumably are passed on to the client.

Level of advisory fees charged to plan sponsors

Plan sponsors often hire financial advisers to help them make decisions concerning the pension plans they sponsor. For 401(k) plans, these decisions relate to the investment options they offer participants, and also to financial education and advice provided to participants. For DB plans, decisions tend to relate to the selection of investments for the pension fund.

No unique source exists for examining fees charged to pension plan sponsors. Edelman Financial Services establishes 401(k) plans for companies for a one-time setup fee that is not disclosed at its website. It will then manage the 401(k) plan, including providing advice to participants for a flat annual fee (also not disclosed at its website; Edelman Financial Services, 2011). To obtain information about those fees, a plan sponsor must directly contact the firm, which makes it more costly in terms of time and effort to compare fees.

Compensation received by financial advisers

Users of financial advice need to understand the fees they pay directly to their adviser or adviser's employer, as well as how their adviser is compensated, including indirect effects on his compensation such as compensation from third parties. Compensation from third parties can also affect the advice that the adviser provides. The US Department of Labor (2011) specifies that compensation a financial adviser receives can include 'commissions, salary, bonuses, awards, promotions, or other things of value,' as well as fees. 'Other things of value' include trips and gifts. The precise level of compensation the adviser receives may be difficult to determine when the adviser receives commissions for products he sells, as well as fees.

Advisers who work independently, including those who sell long-term care insurance, may be paid entirely through commissions they receive for products they sell, or may receive fees, or both. Regarding advisers who work for companies, most companies do not explain how their advisers are compensated, and it can be difficult to obtain information on how compensation by third parties affects the compensation of financial advisers employed by a firm. For example, Benjamin F. Edwards & Co. discloses that it receives third-party payments but indicates that those payments do not directly affect the compensation of employees acting as financial consultants. It discloses further that 'it is possible, through various compensation arrangements, that financial consultants may indirectly benefit from these payments' (Benjamin F. Edwards & Co., 2011), but the firm does not disclose on its website exactly how third-party payments affect a consultant's compensation.

Some financial services companies offer financial advisers options for employment and compensation. Under one option, the advisers are affiliated with the company, but they remain responsible for establishing their office. Under the second option, agents are employees of the company which provides them full office support. Under both options, compensation is based on the business they generate. Agents receive a smaller percentage of their fees and commissions under the second option than the first option.

Some financial advisers also pay CPAs and other professionals referral fees. For example, CPAs may receive referral fees when they refer a client to a financial adviser, ranging from 10–20 percent, to as much as 40 percent, of the fee charged by the adviser (Drucker, 2005). In addition, independent financial advisers recommended by Charles Schwab pay Schwab a fee for referrals (Schwab, 2011a). These fees are at least partly passed on to clients.

Issues concerning financial advice provided to individuals

After identifying a qualified financial adviser with expertise that meets their needs, the consumer receiving financial advice may still encounter difficulties. For example, people may not understand the information or advice they receive, and such problems may be age-related (Karp and Wilson, 2011). In addition, people may receive biased advice that may not be in their best interest when they have difficulty evaluating the quality of the advice received. According to a survey by the Investor Protection Trust, about 20 percent of adults aged 65 or older report having 'been taken advantage of financially in terms of an inappropriate investment, unreasonably high fees for financial services, or outright fraud' (Infogroup/ORC, 2010). Other problems they may encounter are inaccurate information, such as use of overly optimistic rate of return assumptions in financial projections (Turner and Witte, 2009), or lack of advice on certain topics, such as annuitization (Turner, 2010).

Next we turn to problems in understanding advice caused by terminology, advice relating to the marketing of products where a fiduciary duty does not apply, and problems in quality of advice caused by conflicts of interest that advisers may have.

Terminology

Financial advice can be hard to understand because of the terminology advisers use: for instance, consumers may be unclear as to the difference between a fee and a commission, or know what a load is. A fee is a payment the adviser receives from the client for providing advice. A commission is a payment the adviser receives for selling a financial product. A load is the commission investors pay when they purchase retail mutual funds. Other examples include 'wrap fees' and 'discretionary versus non-discretionary assets.' A wrap fee is a fee charged for providing a bundle of services, without breaking out the charges for the different components of the bundle. Discretionary assets are assets for which the client has delegated responsibility for management to the management company. The fine print relating to financial advice is often difficult to comprehend. As an example, prospectuses may mention 12b-1 fees, with no explanation as to what they are. These fees are marketing or distribution fees charged by mutual funds.

Advice related to marketing where a fiduciary duty does not apply

When marketing products to consumers, financial service providers often do not have a duty to provide advice in the best interest of the client (GAO, 2011*a*). For example, many insurance companies market variable annuities. These are investment products until retirement, at which point the investor has the option of converting them to annuities, with one option being converting them to variable annuities whose payouts vary depending on the investment performance of the underlying assets. One firm suggests that variable annuities offer for market appreciation with tax-deferred accumulation and future income. The SEC, however, suggests that many people may be better off investing the maximum amounts in their IRA and 401(k) plans before purchasing variable annuities (SEC, 2011*f*).

Conflicts of interest can arise with financial advisers at several points in the 401(k) decision-making process. For instance, plan participants may be affected by conflicts of interest when sponsors receive advice as to what investment options to include. This determines the choice set, given participation in the plan. In recent court cases, some 401(k) plan participants allege they lost millions of dollars collectively because of investment options with high fees that benefited their plans' investment managers. Participants may pay too much in fees when low-fee options are not available (GAO, 2011a).

Moreover, financial advisers may encourage pension participants to not contribute more than the amount necessary to receive the full employer match, and instead to put extra savings into financial products outside the plan if the adviser receives commissions on those products (Pettus and Kesmodel, 2010).

Plan participants may also be affected by conflicts of interest of advisers when they select funds from among the investment options available to them. Some participants may not distinguish between financial education, where the provider does not have a fiduciary obligation, and financial advice, where the provider may have a fiduciary obligation. Participants may become confused, for example, if advisers highlight only the products of the company providing the education (GAO, 2011a).

Sometimes a financial adviser may fail to explain the value of selecting low-fee funds, for instance when the adviser is connected to a mutual fund family, so he may recommend only those funds without mentioning fees. The potential magnitude of this conflict can be assessed from data on expense ratios. In 2010, according to the Investment Company Institute (ICI), the asset-weighted expense ratio for stock mutual funds invested in 401(k) plans was 71 basis points (ICI, 2011a). This figure represents the result of decisions by plan sponsors as to what funds to offer, as well as decisions by plan participants as to what funds to choose. This figure is higher than the expense ratios for institutional low-cost stock index mutual funds. While 401(k) participants may receive more services than do individual investors, which raises costs, employers could negotiate for institutional rates to lower costs.

Participants may also be adversely affected by conflicts of interest by advisers when participants leave the companies sponsoring their 401(k) plans. That is, some individuals may encounter biased advice when considering whether to roll over a 401(k) plan to an IRA. Research suggests that providers may gain higher fees from consumers moving their money to investments outside 401(k) plans (GAO, 2011a). Mutual fund companies and insurers encourage individuals to roll over their 401(k) plan accounts from former employers into IRAs. This may not be in the best interests of individuals, due to possibly paying higher fees. Individuals may also encounter advice to roll over their 401(k) accounts, even when not seeking advice, since mutual funds advertise their advice on television and in other media. The US Department of Labor (2011) currently does not consider this type of advice to be investment advice, and thus it is not covered by fiduciary standards. Also, individuals may be affected by conflicts of interest when they seek advice as to the investments of their IRAs.

The potential magnitude of the costs resulting from advice concerning rollovers from 401(k) plans to IRAs is large. Between 1998 and 2007, more than 80 percent of funds contributed to IRAs came from rollovers from other plans, primarily 401(k) plans but also including other defined contribution (DC) plans and DB plans (GAO, 2011b). In 2010, IRAs held $4.5 trillion in assets versus $2.9 trillion in 401(k) plans (Investment Company Institute, 2011b); accordingly, IRA rollovers are one of the main drivers of the structure of the US retirement income system. IRA account holders typically pay higher fees than 401(k) plan participants—about 25 to 30 basis points a year higher (GAO, 2011a).

Inertia would tend to cause 401(k) participants to keep their 401(k) accounts with their former employers where sensible. Inertia has been cited as a powerful force regarding employee contributions to 401(k) plans (Choi et al., 2004). The force of inertia, however, has been overcome with respect to rollovers in a major way. One explanation for this phenomenon may be that individuals receive advice from mutual funds and other financial service providers, encouraging them to roll over their 401(k) accounts to earn higher fees.

Conflicts of interest affecting individual investors

For individuals holding non-qualified investments (investments not benefiting from the preferential tax treatment received by pensions), the potential for conflicts of interest depends on the choice of investments. Due to how advisers are compensated, some may provide biased advice to individuals concerning the choices between mutual funds and individual stocks; for example, some advisers are paid by mutual funds that their clients select, biasing them in favor of those funds. Others may receive higher compensation for recommending individual stocks in a portfolio they manage than for recommending low-cost mutual funds. At Schwab, advisers receive 0.0028 percent of assets as a fee for funds invested in individual stocks, 0.0350 percent of assets for money invested in mutual funds, 0.0595 percent for assets invested in Schwab-managed portfolios, and 0.0770 percent for assets enrolled in Schwab Private Client where the adviser provides ongoing services (Schwab, 2011b). At Ameriprise (2011), some employees receive higher compensation if they recommend and sell affiliated mutual funds, than if they sell mutual funds not affiliated with Ameriprise. Conflicts of interest also arise when a firm underwriting an IPO (Initial Public Offering of stock) also provides advice to retail clients, encouraging them to purchase the stock (Loewenstein et al., 2011).

Financial advisers charging ongoing fees may also be biased toward recommending active management associated with higher transaction costs, rather than passive management in index funds, so as to boost the commissions from the broker-dealer that the adviser receives (GAO, 2011*a*). Schwab (2011*b*) compensates some advisers based on the clients increasing the amount of trading that they do.

Issues affecting the quality of financial advice provided to plan sponsors

Conflicts of interest affecting the quality of advice are also relevant to plan sponsors, because some mutual funds pay advisers who recommend funds. These payments can create a conflict of interest, if an adviser directly or indirectly receives compensation from marketing certain funds. Furthermore, low-cost funds tend not to offer such payments. For example, some mutual funds offer share classes with no revenue sharing and lower expense ratios, alongside share classes with revenue sharing and higher expense ratios (Reish and Ashton, 2011). Revenue sharing occurs when a mutual fund pays an adviser to recommend the fund (Moon, 2004). The payments may be characterized as paying for expenses relating to selling the fund. At least one service provider—Securion—deals with the issue of revenue sharing by passing on all revenue sharing to the plan, crediting the amounts to the individual accounts that generated the revenue sharing (Reish and Ashton, 2011).

The amount of revenue-sharing payments advisers receive varies considerably. One study found that payments range from 5 to 125 basis points annually (GAO, 2011*b*). Employee Retirement Income Security Act (ERISA; US private pension law) requires pension plan sponsors to consider conflicts of interest when selecting service providers (GAO, 2011*a*). For example, an investment adviser may purposely not negotiate for the lowest transaction fees for plan participants for buying and selling shares. As a result, the broker-dealer would pay the investment adviser out of these higher fees (GAO, 2011*a*).

Evolving legal and regulatory issues

The US legal system has struggled in recent years with the regulation of financial advisers, including regulation of the services they provide to employee benefit plans sponsored by private-sector employers. The continuing evolution of the legal and regulatory issues may be attributed to a number of factors. The increase in assets held in 401(k)-style plans and

IRAs has drawn the attention of regulators to the importance of investment selection in retirement security (EBSA, 2011). Behavioral economists have contributed to the debate by investigating questions such as whether investors benefit from an expanded set of investment alternatives (Benartzi and Thaler, 2002). Among the research mandated by Congress after the financial crisis was a study of the regulation of financial planners by the Government Accountability Office (GAO), an independent agency of the federal government, and a study of the regulation of investment advisers and broker-dealers by the Staff of the SEC (GAO, 2011b; SEC Staff, 2011b). The SEC is responsible for regulation of the US capital markets and investor protection. Next we explain legal issues as they relate to financial advisers, provide some background on the history of those issues, and update the status of regulatory efforts.

Conflicts of interest

The primary legal issues regarding investment advisers are grounded in identification of the conflicts of interest that may exist in the provision of investment advice and how best to mitigate such conflicts in ways that are understandable to investors. The SEC is concerned with these issues as part of its general mandate to protect investors and specifically in its interpretation and enforcement of the Investment Advisers Act of 1940 (Advisers Act). The Employee Benefits Security Administration (EBSA) of the Department of Labor has an overlapping regulatory interest because of its mandate to regulate private-sector employee benefit plans, such as 401(k) plans, including regulation of the entities that provide services to those plans and to the employees who participate in the plans. As discussed below, the overlapping regulatory authority of the SEC and EBSA increases the complexity of regulatory efforts. That complexity is increased further through the involvement of the self-regulatory agency, FINRA, which regulates broker-dealers including broker-dealers who provide investment advice, and various state agencies that regulate advisers who engage in securities-related transactions and sales of insurance products.

The US legal system uses three methods to mitigate conflicts of interest. Those three methods are: (*a*) requiring disclosure, (*b*) prohibiting specified actions, and (*c*) subjecting actions or actors to fiduciary duties. Each of these methods is used in the context of investment advice. Turning to disclosure first, the relevant legal standard may require that an actor such as an investment adviser disclose its conflicts of interest so that the client can consider the existence of the conflicts when selecting an investment adviser and in evaluating its recommendations. For advisers who are fiduciaries, disclosure of conflicts of interest typically is part of the adviser's general fiduciary duties.

Specific disclosure requirements sometimes go beyond the general fiduciary obligations. For example, advisers who register with the SEC must disclose conflicts of interest in their public filings (SEC Staff, 2011*b*: 19, 22). Federal securities laws require broker-dealers to register with the SEC and prohibit broker-dealers from engaging in fraudulent actions. The prohibition on fraud results in an implied obligation to disclose significant conflicts of interest. FINRA rules require broker-dealers to disclose conflicts of interest in certain situations but the FINRA staff does not believe that there is a general requirement that broker-dealers disclose their conflicts of interest at the beginning of a client relationship or transaction (GAO, 2011*b*).

The second method of mitigating conflicts of interest—prohibition—applies to some investment advice provided regarding benefit plan assets through ERISA's ban on 'prohibited transactions.' Prohibited transactions include transactions where a fiduciary to a plan or an affiliate of the fiduciary is compensated for providing investment advice to participants in the plan (EBSA, 2011: 66,136). Exemptions from these prohibitions do exist and permit actions by any party so long as the actions fit within the terms of the exemption. EBSA has provided guidance and exemptions over time regarding the provision of investment advice on benefit plan assets. As explained later, legislation in 2006 provided a new, statutory prohibited transaction exemption for certain transactions connected with the provision of investment advice (Muir, 2010).

The Advisers Act also contains categorical prohibitions relating to investment advice. For example, it prohibits investment advisers, whether registered with the SEC or not, from charging advisory fees based on account performance. There are limited exceptions from that prohibition, such as for advice provided to high net worth individuals.

The third legal response to conflicts of interest is to designate the conflicted adviser as a fiduciary. Because of the complexity involved in fiduciary obligation and the incentives established by such a designation we address those matters next, and in some detail.

Investment advisers as fiduciaries

First we discuss the standard of conduct a fiduciary investment adviser must meet and compare it with the standards applied to non-fiduciary advisers. Next we describe the lines the current legal definitions draw between when an investment adviser is a fiduciary and when an adviser is not a fiduciary. Then we explain how the standards and the technical legal definitions result in confusion among investors about whether the investment advice they receive is provided by a fiduciary or a non-fiduciary adviser.

The effect of fiduciary regulation on investment advisers

The legal obligations owed by a fiduciary to its clients significantly exceed the obligations owed in traditional contracting relationships. The higher standard is the point of imposing a fiduciary obligation to mitigate conflicts of interest. The precise obligations of a fiduciary vary depending on factors such as context and statutory provisions. There is general agreement though that all fiduciaries must meet the basic duties of: (*a*) loyalty, which requires the fiduciary to act in the client's best interest, and (*b*) care, which requires the fiduciary to act reasonably on the client's behalf (Laby, 2008: 105–6). The duty of loyalty responds directly to the threats imposed by conflicts of interests and generally requires, among other things, that a fiduciary subordinate its own interests to the interests of its client (Laby, 2011: 1055).

ERISA implements the fiduciary duty of loyalty through its statutory 'exclusive purpose rule.' As a result, fiduciaries of employee benefit plans, including 401(k) plans, must act for the purpose of providing plan benefits and paying plan expenses and not for their own benefit. For example, if management fiduciaries advised employees with employer stock in their 401(k) plans not to tender company stock in a tender offer in order to entrench management, that advice probably would violate the exclusive purpose fiduciary obligation (Muir, 2002: 21).

Similarly, the Advisers Act requires an investment adviser to 'serve the best interests of its clients, which includes an obligation not to subordinate the clients' interests to its own' (SEC Staff, 2011*b*: 22). The Advisers Act also requires an investment adviser to disclose information on conflicts of interest (SEC Staff, 2011*b*: 22).

In contrast with the fiduciary duty of loyalty, non-fiduciaries are often referred to as interacting with others at 'arm's length.' At arm's length is the standard that typically is applied to business transactions where each party is expected to work or negotiate in its best interest. Black's law dictionary defines at arm's length as: 'Beyond the reach of personal influence or control... [w]ithout trusting to the other's fairness or integrity' (Black, 1983). Specifically, broker-dealers who are not fiduciaries because they provide financial advice that is incidental to their work as broker-dealers and do not receive 'special compensation' for the investment advice are governed by a suitability standard—the advice must be suitable for the client. Suitability is a lower standard than a requirement to act in a client's best interest. The standard of care required of insurance agents depends on the law of the relevant state but may be a suitability standard (GAO, 2011*b*: 16–17).

Understanding the effect of fiduciary regulation on investment advisers requires understanding not just the obligations imposed on advisers but also the penalties imposed for fiduciary breach. ERISA permits EBSA or individuals to bring lawsuits for breach of fiduciary duties and contains potentially severe penalties. Those harmed by a fiduciary breach may receive a monetary award to compensate for the harm. And, a court may prohibit a breaching person or entity from acting as a fiduciary to other ERISA plans (Stanley, 2000: 701). Some commentators have argued that these relief provisions are insufficient to discourage illegal conduct because punitive damages, pain and suffering, and similar kinds of relief are not available (Schultz, 2011). By contrast, the Advisers Act does not permit individual investors to bring lawsuits alleging fiduciary breach; instead the SEC has enforcement authority (SEC 44). That authority permits the SEC to impose a variety of remedies for fiduciary breach, including monetary penalties and revocation of the adviser's registration (SEC Staff, 2011*b*: 44, A-17).

The law imposes fiduciary standards and penalties for breach of those standards in order to protect investors from conflicts. Entities that provide investment advice may react to the fiduciary standards in one of three ways. First, the investment adviser might comply with the fiduciary standards. This may result in higher costs for advice as a result of compliance efforts (e.g., SEC Staff, 2011*b*: 146). As is typical with regulation, the increased costs that result from compliance may be passed along to the investors who receive advice and to benefit plans that hire advice providers. The increased costs may result in decreased use of investment advice. Second, if the fiduciary standards are imposed by ERISA then the investment adviser might refuse to provide advice regarding benefit plan assets. Again, the result is that the imposition of the fiduciary standard would result in a decrease in the amount of advice available to benefit plans and to the individuals who earn benefits under the plans. The third possibility is that an adviser may avoid the cost of fiduciary regulation by providing investment advice in such a way that the adviser avoids being categorized by the law as a fiduciary. Next we discuss the line drawing that determines fiduciary status and the steps an adviser might take to avoid that status.

Current legal definition of investment advisers as fiduciaries

As we noted earlier, various terms are used in the brokerage and advisory industries to describe individuals and entities that provide advice on financial matters. Most of those terms do not have a precise legal definition. However, since fiduciary status gives rise to significant duties, substantial penalties for breach of those standards, and, thus, possibly an incentive to avoid fiduciary status, the definition of when an investment adviser is a fiduciary is important to both advisers and their clients. The regulators continue to struggle with the definitional questions. Here the complexity resulting from overlapping regulation becomes apparent because each regulator has a different definition for when an investment adviser is a fiduciary.

As a general matter, the Advisers Act defines the term 'investment adviser' in a reasonably straightforward manner as an individual or entity who is compensated for providing advice related to investments in securities. The Advisers Act's requirements, including its fiduciary standards, apply to any entity that fits within the definition. There are, however, a number of exceptions from the definition of 'investment adviser,' including broker-dealers who provide investment advice that is incidental to their work as a broker-dealer and who do not receive 'special compensation' for the advice. The result of the exceptions, especially when combined with the various terminologies used in the industry, can be confusing for investors who then find it difficult to determine whether their adviser is obligated to work in their best interest or owes them only a duty to recommend a suitable investment.

Under ERISA the standards are different. The statute contains alternate ways a person interacting with a benefit plan or its assets might become a fiduciary. The relevant language for investment advisers is that a person is a fiduciary if 'he renders investment advice for a fee or other compensation, direct or indirect...' (ERISA, 1974: Sec. 3(21)). This relatively clear language, however, is complicated by regulations. The regulations have long made clear that provision of investment education is not in itself a fiduciary action (Muir, 2002: 18–19). Thus, a rational provider of investment-related services may choose to provide only investment education or to charge higher fees for investment advice than for investment education. This gives rise to legal issues over the line between investment advice and investment education (Muir, 2002).

A second set of complications results from regulations issued in 1975 that established a significantly narrower, five-part definition of when a provider of investment advice becomes a fiduciary regarding benefit plan assets. In summary, according to the regulations, an investment adviser is not a fiduciary when giving advice regarding benefit plan assets or an IRA unless the adviser (*a*) advises on securities valuation or makes recommendations on the purchase or sale of securities, (*b*) on a regular basis, (*c*) according to a mutual agreement with the plan or a plan fiduciary, (*d*) that provides the advice will serve as the primary basis for decisions on investments, and (*e*) the advice is individualized to the plan's needs (EBSA, 2010). By avoiding meeting this narrower regulatory definition when giving advice, a financial adviser currently may give investment advice for a fee regarding benefit plan assets but avoid the fiduciary obligations imposed on an adviser who provides advice regarding the assets of a benefit plan or IRA.

Investor confusion resulting from industry practice

The complexities in the current definitions of when an adviser is a fiduciary combined with the lack of uniform terminology, the variety of services an adviser may provide, and the many different professional designations have given rise to concerns that investors can be confused about the standard of care owed to them by their adviser. A study by the GAO, an independent, investigative agency that reports to Congress, of financial planners observed that when one individual or firm provides a variety of services, the standard of care may vary with the services. This finding was consistent with an earlier study by the RAND Corporation of various perspectives on investment adviser and broker-dealer services (Hung et al., 2008). The variation of the standard of care with the type of service provided is known as a 'hat-switching' problem. For example, if the financial planner is purchasing securities for the client, the planner is wearing its broker-dealer hat and owes only a duty of suitability. When the planner provides advice under the classic Advisers Act definition of investment advice, the planner is wearing its Advisers Act hat and must act in the client's best interest (GAO, 2011*b*). An additional point of confusion not discussed by the GAO is that if the planner is providing advice regarding benefit plan assets and meets ERISA's definition of a fiduciary then the planner is wearing its ERISA fiduciary hat. This results in application of a standard of care similar to the Advisers Act fiduciary standard but, as explained above, a different set of remedies if the standard of care is breached.

The GAO's observations about the possibility of investor confusion are backed up by other research. Focus group studies indicate that investors do not understand the differences between investment advisers and broker-dealers, including the different types of services the two groups provide and the differences in their legal obligations (SEC Staff, 2011*b*). A larger study identified the interlocking relationships between entities that offer a variety of services, such as both brokerage and advisory services, as one source of the difficulty investors have in teasing apart the obligations. The GAO has recommended that a study the SEC is currently doing on the financial literacy of investors includes an investigation into whether investors are confused by the various certifications used and roles played by financial advisers and, if so, whether the confusion affects investment decisions (GAO, 2011*b*).

Current rule making and reports on fiduciary investment advisers

As noted above, the regulation of investment advisers has long been part of the agendas of the SEC and EBSA. In recent years, the agencies have undertaken studies and proposed regulations regarding investment advice, some of which have come at the direction of Congress. In 2006, the Pension Protection Act (PPA) initiated EBSA regulatory efforts to expand access to investment advice. The SEC and EBSA have issued reports and regulations related to investment advice in the wake of the financial crisis and as directed by Congress in the Dodd-Frank Wall Street Reform and Consumer Protection Act (Dodd-Frank, 2010). To explore these, we begin by discussing the agencies' actions on the definitional question of what types of actions are subject to fiduciary duties. Next we review recent regulations that expand the ways in which advisers may offer investment advice to 401(k)-type plan participants and holders of IRAs. In a final section, we explain efforts to expand the disclosure of fees charged in 401(k) plans.

In early 2011, as required by the Dodd-Frank Act, the Staff of the SEC issued a report evaluating the regulation of investment advice provided by both investment advisers and broker-dealers. As noted above, the Advisers Act contains a broad definition of 'investment adviser' but excludes broker-dealers from its regulation if the broker-dealer's provision of advice is incidental and it does not receive any 'special compensation' for the advice. The SEC Staff's study of this bifurcated regulatory system concluded that a unified federal fiduciary standard and regulatory system should be applied to both investment advisers and to broker-dealers when they provide individualized investment advice to retail customers (SEC Staff, 2011*b*). If adopted, the unified standard would decrease the incidence of the hat-switching problem. The report was controversial even at the highest levels of the SEC. Three of the SEC Commissioners, those who govern the SEC, voted to submit the Staff study to Congress, over the objection of two Commissioners. The Dodd-Frank Act granted the SEC authority to apply the same standards to broker-dealers as apply to investment advisers under the Advisers Act. There were indications that the SEC would propose regulations on the topic in early 2012 (Christie, 2011) but that effort has been delayed indefinitely while the SEC gathers cost–benefit data (Zamansky, 2012). The SEC and Congress also are considering changes to the way compliance examinations of investment advisers are conducted, including the possibility of a self-regulatory organization with authority for additional oversight (SEC Staff, 2011*a*).

On the fiduciary definitional question, in 2010 EBSA proposed a change in its long-standing regulation defining when the provision of investment advice regarding benefit plan or IRA assets results in fiduciary status. The result would be that an investment adviser would no longer have to provide individualized advice on a regular basis according to an agreement that the advice would be the primary basis for the investment decision in order to be considered a fiduciary of a benefit plan or IRA. The proposal would have dramatically increased the scope of financial advisory activities that result in a provider becoming a fiduciary when giving investment advice regarding benefit plan or IRA assets. The proposed regulatory definition tracked the general statutory definition and specifically stated that investment advice or recommendations given to a plan participant or beneficiary or to an investor regarding an IRA are a fiduciary act (EBSA, 2010). By decreasing the ability of individuals and entities to avoid fiduciary status, the proposed standard would have decreased the incidence of the hat-switching problem. In September 2011, EBSA withdrew the proposed regulations, which had generated substantial controversy (DOL, 2011). Current indications are that it will revise and re-propose the regulations in 2013 while continuing to coordinate its efforts with the SEC.

As discussed above, both ERISA's fiduciary and prohibited transactions rules impose constraints on the provision of investment advice regarding benefit plan assets. To date, investment advice provided by ERISA fiduciaries, a role held by many large financial institutions, to holders of 401(k) accounts typically has been structured to meet one of two models approved by EBSA in opinion letters. The first is known as the SunAmerica model. It allows financial entities to provide advice though computer models if the computer models are developed and controlled by an independent third party. The second model is the level fee model. It prohibits the investment adviser's compensation, or the compensation of any employer or affiliate of the adviser, from varying as a result of the investment choices made according to the advice (Muir, 2009).

In 2006, Congress enacted the PPA, which explicitly addressed the regulation of investment advice provided in benefit plans, and theoretically granted more flexibility to investment advice providers than existed under the SunAmerica or level fee models. However, Congress left a number of details in the PPA to be determined by EBSA through the regulatory process. The agency's initial regulations interpreting the PPA provisions were extremely controversial, because they arguably provided more flexibility than the legislation mandated, and were not implemented (Muir, 2009). After making significant revisions, EBSA finalized those regulations and they became effective in December 2011.

The new regulations do not change the old fee leveling and computer model platforms but do give advice providers alternative ways to structure their advice products. In order to utilize either of the new exemptions, an investment advice provider must meet a number of technical requirements. One of the requirements of the new regulations is that advisers must request details from each investor regarding such factors as age, risk tolerance, current investments, and other assets. Another is that any computer model must take into account nearly all of the investment options available in a plan including company stock. The requirements of fee leveling do not extend to the affiliates of the adviser. Thus, if the adviser is affiliated with an entity that provides investment products, the fees of the affiliate that result from the investment advice are permitted to vary depending on the investments made as a result of that advice.

As discussed above, disclosure is one of the general mechanisms the law uses to mitigate conflicts of interest. EBSA has taken action in the last few years to enhance the disclosure of investment-related fees by issuing two new regulations on fees. The first is effective for contracts as of July 2012, requiring service providers who are fiduciaries or registered investment advisers providing a broad array of services and expecting to receive at least $1,000 in compensation to disclose that compensation to plan fiduciaries. For certain services believed to be significant or to present possible conflicts of interest, the services and costs must be described separately even if the services and costs are bundled. The second regulation is linked to the effective date of the fiduciary disclosure regulation and was generally applicable in August 2012. It requires plans to provide participants and beneficiaries in DC (e.g., 401(k)) plans with information about the plan and with investment-related information including performance data and fee and expense information related to investment alternatives (EBSA, 2010).

Conclusion

Because of the dominance of 401(k) plans and IRAs in the US retirement planning landscape, the market for financial advice is of increasing importance to pension policy. Researchers have documented numerous factors, from lack of financial sophistication to lack of interest, that inhibit individuals from making optimal investment decisions. In contrast to the challenges faced by individuals who make their own investment decisions, the US Department of Labor estimated that in 2010 financial advice saved pension participants $15 billion in financial errors (EBSA, 2011). Policymakers and plan sponsors have recognized the potential benefits investment advisers can provide and, thus, have sought to enhance the quantity and quality of financial advice available to individuals with IRA and 401(k) accounts.

Our examination of the market for financial advice establishes several of the market's characteristics provide important flexibility and information to advisory clients. Advisers engage with clients in a variety of ways, from providing individualized advice to managing assets, which permits services to be tailored to individual needs. The scope of advice provided may be shaped to accommodate the level of complexity of a client's financial situation. Similarly, an individual interested in engaging an investment adviser has access to a significant volume of information about the adviser as a result of federal disclosure requirements and numerous potential professional certifications, in addition to the extensive marketing done by some advisers. Finally, fee structures for investment advice vary in numerous ways.

The flexibility and variability in the market for financial advice, however, also result in complexity that poses two related hazards. First, the presence of conflicts of interest, which are inherent in some fee structures, may result in some advisers providing investment advice that is not always in the best interest of their clients. The conflicts may not always be obvious to the individuals and benefit plans that seek investment advice. Second, because of the variety of certifications, different types of financial market participants who provide advice, and layers of disclosure and marketing materials, advisory clients may be unaware or confused about the level of legal protections that govern their relationships with their advisers. This is especially true when an adviser provides a client with various services that are governed by different standards of care, giving rise to the 'hat-switching' problem. The client may not understand that the adviser must act in the client's best interest in some transactions but in others merely must provide advice suitable to the client's situation.

The regulatory framework addresses both conflicts of interest and investors' informational requirements. The three mechanisms utilized by the regulatory system—disclosure requirements, prohibitions on some actions, and the imposition of fiduciary duty—are useful regulatory tools that provide significant protection to participants and establish a floor for industry standards. However, here too complexity has costs. For example, the overlapping regulatory jurisdiction has resulted in a variety of different disclosure requirements depending on the type of service being provided. And, whether an advice provider is a fiduciary or not may depend on whether the advice involves assets of a tax-favored retirement account. These and other complexities sometimes result in confused investors and a subset of advice providers who choose to operate in ways that may be less than optimal for their clients or the advice industry. Regulatory efforts are underway in the United States to address informational issues and to rationalize the application of fiduciary standards, with the ultimate goal being to increase the quality and quantity of investment advice to support retirement security.

We have received excellent research assistance from Alexandra Kahn and Jonathan Roselle, have benefited from discussions with Stephen Utkus and Ron Gebhardtsbauer on some issues discussed in this chapter, and have received valuable comments from Arthur Laby, Olivia S. Mitchell, and Kent Smetters.

Endnotes

1. Due to space limitations, we do not consider a number of related topics including financial advice to individuals as small business owners, such as advice on what type of pension plan to offer, or advice to individuals concerning tax planning, estate planning, insurance, or obtaining a mortgage. We also exclude advice to people with high net worth, because they are relatively few and presumably are more sophisticated investors than people with lower net worth. Having high net worth does not guarantee that people are satisfied with the financial advice they receive; one survey of affluent investors found that 85 percent was sufficiently dissatisfied as to consider switching advisers (Girouard, 2010). The Securities and Exchange Commission (SEC, 2011a) defines for purposes of its ADV Form an individual with high net worth as an individual with at least $750,000 managed by one company, or whose net worth a company reasonably believes exceeds $1,500,000. The net worth of an individual may include assets held jointly with his or her spouse.
2. One financial columnist recommends financial advisers with the Certified Financial Planner designation (Anspach, 2011b) and advisers with the Personal Financial Specialist (PFS) designation, a designation that only Certified Public Accountants (CPAs) can earn. For investment advisers, she recommends Chartered Financial Analysts (CFAs).

References

American Institute of Certified Public Accountants (2011). *Personal Financial Planning.* New York, NY: American Institute of CPAs. http://www.aicpa.org/InterestAreas/Personal%20FinancialPlanning/Pages/default.aspx

Ameriprise (2011). *Purchasing Mutual Funds and 529 Plans through Ameriprise Financial.* Minneapolis, MN: Ameriprise Financial, Inc. http://investment.ameriprise.com/mutual-funds/purchasing-mutual-funds-thru-ameriprise.asp

Anspach, D. (2011a). *6 Ways Financial Advisors Charge Fees.* New York, NY: About.com. http://moneyover55.about.com/od/findingqualifiedadvisors/a/finadvisorfees.htm

—— (2011b). *Understanding Financial Advisor Credentials.* New York, NY: About.com. http://moneyover55.about.com/od/findingqualifiedadvisors/a/advisorcred.htm

Bank of America Merrill Lynch (2011). *Retirement & Benefit Plan Services.* New York, NY: Bank of America Corporation. http://www.benefitplans.baml.com/IR/Pages/ts_er.aspx

Benartzi, S., and R. H. Thaler (2002). 'How Much is Investor Autonomy Worth?' *Journal of Finance,* 57(4): 1593–616.

Benjamin F. Edwards & Co. (2011). *Mutual Fund Sales Charges and Breakpoints.* St. Louis, MO: Benjamin F. Edwards & Co. www.benjaminfedwards.com/content.php?pageID=mut_fund_discl

Black, H. C. (1983). *Black's Law Dictionary.* St. Paul, MN: West Publishing Co.

Bliman, N. (2011). 'BrightScope Roles Out Adviser Data Base,' *PlanAdviser.* Stamford, CT: Asset International, Inc. http://www.planadviser.com/NewsArticleProducts.aspx?id=14286&page=1

BrightScope, Inc. (2011). *Advisor Pages*. San Diego, CA: BrightScope, Inc. http://www.brightscope.com/financial-planning/find/advisor/

Bucks, B. F., A. B. Kennickel, T. L. Mach, and K. B. Moore (2009). 'Changes in US Family Finances from 2004 to 2007: Evidence from the Survey of Consumer Finances,' *Federal Reserve Bulletin*, February: A1–A56. http://www.federalreserve.gov/pubs/bulletin/2009/pdf/scf09.pdf

Certified Financial Planner Board (2011a). *CFP Board Mission*. Washington, DC: Certified Financial Planner Board of Standards, Inc. http://www.cfp.net/

—— (2011b). *Topic List for CFP Certification Examination*. Washington, DC: Certified Financial Planner Board of Standards, Inc. http://www.cfp.net/downloads/Financial%20Planning%20Topics%202006.pdf

—— (2011c). *Types of Financial Advisors*. Washington, DC: Certified Financial Planner Board of Standards, Inc. http://letsmakeaplan.org/Why-You-Need-A-Plan/Types-of-Financial-Advisors.aspx?gclid=CNrpgrKLuKoCFeJ65Qodv%20DYT8A

Chartered Financial Analyst (CFA) Institute (2011). *What We Stand For*. New York, NY: CFA Institute. http://www.cfainstitute.org/about/strategy/Pages/index.aspx

Choi, J. J., D. Laibson, and B. Madrian (2004). 'Plan Design and 401(k) Savings Outcomes,' *National Tax Journal*, 52(2): 275–98.

Christie, S. (2011). 'IAA's Tittsworth: Fiduciary Ruling Likely in Q1 of 2012: RIS,' *AdvisorOne*. Erlanger, KY: AdvisorOne. http://www.advisorone.com/2011/10/21/iaas-tittsworth-fiduciary-ruling-likely-in-q1-of-2

Dodd-Frank Wall Street Reform and Consumer Protection Act (2010). Public Law 111–203.

Drucker, D. J. (2005). 'Accounting for CPA Referrals: Why Are CPAs Selling Client Referrals, and Should You Be Buying?' *Financial Advisor*. Shrewsbury, NJ: Charter Financial Publishing Network, Inc. http://www.fa-mag.com/component/content/article/1126.html?issue=56&magazineID=1&Itemid=27

Edelman Financial Services (2011). *The Edelman 401(k)—Ric Edelman*. Fairfax, VA: Edelman Financial Services. http://www.ricedelman.com/galleries/default-file/401k_brochure_0617.pdf

Employee Retirement Income Security Act (1974). Public Law 93–406.

Financial Engines (2011). *Understanding the Accidental Investor: Baby Boomers on Retirement*. Palo Alto, CA: Financial Engines, Inc. http://corp.financialengines.com/employer/Accidental_Investor_April2011.pdf

FINRA (2011a). *Understanding Professional Designations*. Washington, DC: Financial Industry Regulatory Authority, Inc. http://apps.finra.org/DataDirectory/1/prodesignations.aspx

—— (2011b). 'Use FINRA BrokerCheck to Review Your Broker's Record.' *Investor Newsletter*. Washington, DC: FINRA. July. http://www.finra.org/Investors/Subscriptions/InvestorNews/P123886

Girouard, J. E. (2010). 'Why Clients Distrust Advisors,' *Forbes*. New York, NY: Forbes.com. http://www.forbes.com/2010/04/06/client-retention-financial-advisor-network-high-net-worth.html

GuidedChoice (2011). *Pricing and Fees*. San Diego, CA: GuidedChoice, Inc. http://www.guidedchoice.com/index.php?option=com_content&view=article&id=33&Itemid=15

Hastings, J. S., and O. S. Mitchell (2011). 'How Financial Literacy and Impatience Shape Retirement Wealth and Investment Behaviors,' National Bureau of Economic Research Paper No. 16740. Cambridge, MA: NBER.

Hung, A. K., N. Clancy, J. Dominitz, E. Talley, C. Berrebi, and F. Suvankulov (2008). 'Investor and Industry Perspectives on Investment Advisers and Broker-Dealers,' RAND Technical Report. Santa Monica, CA: RAND. http://www.rand.org/pubs/technical_reports/TR556.html

Infogroup/ORC (2010). *Elder Investment Fraud and Financial Exploitation: A Survey Conducted for Investor Protection Trust.* Papillion, NE: Infogroup/ORC. http://www.investorprotection.org/downloads/EIFFE_Survey_Report.pdf

Investment Adviser Association (2011). *Chartered Investment Counselor Program and Designation.* Washington, DC: Investment Adviser Association. https://www.investmentadviser.org/eweb/dynamicpage.aspx?webcode=cic

Investment Company Institute (2011*a*). 'The Economics of Providing 401(k) Plans: Services, Fees, and Expenses, 2010.' *ICI Research Perspective*, 17(4). Washington, DC: Investment Company Institute.

—— (2011*b*). *The US Retirement Market: Third Quarter 2010.* Washington, DC: Investment Company Institute. http://www.ici.org/pdf/ppr_11_retire_q3_10.pdf

Karp, N., and R. Wilson (2011). 'Protecting Older Investors: The Challenge of Diminished Capacity,' AARP Public Policy Institute Research Report No. 2011–04. New York, NY: AARP Public Policy Institute.

Kolakowski, M. (2011). *Insurance Sales Agents.* New York, NY: About.com. http://financecareers.about.com/od/insurance/a/insuranceagent.htm

Laby, A. B. (2008). 'The Fiduciary Obligation as the Adoption of Ends,' *Buffalo Law Review*, 56(1): 100–67.

—— (2011). '*SEC v. Capital Gains Research Bureau* and the Investment Advisers Act of 1940,' *Boston University Law Review*, 91(3): 1051–104.

Loewenstein, G., M. C. Daylian, M. Cain, and S. Sah (2011). 'The Limits of Transparency: Pitfalls and Potential of Disclosing Conflicts of Interest,' *American Economic Review*, 101(3): 423–28.

Lusardi, A., and O. S. Mitchell (2006). 'Financial Literacy and Planning: Implications for Retirement Wellbeing,' Pension Research Council Working Paper No. WP 2006-1. Philadelphia, PA: Pension Research Council.

Maxey, D. (2011). 'How to Pay Your Financial Adviser.' *The Wall Street Journal.* December 12.

McCarthy, D. M., and J. A. Turner (2000). 'Pension Education: Does It Help? Does It Matter?' *Benefits Quarterly*, 16: 64–72.

Merrill Edge (2011). *Invest with Advisors.* New York, NY: Bank of America Corporation. http://www.merrilledge.com/m/pages/merrill-edge-advisory-center.aspx

Merrill Lynch (2010). *Global Wealth & Investment Management.* New York, NY: Bank of America Corporation. http://www.ml.com/?id=7695_8134_114044

MetLife (2011). *About MetLife Securities, Inc.* New York, NY: Metropolitan Life Insurance Company. http://www.metlife.com/individual/investment-products/mutual-fund/index.html?WT.ac=GN_individual_investment-products_mutual-fund

Moon, Kenneth P. (2004). *Mutual Fund Revenue Sharing and the Role of the Fiduciary.* Washington, DC: Financial Planning Association. http://www.fpanet.

org/journal/BetweentheIssues/LastMonth/Articles/MutualFundRevenueSharingandtheRoleoftheFiduciary/

Muir, D. M. (2002). 'The Dichotomy Between Investment Advice and Investment Education: Is No Advice Really the Best Advice?' *Berkeley Journal of Employment and Labor Law*, 23(1): 1–55.

—— (2009). 'Legislation Pending on Investment Advice to 401(k) Account Clients,' *Bank Accounting & Finance*, 22(6): 38–40.

—— ed. (2010). *Employee Benefits Law 2010 Cumulative Supplement.* Arlington, VA: BNA Books.

New Means Financial Planning (2011). *Services.* Nashua, NH: New Means Financial Planning. http://www.newmeans.com/services.html

Pettus, L., and R. H. Kesmodel, Jr. (2010). 'Impact of the Pension Protection Act on Financial Advice: What Works and What Remains to be Done?' in R. L. Clark and O. S. Mitchell, eds., *Reorienting Retirement Risk Management.* Oxford, UK: Oxford University Press, pp. 86–104.

Reish, F., and B. Ashton (2011). 'Fiduciary Issues Related to the Allocation of Revenue Sharing,' White Paper. Washington, DC: Drinker Biddle. http://www.securiannews.com/sites/securian.newshq.businesswire.com/files/white_paper/file/ReishPaperFinal.pdf

Schultz, E. E. (2011). *Retirement Heist.* New York, NY: Penguin Group.

Schwab (2011a). *Advice Guidelines.* San Francisco, CA: The Charles Schwab Corporation. http://www.schwab.com/public/schwab/nn/legal_compliance/compensation_advice_disclosures/advice_guidelines.html

—— (2011b). *How We Compensate our Investment Professionals.* San Francisco, CA: The Charles Schwab Corporation. http://www.schwab.com/public/schwab/nn/legal_compliance/compensation_advice_disclosures/investment_professionals_compensation.html

Simon, W. S. (2004). 'Fiduciary Focus: How to Bring Value to 401(k) Sponsors,' *Morningstar Advisor.* Chicago, IL: Morningstar, Inc. http://advisors.morningstar.com/advisor/t/54224664/fiduciary-focus-how-to-bring-value-to-401-k-sponsors.htm?&q=how+to+bring+value+to+401%28k%29+sponsors&single=true

Smart401(k) (2011). *Stop Guessing. Start Planning. Take Control of Your Retirement and Invest with Confidence.* Overland Park, KS: Smart401(k). http://www.smart401k.com/Content/Retail/Retail-Landing-Pages/simplify-401k-investing.aspx

Staff of the United States Securities and Exchange Commission (SEC Staff) (2011a). *Study on Enhancing Investment Adviser Examinations.* Washington, DC: SEC. http://www.sec.gov/news/studies/2011/914studyfinal.pdf

—— (2011b). *Study on Investment Advisers and Broker-Dealers.* Washington, DC: SEC. http://www.sec.gov/news/studies/2011/913studyfinal.pdf

Stanley, J. K., ed. (2000). *Employee Benefits Law.* Arlington, VA: BNA Books.

TD Ameritrade (2011). *Amerivest Guided Portfolios.* Omaha, NE: Ameritrade. http://www.tdameritrade.com/offer/ad/investmentservices.html

The American College (2011a). *Chartered Financial Consultant.* Bryn Mawr, PA: The American College. http://www.theamericancollege.edu/financial-planning/chfc-advanced-financial-planning

—— (2011b). *Chartered Life Underwriter.* Bryn Mawr, PA: The American College. http://www.theamericancollege.edu/insurance-education/clu-insurance-specialty

The Motley Fool (2011). *Whom to Hire.* Alexandria, VA: The Motley Fool. http://www.fool.com/financial-advice/whom-to-hire.aspx?source=famp

T. Rowe Price (2011a). *Advisory Planning Services.* Baltimore, MD: T. Rowe Price. http://individual.troweprice.com/public/Retail/Products-&-Services/Advisory-Planning-Services/FAQs

—— (2011b). *Benefits of Advisory Planning Services.* Baltimore, MD: T. Rowe Price. http://individual.troweprice.com/public/Retail/Products-&-Services/Advisory-Planning-Services/Benefits

Turner, J. A. (2010). 'Why Don't People Annuitize? The Role of Advice Provided by Retirement Planning Software,' Pension Research Council Working Paper No. WP2010-07. Philadelphia, PA: Pension Research Council. http://www.pensionresearchcouncil.org/publications/document.php?file=858

—— H. A. Witte (2008). *Fee Disclosure to Pension Participants: Establishing Minimum Standards.* Toronto, Canada: Rotman International Centre for Pension Management. http://www.rotman.utoronto.ca/userfiles/departments/icpm/File/John%20Turner_%20Pension%20Fee%20Disclosure_August%202008_FINAL_for%20webposting.pdf

—— (2009). 'Retirement Planning Software and Post-retirement Risks,' *Society of Actuaries and Actuarial Foundation.* Schaumburg, IL: Society of Actuaries. http://www.soa.org/research/research-projects/pension/retire-planning-software-post-retire-risk.aspx

US Department of Labor (DOL) (2011). *US Labor Department's EBSA to Repropose Rule on Definition of a Fiduciary.* 11-1382-NAT. Washington, DC: DOL.

US Department of Labor, Employee Benefits Security Administration (EBSA) (2010). *Proposed Regulation, Definition of the Term 'Fiduciary.'* 75 Fed. Reg. 65, 263–5, 278. Washington, DC: EBSA.

—— (2011). *Requirements for Fee Disclosure to Plan Fiduciaries and Participants—Applicability Dates.* 76 Fed. Reg. 42,539–42,542. Washington, DC: EBSA.

US Government Accountability Office (GAO) (2011a). *401(k) Plans: Improved Regulation Could Protect Participants from Conflicts of Interest.* GAO-11-119. Washington, DC: GPO.

—— (2011b). *Regulatory Coverage Generally Exists for Financial Planners, But Consumer Protection Issues Remain.* GAO-11-235. Washington, DC: GPO.

US Securities and Exchange Commission (SEC) (2011a). 'Fees Make a Big Difference.' Washington, DC: SEC. http://www.sec.gov/investor/tools/mfcc/fee-comparison-help.htm

—— (2011b). *Frequently Asked Questions on Form ADV and IARD.* Washington, DC: SEC. http://www.sec.gov/divisions/investment/iard/iardfaq.shtml#networth

—— (2011c). *General Information on the Regulation of Investment Advisers.* Washington, DC: SEC. http://www.sec.gov/divisions/investment/iaregulation/memoia.htm

—— (2011d). *Protect Your Money: Check Out Brokers and Investment Advisers.* Washington, DC: SEC. http://www.sec.gov/investor/brokers.htm

—— (2011e). *Rules Implementing Amendments to the Investment Advisers Act of 1940.* 76 Fed. Reg. 42,950. Washington, DC: SEC.

—— (2011f). *Variable Annuities: What You Should Know.* Washington, DC: SEC. http://www.sec.gov/investor/pubs/varannty.htm

Vanguard (2011a). *The Ongoing Advice You Want from a Partner You Can Trust.* Malvern. PA: The Vanguard Group. https://personal.vanguard.com/us/LiteratureRequest?FW_Activity=ViewOnlineActivity&litID=2210056021&FW_Event=start&view_mode=web&usage_cat2=&viewLitID=2210056021&formName=Asset+Management+Services+for+Individuals&vendorID=S177&cbdForceDomain=true

—— (2011b). *Guidance and Advice.* Malvern, PA: The Vanguard Group. https://personal.vanguard.com/us/whatweoffer/advice

Veritat (2011). *Finally, Financial Planning for Everyone.* Philadelphia, PA: Veritat. https://www.veritat.com/

Zamansky, J. (2012). 'SEC Struggles with Investor-Protection Rules,' *Forbes.* New York, NY: Forbes.com. http://www.forbes.com/sites/jakezamansky/2012/01/24/sec-struggles-with-investor-protection-rules/

Chapter 3

Explaining Risk to Clients: An Advisory Perspective

Paula H. Hogan and Frederick H. Miller

The field of financial planning embodies a shifting mosaic of theoretical models. Nevertheless, risk management is a fundamental component of financial planning. This chapter examines current advisory practice with particular emphasis on risk management. We then apply this information to identify questions for further discussion and research. Our views are based on perspectives derived from our ongoing discussions with clients and colleagues,[1] and this chapter seeks to further dialogue between practitioners and academics.

In what follows, we first paint a picture of how financial planning is defined and delivered through three distinct theoretical paradigms. Next, we describe each paradigm, with particular emphasis on how each treats risk tolerance, risk capacity, and risk perception. In doing so, we identify the contributions of each paradigm and also the real-world problems of applying each of them in our daily work with clients. A fourth planning paradigm details several real-world challenges advisors face every day, which the other approaches do not incorporate. We find that unresolved real-world issues confound our daily work along most of the dimensions we use to describe the theoretical models, including, for example, the information clients are assumed to be able to provide and the presumed unit of analysis. Finally, we illustrate some practical implications of each paradigm by suggesting how advisors employing the paradigms would handle three common planning challenges: investment risk management, longevity risk management, and the appropriate planning strategy when the client has more than enough (or less than enough) personal wealth.

It is worth noting that most standard economic models assume consumers know both their utility functions and the world in which they operate; moreover, the models assume them to be capable of perceiving and managing personal risk effectively. In that world, the consumer's task is simply to map personal choices and actions onto the economic model, and then follow what the model provides. In practice, however, advisors help clients every day with such strategic economic decisions as how much to spend, and thus, how much to save; what kinds of insurance to buy, and how much of each; what to do with their savings (how to invest); and, increasingly, how to manage their human capital.

In our daily work, we rely on insights from the academic community and struggle to bridge the gap between theory and practice. This chapter contributes to the ongoing conversation between practitioners and academics.

Planning paradigms

Financial advisors use four main paradigms in their practices: the Traditional paradigm, the Life Cycle paradigm, the Behavioral paradigm, and the Experienced Advisor paradigm. We describe each in turn (see Table 3.1).

The Traditional or Accounting/Budgeting/Modern Portfolio Theory paradigm

The most prominent and dominant approach to financial planning in existence today has been assembled from a variety of sources, and it has brought significant benefits to its practitioners' clients. Clients have become alert to the importance of saving for retirement and other goals, diversifying investment portfolios, managing investment costs, and insuring against loss of income.

Much of modern financial planning draws on stock brokerage and investment advice, perhaps because many clients articulate a desire for assistance with their financial portfolios. In the 1970s, leading-edge investment advisors began to adopt Modern Portfolio Theory, as initiated by Markowitz (1952), elaborated by Sharpe (1964) and others, and popularized by Ibbotson and Sinquefield (1977),[2] as the basis for investment advice; today, most personal financial advisors use this approach.[3] For example, Morningstar's Principia software, which has a strong market position among investment advisors, implements Mean Variance Optimization as its primary method of asset allocation; Morningstar's 'style boxes' for classifying equity securities are also direct descendants of Modern Portfolio Theory as extended by Fama and French (1992) and others.

The theoretical basis of the non-investment aspects of financial planning advice in the Traditional paradigm is less clear. For want of a better term, we call it the 'accounting/budgeting' approach. Most commercial financial planning software adds up income from all sources, subtracts the costs of discretionary and non-discretionary spending and client goals (e.g., college, spending in retirement, etc.), and tracks the net impact on a client's

TABLE 3.1 The current financial planning mosaic

	TRADITIONAL Accounting/ Budgeting/Modern Portfolio Theory	RATIONAL Life Cycle Theory of Saving and Investing	BEHAVIORAL Prospect Theory and Framing	ADVISOR EXPERIENCE Life in the Trenches
Key contributions	Identifies and legitimizes personal financial planning	Human capital and standard of living take center stage	Highlights non-rational aspects of human decision-making, including the propensity for loss aversion, and the central role of framing in decision-making	As we move from left to right, quantitative financial analysis cedes importance to psychology and overall client well-being
Utility	Linear (implicitly a function of wealth)	Nonlinear; diminishing marginal (explicitly a function of consumption and perhaps leisure, wealth is indirect)	Prospect theory—risk aversion at a reference point. Experienced vs. remembered/'mis-wanting'	Economics strives to predict behavior of groups of people. Most empirical work focuses on a point in time (cross-sectional). Advisors deal with individuals, over a long period of time (longitudinally)
Unit of analysis	Portfolio	Rational consumer	Human (frequently not rational) consumer	Many clients are couples, not individuals. Many clients must deal with family member issues, not all of which are obvious to the advisor
Client/advisor goal	Maximize portfolio	Smooth utility (consumption)	Understand and then optimize utility/well-being	Integrate personal values with the management of human and financial capital
Approach to risk	Each risk is discrete. Risk management is comprehensive but not integrated. Primary focus may depend on the	Utility function affords an integrated view of all risks. Risk impact is goal specific, measured through the lens of personal goal priority	Client risk *perception*, both directly and as interpreted through the utility function, becomes more important. Risk is poorly understood and risk	Advisors do not know the probabilities or costs associated with many risks. Advisors are subject to the same (irrational) behavioral heuristics and biases as clients

		advisor's background, e.g., investments vs. insurance. Risks are objective—quantifiable	and risk capacity. Risks are objective—quantifiable	perception is greatly influenced by cultural trends, the economic environment, personal history, and the advisory relationship	
Risk tolerance		Clients assumed to have a measurable risk tolerance, which can be applied to select an appropriate level of (investment) risk from choices based on securities market benchmarks	Risk tolerance derives from risk aversion, which is a parameter of the utility function	Risk assessment and tolerance depend on the frame and can be internally inconsistent. Rational and human assessments can differ. Clients come in with notions of what risk level they 'should' be comfortable with (anchoring). They also define loss in a variety of ways: relative to market, their neighbor, their understanding of a 'good' return, dollars, and sometimes specific goal achievement	Advisors can confuse their own professional 'knowledge' with their own personal risk tolerance. The quality of the client–advisor relationship—and especially the trust between the client and advisor—is a powerful influence during risk discussions
Risk capacity		Risk capacity is not a distinct concept. However, age-based rules of thumb for risk tolerance suggest the need for the concept	Risk capacity is fundamentally important and is calculated by the planner—limiting losses to maintain a minimum utility level	Risk capacity is a slippery concept when risk perception is changeable	Clients are not used to thinking about the difference between risk capacity and risk tolerance
Importance of language/ framing		None	None	Language matters: Framing changes client perception of risk and choices. Advisors 'nudge' clients to a particular point of view, both deliberately and unwittingly	Advisor's ability to interpret client communication improves with experience. Advisors are aware of their power to nudge, and wonder how to use that power effectively and responsibly

(*Continued*)

TABLE 3.1 Continued

	TRADITIONAL Accounting/ Budgeting/Modern Portfolio Theory	RATIONAL Life Cycle Theory of Saving and Investing	BEHAVIORAL Prospect Theory and Framing	ADVISOR EXPERIENCE Life in the Trenches
Model assumptions about clients	Clients understand risk very well, and can specify their tolerance for it. The concept of 'risk capacity' is blended in with and even used interchangeably with 'risk tolerance'	Clients assumed to be able to specify goals and preferences (about risk)	Clients do not have an accurate understanding of their own utility functions or risk	Advisors have learned that client-provided information requires interpretation; expressed goals and preferences can change over time. Clients are in different stages of personal change
Advisor questions (of clients)	What are the facts? What are the numbers? (Spending, assets.) What is your risk tolerance—framed as ability to withstand market volatility?	What is your utility function? What is your risk aversion (parameter)? What are your specific personal goals and likely pattern of lifetime earnings? How much more could you save?	Are we optimizing utility of experiencing, future, or remembering self? What framing do the advisor and the environment (economy and culture) create?	Advisors must frequently define the advisory deliverable for new clients (many believe it is solely portfolio performance). Clients typically first come to an advisor because of some kind of personal change. Sometimes the first part of the client engagement is analogous to a visit to the ER, i.e., quick diagnostics and triage before real planning
Advisor-client relationship focus	Investments and other financial products, in a comprehensive but not integrated manner	Understanding the risk and return features of the client's human capital, and tailoring financial strategies to that human capital. Comprehensive, integrated risk management, centered on goals-based planning	Understanding and improving the client's decision-making ability, 'nudging' client toward better decisions. Framing advice when appropriate as a counterpoint to the environment (economy, personal history, cultural milieu)	Values clarification as a precursor for the goal-setting foundation for the financial plan

Advisor role	Data and analysis provider, and authority who advises mainly about investments and the economy	An authority who provides the calculated result of a goals-based planning process	A coach, resource, and authority for improved decision-making	The advisor shifts from authority figure/technical expert to more of an informed resource, facilitator, and coach (and with couples, sometimes a mediator)
Advisor deliverable	The advisor strives to optimize the financial portfolio. *Deliverable: Product (maximized financial wealth)*	The advisor strives to manage income and outflows/protect financial safety. *Deliverable: Policy (goals-based lifetime consumption [utility] smoothing)*	The advisor strives to clarify decision-making. *Deliverable: Process (improved decision-making around values and goals and risk management)*	The advisor facilitates values clarification to support a personally grounded comprehensive goals-based financial plan, then coaches implementation according to client readiness. *Deliverable: Trust-Based Process (integrating personal values with comprehensive goals-based financial planning)*. The deliverable becomes less distinct and measurable—and less of a commodity
Advisor–client relationship issues	The intertwining of product sales and advice can compromise the deliverable	The process is dependent on the quality of data from the client	The advisor is just as human as the client	Clients are unclear about the purpose of the relationship: many clients expect the conversation to be solely about investments. Clients are in different stages of personal change and advisors must give financial advice calibrated to their perception of the client's personal stage. Advisor training does not include skills for exploring purpose and meaning or motivation for change

Source: Authors' tabulations (see text).

52 The Market for Retirement Financial Advice

portfolio over time. A plan is said to succeed if the portfolio balance is positive at death (or large enough to produce the desired inheritance), and it fails otherwise.

In the Traditional paradigm, most advisors address primarily investment risk, which they frequently evaluate using the Monte Carlo analysis. Measures of success are the size of the portfolio balance at the conclusion of the plan, and the probability of a positive (or sufficiently large) balance. In determining how much investment risk to recommend that a particular client should retain, a Traditional Advisor will attempt to assess the client's comfort with risk, or 'risk tolerance.' Advisors label clients willing to accept large amounts of risk as 'aggressive' or 'growth' investors, while those willing to accept less risk are 'conservative' or 'income' investors. Advisors also consider mortality risk, which can threaten income earning ability. In this paradigm, advisors see life insurance sufficient to cover specific expenses and goals (e.g., including funding the mortgage and college education) as the solution. Disability insurance replaces income lost due to illness or other sources of incapacity to work, and long-term care insurance funds all or some of the cost of custodial care in order to preserve the estate and ensure the desired quality of care in the event care is needed.

Importantly, the Traditional paradigm employs two contrasting approaches to risk management. For 'insurable' risks (for which commercial insurance is available), an advisor is likely to recommend full insurance. That is, the advisor recommends sufficient insurance coverage to produce substantially equal resource levels in both the 'good' and 'bad' states of the world. For investment risk, however, advisors are likely to select a non-zero failure target; for example, an advisor may deem a 5 or 10 percent failure probability to be acceptable. Thus, in 'good' investment states, a client may have very large (unused) resources, while in 'bad' states, a client may exhaust his resources entirely before dying (in some cases several years before) (Scott et al., 2008). In other words, it is not unusual for Traditional Advisors to recommend insurance to transfer as much of insurable (financial) risks as possible, while recommending that clients retain (potentially very) significant amounts of investment risk.

In the Traditional model, the term *risk tolerance* conflates the notion of being able to accept or 'afford' risk (sometimes called risk capacity) and the client's level of comfort with asset price volatility. While both of these concepts are important to advisors and their clients, and it is essential to distinguish between them, the Traditional paradigm does not do so as the use of one term to stand for both concepts suggests.[4] Furthermore, at least in the advisor community, neither concept is well defined by any of the paradigms we consider.

'Risk capacity' in the Traditional paradigm roughly refers to the maximum amount of risk a client can retain, while ensuring that a bad outcome of the risk in question will not impose unacceptable harm. With investments, unacceptable harm occurs when the money runs out before the end of retirement. At least in concept, risk capacity is computable, quantifiable, and related to the client's time horizon. This notion is the root of the rule of thumb that the proper allocation to stocks in a portfolio is 100 minus the client's age, and more generally that younger clients can afford more risk.

The Traditional Advisor also seeks to assess and manage the client's ability to contain his anxiety through the ups and downs of the stock market. Accordingly, advisors will speak of a client's 'stomach' for risk. Clients with high risk tolerance will be psychologically comfortable with maintaining their stock holdings even in the face of sharp stock market price declines, clients with low risk tolerance will not.

Moreover, the Traditional Advisor usually holds a strong belief in the long-term advantage of stocks over bonds and in reversion to the mean in stock returns; this view is implicit in the typical application of the concept of risk tolerance.[5,6] Since stocks are deemed less risky in the long run, boosting client stock exposure to improve the odds of meeting financial goals can be seen as prudent, and stock market price declines mainly trigger advisor coaching to 'stay the course.' Thus, in the Traditional paradigm, risk perception is skewed to the extent of the belief that stocks are not risky in the long run.

Developing a financial plan and investment strategy is straightforward in the Traditional paradigm. The advisor elicits data from the client about goals, resources, risk tolerance, and required retirement income. Then the advisor calculates the impact on the investment portfolio of the implicit plan (funding all of the goals); and discusses which goals to eliminate (if the portfolio is exhausted too early or with too much frequency according to the Monte Carlo analysis) or which to add (in the fortunate circumstance that extra funds are projected with high frequency). Software calculations implicitly assume a linear utility function and usually solve for one gross asset allocation across the entire portfolio. The Traditional Advisor then recommends an asset allocation consistent with the client's risk tolerance and deemed likely to produce the investment returns required to accomplish the plan. He will also recommend specific investments to implement the asset allocation. The discussion then moves to protecting the family against insurable risks with the appropriate insurance products.

In line with the central importance of the financial portfolio, many Traditional Advisors view excellent portfolio management as a key if not the core deliverable. They believe their clients also evaluate their advisors on this basis, speaking about advisors who have 'done well' or 'done poorly' for them in managing their investments. In reality, however, the most important criterion for assessing advisor performance often focuses on advisor attentiveness and service. Many advisors devote considerable time and effort to selecting the investment vehicles and managers that they expect to perform well.[7]

Thus, investment management dominates the Traditional paradigm, with insurance coverage appended to it. Comprehensive personal financial planning is a marginal component, measured as a fraction of revenue or advisor attention, and even of regulatory attention. FINRA and SEC examinations of advisors focus solely on factors relating to portfolio management and associated activities, distinguishing mainly between advisors held to a fiduciary standard and/or those held to a sales suitability standard. Perhaps catering to consumer demand, however, the advertising by Traditional Advisors emphasizes the promise of personal, comprehensive advice designed to make one's lifetime dreams come true. Since there is as yet no legally enforceable definition for the word 'financial advisor,' consumers are left to figure out for themselves which business model provides context for the advice offered, including whether the focus is primarily on portfolio management or comprehensive planning, and whether the advisor is held to a fiduciary and/or a sales suitability standard (Turner and Muir, 2013).

Two factors challenge the Traditional paradigm. One pertains to advisors' compensation and arrangements. Traditional Advisor compensation often depends in (large) part on their investment product sales, via transaction commissions (retail stock brokers), product sales commissions and revenue sharing (retail stock brokers and some investment advisors), and fees proportional to assets (other investment advisors). Important conflicts of interest can arise if clients purchase investment products recommended by advisors rewarded for investment product sales (Bromberg and Cackley, 2013). Perhaps in response, there has been some recent migration toward advisory business models with hourly or flat retainer fees.

Secondly, clients cannot always provide the facts of their financial situation and their personal preferences. Instead, our experience is that a combination of client's unfamiliarity with financial matters and their trust in the advisor can place the advisor in a powerful and influential position. In particular, clients are often unlikely to identify and question this paradigm's inconsistent approach to investment risk (risk retention) and other risks (full insurance).

The Life Cycle paradigm

The Life Cycle approach to planning applies economic analysis and pension fund management perspectives to clients' lifetime financial problems (Bodie et al., 2008),[8] bringing greater coherence and integration to comprehensive financial planning, and highlighting the value and mechanics of goals-based investing. It does so in two ways (Hogan, 2007, 2012). First, it focuses on lifetime income and spending, and thus recognizes human capital, the net present value of lifetime earnings, as the central asset. Absent a large inheritance, human capital is the primary determinant of a client's lifetime standard of living. This emphasis on human capital shifts the planning spotlight from the investment portfolio to the consumer herself, and broadens the scope of the advisory engagement, focusing advisor attention on understanding and managing the client's career path, protecting earned income with appropriate disability and life insurance, and tailoring financial capital to the expected risk and return of the human capital.

Clients are often surprised to learn that their financial portfolio allocation should depend on the expected risk and return of their human capital. For example, a person with the same taste for risk and risk capacity as his friend, but with riskier human capital, should be advised to select less risky asset allocations. In addition, as human capital resiliency lessens (i.e., as the client's ability or willingness to continue earning income declines over time), there is typically a commensurate need to reduce risk in the financial portfolio.[9]

Another insight from the Life Cycle paradigm is that people care more about their lifetime standards of living than about their wealth. This shifts the advisory focus from return management to risk management: from building the largest possible portfolio constrained by risk tolerance to arranging lifetime consumption in the safest way possible given finite lifetime income. One of the most common statements that clients make to advisors is: 'I just want to know how much I can spend and still be safe.' In the Traditional paradigm, an advisor's response to this question is framed in terms of a return target and the implied level of portfolio risk. By contrast, the Life Cycle Advisor frames his response in terms of risk management, by discussing recommended levels of working, saving, insuring, and hedging.

A preference for a stable living standard over time implies consumption smoothing, so that purchasing power is transferred from periods of high earnings (the working years) to those of low earnings (retirement). When health risk is added to the model, this approach also implies moving purchasing power from states of the world with good health (and high earnings capability) toward those with poor health (and low earnings capability). The Life Cycle approach can also incorporate leisure, explaining post-retirement consumption spending declines.[10]

Advisors' practical implementation of the Life Cycle paradigm requires simplifying the economic Life Cycle model. Rather than attempt to estimate risk aversion, advisors instead calculate sustainable levels of consumption, and they illustrate for clients the range of consumption outcomes associated with various portfolio alternatives. Accordingly, clients reveal their risk aversion and risk tolerance levels by selecting the alternatives associated with preferred range of consumption outcomes. Goals-based investing requires that each goal be assigned a distinct investment allocation based on risk capacity, not just risk tolerance; and furthermore that these allocations when optimally set tend to become less risky over time as the share of human capital in the portfolio declines. By contrast, Traditional software programs often assign a global portfolio allocation to address all goals, fixed in time, and based mainly on assessed risk tolerance, not risk capacity.

Because of this goal of smoothing lifetime consumption, Life Cycle Advisors tend to favor inflation-indexed immediate income annuities as a core retirement income vehicle more than advisors who apply the Traditional paradigm (Hogan, 2007). In addition, the development of the derivatives markets opens an array of new possibilities for implementing Life Cycle goals-based planning, as they make it possible to tailor financial products more directly to specific goals. Structured products can allocate each risk to the party most willing and able to bear it, and they allow clients to avoid risks extraneous to accomplishing their objectives. Nevertheless, many advisors have concerns—and lack education—about current structured product packaging, pricing, and distribution. Structured products also create dissonance with most advisory business models; few advisors have malpractice insurance for providing structured product advice and fee-only advisors do not accept product commissions.

The Behavioral paradigm

If the Life Cycle approach focuses a planner's attention on human capital and its implications for consumption smoothing and saving behavior, the Behavioral approach adds prospect theory and loss aversion. That is, the Behavioral approach raises questions not only about clients' rationality but also about what utility function they are and should be maximizing. This approach notes that clients employ heuristics and have biases that produce suboptimal decisions given their utility functions, and that they likely do not fully understand what increases their utility. In the Behavioral paradigm, therefore, it is not enough for advisors to help their clients make more rational decisions. It is also valuable to help clients figure out what will actually make them happier. Moreover, the Behavioral approach emphasizes the importance of communication between advisors and their clients. That is, advisors can influence client decisions not only with accurate analysis and persuasive presentation but also with how they compare and contrast the alternatives they present (framing). Furthermore, apparently irrelevant and innocent comments can also influence client perspectives (anchoring).

Behavioral finance insights help advisors recognize certain human aspects of client thought process and psychology, and even use them to their client's advantage. For example, advisors can take advantage of mental accounting by recommending special savings accounts targeted to specific goals, and by identifying 'savings' (unnecessary spending) that can be used to make previously 'unaffordable' purchases. On the other hand, a client's overconfidence can make it difficult for the advisor to advocate for diversification and a buy and hold investment strategy versus the day trading that the client 'knows' to be successful. It is also not unusual for a client to profess being sufficiently knowledgeable about real estate to identify neighborhoods where housing prices will 'never' go down.

The 'life planning' school of modern financial planning[11] is perhaps the most fully developed form of the Behavioral paradigm. A basic tenet of this approach is that many clients fall into financial behavior inconsistent with their own values and preferences. Accordingly, in a life planning engagement, the advisor facilitates a self-discovery process in which clients identify specific preferences for what they want to be doing with their lives and the implications of those preferences for their personal planning. Life planning, however, is not typically linked to an economic model for financial planning.

From an economic perspective, advisors attempting to apply the Behavioral paradigm face a fundamental unanswered question: What utility function should they be helping their clients maximize? For example, for younger clients, the far future is an unknown country. Some may think that they wish to retire 'early,' or they may believe that they want to stay in the (expensive) part of the country in which they currently live throughout their entire lives. Both of these choices have real consequences, requiring more saving and less spending than an alternative plan. The Behavioral paradigm forces the advisor to ask whether this is a case of 'mis-wanting' or an accurate assessment of preferences.

Furthermore, there is the question of dealing with downside risk aversion. Is this a temporary phenomenon or long-term irrationality? Is the reference point a feature of the moment, the day, the month, the year, or the lifetime? Behavioral finance research suggests that expressed preferences can change when a positive expected value gamble is repeated many times, suggesting that downside risk aversion is short-term irrationality. But this approach does not help much with the investment choices facing a client—since an advisor cannot replicate a repeated game. The client's situation changes from year to year, and the market situation is never the same from one day to the next, let alone at yearly intervals.

When we come to risk tolerance (again focusing on the investment portfolio) in the Behavioral paradigm, the complexity mounts rapidly. Especially early in a client's working life, a relatively large percentage loss in the investment portfolio implies a much smaller percentage decline in lifetime consumption. Rationally, it would seem that sustainable or smoothed consumption spending is the more relevant measure. Moreover, a client's risk assessment and tolerance depend on the advisor's framing of the situation, and can also be internally inconsistent. (For example, the advisor probably could encourage more conservative decision-making by framing the potential loss in terms of the investment portfolio instead of in terms of likely lifetime consumption.) Ideally, an advisor will frame the decision so that the client makes the best (most rational) decision. However, if the client is overconfident (and how will the advisor know just how overconfident the client is?), perhaps the advisor should adopt a framing strategy to counteract the overconfidence.

Furthermore, clients enter advisory relationships with notions of what risk level they 'should' be comfortable with. These initial notions can be based on discussions with colleagues, friends and family, previous advisors' advice, research on investment company websites, the opinions of 'experts' quoted in the media, or just their current level of risk exposure. To some extent, these initial notions are anchors—the client starts from the initial 'should' level and adjusts in the direction the analysis suggests or the advisor recommends.

In the Behavioral paradigm, clients are seen as less reliable information sources than in either the Traditional or the Life Cycle paradigms. Clients may have imperfect understandings of their own utility functions, their capabilities, and of the ways that probability distributions associated with risks influence the opportunities available to them and the risks they face. For this reason, practitioners of the Behavioral paradigm need to distinguish between risk tolerance and risk capacity, as well as do a careful job communicating and presenting recommendations, as all of these may influence client decisions.

Advisors 'nudge' their clients toward the views they finally adopt and the decisions that they make, both deliberately and unwittingly.[12] For example, the client may accept or reject a particular investment alternative depending upon whether the advisor frames the potential outcomes as gains or losses (by choosing different reference points), and introducing selected data about choices can influence clients to adjust their view about what amounts are appropriate. This changes the nature of the advisor–client conversation in ways we are just beginning to understand. Indeed, now the advisor takes on the new roles of process facilitator and counselor. Moreover, advisors are just as human as the clients and may display the same—or other—behavioral biases. In the future, we must learn more about the conditions under which advisors learn from their professional experience.

In summary, advisors have more questions about applying the Behavioral paradigm than concrete tools. Just having the questions is very helpful. And knowing about the pitfalls encourages advisors to be more cautious with communication, persuasion, and advice. It is also clear that behavioral economics research focused on improving the effectiveness of the advisor–client process and relationship could be enormously productive.

The Experienced Advisor paradigm

As practicing advisors, we wrestle with a number of issues that the economic models do not yet address. Accordingly, we propose that a new paradigm can fruitfully be added to the set of advisor practices. Specifically, we believe that advisors are moving beyond providing mainly portfolio management, and toward the role of financial counselors who facilitate a process designed to both define and support client financial safety and well-being. Advisors who participate in this emerging trend increasingly describe themselves as *comprehensive planners*, and especially *holistic comprehensive planners*.

Here the focus is on a client's well-being, and quantitative financial analysis cedes importance to psychology (Anderson and Sharpe, 2008), requiring values clarification and personal coaching as supplements to economic models and methodologies. Human capital is deemed to be both of central importance and also personal. Hence, the advisor becomes a counselor and process facilitator in addition to offering expert advice. As a result, the Experienced Advisor deliverable becomes more process based, less measurable, and more valued.[13]

Values clarification precedes goal-setting

In the Experienced Advisor paradigm, values clarification is a prerequisite for goal-setting, and it is also a risk management strategy. Advisors invite their clients to discuss such questions as: 'What do I care about and value? Where do I find meaning and purpose? How can I align meaning and purpose with money habits? How do I go about bringing about the personal change that I desire? What is the difference between my needs and my wants?' Values clarification leads to a more robust goal-setting process and hence it improves the quality of the data input for the economic model. In addition, the values clarification process is a self-discovery process, serving as a foundation for positive personal change (Hogan, 2012). The resulting self-knowledge and personal resiliency influence decisions about investment risk and about tailoring personal habits for earning, saving, and spending. Absent such a process, clients may not be well prepared to articulate personal goals reliably. For example, it is not unusual that, after the advisor asks a client couple about the family's goals for financing their children's schooling, the spouses will look at each other and comment: 'We've never talked about that.' Asking a client to describe a desired typical day in retirement can be similarly startling and confusing, as is the question 'What is your preferred living arrangement if you were to need custodial care?'

Plan implementation is part of the planning process

In the Experienced Advisor paradigm, implementation of the plan following the economic modeling is also a core part of the planning process, and as with the values clarification process, is also personal. After the client envisions his desired future, and after the economic modeling, the advisor helps the client specify and then take a series of frequently small steps that cumulatively result in plan implementation. Along the way, the advisor offers encouragement, information, affirmation, motivation, measurement, and accountability. This implementation process is an extension of traditional risk management; it is designed to align spending habits and investment risk choices with money values and personal safety.

Client engagement relies on iterative small steps

Perhaps analogous to the behavioral finance discovery that people get better—more rational—when allowed to repeat a game of chance, it may be that people get better at the game of life when they have repeated small opportunities to make informed and meaningful choices. Absent a focus on a series of small meaningful choices derived from the plan, the client may not feel a part of the planning process. Successful plan implementation usually involves some combination of nudged default decisions with a series of small and manageable decisions usually cash-flow related, made in context and in real time. For example, reducing spending in order to increase savings to the desired level usually requires identifying specific habit changes in addition to setting up nudged default saving policies. Daily cash-flow management is central to the values clarification process.

The client is at the center of the planning process; the advisor is a trusted counselor

A core assumption in the Experienced Advisor paradigm is that an iterative process of putting the client at the center of values clarification, goal specification, and plan implementation will result in the client getting better at personal wealth management and more resilient as the client's life unfolds. The advisory deliverable shifts strongly toward process and the advisor's role shifts toward counselor and process facilitator, in addition to expert resource and technical consultant. Personal trust as the foundation for the advisory relationship rises in importance.

Client couples

The Experienced Advisor paradigm incorporates the fact that many clients are couples. Rarely do partners have identical goals and values, nor do they necessarily grow and change in sync with each other with respect to either speed or direction. In this model, the advisor will thus also interact with couples as coach, and sometimes ad hoc mediator, in order to help them make fundamental planning decisions, including decisions about personal risk management. A common challenge arises when one partner has higher risk tolerance than the other.

Clients are often undergoing change

In our experience, clients often seek financial advice in response to a dramatic life transition, such as new widowhood, or a sudden wealth loss or gain. In these cases, the first part of the advisory relationship can be analogous to a hospital emergency room visit: the focus is on quick diagnostics, addressing life-threatening conditions, stabilizing, and then triaging or specifying further follow-up. Advisors often do not see clients at their best at the beginning of the financial advisory relationship, and we have found that risk perceptions, goals, and decision-making abilities shift as clients begin to feel calmer and safer. Often of equal impact are the subtler changes in preferences and judgments that can develop as a client ages, with the consequent impact on financial planning. In the Experienced Advisor paradigm, deciding when and how and how fast to get the client into the driver's seat for planning decisions is a routine challenge confounded by the client being in a constant state of personal change.

Clients often cannot accurately articulate basic facts about their finances

Clients are busy people, and their financial situation represents only one dimension of their lives. In practice, it is unusual that clients can accurately report all of the basic facts, including their total income, how much debt they have and what it costs, details of their employee benefit package, insurance coverage in place, the substance of their estate plan, how much they pay in taxes, and how their portfolio has performed over time, or how much they spend on needs versus wants. Most clients are also unable to report accurately where their money goes each year for discretionary spending. Most have no idea how much a change in income would change their standard of living, and many do not know whether they are currently living within their income or not. Clients often cannot accurately report the value of their financial assets, and sometimes do not have a full list of assets. Discovering 'lost' or forgotten assets during a client engagement is not uncommon.

Data collection is also confounded by lack of financial education. Most advisors have learned, after asking a client whether he has any debt, to ask the follow-up question: 'Do you have a mortgage?' Clients do not always perceive mortgage as debt.

Several implications follow from client's unfamiliarity with financial matters. First, financial plans are vulnerable to inaccurate data inputs, so advisors must often look hard to confirm the data. Second, the results of a financial plan can be difficult for a client to understand, if the advisor does not address from the outset the client's unfamiliarity with their current situation. In addition, client ignorance of finances combined with trust in the advisor places the advisor in a very powerful position, not dissimilar to that of physicians, attorneys, and other professionals with specialized knowledge. For many clients, the simple process of getting their finances organized is a highly valued feature of the advisory deliverable, and indeed for some clients, almost sufficient to justify the whole planning engagement. It is not unusual to hear a client express gratitude for showing them the facts about their own finances.

Clients may see the financial advisor as 'healer'

In this context, 'healer' implies someone experienced by members of the culture as the 'go-to' source for wisdom and knowledge. The value of the healer comes from the sense that this person represents the wisdom of the culture, offers a trusted relationship, and will be there through life events. We believe that clients often relate to advisors as healers, and a large part of our value is simply to provide a connection or affirmation, known in the field as 'unconditional positive regard.' Advisors sometimes take on this role in lieu of medical, legal, and in some instances, religious entities, and also because of the reduced emphasis on extended family connections today.

Information gaps confound risk measurement

It is challenging to measure human capital risk precisely, especially as clients develop interests and skills over a period of years. It is also difficult to assign precise probabilities for many risks, such as disability or the need for custodial care. Nor can advisors reliably predict the financial value and cost of divorce or a successful marriage, or the odds of remarriage subsequent to the loss of a spouse. Given such incomplete knowledge, advisors may sometimes confuse their own personal experiences and risk tolerance levels with actual expert knowledge, just as behavioral finance suggests will happen. Thus, advisors offer the best advice they can, based on limited data and with few reference points, to help people manage well-being over their lifetimes.

The advisory deliverable is changing faster than advisor training

The psychology literature offers insights about typical stages of personal change and effective strategies for fostering positive personal change. For example, the Prochaska model makes the point that the stages of personal change are recognizable, reliable, and repeating, and that counseling and advising should be specific to each stage of change (Prochaska et al., 1994). Counselors and medical professionals are specifically trained and tested for this skill. By contrast, most financial advisors have no formal training in this area, yet we routinely coach clients through personal change as a part of our daily work. This means that our financial advice is calibrated to what we perceive to be a client's state of mind, though our training may not include psychology.

On a positive note, the financial advisory industry is beginning to focus on the emerging field of *life planning*. This is designed to develop effective processes for clarifying personal values and coaching clients toward positive personal change. Nevertheless, life planning is not linked to any economic model, and hence may become disassociated with the delivery of financial advice.

Within the financial realm, the growth of the derivatives market and the many other new possibilities for structured products and insurance represents another area where the deliverables are outpacing advisor training. Only a small subset of advisors has substantive training in finance, and yet advisors are increasingly in a position where they are asked to evaluate structured products.

Lack of advisory standards creates confusion

Best practice standards for advisors are similarly changing and under construction. As a result, clients do not know what to expect when they go to an advisor's office. The deliverable could be anything from portfolio management with little to no values clarification, to data-driven goals-based projections, to a full-blown values clarification process with some appended planning calculations and portfolio management that may or may not be goals based.

Three tasks as viewed by each paradigm

Next we offer a brief look at how three very typical planning challenges might be addressed through the lens of each paradigm. Table 3.2 illustrates the outlines.

TABLE 3.2 How it all plays out

	TRADITIONAL Accounting/ Budgeting/Modern Portfolio Theory	RATIONAL Life Cycle Theory of Saving and Investing	BEHAVIORAL Prospect Theory and Framing	ADVISOR EXPERIENCE Life in the Trenches
Investment risk management	Diversification—'stay the course.' Precautionary saving. Relatively high comfort level with stock investing	Hedging and insuring. Identifying human capital as the central asset and tailoring financial capital to it. Asset liability matching (TIPS)	Guarantees	Clients expect only portfolio management from their advisors. Early conversations can be confused as advisor strives to establish expectations about nature of the service. Clients present with investment opinions already framed by the trends in the economy, current culture, and personal history
Longevity risk management	Sustainable withdrawal program	Annuitization	Annuitization with guarantees and upside potential	Perceptions and feelings about aging create denial and unrealistic expectations
Strategy when there is more than or less than enough	Change level of saving or gifting. Change level of risk	Change level of saving or gifting. Change level of risk. Work shorter/longer/differently	Change level of saving. Change level of risk. Work shorter/longer/differently. Choose to spend less. Recheck values and framing. Are you sure there is not enough for your well-being? And which well-being are we optimizing: experiencing self, remembering self, future self, or legacy?	Help client with: What do I care about and value? Where do I find meaning and purpose? What are my money values? How can I align meaning and purpose with money habits? How do I bring about the personal change that I desire?

Source: Authors' tabulations (see text).

Investment risk management

When designing portfolio strategy, the Traditional paradigm advisor would focus on building a large portfolio, mainly using the strategies of diversification and precautionary saving. Financial risk would be tailored to perceived risk tolerance. The Traditional Advisor would emphasize the expected outperformance of stocks over the long run, would tend to advise 'staying the course' when markets are volatile, and would feature his authoritative view on investments as the central deliverable. A colleague coming from the Life Cycle viewpoint would reframe the portfolio goal to funding highly valued personal goals with the least possible risk, and so would add hedging and insuring, and asset/liability matching to standard risk management strategies. The Life Cycle Advisor would also tailor risk in the client's financial capital to the expected risk and return of the client's human capital, using safety of lifetime spending as a key measure of success. The advisor informed by the Behavioral approach would emphasize portfolio guarantees, to address the possibility of loss aversion. He would also seek to frame decisions correctly about how much portfolio risk to take and how to view portfolio performance. Finally, an advisor from the Experienced Advisor paradigm would devote effort at the outset to discovering and resetting as necessary client preconceptions about risk, return expectations, and benchmarking.

Longevity risk management

A Traditional Advisor would be likely to design a portfolio withdrawal program centered on, for example, a simple 4 percent per year withdrawal pattern and rising with inflation thereafter. Variations on the fixed percentage withdrawal strategy could include a buffer of cash reserves, smoothed withdrawal rates, and/or withdrawal rates adjusted in response to market valuations. Long-term care insurance might be suggested as a complement to portfolio wealth. The Life Cycle Advisor would fund the most highly valued personal goals first, seeking to match assets and liabilities through some combination of TIPS ladders and immediate inflation-protected annuities. More aspirational goals would be funded with commensurately riskier investment strategies. The Behavioral Finance Advisor would tend to focus on annuitization strategies with downside protection guarantees paired with some upside potential, after sorting through client and advisor biases. And unless the client had been close to someone needing custodial care in old age, both the Behavioral Advisor and the Advisor Experience advisors would likely devote attention to client denial or implausible expectations about aging before developing an appropriate recommended financial strategy.

Planning strategy for when the client has more than (or less than) enough

If the economic analysis suggests that a client has too little or too much wealth relative to the client's notion of financial sufficiency, some aspect of the plan must change. The Traditional Advisor might propose ramping up risk and advise changing saving or gifting as well. The Life Cycle Advisor will instead illustrate which goals may not be feasible in the case of too little wealth and might suggest working shorter, longer, or differently as a core strategy. A Behavioral Finance Advisor would also suggest changing the levels of saving, risk-taking, and work duration, but he will also work with the client to recheck values and framing around money issues to improve decision-making. The advisor informed by the Experienced Advisor paradigm would also deploy strategies of changing the levels of saving, spending, working, and risk-taking, but he will also initiate a valued discussion and also a personal action plan likely characterized by measured small step progress.

Conclusion

Advisors seek an integrated approach that improves our ability to produce better outcomes for clients. This requires selecting from various paradigms, incorporating increased realism (as illuminated by the advisor experience), and recognizing that the financial advisory problem is more complex than extant models allow. The financial planning problem is fundamentally about resource allocation over time and matching personal values to the management of both financial and human capital. To do so, advisors and their clients need to understand the value of the resources, the risks to that value, the terms under which the value can be moved from one point in time to another, and the ideal resource allocation over time.

Rigorously addressing these issues, especially given the implications of behavioral finance discoveries, will help advisors develop more effective strategies and tactics for serving their clients. It will also pave the way for consistent practice standards which are essential for better consumer protection. It is also worth noting that the rapidly declining cost of analytical software should allow personalized rational advice to become less expensive. Internet communications software and social media should allow personal advice to become less expensive. Yet until 'the answer' to behavioral economic biases in the financial planning setting is developed, it is not clear how much technology can facilitate planning. Research is needed on which components of financial planning are essentially personal versus product, policy, and process that can be delivered through technology. Additionally, the answers to these questions may change as Baby Boomers age, and the next generation of clients grows dominant.

Endnotes

1. One author (Miller) served on the 2009 Certified Financial Planner Board of Standards Job Analysis Task Force which assessed then-current Certified Financial Planner practices. Both authors served on the 2009 Certified Financial Planner Board of Standards Task Force on the Future of Financial Planning.
2. This seminal work remains popular today, and updated editions are published annually.
3. There are many descriptors for personal financial advisors in use today. To list just a few: 'financial planners' adopt a holistic approach to financial advice, incorporating retirement or cash-flow planning, investments, insurance, taxes, estate planning, and employee benefits (this is the CFP Board's definition); investment advisors focus on investments; 'wealth managers' apply a holistic approach for clients with higher net worth; 'life planners' emphasize values clarification (about which more below); 'financial advisor' is less specific, and could encompass all of the foregoing. We will use 'advisor' to stand for a practitioner who advises clients about financial issues.
4. For example, see Kiplinger (2012). The six-question quiz includes 'quantitative' questions about age and home equity, and 'qualitative' questions about the respondent's ability to stay with a strategy.
5. See for instance Siegel (1994).
6. Each year, an updated 'Ibbotson chart' (e.g., Ibbotson and Sinquefield, 2012) is published, and many Traditional investment advisors refer to it regularly.
7. The popularity of the Morningstar Principia software (used largely to compare stocks, mutual funds, and variable annuity accounts) with advisors, and the prevalence of investment managers among sponsoring vendors at advisor conferences both support this view.
8. The economics Life Cycle literature goes back at least to Fisher (1930), with notable contributions from Modigliani and Brumberg (1954), Friedman (1957), Heckman (1974), and Bodie et al. (1992).
9. Lower remaining potential income means less ability to recover from a poor financial investment outcome, thus less risk capacity. Also, as the client ages, human capital declines and financial capital tends to grow, the importance of human capital in the total portfolio diminishes. To keep the portfolio risk level the same, the client must reduce the risk of the financial component, since for most clients, human capital is less risky than stocks. See Taleb (2001); Ibbotson et al. (2007); and Milevsky (2008).
10. Chai et al. (2011) suggest that if leisure and consumption are substitutes, it is natural for consumption to decline post-retirement, when leisure increases.
11. Anthes and Lee (2001) provide an introduction to life planning.
12. Thaler and Sunstein (2008) introduce the notion that the emerging understanding of how people make choices allows 'choice architects' to purposefully influence the choices users of their architectures ultimately make.
13. Anderson (2012) is a prominent resource for life planning process.

References

Anderson, C. (2012). Money Quotient website. http://moneyquotient.org/
—— D. L. Sharpe (2008). 'The Efficacy of Life Planning Communication Tasks in Developing Successful Planner-Client Relationships,' *Journal of Financial Planning*, 21(June): 66–77.
Anthes, W., and S. A. Lee (2001). 'Experts Examine Emerging Concept of Life Planning,' *Journal of Financial Planning*, 14(June): 90–101.
Bodie, Z., R. C. Merton, and W. Samuelson (1992). 'Labor Supply Flexibility and Portfolio Choice in a Life-Cycle Model,' *Journal of Economic Dynamics and Control*, 16(3–4): 427–49.
—— L. B. Siegel, and R. N. Sullivan, eds. (2008). *The Future of Life Cycle Saving and Investing*, Second Edition. New York, NY: The Research Foundation of CFA Institute. http://www.cfapubs.org/toc/rf/2008/2008/1
Bromberg, J., and A. P. Cackley (2013). 'Regulating Financial Planners: Assessing the Current System and Some Alternatives,' in O. S. Mitchell and K. Smetters, eds., *The Market for Retirement Financial Advice*. Oxford, UK: Oxford University Press.
Chai, J., W. Horneff, R. Maurer, and O. S. Mitchell (2011). 'Optimal Portfolio Choice over the Life Cycle with Flexible Work, Endogenous Retirement, and Lifetime Payouts,' *Review of Finance*, 15(4): 875–907.
Fama, E. F., and K. R. French (1992). 'The Cross-Section of Expected Stock Returns,' *Journal of Finance*, 47(2): 427–65.
Fisher, I. (1930). *The Theory of Interest*. London: Macmillan.
Friedman, M. (1957). 'The Permanent Income Hypothesis,' in M. Friedman, ed., *A Theory of the Consumption Function*. Princeton, NJ: Princeton University Press, pp. 20–37.
Heckman, J. (1974). 'Life Cycle Consumption and Labor Supply: An Explanation of the Relationship between Income and Consumption Over the Life Cycle,' *The American Economic Review*, 64(1): 188–94.
Hogan, P. (2007). 'Life Cycle Investing Is Rolling Our Way,' *Journal of Financial Planning*, 20(May): 46–54.
—— (2012). 'Financial Planning: A Look from the Outside In,' *Journal of Financial Planning*, 25(June): 54–60.
Ibbotson, R. G., P. Chen, M. A. Milevsky, and X. Zhu (2007). *Lifetime Financial Advice: Human Capital, Asset Allocation, and Life Insurance*. Charlottesville, VA: The CFA Institute.
—— R. A. Sinquefield (1977). *Stocks, Bonds, Bills, and Inflation: The Past (1926–1976) and the Future (1977–2000)*. Charlottesville, VA: Financial Analysts Research Foundation.
—— —— (2012). *Stocks, Bonds, Bills, and Inflation 1926–2011*. Chicago, IL: Morningstar. http://corporate.morningstar.com/ib/documents/Brochures/2012_SBBIHandout_SAMPLE.pdf
Kiplinger (2012). Test Your Risk Tolerance. http://www.kiplinger.com/tools/risk-find.html
Markowitz, H. M. (1952). 'Portfolio Selection,' *Journal of Finance*, 7(1): 77–91.
Milevsky, M. A. (2008). *Are You a Stock or a Bond? Create Your Own Pension Plan for a Secure Financial Future*. Upper Saddle River, NJ: FT Press, pp. 13–45.

Modigliani, F., and R. H. Brumberg (1954). 'Utility Analysis and the Consumption Function: An Interpretation of Cross-section Data,' in K. K. Kurihara, ed., *Post-Keynesian Economics*. New Brunswick, NJ: Rutgers University Press.

Prochaska, J. O., J. C. Norcross, and C. Diclemente (1994). *Changing for Good*. New York: William Morrow.

Scott, J. S., W. F. Sharpe, and J. G. Watson (2008). 'The 4% Rule—At What Price?' *Journal of Investment Management (JOIM)*, 7(3): 1–18.

Sharpe, W. F. (1964). 'Capital Asset Prices—A Theory of Market Equilibrium Under Conditions of Risk,' *Journal of Finance*, 19(3): 425–42.

Siegel, J. J. (1994). *Stocks for the Long Run*. New York: McGraw-Hill.

Taleb, N. N. (2001). *Fooled by Randomness: The Hidden Role of Chance in Life and in the Markets*. New York: Random House.

Thaler, R., and C. Sunstein (2008). *Nudge: Improving Decisions About Health, Wealth, and Happiness*. New Haven, CT, and London: Yale University Press.

Turner, J. A., and D. M. Muir (2013). 'The Market for Financial Advisers,' in O. S. Mitchell and K. Smetters, eds., *The Market for Retirement Financial Advice*. Oxford, UK: Oxford University Press.

Chapter 4

How Financial Advisers and Defined Contribution Plan Providers Educate Clients and Participants about Social Security

Mathew Greenwald, Andrew G. Biggs, and Lisa Schneider

Many experts believe that a number of older workers have not accumulated enough money to enable them to maintain financial security throughout their retirements, especially if they live beyond their life expectancies. One way to enhance retirement financial security would be to better educate people about when to claim Social Security benefits so they can make an informed choice. Sass (2012) has estimated that a worker who delays claiming from age 62 to age 70 will get a 76 percent inflation-adjusted increase in monthly Social Security benefits. Even waiting from age 66 to age 70 will increase, he estimates, inflation-adjusted monthly benefits by 32 percent. Furthermore, the benefits are also adjusted upward by inflation every year. These benefit increases are calculated to be actuarially fair: thus, a person in average health can expect no decrease in the total benefits received over his lifetime. Those in better-than-average health can expect to get more over their lifetimes than is lost by delaying and forsaking benefits. Also, those in poor health can 'select' against the Social Security Administration and claim benefits early. Claiming later leads to substantially increased benefits, which would give workers extra protection should they live to a very old age, when they would have the most financial pressure. For the majority of people who have not accumulated enough, an informed decision about when to claim benefits offers an opportunity to substantially enhance financial security in later years.

Currently, many Americans are not well informed about when to claim and, for some, the timing of claiming is likely to be sub-optimal. Two channels are often used to educate workers about Social Security and the optimal time to claim: financial advisers, and defined contribution (DC) plan providers. This chapter examines current practices in terms of how financial advisers and plan participants educate those they serve. We identify some shortcomings and offer suggestions to enhance education and advice.

Background

Social Security benefits are the major source of income for Americans aged 65 and over, especially women. Indeed, 51 percent of women aged 65 and older receive at least three-quarters of their income from Social Security (Employee Benefits Research Institute, 2010). Even with this support, many older people have modest incomes; this is especially pronounced for those aged 85 and older.

New emphasis on benefit claiming strategies

Over half of workers fully covered by the Social Security program (and not already getting disability benefits) claimed their benefits at age 62, the first year of eligibility; 69 percent claimed prior to age 65 (Aaron and Callan, 2011). Many economists and financial planners believe current claiming strategies are sub-optimal (Tacchino et al., 2012). The impact is strongest on women because they live longer than men on average, depend to a larger extent than men on their Social Security income in retirement, and are more likely to end their lives living in or near poverty. Coile et al. (2002) used an expected utility model to measure the welfare gains from delayed claiming and found that delayed claiming is optimal in many cases and often makes a significant difference.

Sass et al. (2007) analyzed Health and Retirement Study data on the impact of claiming age on the expected present value of Social Security benefits for couples who both retired before becoming eligible for Social Security. Typically, advisers suggest that couples can maximize the expected present value of benefits in this circumstance by having the wife claim benefits at age 62 and the husband claim at age 66. Among those surveyed, however, over 90 percent of the husbands claimed benefits at age 62. While such behavior had little impact on the expected present value of benefits while the husband was alive, it reduced by 25 percent the expected present value of the survivor's benefit (which widowed wives receive). The authors reported that '[t]wo factors that could plausibly explain early claiming by married men are ignorance and a caddish disregard for the well-being of the spouse' (Sass et al., 2007: 3). Their empirical results 'produced no evidence to attribute early claiming to caddishness' but 'do provide evidence that financial awareness has an effect' (Sass et al., 2007: 3).

More complex strategies were examined by Munnell et al. (2009), going beyond simple choices regarding the age of claiming. Such strategies include a 'Free Loan' in which individuals would claim benefits and then later repay them, thus resetting their benefits to a higher level. Moreover, the repayment included no interest charges. Responding to increased utilization of this strategy, the Social Security Administration (SSA) in 2011 proposed a regulation allowing individuals only a single repayment and restart of benefits, which must take place within one year of initial claiming.

Another strategy includes the 'Claim and Suspend' tactic in which an individual claims benefits but then immediately suspends them. This allows a spouse to claim a spousal benefit while the individual defers claiming, an option not otherwise allowed under Social Security rules. A third strategy, termed 'Claim Now, Claim More Later,' allows the high earner in a married couple to claim a spousal benefit based on the lower earning spouse's record, while delaying his own retired worker benefit. This strategy allows for higher benefits both for the individual employing it as well as for higher survivor benefits for his widow.

Widows' claiming strategies are examined by Shuart et al. (2010). A surviving spouse who accrued no benefits under her own earnings record receives roughly the same lifetime benefits, in present value terms, regardless of when she claimed. But many widows can claim benefits both under their own earnings record and that of their deceased spouse. The authors found that claiming one type of benefit and then shifting to the second later in retirement tend to maximize lifetime benefits. Yet deciding which benefit to claim first, and when to reclaim, depends on the ratio of the widow's earned benefit versus the survivors' benefit for which she is eligible. Enhanced claiming strategies such as these have been adopted by some financial advisers.

Public understanding of Social Security benefit rules

The general public has a low level of understanding of the Social Security system and the impact of claiming on long-term financial well-being. Greenwald et al. (2010) conducted a survey of 2,000 people in 2010 and reported that levels of knowledge about Social Security are 'disturbingly low.' Only one-quarter could correctly answer a question about how Social Security benefits are calculated. Forty-three percent did not understand that Social Security benefits can be taxed, and the same proportion did not know that benefits are adjusted for inflation.

Moreover, few people know the relationship between their retirement age, claiming age, and the level of benefit they can receive. While a significant proportion of workers feel they know a lot about the eligibility age for full Social Security retirement benefits, the survey demonstrated poor levels of actual knowledge. One-quarter (25 percent) did not know that benefits can be deferred rather than claiming them at the time of retirement only. Just 29 percent feel 'very knowledgeable' about the impact of age the claiming on benefit level and fully 36 percent claimed not to know that their benefit would rise if they delayed claiming.

Similarly, a survey by AARP (Brown, 2012) of individuals aged 52–70 found that many knew that waiting to claim increased monthly benefit amounts, but knowledge of other issues affecting claiming was weak. For instance, only around one-third could correctly identify (within two percentage points) the amount by which benefits increased with delayed claiming. Likewise, only 7 percent could correctly identify the number of working years on which retirement benefits are calculated 35, with most believing that benefits were based on the highest earning five or ten years of employment. Similarly, 71 percent of respondents incorrectly believed that a permanent reduction in benefits resulted from the earnings test applied to early retirees who continued to work. In reality, benefits are increased at the full retirement age to compensate for any losses due to the earnings test earlier in retirement.

The importance of financial advice

One of the most effective methods for increasing retiree financial security would be to provide them with financial education and advice to help them make more informed decisions about when to claim Social Security benefits. Two channels are available to both increase Americans' knowledge of Social Security and optimize their Social Security claiming decisions: financial advisers and DC plan providers. Both these channels reach a large segment of Americans, have as a key objective increasing clients' financial security, have a high level of knowledge of financial issues, have access to their clients, and have established a level of trust. There were 334,162 financial advisers in the United States in 2010 (Cerulli Quantitative Update: Advisor Metrics). A 2008 survey found that 38 percent of Americans had a financial adviser (Mathew Greenwald & Associates, 2008). According to the Bureau of Labor Statistics (2010), 37 percent of all workers participated in a DC plan in 2010. Among the key issues concerning financial advisers are the extent to which they advise their clients on Social Security; the sources of information they rely on concerning Social Security; the quality of the advice they currently provide about Social Security and claiming behavior; their interest in receiving more education and information on this subject; and which organizations they would prefer to get this information from. This information could be used to design programs to improve how the financial adviser community provides education and information to their clients and to help them more effectively guide their clients on when to claim Social Security benefits and, hence, how to increase clients' financial security throughout retirement. Among the key issues for retirement plan providers is their degree of interest in educating plan participants on Social Security, and what types of programs would be most effective in allowing them to help participants make informed decisions about when to claim benefits. To gain insight on the role financial advisers play in educating Americans about Social Security and what might be done to increase the capability of advisers to increase the effectiveness of claiming decisions, Greenwald et al. (2011) surveyed 406 financial advisers about Social Security and their role in advising clients on claiming strategies. Among the areas covered were advisers' knowledge of what the SSA provides; their roles in providing information and advice on Social Security to their clients; the prevalence of discussions with clients about Social Security; strategies on claiming Social Security; how they frame the issue; and evaluation and use of information about Social Security.

The survey was conducted online by Mathew Greenwald & Associates. Advisers were first selected at random from a list provided by Financial Media Group (FMG), which maintains the industry's most comprehensive database of licensed life insurance professionals and FINRA- and SEC-licensed professionals in the United States. The advisers surveyed work for a variety of organizations, including national investment companies and 'wirehouses' (such as Merrill Lynch), regional firms (such as LPL), independently owned firms and local firms, banks, and insurance companies.

To qualify for the survey, financial advisers had to have at least three years of experience, $50,000 of annual personal income from their work as advisers, 40 percent of their clients had to be at least age 55, and they had to regularly provide clients with advice on saving for retirement and managing money in retirement. These criteria were checked in the phone interview: if advisers qualified, they were asked to answer a questionnaire online and received a link to the questionnaire. Data collection took place from March to May 2011.

To obtain greater understanding of the role played by retirement plan providers, Schneider and Greenwald conducted eighteen in-depth interviews: sixteen with executives of leading plan providers, and two with executives in associated businesses. Results of these in-depth interviews and more detail on methodology are presented below, following a discussion of the survey of financial advisers.

Key results: survey of financial advisers

Our analysis confirms that financial advisers consider addressing the issue of Social Security with their clients to be a central and important task. Around nine in ten (88 percent) of advisers believed that it was incumbent on them to educate their clients about how Social Security fit into their

How Financial Advisers and Providers Educate Clients 75

TABLE 4.1 Financial advisers' role in advising clients on Social Security (%)

To what extent do you agree or disagree with the following statement?	Total (n = 406)	Wirehouse (n = 90)	Regional broker/ dealer (n = 91)	Bank represen- tatives (n = 44)	Life insurance agents (n = 91)	Independent financial advisers (n = 90)
Financial advisers should help their clients make informed decisions about their Social Security benefits						
Strongly agree (5)	55	51	57	45	53	63
4	33	38	33	34	31	30
3	10	9	9	14	13	6
2	2	2	1	7	3	1
Strongly disagree (1)	–	–	–	–	–	–
Advising my clients on when to claim Social Security benefits or how Social Security works is not an important part of my practice						
Strongly agree (5)	6	3	5	5	8	8
4	12	12	12	11	12	10
3	20	17	14	25	29	20
2	34	37	37	36	33	29
Strongly disagree (1)	28	31	31	23	19	33

Source: Greenwald et al. (2011).

retirement finances. Independent financial advisers (93 percent) were particularly aware of the responsibility to address Social Security with their clients, especially compared to bank representatives (80 percent). Furthermore, most advisers specifically believed they should help their clients decide when to claim Social Security benefits. Wirehouses and regional broker dealers (68 percent each) were most likely to suggest advising clients about claiming, while life insurance agents (62 percent) were least likely to feel they should do this (see Table 4.1).

Advisers' perceived knowledge of Social Security

Financial advisers felt they were knowledgeable about Social Security and understood several key details about its benefits. Nearly all advisers (93 percent) said they were knowledgeable about how Social Security works, with 22 percent describing themselves as very knowledgeable, and an additional 71 percent saying they were somewhat knowledgeable. Six percent asserted they were not knowledgeable about Social Security, while only 22 percent felt very knowledgeable. Most (71 percent) reported that they were somewhat knowledgeable. Accordingly, while most financial advisers believed they had knowledge of Social Security, most were not expert. Interestingly, life insurance agents (34 percent) were most likely to believe they were very knowledgeable about Social Security.

Among all advisers, almost half (44 percent) believed they were very knowledgeable about how retirement benefits rise with age, and only one-quarter (24 percent) stated they were very knowledgeable about how spousal benefits work. The rules of spousal benefits are quite complex so workers are not particularly well informed about this issue. Evidently, there are gaps in advisers' knowledge as well. Most advisers were also underinformed about the Retirement Earnings Test: only one in five (19 percent) felt very knowledgeable about it.

Advisers' role in educating clients

The advisers surveyed strongly believed that helping their clients make decisions about their Social Security benefits was an important part of their role. Moreover, for most clients, Social Security benefits made up a significant portion of their incomes in retirement.

Prevalence of Social Security conversations

Three-quarters of advisers (76 percent) discussed Social Security with most of their clients, including the 41 percent who raised this subject with virtually all of their clients (90–100 percent). In around half the cases, the advisers tended to bring up Social Security, but many times it was the client who brought up the topic. Advisers generally raised the issue of Social Security to clients around a median age of 55. When clients raised the issue, the discussion started later, at a median age of 60.

A frequently discussed topic concerning Social Security was system solvency. Advisers tended to advise their clients that they should count on getting at least some of their scheduled benefits, while only one-third told their clients to count on receiving all of their scheduled benefits. For context, under current law, Social Security is projected to pay scheduled benefits until around 2037, when the program's trust fund is projected to be exhausted. If taxes were not increased thereafter, the program would reduce benefits by approximately 23 percent (SSA, 2011).

More than three out of five advisers (62 percent) talked to most of their clients about strategies for maximizing Social Security benefits. That same proportion (62 percent) said they also addressed the subject of taxation of benefits. Almost that many (57 percent) explained the Retirement Earnings Test to most clients. Fifty-six percent of advisers helped at least three-fifths of their clients estimate their Social Security benefits, but fewer, 46 percent, advised that proportion of clients about how spousal benefits worked.

What do advisers say about claiming?

Three of four financial advisers (75 percent) asserted that they advised clients about claiming Social Security benefits. Independent financial advisers and regional broker dealers were most likely to provide this advice (82 percent each), while bank representatives (67 percent) and life insurance agents (63 percent) were least likely. More specifically, two-thirds (66 percent) advised clients about the best age to claim Social Security benefits: the median age recommended was 66. Four in ten (38 percent) believed most clients claimed too early, half (52 percent) felt clients tended to claim at about the best time, and 3 percent believed delay claiming was preferred. Just 8 percent of financial advisers strongly agreed that their clients made good decisions about when to claim their Social Security benefits and fewer than half (46 percent) believed that clients made good decisions regarding Social Security (see Table 4.2).

Advisers often use, or recommend that their clients obtain, information on Social Security. The source used or recommended most often is the SSA, used or referred by half of advisers (51 percent). Another three in ten (29 percent) used material from their primary company or referred their clients to material from their primary company.

TABLE 4.2 Adviser input on the timing of claiming Social Security benefits (%)

In advising clients about the role of Social Security in their retirement finances, did you...?	Total (n = 402)	Wirehouse (n = 90)	Regional broker/ dealer (n = 91)	Bank representatives (n = 43)	Life insurance agents (n = 88)	Independent financial advisers (n = 90)
Provide advice on when to claim their Social Security benefits?						
Yes	75	78	82	67	63	82
No	21	19	14	28	35	13
Not sure	3	3	3	5	2	4
With what proportion of clients do you discuss the following specific issue related to Social Security? The best age to claim Social Security benefits						
Virtually all clients (90–100%)	31	32	40	23	26	31
60–89%	35	33	35	35	32	38
40–59%	20	19	14	26	28	18
10–39%	10	10	9	9	11	11
Very few clients (0–9%)	3	6	2	7	2	2

Source: Greenwald et al. (2011).

Methods and strategies for deciding when to claim

Almost all advisers believed that a variety of factors should be considered when deciding on an age to claim Social Security benefits. Nine out of ten believed it would be important to take into consideration the availability of guaranteed sources of income (93 percent) along with a client's health. Most thought it was important to consider the level of household assets (90 percent) and desired lifestyles in retirement (91 percent). Six in seven advisers (86 percent) indicated that clients' projected benefit amounts were also an important factor. Eighty-eight percent of advisers suggested it was important to consider whether a client wished to continue working, and four in five placed importance on the spouse's age and health (80 percent rated each as an important consideration). Three in four (76 percent) thought it was important to consider their clients' current tax liability.

Framing the claiming decision

There is strong evidence that the way a decision is described has a meaningful impact on what people decide (Brown et al., 2011). Due to this 'framing impact,' respondents were asked which of three concepts best described their perspectives on potential client decisions to delay claiming: (*a*) as a gamble, (*b*) as a way of buying insurance, or (*c*) as a way to save money. The concept of saving was chosen most often, by two in five (41 percent). However, almost as many, 38 percent, stated that the best way to frame the decision when to claim is like a gamble. There is strong evidence that this type of framing encourages people to claim early, which is often sub-optimal (see Table 4.3).

One approach to determine when Social Security benefits should be claimed uses a 'Break-Even Analysis,' which asks how long it will take for higher benefits earned by delaying claiming to offset benefits that would have been earned by claiming earlier. Indeed, the Break-Even Analysis prompts earlier claiming benefits as noted by Brown et al. (2011). This impact is ascribed to loss aversion: when people learn they will be better off if they live beyond the 'break-even point' but worse off if they die prior to the 'break-even point,' they become concerned about the possibility of loss. Over half of advisers (55 percent) considered 'Break-Even Analysis' to be an excellent or very good way to help clients determine when they should claim their Social Security benefits, and 56 percent of advisers used 'Break-Even Analysis' with at least half their clients. The research conducted by Brown et al. suggests that this approach could lead clients of financial

How Financial Advisers and Providers Educate Clients 79

TABLE 4.3 Adviser framing of the decision of when to claim Social Security benefits (%)

Which one of the following do you think is the best way of describing the decision to delay claiming to clients?	Total (n = 406)	Wirehouse (n = 90)	Regional broker/ dealer (n = 91)	Bank representatives (n = 44)	Life insurance agents (n = 91)	Independent financial advisers (n = 90)
The decision to delay claiming is like saving money. You give up income today in order to receive a larger monthly income later in life	41	39	40	41	35	49
The decision to delay claiming is a gamble. If you live longer than your life expectancy, you will 'win' the gamble and get more in Social Security benefits	38	37	41	41	40	34
The decision to delay claiming is like buying insurance, because delaying will yield a higher monthly income guaranteed for life. This provides greater protection against running out of money in old age	21	24	20	18	25	17

Source: Greenwald et al. (2011).

advisers to claim earlier, even though advisers themselves believe that clients often claimed too early (see Table 4.4).

Advisers in our survey were also asked to consider five hypothetical scenarios of 62-year-olds and select one of three strategies they would be most likely to suggest in each situation. The strategies offered as options were: (*a*) people should claim Social Security retirement benefits as soon as they can, at age 62, even if they keep working; (*b*) people should claim Social Security benefits when they stop working full-time at some point after age 62; and (*c*) people should delay claiming Social Security benefits as long as they can, regardless of when they stop working. In each scenario, the hypothetical 62-year-old had financial assets of at least $700,000, an amount that clearly provides enough liquidity to delay claiming Social Security benefits for at least a short period of time.

On the basis of the strategies recommended in these hypothetical situations, the client's health appears to be a leading driver in the approach advisers take to determining optimal Social Security claiming ages (Table 4.5). For example, in one case where the hypothetical client's health was excellent, 60 percent of advisers prefer the third strategy (delay as long as possible). But when shown a similar hypothetical client in poor health, six in ten (60 percent) suggested the first approach (claim

TABLE 4.4 Adviser evaluation of Break-Even Analysis (%)

How would you rate the Break-Even Analysis as a way to help clients determine when they should claim their Social Security benefits?	Total (n = 406)	Wirehouse (n = 90)	Regional broker/ dealer (n = 91)	Bank represen- tatives (n = 44)	Life insurance agents (n = 91)	Independent financial advisers (n = 90)
Excellent	14	18	18	9	8	16
Very good	41	43	42	34	48	32
Good	34	31	30	45	32	38
Fair	9	7	5	9	10	14
Poor	2	1	5	2	2	–

Source: Greenwald et al. (2011).

as soon as you can). A second factor influencing adviser recommendations for claiming is the client's desired retirement age. For instance, where the hypothetical client was in average or excellent health but stated he wished to stop working at age 62 or 'as soon as possible,' far fewer advisers suggested delaying claiming for as long as possible (20 and 19 percent, respectively) and the largest number recommended the second strategy (stopping work and claiming at the same time). By comparison, in a scenario with a comparable client in average health who indicated that he planned to work until age 66, half of advisers (49 percent) suggested he delay as long as possible, while 44 percent recommended that he retire and claim Social Security benefits at the same time. Taken together, client's health and desires to continue working have a clear impact on what advisers suggest their clients do with regards to claiming Social Security retirement benefits.

Two other aspects of these findings are noteworthy. First, in only one case of the five did a majority of advisers suggest delaying claiming as long as possible, even though in each case the couple or individual had at least $700,000 of assets, which would appear to give them the ability to delay claiming. This includes the example of the woman in excellent health who was very likely to have a much higher expected present value of benefits by delaying claiming past age 62.

Second, it is clear that many financial experts considered at least two, and probably more, of these recommendations to be sub-optimal. In the case of the man in average health earning more than his wife and intending to retire at age 62 with assets of at least $800,000, it would clearly be advantageous to the wife if the husband delayed claiming; nevertheless, only 32

TABLE 4.5 Adviser recommendations on when to claim benefits in different scenarios (%)

If the following type of person came to you at age 62 seeking advice about when to claim Social Security benefits, which strategy are you most likely to suggest?	Total (n = 406)	Wirehouse (n = 90)	Regional broker/ dealer (n = 91)	Bank represen- tatives (n = 44)	Life insurance agents (n = 91)	Independent financial advisers (n = 90)
A woman in poor health, earning $100,000 a year, with a retired husband who gets $2,000 a month from Social Security, and has investable assets of $700,000						
Strategy 1	60	53	60	66	62	60
Strategy 2	34	38	35	30	33	31
Strategy 3	7	9	4	5	5	9
A man who is in average health, earning $50,000 a year, with a wife earning $40,000 a year, who plans on working until age 62, and has investable assets of $800,000						
Strategy 1	32	32	33	36	34	27
Strategy 2	48	47	49	52	46	46
Strategy 3	20	21	18	11	20	28
An unmarried woman in excellent health, earning $80,000 a year, who hopes to retire as soon as possible, and has investable assets of $700,000						
Strategy 1	28	27	23	45	32	23
Strategy 2	52	56	54	36	49	58
Strategy 3	19	18	23	18	19	19
A woman who is in average health, earning $75,000 a year, with a husband earning $60,000 a year, who plans to work until age 66, and has investable assets of $700,000						
Strategy 1	8	9	4	14	7	8
Strategy 2	44	43	47	45	46	38
Strategy 3	49	48	48	41	47	54
A man who is in excellent health, earning $75,000 a year, with a wife earning $60,000 a year, who plans to work until age 66, and has investable assets of $700,000						
Strategy 1	6	10	2	14	5	4
Strategy 2	33	31	42	32	31	31
Strategy 3	60	59	56	55	64	64

Notes: Strategy 1 = Claim as soon as you can; Strategy 2 = Claim when you stop working; Strategy 3 = Delay as long as you can.

Source: Greenwald et al. (2011).

percent suggested the husband should claim at age 62 and only 20 percent suggested that the man delay as long as possible. Claiming at 62 would result in a significantly lower survivor benefit for the widow later in life.

Conversely, experts would tend to recommend that a single woman in excellent health delay claiming for as long as she can: this would provide her the greatest protection against longevity risk. In the example given, she had $700,000, was aged 62, and planned to retire 'as soon as possible.' However, 49 percent of the advisers suggested that she delay claiming. In other words, many advisers do not display an understanding of how spousal benefits work. This includes the value of the increase in inflation-adjusted lifetime income gained by each month of delay in claiming benefits, and continuing beyond the covered worker's life to a spouse that has a lower benefit on her own.

Financial advisers' use of information

Financial advisers are often critical of the material on Social Security provided to them and their clients: only 26 percent feel that the material their primary company provides for their clients is useful. Moreover, only 13 percent agree with the statement that '[t]he Social Security Administration does a good job educating financial professionals about how Social Security works.' Fifty-one percent disagree with the statement.

Although two in three advisers (65 percent) have visited the basic Social Security website, there is low awareness that Social Security has a website especially for financial planners. Two in five who visited the website rated it excellent or good, but 13 percent felt it was fair or poor. Younger financial advisers—under age 40 (74 percent)—were more likely to visit the SSA site than older advisers, but they were less likely to have a positive opinion of it.

Although financial advisers often used or referred clients to SSA sources, they tended not to give the Social Security website a high rating as a source of information. One in three rated the website excellent or very good (34 percent), while one in five (21 percent) rated it fair or poor.

Two of the most common reasons advisers visit the official Social Security website are to gather general information (28 percent) and to find information on benefits (26 percent). Seventeen percent went to the website for an estimate of benefits or to research spousal benefits, while 10 percent have used the website to check on a specific issue or do research for their clients. Fewer than one in ten reported having accessed the website to stay up-to-date on changes (7 percent), get contact or administrative information (6 percent), research disability or Medicare coverage (5 percent), or to research tax information (3 percent).

Retirement plan provider perspectives

To obtain insights on retirement plan provider views on educating participants about Social Security and how to optimize the use of Social Security benefits, we also conducted in-depth interviews with executives in the nation's leading DC plan provider companies and executives in related companies. Companies were identified from a list of leading DC plan companies, and contacts were recruited using referrals and snowball sampling techniques. In total, eighteen in-depth interviews were conducted, including sixteen with representatives from the nation's largest DC plan providers (by assets under management), and two with industry experts in organizations associated with DC providers (a plan record keeper and an investment advice service provider). Respondents were high-level executives, directors, and managers, many of whom had direct oversight of their company DC plan operations or were responsible for overseeing the content and delivery of educational materials. On average, the telephone interviews lasted about 30 minutes. All but one interview were conducted by Lisa Schneider, a Director of Research at Mathew Greenwald & Associates. The interviews took place between July and September 2011 (Greenwald and Schneider 2011).

Educating on saving

DC retirement plan providers defined their roles as including: (*a*) encouraging plan participation and boosting contributions at high levels; (*b*) educating employees about the importance of saving for retirement overall; and (*c*) helping employees understand the benefits of using tax-advantaged DC plans for retirement savings. Plan providers encourage plan participants to set savings goals and provide information about how much participants need for a financially secure retirement.

All of the plan providers made a variety of tools available to participants, including online calculators and/or worksheets, to help participants make judgments about how much they needed to accumulate by their target retirement dates. The calculators also tended to include Social Security benefits as a factor to be considered in calculating retirement saving needs. Often the calculators allowed participants to enter their own age for claiming benefits, and often participants were advised to go the Social Security website to obtain information about estimated benefit amounts. Nevertheless, in interviews with plan providers, we heard comments of the following sort: 'We frequently reference ssa.gov in our material for more information, but it is extremely difficult to navigate'; and 'We need to help individuals understand the holistic picture. With Social Security being a component of that, anything that can be done to help individuals understand the need to aggregate their sources of income in retirement to get that complete picture and view of it is incredibly powerful.'

All reported having website content on the topic, including articles, content in seminars, and links to the Social Security website. Some providers arranged for representatives from the SSA to participate in webinars and seminars. The input provided by these SSA representatives was considered of high value. Despite all of these educational efforts, most of the plan providers believed that participants still did not have a good understanding of the way the Social Security benefit structure works, what level of benefits they can expect, and how to evaluate the most effective time to claim benefits.

The plan providers who were interviewed offered several suggestions for how they and the SSA should work together. These included the following.

Social Security Optimizer

One respondent asked for an online 'Social Security Optimizer' to help plan representatives work with participants as they figure out the best age for them to claim their Social Security retirement benefits. This material would be given to advisers and plan participant representatives who interact with and educate plan participants. Some participants believe that a publicly available web planner provided by Social Security would likely be accurate due to SSA's access to demographic data and its actuarial and economic expertise.

More effective material

Some plan providers suggested they could help the SSA create more user-friendly content and improve the presentation of the valuable information currently offered online. For instance, they recommended the completion of a Frequently Asked Questions list, and a set of strategies for claiming Social Security, including some for married couples.

Plan providers would like to integrate data with SSA information. This, for example, would permit plan providers to show participants their estimated Social Security retirement benefits (and even spousal benefits), and help provide participants with a much better integrated understanding of how much income they can expect in retirement.

Training of representatives

Several plan providers suggested that the SSA could develop a capacity to train plan provider representatives about Social Security. For instance, it was mentioned that plan representatives and other financial professionals could become 'certified' Social Security experts, especially if that training could be counted toward Continuing Education (CE).

Conclusion

When to claim Social Security retirement benefits is one of the most important, yet least examined, financial decisions that older workers must make. Unmarried individuals must consider how their claiming age affects the balance between present and future benefits, as well as the need to ensure adequate income in old age. Married individuals face additional and even more complex choices including interactions between Social Security retirement, spousal, and survivor benefit formulas. Few individuals are well equipped to analyze these decisions on their own.

Yet until this study, little was known about the specific advice that financial advisers proffer, the criteria advisers use in forming this advice, and how the advice matches up with academic research regarding Social Security and retirement. Put simply, we knew little about what financial advisers say, why they say it, or whether it is likely to be correct. Our survey of over 400 financial advisers gathered information on advisers' own views of their knowledge levels regarding Social Security claiming decisions, the principal sources they relied on to buttress their knowledge, their views regarding educational resources available through the SSA, and the financial services companies they work with.

We found that most financial advisers regard themselves as at least somewhat knowledgeable regarding the Social Security program, and many take a role in educating their clients regarding Social Security. Yet much of the adviser–client discussion has focused on Social Security's solvency, an issue that is often in the news but which, in our view, has relatively little practical impact on workers nearing retirement today. Moreover, advisers often frame claiming decisions in terms such as 'break even ages' and 'gambles' that may inadvertently encourage individuals to claim earlier. This approach ignores the insurance value of a higher Social Security benefit, which protects the individual from the risk of running out of money in old age.

Financial advisers report speaking with their clients regarding practical issues such as how the timing of retirement affects monthly and lifetime benefit amounts. Spousal and survivor benefits are less frequently addressed, and some advisers fail to take a spouse's health and age into consideration when determining a client's optimal claiming age. It appears many advisers still approach Social Security claiming as an individual decision rather than a household decision. But clients would be better served if a household approach was utilized.

Social Security benefit rules are far more complex than most Americans realize, and it is only in recent years that financial planners and other analysts have begun devising claiming strategies that exploit these rules to the fullest. While to date only a small fraction of claimants has exploited these strategies, the response to the 'Free Loan' strategy was sufficiently large that the SSA was prompted to limit its application. This hints that greater use of claiming strategies is likely to be seen in the future.

Financial advisers reported that they utilize the SSA's website and publications as a tool in assisting their clients. Over half of financial advisers called the SSA a major source of information about Social Security and nine out of ten advisers pointed their clients toward SSA as an additional source of information. Ninety-one percent of advisers said they discussed the Social Security Statement with their clients, and 78 percent review clients' statements themselves.

Yet financial advisers also believed that the SSA could do a better job of providing financial advice. Only 13 percent of advisers offered positive ratings on SSA's material for educating financial advisers and only 24 percent agreed that the SSA does a good job of educating the public. Only one-third of advisers were aware that the SSA has a webpage designed especially for financial professionals. Given the new educational material Social Security has produced, outreach to financial advisers could generate greater awareness of resources available both to financial advisers and their clients.

Greater outreach by SSA is especially important given that recent field experiments have shown that modest, low-cost provision of additional information on Social Security could have significant effects on benefit claiming and labor force participation decisions (Liebman et al., 2011). Financial advisers suggested a number of ways in which the SSA could better interact with the financial planning community. Among potential steps for SSA are: greater outreach to notify planners of SSA source materials that could be useful to them; integration of the online Social Security Statement into financial planners' software used to estimate total retirement income needs; and review and enhancement of SSA's existing web and print materials in consultation with financial advisers.

All of these steps could potentially increase knowledge of Social Security claiming issues among financial planners and improve the claiming decisions of their clients, at relatively little cost to SSA or the taxpayer.

Our interviews with plan providers indicated an interest in assistance from the SSA to help these plan providers extend more effective retirement planning education and guidance to their participants. While there are surely obstacles to the provision of this assistance, some consideration should be given to how the SSA can use this channel to help workers make more informed decisions about their Social Security benefits.

References

Aaron, H. J., and J. M. Callan (2011). 'Who Retires Early?' Center for Retirement Research Working Paper No. 2011-10. Chestnut Hill, MA: Center for Retirement Research, Boston College.

Brown, J. R., A. Kapteyn, and O. S. Mitchell (2011). 'Framing Effects and Expected Social Security Claiming Behavior,' RAND Working Paper No. WR-854. Santa Monica, CA: RAND.

Brown, S. K. (2012). 'The Impact of Claiming Age on Monthly Social Security Retirement Benefits: How Knowledgeable Are Future Beneficiaries?' AARP Report. Washington, DC: AARP.

Bureau of Labor Statistics (BLS) (2010). *National Compensation Survey*. Washington, DC: BLS.

Cerulli Associates (2010). *Cerulli Quantitative Update: Advisor Metrics 2010*. Boston, MA: Cerulli Associates. http://clients.cerulli.com/Files/pdf/2010-Cerulli_Quant_Update-Advisor_Metrics_Info-Packet.pdf

Coile, C., P. Diamond, J. Gruber, and A. Jousten (2002). 'Delays in Claiming Social Security Benefits,' *Journal of Public Economics*, 84(3): 357–85.

Employee Benefit Research Institute (2010). 'Estimates Based on U.S. Census Bureau 2011 Current Population Survey.' Personal communication to the authors from Craig Copeland, EBRI.

Greenwald, M., and L. Schneider (2011). 'How to Improve Social Security Education: Retirement Plan Providers' Perspectives,' RAND Working Paper No. WR-898-SSA. Santa Monica, CA: RAND.

—— A. Kapteyn, O. S. Mitchell, and L. Schneider (2010). 'What Do People Know About Social Security?' RAND Working Paper No. WR-792-SSA. Santa Monica, CA: RAND.

—— A. Biggs, and L. Schneider (2011). 'Financial Advisors' Role in Influencing Social Security Claiming,' RAND Working Paper No. WR-894-SSA. Santa Monica, CA: RAND.

Liebman, J. B., and E. F. P. Luttmer (2011). 'Would People Behave Differently If They Better Understood Social Security? Evidence from a Field Experiment,' NBER Working Paper No. 17287. Cambridge, MA: National Bureau of Economic Research.

Mathew Greenwald & Associates (2008). *2008 MoneyTrack Survey of Consumers*. Washington, DC: Mathew Greenwald & Associates, Inc.

Munnell, A. H., S. A. Sass, A. Golub-Sass, and N. Karamcheva (2009). 'Unusual Social Security Claiming Strategies: Costs and Distributional Effects,' Center for Retirement Research Working Paper No. 2009-17. Chestnut Hill, MA: Center for Retirement Research, Boston College.

Sass, S. A. (2012). 'Should You Buy an Annuity from Social Security?' Center for Retirement Research Working Paper No. 2012-10. Chestnut Hill, MA: Center for Retirement Research, Boston College, pp. 12–60.

—— W. Sun, and A. Webb (2007). 'When Should Married Men Claim Social Security Benefits?' Center for Retirement Research Working Paper No. 2008-04. Chestnut Hill, MA: Center for Retirement Research, Boston College, pp. 8.1–8.8.

Shuart, A. N., D. A. Weaver, and K. Whitman (2010). 'Widowed Before Retirement: Social Security Benefit Claiming Strategies,' *Journal of Financial Planning*, 23(4): 45–53 April.

Social Security Administration (SSA) (2011). *Trustees Summary of the 2011 Social Security and Medicare Trustees Reports*. Washington, DC: Social Security Administration. http://www.ssa.gov/OACT/TRSUM/tr11summary.pdf

Tacchino, K. B., D. Littell, and B. D. Schobel (2012). 'A Decision Framework for Optimizing the Social Security Claiming Age,' *Benefits Quarterly*, Second Quarter 2012: 48.

Chapter 5

How Important is Asset Allocation to Americans' Financial Retirement Security?

Alicia H. Munnell, Natalia Orlova, and Anthony Webb

Financial advice—the topic of this volume—tends to focus on financial assets, applying tools that give prominence to the asset allocation decision. But most Americans have little financial wealth, and financial tools are often silent about the levers that will have a much more powerful effect on retirement security for such individuals. These levers include delaying retirement, tapping housing equity through a reverse mortgage, and controlling spending. Moreover, even for many with substantial assets, these non-financial levers may be as powerful as asset allocation in attaining retirement security.

Our analysis begins with a simple exercise that provides a stylized example of the tradeoff between investment returns and time spent in the labor force. The second section uses data from the Health and Retirement Study (HRS) on pre-retirees aged 51–64, to investigate how the gap between retirement needs and retirement resources is affected by working longer, taking out a reverse mortgage, controlling spending, and shifting funds to assets with no risk. Finally, we use a simple dynamic programming model to calculate a risk-adjusted measure of the value of moving from a typical conservative portfolio to an optimal portfolio for the average household.

We conclude that a focus on asset allocation alone is misplaced, since households have much more potent levers for achieving retirement security.

A simple model

It is useful to begin by estimating what percent of earnings individuals must save to ensure a financially secure retirement, depending on when they start saving, when they retire, and how they invest their retirement savings. Naturally, the age at which one begins to save and the age at which one retires are pivotal decisions in determining the required saving rate, and these can make the difference between a secure or insecure retirement.

TABLE 5.1 Percent of pre-retirement salary required to maintain living standards, 2008

Pre-retirement earnings	Two-earner couples	Single workers
$20,000	94	88
$50,000	81	80
$90,000	78	81

Source: Palmer (2008).

Our approach uses replacement rates—the ratio of retirement income to earnings before retirement—to gauge the extent to which older people can maintain their pre-retirement levels of consumption once they stop working.[1] People typically need less than their full pre-retirement earnings to maintain their standard of living once they stop working. First, they pay less tax: they no longer pay Social Security and Medicare payroll taxes, and they also pay lower federal income tax because—at most—only a portion of their Social Security benefits is taxable.[2] Second, they no longer need to save for retirement. And finally, most households pay off their mortgages before they retire, or soon thereafter.

The RETIRE Project at Georgia State University has been calculating required replacement rates for decades.[3] As of 2008, the Project estimated that households with earnings of $50,000 and over needed about 80 percent of pre-retirement earnings to maintain the same level of consumption (see Table 5.1). Households earning less required more to reach this adequacy goal because they generally save very little for retirement and pay much less tax while working.

How much individuals need to save in order to end up with an 80 percent replacement rate depends on a number of factors, including the household's earnings. The lower the earnings, the greater the portion provided by Social Security, so the individual would have to save less on his own. Also, the higher the rate of return on investments, the lower his required saving rate. The earlier the individual starts saving, the lower the required rate would be for any given retirement age, and the later the individual retires, the lower his required saving rate.

The Social Security Trustees (SSA, 2012) publish the percent of earnings that Social Security will replace at age 65 and at the eventual Full Retirement Age of 67 for low, medium, high, and maximum earners (see Table 5.2).[4] Replacement rates for other ages from 62 to 70 have been calculated using the appropriate actuarial adjustment for early retirement or the delayed retirement credit for later retirement. Subtracting Social Security's replacement rate from 80 percent determines the percent of earnings that would need to be replaced by individual savings.

How Important is Asset Allocation? 91

TABLE 5.2 Current law Social Security replacement rates, 2030 and later (%)

Earnings level	Age	
	65	67
Low	49.0	55.3
Medium	36.3	41.0
High	30.1	34.0
Maximum	23.9	27.2

Source: SSA (2012: table V.C7).

A final issue is to determine how much income may be drawn from retirement savings. Our calculations assume the '4 percent rule,' that is, an individual who retires at age 65 annually withdraws 4 percent of savings in that year. Those who retire earlier would withdraw somewhat less and those who retire later somewhat more.[5] Another option would be to purchase an inflation-indexed annuity, which yields very similar results in terms of the required saving rate.

The implied saving rate depends on the assumed real return earned on accumulated assets, when the individual begins saving, and when the individual retires.[6] In our model, we assume real rates of return from 1 to 7 percent; all individuals are assumed to be age 25 in 2010 and start saving at ages 25, 35, or 45, and retirement ages are assumed to range from 62 to 70.[7] A wage growth assumption of 1.2 percent above inflation is used.[8]

To illustrate, we consider an individual aged 25 in 2010, who earns Social Security's medium earnings of $43,000 and retires at the Full Retirement Age of 67 in 2052. Under current law, Social Security will replace 41 percent of this individual's final inflation-adjusted earnings of $71,000; so the individual would need to save enough to replace 39 percent (80 percent minus 41 percent), or about $27,700. With the 4 percent spending rule, the individual needs just under $660,000 in 2052.[9] If the individual started saving at 35 and earned a real return of 4 percent, he will need to save 18 percent of earnings each year.

Required saving rates for the medium earner, assuming a rate of return of 4 percent are presented in Table 5.3. Two messages emerge. First, starting to save at age 25, rather than age 45, cuts the required saving rate by about two-thirds. Second, delaying retirement from age 62 to age 70 also reduces the required saving rate by about two-thirds. As a result, the individual who starts at 25 and retires at 70 needs to save only 7 percent of earnings to achieve an 80 percent replacement rate at retirement, one-tenth of the rate for an individual who started at 45 and retires at 62—an impossible 65 percent.[10] But note that even an individual who started

TABLE 5.3 Saving rates required for a medium earner to attain an 80 percent replacement rate with a 4 percent rate of return (%)

Retire at	Start saving at		
	25	35	45
62	22	35	65
65	15	24	41
67	12	18	31
70	7	11	18

Source: Authors' calculations; see text.

TABLE 5.4 Saving rate required for a medium earner to attain an 80 percent replacement rate with a starting age for saving of 35, by rate of return (%)

Retire at	Real rate of return		
	2 percent	4 percent	6 percent
62	46	35	26
65	32	24	17
67	26	18	13
70	16	11	7

Source: Authors' calculations; see text.

saving at 45 has a plausible 18 percent required saving rate if he could postpone retirement to age 70.[11]

Retiring later is an extremely powerful lever for several reasons. First, because Social Security monthly benefits are actuarially adjusted, they are more than 75 percent higher at age 70 than age 62. As a result, they replace a much larger share of pre-retirement earnings at later ages—29 percent at 62 and 52 percent at 70 in our example—thus reducing the amount required from savings. Second, by postponing retirement, people have additional years to contribute to their 401(k) and allow their balances to grow. Finally, a later retirement age means that people have fewer years to support themselves by drawing on their accumulated retirement assets. Accordingly, this approach highlights the impact of delayed retirement on the required saving rates.

Of course, these results depend on an assumed rate of return on assets of 4 percent. Table 5.4 shows the impact of lower and higher rates of return for individuals who start at age 35. A 2 percent return is slightly less than the long-run rate of return on intermediate-term government bonds and the 6 percent return is slightly less than the long-run rate of return on large capitalization stocks.[12] While higher returns do permit smaller contribution rates to reach the target, they also bring increased risk. Even ignoring risk, the required saving differentials are less than those associated with ages for starting to save and the age of retirement. In fact, an individual can offset the impact of a 2 percent return instead of a 6 percent return by retiring at age 67 instead of 62.

In summary, starting early and working longer can be more effective in boosting the chances of an adequate retirement than earning a higher return. This strategy of saving for a longer period of time is especially effective given the greater risk that comes from attempting to earn that higher return. Moreover, the further along people are in their careers, the more effective working a few years longer becomes. Next, we examine the effects of alternative strategies on actual households in the HRS.

Retirement income targets and resources

The HRS is a nationally representative panel of older American households; it began in 1992 by interviewing about 12,650 individuals from about 7,600 households ages 51–61 and their spouses (regardless of age), and it has been re-administered every two years since.[13] Over time, other cohorts have been added to the survey, substantially increasing the sample size. War Babies (born between 1942 and 1947) were added in 1998; Early Boomers (born between 1948 and 1953) were added in 2004; and Mid Boomers (born between 1954 and 1959) were added in 2010. Like the original sample, these three additional cohorts are interviewed every two years.

Our sample focuses on households with a working head under age 65. All individuals who reported being single are defined as household heads; for couples, we identify the male as the head. In the case of same-sex couples, we define the higher-earning spouse as the head (or the older one if earnings were equivalent).

HRS households for whom complete data are available may be observed repeatedly until they reach age 64. As a result, the sample begins with 21,423 observations of households with heads under age 65 (in waves five to nine of the HRS, or 2000 to 2008). From that total, 7,203 observations were dropped because the household head was not working, and a further 1,604 observations were dropped because the data were incomplete or inconsistent. These deletions produced a final sample of 12,626 observations.[14] Our sample is of somewhat higher socioeconomic status than the population as a whole, because working households tend to have more education and better health than those not working (Appendix Table 5.A1).[15]

Our goal is to create target replacement rates and projected replacement rates for each age from 60 to 70 for each household observation. Once constructed, the levers identified in the introduction can be applied to test their relative power in helping households achieve a secure retirement income.

Target replacement rates

We calculate a target replacement rate that would enable each household to maintain its current standard of living at each age from 60 to 70, covering both pre-retirement income and required mortgage payments. These targets come from the RETIRE Project and are discussed in the Appendix.

Projected retirement replacement rates

The next step is to project retirement replacement rates that each household will achieve if it continues its present course, maintaining its current saving rate and asset allocation, and not taking a reverse mortgage. Retirement income in our baseline scenario thus consists of Social Security benefits, employer pension payments, and income from financial assets. (Further details on the replacement rate calculations appear in the Appendix.)

Applying the levers

The difference between target replacement rates and projected replacement rates measures the extent to which household needs fall short of resources. This measure provides the baseline against which to assess the respective contributions of four possible interventions to bridge the gap. Such interventions might not be utility maximizing; that is, another strategy could be to accept lower consumption, both now and in retirement. Our objective, however, is not to identify an optimal strategy, but rather to calculate the effectiveness of each intervention in bridging the gap between post-retirement needs and resources.

Reverse mortgage income

Our first experiment has households take out reverse mortgages. These are calculated as follows: for homeowners without a mortgage, the household is assumed to take the maximum available loan, given the age of the younger spouse and the house value, and to exercise the lifetime income option. The proceeds from that option are based on January 2012 interest rates and typical closing costs and expenses. For homeowners with a mortgage, the household is assumed to use its financial assets to clear its mortgage debt at retirement. If financial assets are insufficient to clear the mortgage, the household then takes part of its reverse mortgage in the

How Important is Asset Allocation? 95

form of a lump sum, reducing the amount payable under the reverse mortgage lifetime income option. These reverse mortgage calculations produce a new set of projected retirement incomes for homeowners.

Delay retirement

The second experiment involves postponing retirement and the claiming of Social Security benefits. Postponing retirement gives the household the opportunity to make additional 401(k) contributions, earn additional returns on investments, and increase Social Security benefits, and it also reduces the period that accumulated assets must finance. Our baseline results provide information on the effect of later retirement on the gap, because they present targets and projected replacement rates for each age.

Asset allocation

Next we assume each household invests all of its assets in equities earning a 6.5 percent real return. We also assume no costs associated with the increased risk. Investing 100 percent in 'riskless equities' has an impact on both projected wealth at retirement and the amount that the household can consume during the course of retirement. Our notion is that if asset allocation did not dominate the other levers with 'riskless equities,' it would never dominate.

Control spending

Finally, we control spending, using the extra funds to increase savings. This intervention has two effects. First, the additional 401(k) contributions boost household retirement wealth and retirement income. Second, they reduce post-retirement needs by reducing the level of pre-retirement consumption that the household must maintain in retirement. For this exercise, the household increases its 401(k) contribution by five percentage points, which produces a commensurate decline in the replacement rate target.

Our results for each of the experiments appear in Table 5.5. In the base case, 74 percent of households are found to fall short of their targets at age 62. If households worked to age 67, Social Security's ultimate Full Retirement Age, that share would drop to 45 percent. If households who own a home were to take out a reverse mortgage, the share falling short would reach 45 percent at age 65. If all households cut their spending by five percentage points—thereby increasing their saving and lowering their targets—the percent at risk would fall to 45 percent at age 66. If all households invested all of their assets in 'riskless equities' over their remaining work lives, they would reach the 45 percent figure six months earlier than the base case—at age 66.5. In other words, working six months longer—from 66.5 to 67—produces the same outcome as having all assets invested in 'riskless equities.' As shown in the following section, taking risk into consideration shifts the balance in favor of working longer. The fact that asset allocation has only a minor impact is not surprising, given that most households have little financial wealth (see Table 5.6).

A second set of results focuses just on the top decile of the wealth distribution, which includes households with over $580,000 of financial wealth. Since these households are wealthier, a smaller percentage of households falls short at 62 even in the base case—39 percent for the

TABLE 5.5 Households falling short of target (%)

Lever	60	61	62	63	64	65	66	67	68	69	70
Full sample											
Base case	89.5	88.9	73.6	69.4	64.1	57.4	51.4	45.3	38.8	32.3	26.2
Take out reverse mortgage	89.5	88.9	66.7	61.1	54.4	47.0	40.8	34.8	29.1	23.9	19.2
Control spending	88.7	87.9	70.7	66.0	59.6	52.2	46.4	39.5	33.1	26.8	21.4
Hold all 'riskless equities'	89.2	88.4	72.7	68.3	62.6	55.5	49.3	42.8	36.3	29.7	23.8
Top wealth decile											
Base case	56.3	54.3	38.5	34.4	29.5	23.5	19.1	16.3	12.4	10.4	7.8
Take out reverse mortgage	56.3	54.3	37.0	31.6	25.1	19.8	16.8	13.8	9.9	7.8	5.7
Control spending	54.2	52.0	35.8	30.5	24.7	19.6	16.8	12.8	10.3	7.9	5.6
Hold all 'riskless equities'	55.7	53.5	37.4	32.5	26.2	20.5	17.0	13.0	9.4	6.5	4.0

Source: Authors' estimates; see text.

TABLE 5.6 Wealth levels by wealth deciles ($ 2011)

Wealth decile	Financial wealth	
	Minimum	Maximum
1	0	418
2	438	4,168
3	4,179	14,369
4	14,369	33,642
5	33,654	63,393
6	63,438	108,692
7	108,796	176,346
8	176,534	312,415
9	312,589	579,013
10	579,912	–

Source: Authors' tabulations from the HRS.

top decile, versus 74 percent for the population as a whole (see Table 5.5). If top-decile households worked to 67, the share falling short drops to 16 percent. If these households took out a reverse mortgage, the 16 percent threshold would be reached at age 66. The relative impact of a reverse mortgage is smaller for the wealthy, because their homes are a much smaller component of total wealth. If households controlled their spending, the fraction at risk would fall to 16 percent at age 66. Finally, investing all assets in 'riskless equities' allows the top decile to reach the 16 percent threshold at 66. So, even for the top decile, asset allocation is no more powerful than the other levers.

Dynamic modeling

Our final exercise uses dynamic programming techniques to calculate a risk-adjusted measure of the potential gain from portfolio rebalancing. In contrast to the two previous approaches, this approach enables us to calculate an optimal savings rate and portfolio allocation, and to calculate the benefit to the household of adopting an optimal portfolio allocation taking into account changes in the riskiness of that portfolio. The analysis focuses first on the typical household approaching retirement, and next on a household typical of those in the top financial wealth decile.

In our data, the typical household is aged 57, has a household income of $62,600, and financial wealth of $60,500. The household's portfolio is held in tax-deferred accounts, and the portfolio allocation is 36 percent in stocks, 16 percent in bonds, and 50 percent in cash.[16] The assumption is that stock returns are independent and identically distributed (i.i.d.) with a mean of 6.5 percent and a standard deviation of 20 percent, the average for the period 1926–2010. Bonds and short-term deposits are both assumed to be risk-free, with real returns of 3 and 1 percent, respectively.[17]

Following Scholz et al. (2006), earnings are assumed to follow an autoregressive process of order one (AR(1)).[18] The retirement age is 66, and the household's 401(k) deferral is 9 percent of salary. The household is posited to receive Social Security benefits of $20,800 a year, the median for this birth cohort.[19] Earnings before retirement are subject to federal income and payroll taxes, and withdrawals from tax-deferred accounts and Social Security benefits are subject to federal income taxation after retirement. Prior to retirement, the household's consumption equals labor market earnings minus taxes and 401(k) deferrals.

To calculate an optimal decumulation of financial assets in retirement from the typical portfolio allocation described above, the household is assumed to have a constant relative risk aversion utility function over consumption in excess of the federal poverty guideline. The household has a coefficient of relative risk aversion (CRRA) of five or two, and population average mortality for the 1950 birth cohort.[20] The rate of time preference is assumed to be 3 percent. We also have the household switch from the typical portfolio described above to an optimal portfolio, which varies with age. The goal is to calculate the dollar amount by which the wealth of the household retaining the typical portfolio must be increased, so that the household is as well off in expected utility terms as when it adopts the optimal allocation. Finally, we have the household switch from the typical portfolio to one invested entirely in stocks. We then calculate the dollar amount, if any, by which the current wealth of a household retaining the typical portfolio must be increased, so that it is as well off in expected utility terms as when it switches to a portfolio invested exclusively in stocks. This represents the value or cost to the household of switching to the all-stock portfolio analyzed in the preceding pages.

Results for the hypothetical household at two levels of risk aversion are reported in the upper panel of Table 5.7. One piece of information that helps provide some intuition behind the findings is that a large portion of the total wealth of the typical household is the present discounted value of future Social Security benefits. Since Social Security wealth is a bond-like asset, the optimal allocation for these households involves a large share of financial wealth invested in equities under the assumption of CRRA utility (see Table 5.8).

Assuming a CRRA of five, the amount required to compensate the household for retaining a typical portfolio (where 36 percent of assets are invested in equities), rather than switching to an optimal portfolio allocation (where 51 percent of assets are invested in equities) is $5,800, or approximately the amount the household would earn if it delayed retirement by one month. In contrast, when the comparison is between a typical

TABLE 5.7 Amount required as compensation for retaining typical portfolio allocation ($ 2011)

Household type and risk aversion	Retaining typical portfolio rather than switching to optimal portfolio	Retaining typical portfolio rather than switching to all-stock portfolio
Typical wealth household		
CRRA = 5	$5,800	−$3,800
CRRA = 2	26,800	26,800
Top wealth decile household		
CRRA = 5	$91,000	−$316,000
CRRA = 2	21,000	−11,600

Note: CRRA = constant relative risk aversion utility function.
Source: Authors' calculations.

TABLE 5.8 Typical and optimal portfolio allocations (%)

Household type and risk aversion	
Typical household	
Typical stock allocation	36
Optimal stock allocation—CRRA = 5	51%
Optimal stock allocation—CRRA = 2	100%
Top-decile household	
Typical stock allocation	57
Optimal stock allocation—CRRA = 5	29%
Optimal stock allocation—CRRA = 2	70%

Note: Optimal stock allocations are calculated as of age 65. CRRA = constant relative risk aversion utility function. The typical portfolio allocation is calculated over all households with non-zero financial wealth.

Source: Authors' calculations.

portfolio and an all-stock portfolio, the household is better off by approximately $3,800 if it retains the typical portfolio, or less than one month's salary. That is, an all-stock portfolio is even more sub-optimal than the typical conservative portfolio. In any event, however, the dollar amounts are small, implying that asset allocation is relatively unimportant for the typical risk-averse household.

Even if the household were less risk averse (CRRA of two), the story is similar. In this case, as shown in Table 5.8, the optimal portfolio would be all in stocks. The cost of retaining a typical portfolio (57 percent in equities), rather than switching to an optimal portfolio (all equities), is $26,800 or just over four months' salary. As the optimal portfolio in this model is 100 percent in equities, the cost of retaining a typical portfolio relative to an all-stock portfolio is also $26,800. In short, regardless of the degree of risk aversion, asset allocation has a relatively small impact on the typical household.

The lower panel of Table 5.7 reports results for the wealthy household in the top decile of financial wealth. This household has income of $137,800 and financial assets of $889,000: 57 percent in stocks, 22 percent in bonds, and 21 percent in short-term deposits. Because Social Security wealth is a much smaller share of this household's wealth, optimal equity holdings are lower than for the typical household (Table 5.8). If the household had a CRRA of five, the cost of retaining a typical portfolio (57 percent in equities), rather than switching to an optimal portfolio (29 percent in equities), is $91,000. Again, as above, the top-decile household is *better off* retaining a typical portfolio rather than switching to an all-stock portfolio; the benefit is $316,000. The comparable amounts for a household with a CRRA of two are a cost of $21,000 and a benefit of $11,600. Although the amounts required as compensation are larger for the top-decile household than for the typical household, they are still small relative to working longer.

Conclusion

Financial planners frequently highlight the asset allocation decision, suggesting that individuals may gain substantially from a different allocation of stocks and bonds. Yet they are often silent on the benefits of other behaviors such as delaying retirement, controlling spending, or taking out a reverse mortgage. We show that the typical 401(k)/IRA balances of households approaching retirement are below $100,000, suggesting that the net benefits of portfolio reallocation for typical households would be modest, compared to other levers. Higher income households may have slightly more to gain.

In view of the relative unimportance of asset allocations for most Americans, financial advisers would likely be of greater help to their clients if they focused on a broad array of tools—including working longer, controlling spending, and taking out a reverse mortgage.

Appendix

This appendix explains the calculation of components of the replacement rate.

Target replacement rates

Georgia State University's RETIRE Project provides four sets of retirement income replacement rates that vary by marital status, age, and labor force participation status. Each set of replacement rates is for incomes of $20,000 to $90,000 in increments of $10,000. HRS households were assigned target replacement rates based on these factors. The assumption was that households were aiming to replace the relevant percentage of the average of the last ten years' earnings.[21]

The RETIRE report does not explicitly model mortgage debt, so the targets need to be adjusted to reflect our projection that a significant proportion of the sample will have either repaid their mortgage by retirement or be able to repay all or part of the balance outstanding at that time by drawing on financial assets. The adjustment involved subtracting annual mortgage payments reported by respondents from their target retirement incomes, and then adding annual mortgage payments multiplied by the ratio of remaining mortgage debt (mortgage debt less financial assets) to initial debt at retirement. The adjusted targets were calculated for each household observation for ages 60 through 70.

Projected retirement replacement rates

Social Security. Projected Social Security benefits are calculated using the HRS Social Security earnings records, available to qualified researchers on a restricted basis. When the Social Security earnings records are not available, earnings histories were imputed using current earnings, earnings at the first HRS interview, and final earnings in previous jobs.[22] Wages between the age the household is observed and the retirement age are projected using Social Security's Average Wage Index (AWI; SSA 2011). The entire wage history is then indexed by the AWI, and the highest 35 years of indexed wages are used to calculate the Average Indexed Monthly Earnings (AIME). The benefit formula is then applied to the AIME to derive the individual's Primary Insurance Amount.

Pension income. Pension income is based on the 1998 and 2004 HRS imputed data for employer-sponsored pension plan wealth in current jobs.[23] Households in waves seven through nine (2004, 2006, and 2008) were assigned pensions from the 2004 data set; households in waves five and six (2000 and 2002) from the 1998 data. The data sets differ slightly. The 2004 data set includes values for retirement ages 60, 62, 65, and 70. For the 1998 data set, pension values were available only for ages 60, 62, and 65. The 2004 data set discounts defined benefit pension wealth to the survey year, while the 1998 data set projects defined benefit wealth to the retirement age. The 1998 values are extrapolated to age 70 based on the average increase in retirement wealth from 65 to 70 in the 2004 data. For both data sets, values for ages 63, 64, and 66 through 69 are interpolated based on the reported numbers.

Defined benefit pension wealth is converted into pension income using the interest and inflation rate assumptions embedded in the pension wealth calculations.[24] In the case of defined contribution pension wealth, the starting point is the account balance. Balances then grow as participants contribute 6 percent of salary, receive a 50 percent employer match, and earn a 4.6 percent real return until retirement. The contributions are based on the assumption that the salary rises by 1.2 percent a year. People who started their jobs after 1998 (waves five and six) or 2004 (waves seven, eight, and nine) are assumed to receive no pension benefits on their new job. The conversion of defined contribution wealth to income is discussed in the next section on financial assets.

TABLE 5.A1 Comparison of workers with all HRS households under age 65

	Working (our sample)	All
Age	56.9***	57.4
Married couple	0.644***	0.605
Ethnicity		
Black	0.098***	0.120
Hispanic	0.078***	0.085
Education		
Less than high school	0.094***	0.143
Some college	0.602***	0.542
Homeowner	0.838***	0.796
Median house value (homeowners only)	$189,000***	$179,000
Has mortgage	0.546***	0.468
Median mortgage balance (households with mortgages only)	$93,800***	$89,300
Pension		
DB or both	0.286***	0.096
DC	0.277***	0.134
Earnings		
Median	$65,400***	$38,000
75th percentile	$108,500***	$81,000
Financial assets		
Median	$63,400***	$35,700
75th percentile	$233,200***	$181,800
Sample size	12,626	21,423

Notes: HRS sample weights. *** denotes that the values are significantly different at the 1 percent level, adjusted for household level clustering.

Source: Authors' tabulations from the HRS.

Financial assets. Household financial wealth invested in stocks, bonds, and short-term deposits is assumed to earn returns of 6.5, 3, and 1 percent, respectively, from the date of the interview until retirement. These rates approximate the long-run average rates of return on each of the three asset classes. Importantly, these assumptions are used throughout for projecting asset returns rather than incorporating any actual fluctuations. The objective is to assess whether households are on track to meet their replacement rate targets, not whether they actually succeeded in meeting them.

At retirement, the household is assumed to purchase a nominal joint or single life annuity with all its financial assets, including 401(k) and IRA balances. Currently, annuity rates are extremely low, reflecting depressed interest rates. The objective of this exercise is to calculate financial preparedness for retirement, given the beliefs of respondents at the date of the HRS interviews. Therefore, the assumed annuity rates are based on a 5.1 percent ten-year Treasury Bond interest rate, projected mortality improvements based on Social Security Administration cohort mortality tables, and current expense loads.[25] At this point, target and projected replacement rates are available for each household observation for ages 60 through 70.

Endnotes

1. Technically, economists posit that individuals are interested in smoothing marginal utility, not consumption. If additional leisure enables the household to attain the same marginal utility at lower levels of consumption, it may be optimal to accept lower consumption after retirement. This is one explanation for what the literature calls the 'retirement-consumption puzzle'—namely, the fact that consumption appears to drop as people retire. See Banks et al. (1998); Bernheim et al. (2001); and Hurd and Rohwedder (2003). We abstract from this approach in the present chapter.
2. The taxation treatment of Social Security benefits is as follows. First, the household calculates its 'combined income.' Combined income is regular taxable income plus 50 percent of Social Security benefits. The taxable amount of Social Security benefits is the minimum of three tests: (*a*) 50 percent of combined income over the first threshold ($25,000 for singles and $32,000 for married couples) plus 35 percent of combined income over the second threshold ($34,000 for singles and $44,000 for married couples); (*b*) 50 percent of benefits plus 85 percent of combined income over the second threshold; or (*c*) 85 percent of benefits (Internal Revenue Service, 2012).
3. For an array of pre-retirement earnings levels, they calculate federal, state, and local income taxes and Social Security taxes before and after retirement. They also use the Bureau of Labor Statistics' Consumer Expenditure Survey to estimate consumer savings and expenditures for different earnings levels (Palmer, 2008).
4. The low earner has career average earnings equal to about 45 percent of the national Average Wage Index (AWI). The medium earner has career average earnings equal to about 100 percent of the AWI. The high earner has career average earnings equal to about 160 percent of the AWI. The AWI in 2010 was $43,084 and maximum taxable earnings were $106,800. Thus, the low-wage worker would earn $19,388 and the high-wage worker would earn $68,934. For a further discussion of the AWI, see Mitchell and Phillips (2008) and Munnell and Soto (2005).
5. Bengen (1994) showed that households adopting this strategy and who invest in a mixed stock-bond portfolio face a relatively low risk of outliving their wealth. Although sub-optimal, we assume that the appropriate percentage drawdown rate is not affected by realized returns during the accumulation phase (i.e., that realized returns do not provide information about the distribution of prospective returns).

6. As most saving in the United States is done through employer-sponsored plans—primarily 401(k)s—the required saving rate should be viewed as the combined employer–employee contribution rate.
7. The calculation abstracts from investment risk; in reality, an expected 7 percent real return can only be earned at the cost of assuming very considerable risk. It also abstracts from the notion of optimal saving. Indeed, for households that are middle-aged and have yet to start saving for retirement, the optimal strategy will likely be not only to delay retirement but also to cut post-retirement consumption targets (Kotlikoff, 2008).
8. This assumption is used by the Social Security Trustees (SSA, 2011) for the economy as a whole. Individual workers may experience more rapid increases as they gain seniority in jobs. More rapid wage growth will increase the required saving rate, all else equal.
9. Under current law, benefits will be cut when the Social Security Trust Fund is exhausted.
10. A more sophisticated analysis would adjust the target replacement rate. That is, if an individual was indeed saving 65 percent of earnings, he would be living on 35 percent. The 80-percent target would no longer be appropriate.
11. These results are similar to those reported by Mitchell and Moore (1998).
12. Data from Ibbotson (2010) show that, over the period 1926–2010, real stock returns have averaged 6.5 percent and the real return on the ten-year Treasury was 2.4 percent.
13. The HRS is conducted by the Institute for Social Research (ISR) at the University of Michigan and is made possible by funding from the National Institute on Aging. More information is available at the ISR website: http://hrsonline.isr.umich.edu/.
14. The primary reason for dropping observations was that the head reported working but had zero earnings. We retained the observation if the head reported that he was in the same job as in the previous wave and reported non-zero earnings in the previous wave.
15. Wealth levels are similar to those reported by Moore and Mitchell (2000), after making allowance for inflation.
16. Introducing both taxable and tax-deferred accounts and allowing households to choose the order in which the household draws on these accounts would greatly complicate the model without yielding additional insight.
17. In a single-period model, both stocks and bonds carry risk. Campbell and Viceira (2002) argue that over a long time horizon, bonds and, in particular, Treasury Inflation Protected Securities are the true risk-free asset, because they guarantee a return on capital. If a long-term investor knew his consumption requirements with certainty, he could fund them by buying a portfolio of bonds of appropriate maturities. We therefore assume that corporate bonds yield a fixed real 3 percent return. Our assumed real rate of return is considerably in

excess of the current negative real interest rates, reflecting an assumption that short-term interest rates will eventually revert to more normal levels.
18. An alternative would be to assume that the household experiences both permanent and transitory wage shocks (as in Chai et al., 2011).
19. Given our assumption of labor income uncertainty, the household also faces some level of uncertainty as to Social Security benefit levels.
20. Estimated coefficients of risk aversion in the academic literature range between two and ten, depending in part on whether the estimates are derived from portfolio theory, purchases of insurance, economic experiments, or preferences over lotteries (Chetty, 2003).
21. The ten-year period refers to the decade before the observation, not the ten years prior to retirement.
22. When the Social Security earnings records are not available, the procedure followed Gustman and Steinmeier (2001) and estimated earnings histories based on HRS data on previous jobs and wages, using the estimated returns to tenure from Anderson et al. (1999).
23. Participants in the HRS are asked about projected benefits from employer pensions. The HRS also obtains pension plan data from participants' employers. Also, the HRS pension data collected from participants suffers from high levels of non-response and misreporting of pension type. We considered using data that the HRS has collected from respondents' employers, but these data are only available for about two-thirds of participants.
24. The interest rate assumption is irrelevant, provided that the same assumption is used to calculate pension wealth from respondents' estimates of their pension income, and then to recover pension income from pension wealth.
25. To simplify the calculations, the spouse is assumed to be the same age as the head of the household.

References

Anderson, P. M., A. L. Gustman and T. L. Steinmeier (1999). 'Trends in Male Labor Force Participation and Retirement: Some Evidence on the Role of Pension and Social Security in the 1970s and 1980s,' *Journal of Labor Economics*, 17(4), Part 1: 757–83.

Banks, J., R. Blundell, and S. Tanner (1998). 'Is There a Retirement-Savings Puzzle?' *The American Economic Review*, 88(4): 769–88.

Bengen, W. (1994). 'Determining Withdrawal Rates Using Historical Data,' *Journal of Financial Planning*, 17(3): 64–73.

Bernheim, D., J. Skinner, and S. Weinberg (2001). 'What Accounts for the Variation in Retirement Wealth Among U.S. Households?' *The American Economic Review*, 91(4): 832–57.

Campbell, J. Y., and L. M. Viceira (2002). *Strategic Asset Allocation: Portfolio Choice for Long-Term Investors*. Oxford, UK: Oxford University Press.

Chai, J., W. Horneff, R. Maurer, and O. S. Mitchell (2011). 'Optimal Portfolio Choice Over the Life-Cycle with Flexible Work, Endogenous Retirement, and Lifetime Payouts,' *Review of Finance*, 15(1): 875–907.

Chetty, R. (2003). 'A New Method of Estimating Risk Aversion,' NBER Working Paper No. 9988. Cambridge, MA: National Bureau of Economic Research.

Gustman, Alan L. and Thomas L. Steinmeier (2001). 'How Effective is Redistribution under the Social Security Benefit Formula?' *Journal of Public Economics*, 82(1): 1–28.

Hurd, M., and S. Rohwedder (2003). 'The Retirement-Consumption Puzzle: Anticipated and Actual Decline in Spending at Retirement,' NBER Working Paper No. 9586. Cambridge, MA: National Bureau of Economic Research.

Ibbotson Associates (2010). *2010 Ibbotson Stocks, Bonds, Bills, and Inflation (SBBI) Classic Year-Book*. Chicago, IL: Morningstar, Inc.

Internal Revenue Service (IRS) (2012). *Individual Retirement Arrangements*. Publication 590. Washington, DC: United States Department of the Treasury. http://www.irs.gov/pub/irs-pdf/p590.pdf

Kotlikoff, L. J. (2008). 'Economics' Approach to Financial Planning,' *Journal of Financial Planning*, 21(3): 42–52.

Mitchell, O. S., and J. F. Moore (1998). 'Can Americans Afford to Retire? New Evidence on Retirement Saving Adequacy,' *Journal of Risk and Insurance*, 65(3): 371–400.

—— J. W. R. Phillips (2008). 'Hypothetical versus Actual Earnings Profiles: Implications for Social Security Reform,' *Journal of Financial Transformation*, 24: 102–4.

Moore, J. F., and O. S. Mitchell (2000). 'Projected Retirement Wealth and Savings Adequacy in the Health and Retirement Study,' in O. S. Mitchell, P. B. Hammond, and A. M. Rappaport, eds., *Forecasting Retirement Needs and Retirement Wealth*. Philadelphia, PA: University of Pennsylvania Press, pp. 68–94.

Munnell, A. H., and M. Soto (2005). 'What Replacement Rates Do Households Actually Experience in Retirement?' Center for Retirement Research at Boston College Working Paper 2005-10. Cambridge, MA: National Bureau of Economic Research.

Palmer, B. A. (2008). 'Aon Consulting's Replacement Ratio Study,' Global Corporate Marketing and Communications.

Scholz, J. K., A. Seshadri, and K. Surachai (2006). 'Are Americans Saving "Optimally" for Retirement?' *Journal of Political Economy*, 114(4): 607–43.

United States Social Security Administration (SSA) (2011). *The Annual Report of the Board of Trustees of the Federal Old-Age and Survivors Insurance and Federal Disability Insurance Trust Funds*. SSA-66-327. Washington, DC: GPO.

—— (2012). *The Annual Report of the Board of Trustees of the Federal Old-Age and Survivors Insurance and Federal Disability Insurance Trust Funds*. SSA-66-327. Washington, DC: GPO.

Chapter 6

The Evolution of Workplace Advice

Christopher L. Jones and Jason S. Scott

The past few decades have brought a profound shift in employer retirement plans, away from professionally managed pension assets, and toward individuals bearing the burdens of their own investment and saving decisions. Tens of millions of employees today are faced with making investing and saving decisions in defined contribution (DC) plans that will have a significant impact on their future quality of life. In response to these changes, employers are increasingly providing employees with access to specific investment advice. Yet the workplace environment creates substantial challenges for traditional methods of providing investment advice. This chapter shows how the workplace advice market has evolved over the last fifteen years, how technology has changed the creation and delivery of investment advice, and how the regulatory environment has influenced the availability and usage of advice in DC plans.

A key characteristic of workplace investment advisory services in the United States is that they must address the requirements and preferences of three distinct groups of stakeholders: government regulators, plan sponsors (employers), and plan participants (employees). One can think of each of these stakeholders as representing filters through which any successful advice solution must be able to pass. For instance, a workplace advice solution that fails to meet regulatory requirements is a non-starter in the marketplace. Likewise, one that meets regulatory requirements but fails to address plan sponsor concerns will not be provided. And individual participants must also want to use the advisory services if they are to have any impact on investment behavior. Finally, an advisory service must be able to cost-effectively meet the needs of a wide spectrum of plan participants.

Successful workplace advisory services must also address the needs of varied workforces, helping employees create appropriate investment strategies to achieve their retirement goals. Many plan participants have little experience with investing and hold modest account balances, unlike the affluent customers of traditional registered investment advisors (RIAs). For instance, the median 401(k) account balance in Financial Engines' member base in 2011 was approximately $38,000.[1] Providing personalized investment advice to clients with such modest balances places additional requirements on the scalability of the advice provider's business model. Moreover, plan participants differ in terms of their knowledge, level of engagement, risk preferences, and financial circumstances. Addressing the advice needs of such participants therefore requires a multi-faceted approach to engagement and communication. As gatekeepers to the employee population, plan sponsors play an important role in determining which advisory services are available to their plans. Fiduciary responsibilities under the Employee Retirement Income Security Act (ERISA) require plan sponsors to engage in an appropriate selection process in hiring a provider of workplace advisory services. Because of this due diligence requirement, plan sponsors are an important constituency in the development and distribution of workplace advisory services. Finally, as we will see, the actions of government regulators and policymakers, particularly the Department of Labor (DOL) and Congress, have played an important role in shaping evolution of workplace investment advice.

Workplace advice: filling the vacuum

In the mid-1990s, DC plans, and especially 401(k) plans, began to play a central role for many US workers. Originally viewed as supplemental plans to augment traditional defined benefit (DB) pensions, many companies now use the 401(k) as the primary retirement vehicle offered to employees. This move shifted the burden for making investment decisions and bearing investment risk onto individual investors. Many plan sponsors and policymakers began to recognize the large gap between the knowledge and expertise of typical plan participants, as well as the need to make informed investment decisions to shape retirement outcomes.

During most of the 1980s and 1990s, help offered to rank-and-file employees was mainly limited to generic education about investing concepts. Communications provided to plan participants discussed general concepts of diversification and asset allocation, but most did little to provide specific help in constructing an appropriate portfolio using plan investment options. Moreover, many firms provided simple deterministic retirement calculators designed to illustrate the value of compounding and regular saving.

A key problem with these simple models was that they encouraged risk-taking by characterizing asset allocation as a 'return-return' tradeoff. That is, many such calculators asked participants to provide an assumed rate of return used to compound uniformly over the investment horizon, so as to produce an estimate of future retirement wealth. But because these calculations were purely deterministic, it appeared that there was no downside to simply picking the asset allocation with the highest expected return; they ignored investment risk. While institutional investors, notably DB pension plans, had long used sophisticated simulation techniques to help assess the impact of investment risk and make informed choices about risk preferences, such tools were not widely available to individual investors until the mid-1990s. The complexity and costs of developing such models put them out of reach for all but the most affluent investors and their advisors.

Economics and technology were not the only barriers to participants obtaining access to high-quality investment advice in the workplace: sponsor concerns played a role as well. Plans sponsors were wary of jeopardizing their fiduciary protections under Section 404(c) of ERISA.[2] Many sponsors became concerned about providing assistance that might be construed as offering direct investment advice to their employees, fearing that if participants followed such advice and subsequently lost money, employers might be sued. Nevertheless, it grew increasingly clear that many plan participants did a poor job of investing their 401(k) accounts. Common mistakes included overconcentration in employer stock, chasing past performance, selecting inappropriate risk levels, and failing to take advantage of savings opportunities including employer matching contributions. Both employers and government regulators began to view participants' decision-making with alarm, finding that most participants were neither well informed about retirement investing, nor adequately engaged in managing their investments.

The regulatory environment also played a key role in explaining the dearth of workplace advice during the early 1990s. In the United States, 401(k) plans are subject to ERISA which imposes strict limitations on entities providing advice to qualified plan participants. At its core, ERISA seeks to protect plan participants from self-dealing and other conflicts of interest. In the early years of the 401(k) industry, the natural providers of investment advice at large scale, namely large record keepers and asset management firms, were generally prohibited from offering plan participants investment advice. Under ERISA, such advice from an investment manager in the plan would trigger a *prohibited transaction*, with severe penalties for the infracting institution. The ERISA prohibited transaction rules prevent an investment manager from offering advice on its own products, when there is an economic incentive for self-dealing. Since neither plan sponsors nor plan providers showed much interest in offering investment advice due to these legal and compliance concerns, plan participants were largely left on their own.

Recognizing the reluctance of sponsors to offer needed help to plan participants, regulators looked for ways to clarify how such help could be provided safely. In 1996, the US Department of Labor (DOL) issued

Interpretive Bulletin 96-1, which sought to encourage plan sponsors to offer more help to struggling employees. The bulletin marked a milestone in the market for workplace advisory services, as it helped in two important ways: it provided a clear definition of the line between educational guidance and investment advice for plan sponsors under ERISA, and it showed that the DOL favored making more help available to plan participants. Through subsequent related communications, the DOL offered a roadmap for sponsors on how to provide advice safely by hiring an independent fiduciary to give advice to plan participants. In this way, plan sponsors could avoid liability for the advice provided as long as they engaged in a prudent selection and monitoring process. This signaled a shift in the historical view that participants were 'on their own' when it came to making investment decisions in their retirement plans, and it led to many sponsors playing a role in helping their employees with this important and challenging burden.

A new model for workplace advice

The US workplace advice market began to take off in the mid-1990s with the rapid rise in employee access to the Internet. This provided a conduit to reach millions of participants in retirement plans at low cost, and to provide them with interactive advisory services to help them manage their investment choices. In 1995 and 1996, two venture capital-backed startup firms, 401(k) Forum (later mPower) and Financial Engines, were founded in California to provide independent, cost-effective, investment advice for 401(k) plan participants. Both firms adopted the business model of selling independent advisory services to employers who would in turn make these available to their plan participants.

A key attribute of the new approach was to avert the potential for prohibited transactions under ERISA by avoiding the sale or manufacture of investment products. To prevent any incentives for self-dealing, it was necessary to have a business model where advisory services revenues did not depend on the advice itself. By structuring the firm to be independent of the plan funds, it was possible to provide investment advice without violating ERISA rules against self-dealing.

Financial Engines was co-founded in 1996 by William Sharpe, a financial economist and Nobel Laureate at Stanford University, and Joseph Grundfest, a professor at the Stanford Law School and a former Commissioner at the Securities and Exchange Commission (SEC). The founding vision for the company was to bring best practices from academic finance and institutional money management to bear on the needs of everyday investors. With the explosive growth of the Internet, Sharpe saw an opportunity to apply technology to the problem of delivering high-quality personalized investment advice to plan participants, irrespective of their account balances.

Until this point, it had been too expensive to rigorously apply the techniques of modern financial economics to individual investment problems on a mass basis. Investment advisors had historically focused on high-net-worth investors, personally interacting with each client to develop a personalized investment strategy. These advisors were expected to have deep expertise in finance and other domains, and as a part of their services, they spent substantial time developing relationships with each client. The costs of providing investment advisory through this model were and still are considerable. For instance, most independent investment advisors charge for their services as an annual percentage of a client's assets. Fees for investment advisory services generally range from 50 basis points (0.5 percent) to more than 200 basis points (2 percent) of assets under management, depending on the types of services provided and the size of the client account. For the process to be profitable for the advisor, the client account must generate sufficient fees to cover advisors' overhead and compensation. This model is not economically feasible for clients with only a few thousand dollars in their 401(k) accounts. The advance offered by Financial Engines and other firms targeting the 401(k) advice market was technology infrastructure that made it economically feasible at large scale to provide personalized investment advice to participants with modest balances. Plan sponsors demanded services that could help all their employees, not just the affluent. By using technology to automate much of the investment analysis process, it now became possible to provide high-quality advice at a much lower cost than in the past.

Experience with online advice

Financial Engines went live with its first online investment advisory service for 401(k) plan participants in 1998. The online advice service provided plan participants with specific recommendations on which funds to buy and sell, so as to create appropriate retirement investment strategies. Users would log onto the service and interactively explore the tradeoffs associated with different combinations of investment risk, saving, and retirement horizons. This 'outcomes-based' approach emulated techniques used in asset-liabilities studies performed for large pension plans, but now at the scale of individual participants instead of a large DB plan with thousands of beneficiaries. For the first time, plan participants could get realistic views of their retirement outcomes via sophisticated Monte Carlo simulation. Moreover, they could explore how different decisions might alter the probabilities of reaching their goals. Finally, leveraging the expertise built into the optimization engine, they could receive specific recommendations on how to take the best advantage of investment options available in their 401(k) plans. The cost of the service was picked up by the employer, so that participants could use it without any out-of-pocket expense. This was an important consideration in getting plan participants to take advantage of the service, since requiring participant-initiated payments up front would have placed an additional barrier to adoption of the service.

Sponsors who were early adopters of these new services and benefits generally reacted favorably to the availability of personalized investment advice for their employees. Many sponsors were familiar with the failure of generic education to 'move the needle' and change investor behavior, and some were concerned about the potential litigation risk associated with high levels of company stock held by some employees.

Larger plan sponsors also played an important role in the evolution of online advice programs, demanding on close integration with their record-keeping platforms to provide participants with convenient access to their own data, as well as the ability to execute transactions at the press of a button. In addition, various plan complexities needed to be handled gracefully. For instance, some plans had trading restrictions that shaped how participants could trade over time. Plans with stable value funds often had equity wash provisions that constrained how money could flow out of the stable value fund into other fixed income options. Other sponsors had multiple plans for certain participants. Between 1998 and 2011, Financial Engines expanded the capabilities of the online advice service to address these needs and provide a more convenient experience for plan participants.

Nevertheless, there were still challenges in getting some participants to pay attention to personalized advice. Many did respond more favorably to personalized advice than they did to generic education, but the uptake of professional advice was not universal. Convenience proved to be a major factor in the adoption of online advisory services. One of the most important convenience features was the ability to download participant data from the record-keeping system so as to minimize the amount of information that had to be manually entered by each plan participant. Financial Engines also found that sponsor endorsement of the advisory services was important in driving adoption. To this end, participants needed to be made aware of the service, as well as how it could benefit their futures. Participants tended to value the due diligence provided by their employers, and they were more likely to trust the advice when it was endorsed by their employers.

As Financial Engines gained experience with different plan populations, it became apparent that demographic factors influenced adoption patterns

The Evolution of Workplace Advice 113

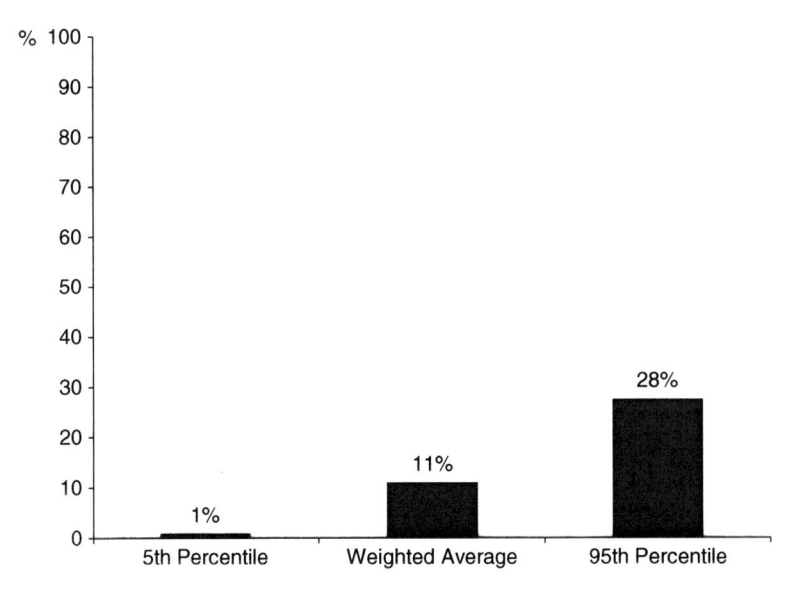

```
%  100
     90
     80
     70
     60
     50
     40
                                                        28%
     30
     20
                                  11%
     10      1%
      0
        5th Percentile    Weighted Average    95th Percentile
```

Figure 6.1 Online advice usage
Source: Authors' computation from the Financial Engines database (December 31, 2011).

for online advice. The usage of online advice was also observed to vary widely by plan sponsor. In the first year of deployment, an average plan sponsor might see around 10–15 percent of the workforce use online advice. Yet white collar workers, particularly those in technology-related fields, often had adoption rates that were double or triple this average. By contrast, plan sponsors with a population dominated by factory workers in manufacturing or transportation often saw lower usage. Figure 6.1 shows the distribution of online advice adoption across a sample of more than 450 plan sponsors at Financial Engines as of the end of Q4 2011.

The variation in usage is striking, varying from 28 percent at the 95th percentile, to only 1 percent at the 5th percentile. The average usage weighted by participants was 11 percent. The top end of usage was generally the result of favorable demographics and aggressive communication programs. The lower end of the distribution included firms that either had recently introduced advice or had made no communication offers.

Online advice users also differ somewhat from the broader plan participant population: they tend to be slightly younger and significantly wealthier than average participants. They also save more and are generally more engaged with the 401(k) plan than their average co-workers. Table 6.1 provides a comparison of online advice users and the general plan population.[3]

TABLE 6.1 Demographic comparison of online advice users

	Online advice users	Overall covered workforce
Average age (years)	46.3	46.4
Average balance ($)	159,103	89,549
Median balance ($)	74,828	30,579
Average salary ($)	87,813	69,358
Average savings rate (as percent of salary)	9.0	7.0

Source: Authors' calculations from a Financial Engines database query Q1, 2012.

Overall, online advice services tend to appeal to wealthier, more engaged plan participants, who tend to be influential in plan sponsor decisions around plan design. In this sense, they differ from the average participant in most companies offering advisory services.

The 2001 SunAmerica Advisory Opinion

There was a significant regulatory development having an important impact on the workplace advice market in 2001. The SunAmerica corporation petitioned the DOL for an Advisory Opinion to permit the company to provide investment advice under its own brand to 401(k) participants in plans where its products were included in the lineup, but with the condition that the advice would be generated by an independent third-party expert. The DOL (2001) issued the SunAmerica Advisory Opinion providing specific conditions under which this arrangement could avoid prohibited transaction prohibitions under ERISA. The practical impact of this Advisory Opinion was that now, larger asset management firms and record keepers in the 401(k) space could work with independent advisory firms to bundle investment advice with other services offered to plan participants and do so under their own branding. Over the next few years, many 401(k) financial service firms joined forces with independent advisors like Financial Engines to provide integrated advisory services on their platforms. By allowing 401(k) firms to offer advice under their own brands, it become easier to deeply integrate investment advice into the 401(k) platform and further increase customer convenience. This also accelerated the adoption of advisory services by plan sponsors, as often the advice was bundled in with other 401(k) services.

These developments offered independent advisory firms like Financial Engines an opportunity to expand the reach of advisory services and thus further leverage the large fixed costs associated with building sophisticated advisory platforms. They also accelerated the view that independent advisory services in 401(k) plans were an emerging 'best practice' among larger employers. As the market for online advisory services matured, it became increasingly clear that only a subset of plan participants was willing to spend the time and effort to interact with an online advisory service to interactively build and implement retirement plans. Despite ongoing communications campaigns, it was difficult to achieve adoption rates much beyond one-quarter of the plan population for most sponsors. The key question then became, how to reach the other three-quarters of the participant population?

Managed accounts

Financial Engines embarked on a development effort to design services to better address the needs of the participants disinclined to use online advice in 2003. Extensive participant interviews and focus groups were conducted to determine what this population of 'reluctant investors' was looking for in terms of retirement help, and two key themes emerged. First, many participants were not interested in, or did not have the time to, engaging in an interactive online planning experience. Instead, they sought a 'hands-off' solution that would allow them to delegate the responsibility of managing their accounts with minimal day-to-day involvement. For such participants, managing a retirement portfolio was a burden they preferred not to bear. Another segment of the population, particularly older participants closer to their retirement dates, was looking for access to human advisors to whom they could address questions and validate their decisions. At times, the latter participants were nervous about implementing decisions without consulting with an expert. Combining insights from these two population segments, it became apparent that a service was needed that offered access to telephone-based advisors with a discretionary account management structure.

The idea of discretionary management in a 401(k) account was easily accommodated within ERISA through Section 3(38), which permits fiduciary investment managers to make decisions on behalf of plan participants while shielding the plan sponsor who selects the investment manager from liability associated with the investment decisions of the manager. This long-established framework, in place for decades in traditional DB plans, was familiar to plan sponsors. Of course, prohibited transaction prohibitions still apply, as they do for investment advice. Since Financial Engines and other independent vendors of managed accounts were not selling or managing the plan funds, they could avoid the potential for self-dealing. In practice, getting sponsors comfortable with hiring an investment manager to offer managed accounts was actually easier than overcoming liability concerns in the early years of selling online investment advice.

Financial Engines launched its first managed account clients in 2004, and by year-end it had amassed over $1 billion in assets under management. The service was structured as a discretionary managed account program, where Financial Engines took over control of the investment portfolios on behalf of participants. Once a participant enrolled, Financial Engines would generate a Plan Preview illustrating the proposed portfolio allocation based on information drawn from the record-keeping platform. The Plan Preview disclosed the data and assumptions on which the advice was based, and it provided participants with the ability to further personalize their proposals online or by calling phone-based investment advisor representatives. Program members could customize their risk preferences, retirement ages, outside assets, and preferences for holding company stock within the program. If a member personalized his or her account, a revised Plan Preview would be generated showing the new recommendations. At any point along the way, managed account users had the ability to speak with investment advisory representatives who could answer general retirement questions, help participants personalize their retirement plans, and provide help with retirement income planning. In the case of Financial Engines, investment advisors use specialized software to generate these investment recommendations and provide forecasts and diagnostic statistics. As with online advice, these investment recommendations are strictly generated by the advice platform, insuring consistent high-quality advice independent of which advisor a participant works with.

A key distinction between online advice and managed accounts is that a member need not take any action to have the plan implemented. Once a member joins the program, Financial Engines takes care of the transactions required to move funds to the target portfolio, and then it monitors each account on an ongoing basis, making adjustments as required. Similar to target date fund strategies, the allocation of the managed account portfolio gradually becomes more conservative as a member approaches his or her retirement date. Unlike a target date fund, each portfolio is individually tailored to the participant. For instance, a more risk-averse participant might see an allocation tilted toward fixed income investments, compared to a risk-seeking participant. Also, a managed account approach can adapt to plan-specific circumstances such as the existence of a cash balance plan or a position in restricted company stock. By personalizing fund allocations to account for such individual and plan differences, the program can offer participants more efficient allocations better suited to their needs.

Another important attribute of managed accounts is that plan participants pay the fees for the program from their DC accounts. As a rule, managed account participants pay an asset-based fee for the discretionary management of their accounts, similar to the way in which fee-only investment advisors charge for their services. This account fee is usually deducted from the participant's account balance once a quarter (in arrears). Since plan sponsors do not have to pay for the services, there are fewer barriers to offering such a program to a plan population. Naturally, since participants pay for this service, it is still necessary to overcome the potential reluctance to pay for account management. But because of the scale economies provided by the large plan market, 401(k) managed account services are typically offered at a fraction of the standard discretionary management fees charged in the retail marketplace. Typical retail fees for discretionary management range from 75 to more than 150 basis points of assets under management annually, whereas the fees for Financial Engines' managed account services range from 20 to 60 basis points, depending on the enrollment method and the size of the participant's account balance.

We have also found that participants who select managed accounts differ from the larger plan population.[4] First, managed account users tend to be older on average, by about one to two years. Second, average account balances of managed account clients are similar to the overall plan average, but median account balances are higher. For instance, in our managed account population, the average balance is 105 percent of the overall participant population, but the median balance is 145 percent of the overall average. This implies that managed account users tend to have fewer very large accounts, and fewer very small accounts. Many plan participants with very large balances often have established relationships with outside investment advisors. For participants with very small balances, there is generally little urgency to getting help with an investment strategy for retirement. Third, in terms of salary and savings rates, managed account users are similar to the overall participant average (see Table 6.2).

Interestingly, online advice users tend to place a high premium on maintaining control over their accounts and investment decisions.

TABLE 6.2 Demographic comparison of managed account users

	Managed account users	Overall population
Average age (years)	47.5	46.4
Average balance ($)	93,884	89,549
Median balance ($)	44,301	30,579
Average salary ($)	70,138	69,358
Average savings rate (as percent of salary)	7.2	7.0

Source: Authors' calculations from a Financial Engines database query Q1, 2012.

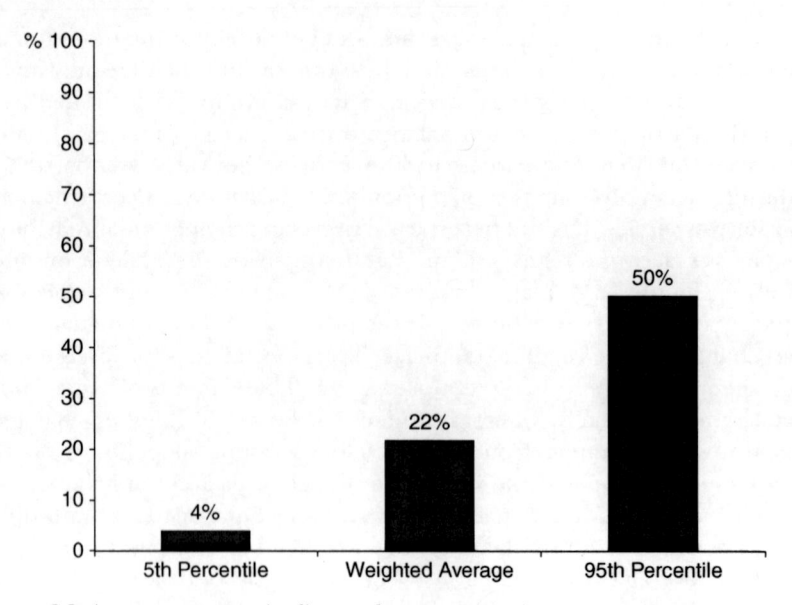

118 The Market for Retirement Financial Advice

Figure 6.2 Aggregate usage (online and management)
Source: Authors' computations from the Financial Engines database (December 31, 2011).

By contrast, most managed account users see value in being able to delegate investment decisions to a trustworthy expert. Consequently, the usage of managed accounts in plans that previously offered online advice tends to be additive. Figure 6.2 shows the total usage distribution for Financial Engines sponsors (as of year-end 2011). Overall, the usage rates of managed account participants appear similar to that of online advice users, but a different subset of the participant population is involved. With the addition of managed accounts, overall usage of advisory services doubled from 11 to 22 percent. Of course, usage of managed accounts will differ according to participant demographics and the level of communications provided to create awareness and understanding of the program.

From a plan sponsor's perspective, managed accounts can be a valuable addition because they have a demonstrable impact on investor behavior. Unlike online investment advice, where participants are free to ignore the advice or only partially implement a set of recommendations, managed accounts insure compliance by construction. Once participants turn over control of their accounts to the investment manager, the account is optimized and periodically reviewed for any required changes. No participant action is required to implement the advice. By taking the responsibility for implementation of the recommendations out of participants' hands, it is possible to insure that appropriate adjustments to the investment allocation are made on a timely basis. This is particularly helpful in persuading participants to reduce their exposure to company stock, a common mistake in 401(k) plans (which can elicit emotional and behavioral reactions). Many participants make the mistake of equating familiarity with safety when it comes to their employer's stock, but company stock is the largest contributor to undiversified risk in many participant portfolios and can be a potential source of litigation risk for employers. Over the course of Financial Engines' managed account program since 2004, over $6.5 billion of company stock positions have been diversified into fixed income and equity positions.[5]

The introduction of managed accounts also had a profound impact on participants' utilization of workplace advisory services. The innovation made it possible for 'reluctant investors' to receive similar benefits from professional help that had been previously limited to the most engaged participants. But events in 2006 provided a further push toward more widespread usage of advice in the workplace.

The Pension Protection Act of 2006

In the early 2000s, researchers found that 401(k) plans which changed their default options often saw dramatic changes in the choices made by their participants. Specifically, automatic enrollment substantially increased plan participation across the board. Yet, for all its benefits, auto-enrollment created new challenges for plan sponsors. Concerns regarding fiduciary responsibility again became central, since implementation required plan sponsors to select a default investment. Given the realities of auto-enrollment, a large fraction of employees would likely be fully invested in whichever investment was selected as the plan's default. Many sponsors worried about potential liability if they selected a default investment that subsequently lost money. To avoid this problem, sponsors pioneering auto-enrollment techniques often selected a money market or stable value fund as their plan default. This approach avoided the potential for subsequent losses, but it created the chance that defaulted employees might spend their entire investment careers fully allocated to short-term fixed income investments.

The Pension Protection Act of 2006 (PPA) was passed, in large part, to encourage widespread use of automatic enrollment, and to address sponsor fiduciary concerns. The PPA created a safe harbor for the investment allocation by identifying three Qualified Default Investment Alternatives (QDIAs). Utilizing a QDIA as the default investment provides a safe-harbor shielding employers against liability from automatic enrollment should the

120   The Market for Retirement Financial Advice

QDIA suffer a loss. The three QDIAs identified were (*a*) a professionally managed account, (*b*) a target date fund, or (*c*) a balanced fund.

Post-PPA, many plan sponsors selected either a target date fund menu or a professionally managed account as their QDIA, primarily because these two options were more personalized to the plan participant. Both decreased investment risk as participants aged, with the managed account option providing additional levels of personalization. The PPA was a boon to the managed account business, since the halo associated with being a QDIA caused many sponsors to consider managed accounts even if they had not considered switching to automatic enrollment. As Figure 6.3 illustrates, the net increase in managed account clients peaked at over 120,000 in 2007, the year following enactment of the PPA.

The PPA described a mechanism to automatically enroll new employees into a DC pension plan and created a safe harbor if the default investment option was a QDIA. But by focusing exclusively on new hires, the vast majority of plan participants were ignored. This led many sponsors to adapt auto-enrollment for the entire workforce, a step made possible because of the guidance and safe harbors provided by the PPA: plan sponsors essentially

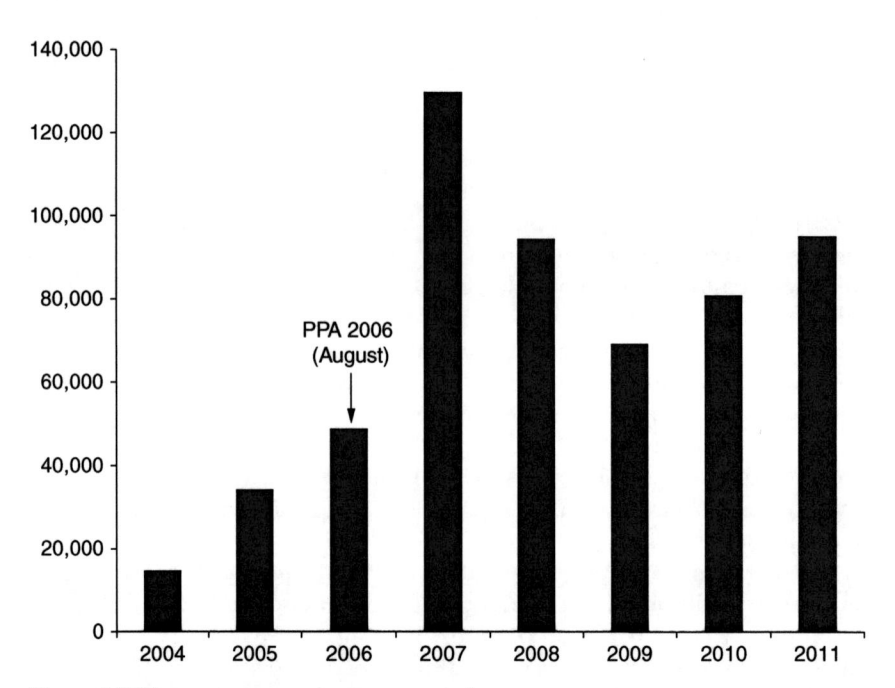

Figure 6.3 Net new managed account members
Source: Authors' computations from the Financial Engines SEC Filings.

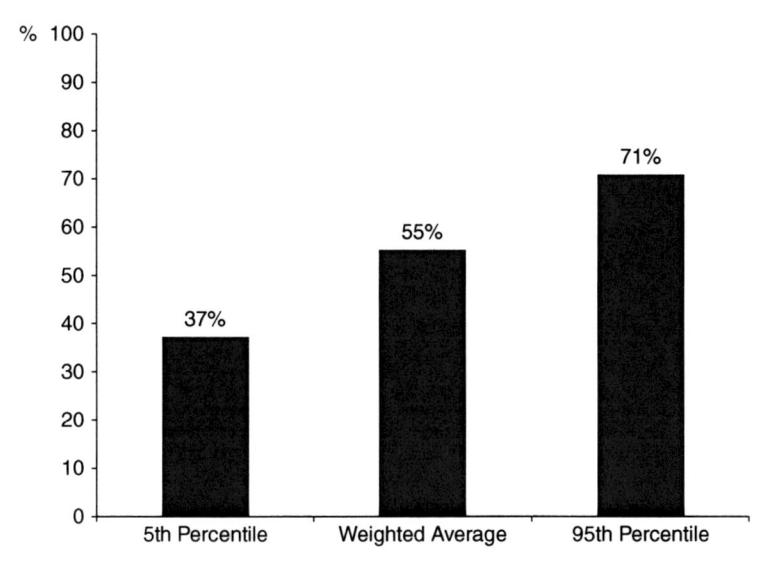

Figure 6.4 Aggregate usage with defaults
Source: Authors' computations from the Financial Engines database (December 31, 2011).

're-enroll' existing participants into a default investment option and follow the same procedures outlined by the PPA. The main advantage of plan re-enrollment is that all participants are provided with a reasonable asset allocation, and participants must make an active election to alter their portfolios. For example, a company might be concerned with high levels of employer stock held inside its 401(k) plan. To make clear that company stock holdings were the result of an active participant decision, a company could re-enroll the entire plan into a QDIA. Then participants wishing to hold company stock, or any other investment allocation, would need to either opt out of the QDIA prior to the re-enrollment, or subsequently proactively alter their investment allocations.

Results illustrate that inertia proves to be a powerful factor. Figure 6.4 reports usage statistics as of year-end 2011 in pension plans that included some form of default (either for new hire or via plan re-enrollment). Clearly, the difference in usage was dramatic. The 5th percentile increased from 4 to 37 percent, indicating that even the lower range usage was substantial. At the high end, defaulted plans had overall usage rates of over 70 percent. The participant weighted average overall usage was 55 percent for clients with some form of default, so usage in a default context was more than double the average usage otherwise.

Retirement income in DC plans

With trillions of dollars now accumulating in DC plans and Baby Boomers retiring in large numbers, a key question becomes: how can participants turn their DC assets into retirement income? Unlike DB plans, the 401(k) and other DC plans were not designed to produce a steady stream of retirement income. But recent regulatory changes have been targeted at helping develop the DC marketplace for retirement income. The same factors that governed the development of accumulation help for DC participants are again in play: that is, regulations will define the environment, sponsor preferences will determine which solutions get offered, and, assuming a workable business model, individual preferences will largely determine what gets used.

Since DC plans are increasingly displacing DB plans, a natural starting point is to try and make income from DC plans seem comparable to income from DB plans. This intuition has led sponsors and regulators to focus on annuities as potential income solutions for DC plans. Nevertheless, participant behavior, sponsor preferences, and the current regulatory environment, all suggest that annuity solutions are a difficult sell in the DC marketplace. The core reason is that many people seem reluctant to annuitize assets at retirement. Numerous researchers have studied this 'annuity puzzle,' a term referring to the gap between predicted and actual annuity demand. For example, Warner and Pleeter (2001) examined a group of 66,000 military personnel offered the option of a lump-sum or annuity payout; they found that, even though the annuity payout was typically twice as valuable as the lump sum, 90 percent of enlisted personnel and 50 percent of officers opted for the lump-sum payout. Even more relevant, Vanguard recently analyzed the decisions of participants in DB pension plans who were given the option of taking their annuity benefit as a lump sum (Mottola and Utkus, 2007). The results were striking: even in a traditional DB plan where the pension benefit was consistently communicated as an income payout, fully 73 percent of participants over the age of 55 selected a lump-sum payout. For a cash balance type pension plan, where the annuity cash value was more salient, 83 percent of participants over the age of 55 elected the lump-sum payout option. This analysis also dealt a blow to the idea that plan defaults result in high levels of annuity utilization, reporting that:

> Less than one-quarter of married participants in our study chose an annuity, even though it is the federally mandated default option for married couples. Married participants worked actively to overcome the default annuity option by submitting a written, notarized waiver. (Mottola and Utkus, 2007: 1)

Given the evident preference for liquidity over annuity income (even for long-standing DB participants), it is small wonder that very few individuals with 401(k) or IRA assets annuitize any, much less a majority, of their retirement portfolios.

When people do not elect payout annuities, it remains to be seen what type of retirement income solutions will interest them. A number of possibilities emerge, ranging from solutions that provide income while preserving liquidity, to those that use early retirement payouts from the 401(k) plans to finance Social Security deferrals. While the options that will succeed are not yet known, it is clear that inertia, participant demand, sponsor support, and regulatory clarity will all likely play a large role in shaping the evolving marketplace.

Conclusion

The current US pension system asks millions of Americans to rely on their employer-sponsored DC pension plans for retirement income security. Yet saving, investing, and creating retirement income from DC plans require a level of financial expertise that many people lack. A positive development is that the economies of scale achievable in the workplace now offer an opportunity to provide financial advisory help to those with insufficient assets to attract the interest of a typical retail advisor. To take advantage of these economies of scale, successful workplace offerings must be aware of a complex environment and satisfy the preferences of many different constituencies.

The regulatory environment is an important framework for such services. This creates some barriers, but more often it can influence plan sponsor perceptions as to the riskiness of specific approaches. If an approach does meet regulatory requirements, the next relevant hurdle is plan sponsor acceptance. Since plan sponsors exercise wide latitude regarding services for their pension plans, sponsor approval is required to achieve widespread success. But ultimately, participants themselves must decide to take advantage of the available help. Solutions that individuals ignore or dislike will not enjoy long-term success. In the process, the importance of a workable business model cannot be over-emphasized. Many approaches to financial advice might meet with regulatory, sponsor, and individual approval, but these are irrelevant if they cannot service the typical 401(k) participant with less than $40,000 in investible assets.

Endnotes

1. This datum was derived from a query to the Financial Engines database. Population median account balances were calculated on a sample of approximately 567,000 professional management (managed account) members.

2. This provides certain fiduciary protections to plan sponsors with respect to the liability arising from investment decisions made by their participants. The protections are conditional on various requirements, including adequate diversification opportunities and other plan characteristics. If the 404(c) conditions are met by the plan sponsor, then it would be shielded from liability deriving from investment decisions made by plan participants.
3. Balances include total sponsored assets collected by Financial Engines (e.g., DC, deferred compensation, cash balance, Employee Stock Ownership Plan (ESOP), profit sharing, and money purchase). In some cases, accounts ineligible for online advice may be included. Traditional DB pension assets are excluded.
4. Balances include total sponsored assets collected by Financial Engines (e.g., DC, deferred compensation, cash balance, ESOP, profit sharing, and money purchase). In some cases, accounts ineligible for management may be included. Traditional DB pension assets are excluded.
5. This evidence was derived from a query to the Financial Engines database (December 31, 2011).

References

Mottola, G. R., and S. P. Utkus (2007). 'Lump Sum or Annuity? An Analysis of Choice in DB Pension Payouts,' Vanguard Center for Retirement Research.

US Department of Labor (DOL) (1996). Pension and Welfare Benefits Administration. 29 CFR Part 2509. Federal Register, 61(113): 29586–90. Washington, DC.

—— (2001). *Advisory Opinion.* 2001-09A. Washington, DC: DOL. http://www.dol.gov/ebsa/regs/AOs/ao2001-09a.html

Warner, J. T., and S. Pleeter (2001). 'The Personal Discount Rate: Evidence from Military Downsizing Programs,' *American Economic Review*, 19(1): 33–53.

Chapter 7

The Role of Guidance in the Annuity Decision-Making Process

Kelli Hueler and Anna Rappaport

Some of the most important decisions that employees and retirees ever make pertain to evaluating lifetime income streams and deciding how to draw down their retirement incomes. Yet because these decisions involve complex trade-offs that are often poorly understood, most people would benefit from guidance. This chapter reviews the roles of plan sponsors, plan administrators, advice providers, and public policy surrounding the decision to buy annuities as payout vehicles providing lifelong income. We examine how these roles can be handled using an institutional platform offering structural and active guidance in the purchasing process. This system requires informing individuals about available options, designing websites for presenting information and education, and purchasing through a competitive bidding process. Active guidance involves information provided by salaried professionals who answer questions and have conversations with individuals about the annuity purchase process. We draw for our analysis on the experiences of Income Solutions®, Hueler Companies' institutional purchasing platform in the United States (Hueler, 2012). We also draw lessons from experiences in Chile and the United Kingdom.

Setting the stage

In the past, employees in the United States tended not to receive much guidance about how to handle their retirement assets. If advice was offered, it was normally relegated to at or near retirement, and rarely did employers offer advice about annuitization, or the conversion of retirement assets into a lifetime income stream. Now that defined contribution (DC) plans are more common, most (except for money purchase pension plans) tend not to offer annuity payouts, and if annuities are not offered through the plan, retirees traditionally have gone to the retail market to purchase annuities. Yet annuities can also be offered through an institutional purchasing platform (discussed in more detail below) that can bring the benefits of group purchasing to individual retirees.

If people do not annuitize, they may take a structured or phased withdrawal from their investment portfolios, and then they have no lifetime protection against running out of money. Some favor the '4 percent rule,' where the retiree can spend 4 percent of the initial asset balance annually, perhaps with the withdrawal amount increased by inflation each year. Many financial advisors and advice providers,[1] particularly those who offer managed accounts, tend to favor such a structured withdrawal approach over the use of lifetime income annuities during the paydown phase. This bias exposes the retiree to both investment and mortality risk. Some advice providers have begun promoting late-in-life deferred annuities that begin payments at ages 80 to 85 to address longevity risk, but they still discourage the use of lifetime income annuities earlier in the drawdown phase.

US policy toward retirement payouts has been of two minds, in that some efforts have promoted annuitization, while others discouraged it. For instance, social security benefits are an inflation-indexed lifetime income stream, and defined benefit (DB) pensions also traditionally provided lifetime income. By contrast, funds in Individual Retirement Accounts (IRAs) or DC plans other than money purchase plans are generally not annuitized (Rappaport, 2011). As shown by Turner and Muir (2013), the time of rollover is one of several situations when 401(k) plans are vulnerable with regard to potential conflicts of interest. There is also no requirement to provide employees or retirees with information on payout strategies or options beyond what is provided by the plan, and there is also no requirement to provide information about the possibility of lifetime income while plan assets are being accumulated. Some legislators have recommended including illustrations of lifetime income streams as well as account balances in the DC accounts, but this practice has not been widely adopted (United States Senate, 2011).

The US Internal Revenue Code allows contributions to and investment earnings in employer-sponsored pensions to benefit from tax deferral, until the age of 70 and a half. Thereafter, the Required Minimum Distributions (RMD) rule requires that people withdraw at least a minimum amount from their tax-deferred accounts each year, in order to limit tax deferral. This minimum is calculated to spread withdrawals over the retiree's life expectancy, and the withdrawal fraction is recalculated each year. Because the RMD provides for gradual withdrawals, it takes the focus away from annuitization and other income options for people who do not need to withdraw more from their qualified funds. For this reason, it has come to be viewed as a recommendation or guidance offered by policymakers on about how to spend one's funds. One problem is that an individual who takes the RMD each year will have continued growth in funds when investment returns are high, but will deplete his assets too rapidly when markets are low. As a consequence, the individual could run out of money too soon.

It has also been difficult for pension plan sponsors to offer annuity options, since regulations often impose barriers and create legal risks (Iwry and Turner, 2009). Proposed regulations and two revenue rulings issued in 2012 by the United States Treasury Department sought to remove some of the barriers and make it easier to offer lifetime income options to participants in certain instances. The new proposals sought to (*a*) move away from the idea that choice of distribution option in employer-sponsored DB and DC plans must be an all-or-nothing decision; (*b*) remove the barriers to the use of advanced life deferred annuities that arise from the structure of the RMD requirements;[2] (*c*) clarify that DC sponsors who also have DB plans may permit participants access to lifetime income through rollover of DC funds into DB plans;[3] and (*d*) make it easier for DC plan sponsors to include deferred annuity options as plan investments prior to retirement (United States Department of the Treasury, 2012). There has also been US Department of Labor regulation requiring the disclosure and explanation of all DC plan fees. These changes are signaling to plan sponsors and the broader population how important it is to have lifetime income and transparency (Council of Economic Advisers, 2012). These developments reflect new support for lifetime income plans using qualified retirement plan assets.

Even if these initiatives are positive, the state of the regulatory environment remains complex. US employer-sponsored retirement programs are regulated by the Federal government, while insurance contracts are regulated by separate state insurance departments. Moreover, the annuity sales process includes a requirement for a suitability review when individual annuity contracts are sold, and the standards are evolving. In 2010, the National Association of Insurance Commissioners (NAIC) adopted the 'Suitability in Annuity Transactions' model regulation seeking to set up a regulatory framework holding insurers responsible for ensuring that annuity transactions are suitable. This approach also required training for agents, and where feasible, coordinated standards with requirements of Financial Industry Regulatory Authority (FINRA; see NAIC, 2010). Some might see this suitability review process as a form of guidance.

Guidance and the annuitization decision

In the United States, pension participants receive signals on strategies for asset drawdowns from many sources. Information can be provided by the plan sponsor, the plan's architecture, the media, an advisor or financial services firm, guidance during the annuity purchase process, and government via policy and regulation. As discussed below, such guidance can either support or discourage annuitization.

US DB plans must offer annuities as the default distribution option, so here plan architecture imparts strong signals about the importance of lifetime income. By contrast, most DC plans pay out lump sums that are often rolled over to an IRA. Currently, only about one-fifth of DC plans offer in-plan annuity options, and these are rarely utilized even when offered (Wray, 2008).[4] The 2012 Treasury releases may change how DC balances are used, inasmuch as these assets now may be rolled over to DB plans to provide lifetime income. A complementary model to this idea is to offer participants who roll their funds to an IRA access to a favorable purchasing program for annuities as part of the employer-sponsored program design. At least one large plan is currently offering such an approach, giving participants the alternative of moving DC funds to DB and the choice of using DC funds to find the best customized arrangement from the private market. Structural guidance in this case would include basic education about lifetime income, information about specific annuity options provided, and the pros and cons of each option.

Another example of plan architecture that highlights lifetime income offers workers an option to buy lifetime income on a deferred basis, as one of the plan's investment options. Several insurance companies offer products to support such options, some using a fixed annuity, and some using a variable annuity. The variable annuity options guarantee floor benefits and offer upside potential through the use of a guaranteed minimum income benefit or a guaranteed minimum withdrawal benefit. The options have important differences with regard to portability and guaranteed provisions. With these options, plan assets are invested during the working years in a fund that offers lifetime income in retirement (Institutional Retirement Income Council, 2011). These models blend features of traditional group deferred annuity products with newer investment structures. Under these models, the individual has no choice of insurance company and is limited to the choice of payment forms embedded in the plan architecture. As yet, the modern versions of this model have been adopted by few employers so it remains to be seen how effective they will be.

To date, the role of the employer in supporting and encouraging the use of lifetime income alternatives has been limited. Some plans have begun to offer education around lifetime income and access to institutionally priced annuities. As shown in Table 7.1, according to a Plan Sponsor Council of America survey, about one-third of employers provide access to an employer-selected financial planner or offer a seminar regarding retirement assets and income planning (Wray, 2008). Nevertheless, it is not known whether much information about annuities is provided, or whether the messages favor or discourage consideration of annuitization. Moreover,

TABLE 7.1 Types of retirement guidance or education provided by companies to their employees

Percentage	Type of education
11	None, except notices required by law
34	Access to an employer-selected financial advisor
78	Provides educational materials explaining plan options
68	Offers retirement income calculator online
31	Offers seminar regarding retirement assets and income planning

Source: Derived from Wray (2008) using a 2008 survey of Profit Sharing Council of America (now Plan Sponsor Council of America) members.

the choice of options to be presented and how they are positioned may be impacted by the products and services offered by the firm conducting the seminar, as well as the compensation model. Of survey respondents, 5 percent indicated that they actively encouraged retirees to leave their accumulations in the plan, 11 percent required or encouraged withdrawal, and the remaining 84 percent were ambivalent (Wray, 2008).

When they do not offer access to annuities directly through the plans, some employers do provide access to institutionally priced annuities through a purchasing platform such as Income Solutions®. This platform is most often utilized as an IRA rollover alternative. In such cases, structural guidance varies widely: some regularly mention the availability of the annuity purchasing option, while others provide little or no information about the program. In addition, some employers make the program visibly prominent at the benefits portal and facilitate easy access, while others bury the offering in the benefits website, making it difficult to locate and access.

In our experience, the employer representative (either in-house or at the record keeper) is the first point of contact regarding information at the time of retirement plan distributions. How the process of such participant communication is designed has a potent impact on what alternatives retirees elect to explore. Very few employers offer education emphasizing the importance of lifetime income and the value of annuitization, though if, over time, a plan sponsor does explain such benefits in newsletters or employee publications, this drives an increase in annuity quotations, inquiries, and ultimately purchase activity. In other words, such an approach can take several years to take hold, but it does produce increased activity with time. On the other hand, experience across multiple program partners suggests that even when a plan sponsor encourages consideration of annuities, the primary driver behind purchasing behavior is whether the benefits representative is objective and knowledgeable about retirement distribution options. If the benefits representative dissuades participants

130 The Market for Retirement Financial Advice

from utilizing the competitive platform, or annuitizing a portion of their balances, or steers the participant to a proprietary higher cost alternative, this can trump employer efforts.

Many employers today offer advice to their DC plan participants; in fact, a recent survey indicated that 79 percent of plan providers offered their employees some type of investment advice (Callan Investment Institute, 2012). An advice provider may be an independent third party or affiliated with the plan administrator, and such advisors generally seek to help employees save more and make better investment decisions. Since plans differ with regard to whether they encourage or permit leaving funds in the plan post-retirement, and what options they offer, naturally the advice providers will also differ as to whether they supply information and advice for the payout period, what advice they provide, and how they help people transition to the payout period. In our experience, some advice providers do discuss a wide array of post-retirement options including annuitization and explain the options well, but others clearly discourage annuitization as part of a drawdown strategy and instead seek to keep the funds in a managed account using a structured payout or systematic withdrawal method. This is important since the conversations taking place around retirement are likely to have a major impact on retirees' distribution strategies.

Employers also build expectations about the importance (or lack thereof) of retirement income by how they depict retirement plan account values during the working years. Some show only the account balances, whereas others include retirement income projections.[5] Callan Investment Institute (2012) recently indicated that 58 percent of employers offered or provided retirement income projections for participants; of these, 31 percent showed them on the employee statements, 13 percent provided the information through a separate mailed statement, 74 percent provided access to a calculator on the benefits website, and 15 percent provided the projection through a third party advice provider. More research is required to better understand the range of practice in such statements and projections, and their impacts on later decisions about lifetime income and structured payouts.

An institutional purchasing platform and guidance

Plan sponsors can elect to offer an institutional purchasing program for lifetime incomes, via an Internet-based competitive bidding platform for immediate and deferred income annuities. This platform has two primary modes for implementation: as a distribution option within the plan, or as an IRA rollover alternative. To date, the most common method—with over 90 percent of programs implemented—is the IRA rollover alternative. The

The Role of Guidance in the Annuity Decision-Making Process 131

platform relies on participating insurance companies' willingness to offer annuities through a low-cost competitive distribution channel.

Within the various program partner offerings, the individual purchaser may learn about annuities through general financial education, basic annuity education provided on the website, employer-provided information about the programs, or through facilitators or advisors. The system architecture offers structural online guidance and information to support a self-service model, including general annuity education, educational videos discussing the importance of inflation-adjusted annuitization, tools for calculating gaps between other sources of income and regular expenditures to establish income levels needed, standardized competitive annuity quotes across multiple issuers, and information about the financial status of the participating insurance companies. The structural guidance does not recommend whether to buy an annuity or how much to buy; instead the program is designed to educate individuals about annuity options, lower costs, standardize fees, create transparency, and produce the best possible market result for each individual. There is no incentive to use one annuity provider versus another, or to constrain individual purchase decisions.

Access to program and guidance models

Access to the platform occurs mainly through a retirement plan sponsor, a program partner such as a financial services firm, a record keeper, an association, or through an advisor linked to the program. The partner plays a critical role in setting the stage for consideration of lifetime income alternatives (or, as noted above, in effectively foreclosing such options). Programs that offer a menu of alternatives and integrate annuitization into the discussion not just for those on the verge of retirement but also after retirement show the highest level of annuity purchase activity. By contrast, if a program presents onerous disclaimers and/or uses an advice provider who discourages annuitization in the drawdown phase this creates the highest user drop-off rate.

The platform also provides individuals with access to active personal guidance. This can range from basic assistance to more in-depth advice, depending on the program partner. Currently, most programs do not offer comprehensive financial planning or advice; rather, active guidance is delivered through licensed salaried professionals able to talk with individuals about options accessible through their employers, and/or additional lifetime income alternatives available to them through their personal IRA.

Table 7.2 shows how the delivery of guidance differs across the program models. Three models of guidance are available.

TABLE 7.2 Comparison of structural and active guidance in institutional platform delivery models through different channels

Element of purchase process	Institutional individual	Institutional facilitator	Institutional advisor
Structural guidance			
Information provided about program availability	Program partner	Program partner	Advisor
Who secures quote	Individual	Facilitator or individual	Advisor
Who executes purchase	Individual	Facilitator or individual	Advisor
How platform impacts decision to annuitize	Provides information about value of annuity and considerations—text and video on website	Facilitator may add to what is on website, but limits discussion to pros, cons, and issues vs. recommendations	Depends on how it is used by advisor
Issues to be considered and pros/cons provided	By website	Additional information may be provided by facilitator; depends on program partner	Depends on advisor
Tools provided	Yes, competitive quote, insurance company ratings, tool to calculate income gap	Yes, how much additional beyond program platform depends on program partner	Advisor may provide evaluation or offer tools beyond program platform
Universe of insurance carriers providing annuity quotes[a]	Platform does this automatically	Platform does this automatically	Platform does this automatically
Can individual access website directly	Yes	Yes	No
Active guidance			
Who answers individual questions	Help center or staff	Facilitator	Advisor
Recommendations provided	No	No	Yes

[a] Participating insurance carriers may vary depending on program partner, annuity type, and employee demographics such as state of residence.

Source: Authors' analysis; see text.

The Role of Guidance in the Annuity Decision-Making Process 133

Online direct to individual

Here access is by the individual who initiates the quote and purchase process through an online platform. This program includes structural guidance with general information about immediate annuities, an explanation of the benefits of institutional purchasing, a calculator to help the individual estimate the gap between existing income and expenses, and a place for requesting annuity quotes online. Individuals can telephone the help center with questions and are provided basic assistance. Callers are provided with active guidance in the form of assistance to help them use the online platform and answers to questions regarding annuity terminology, features, and the purchase process.

Facilitated

Here active guidance is provided through partnerships offering additional professional assistance through a facilitator: salaried and licensed professionals help participants submit requests for quotations, consider the purchase, answer questions, and submit purchase requests through the platform. Such facilitators may communicate with individual buyers by telephone or e-mail; they are typically employees of the program partner who specialize in annuities and income alternatives for retirement. In some transactions, the facilitator does all of these steps, while in others, the participant secures quotes or places transactions, while the facilitator provides some assistance. The system has an interactive design so that facilitators and individuals can both review annuity quotes at the same time.

Advisor

Here the advisor provides broader financial advice, including advice about the individual's overall portfolio; in this case, the expert would initiate the discussion. Advisors using this program are normally fee-based advisors paid by the client; their job is to secure quotations, explain the options to the client, advise them regarding the best annuity option, and in some cases make the annuity placements.[6]

Table 7.3 compares the guidance models with individual purchase and DB plan elections. Here we see that DB plan elections have a fixed period when the election must be made; all the other purchase models allow flexibility with regard to when the annuity purchase can take place and features that can be selected. These models differ with regard to how the contact is initiated, the options available, the timing, and the type of guidance that is offered. The three models in the institutional purchase

134 The Market for Retirement Financial Advice

TABLE 7.3 Obtaining annuity income through retail purchase, institutional purchase, and/or DB payout

Characteristic	Retail[a]	Institutional individual[b]	Institutional facilitator[c]	Institutional advisor[d]	Annuity as a DB payout
Contact re-purchase of annuity	Agent	Self	Facilitator, seen as affiliated with plan and hired by program partner	Advisor, hired by buyer	Plan sponsor or administrator
Pricing	Retail	Institutional	Institutional	Institutional	Defined in plan
Competitive quotes	Maybe	Yes	Yes	Yes	NA
Fee disclosure	Maybe	Yes	Yes	Yes	NA
Fee level	Retail	Institutional	Institutional	Institutional	NA
Timing constraints	No	No	No	No	Yes
Initial communication	Usually agent	Plan or program partner	Plan or program partner	Advisor	Plan sponsor
Initiator of first step	Usually agent	Self or help center staff	Self or program partner	Advisor	Plan sponsor must follow plan

[a] Applies to purchase by the individual in the retail insurance market, usually using an agent.
[b] Applies to purchase through the institutional purchasing platform, where the individual directly uses the platform after an introduction by the program partner.
[c] Applies to institutional purchasing platform where a facilitator, or salaried representative of a program partner, assists in the purchase and secures quotations, answers questions, and executes the purchase.
[d] Applies to situations where an advisor initiates the contact and executes on behalf of their client.

Source: Authors' analysis; see text.

platform are similar except for the content and method of active guidance and the method of initiation of the discussion.

Table 7.4 shows how the annuity purchases differ depending on the delivery channel used. It must be noted that the groups purchasing through different channels are not necessarily similar demographically or by wealth levels; we do not yet know the reasons for the observed differences by channel. Individuals purchasing directly via the online platform have the highest average premium, are heavily male, and are most likely to select a joint life annuity; they also consider the purchase for quite a while and request multiple quotes. Those purchasing through facilitators tend to have several conversations before securing quotations, suggesting consideration of needs prior to obtaining quotes. Our analysis of purchases where active guidance was available showed an average of five calls per purchaser (and a

TABLE 7.4 Characteristics of annuity purchasers and what they purchased through different channels

	Total across all channels	Institutional individual	Institutional facilitator	Institutional advisor
Average amount of premium	$139,000	$158,000	$142,000	$50,000
Female (%)	37	25	40	49
Male (%)	63	75	60	51
Joint life (%)	37	47	31	53
Single life (%)	50	40	55	46
Fixed period only (%)	13	13	14	1
Buying within two weeks of first quote (%)	63	50	70	53
Buying within four weeks (%)	78	67	83	69
Buying within six months (%)	94	90	98	81
Buying after six months (%)	6	10	2	19

Source: Authors' analysis of data provided by the Hueler Companies.

maximum of fourteen). Those purchasing through advisors had the lowest premium per single purchase and a greater number of individual purchases, perhaps reflecting the positioning of the annuity in their portfolios. Advisors and their clients are more likely to view the purchase as part of a longer-term lifetime income planning process, whereas a facilitator tends to act as a specialist dealing with the client specifically on the annuity decision.

Structural guidance and decision-making

Individual purchasers of annuities have many choices to make, including when to buy, how much to buy, whether to make multiple purchases, which carrier(s) to choose, and what forms of annuity to take. Accordingly, the competitive quotes provided on the platform include multiple carriers, the form of annuity requested as well as alternatives, and the financial rating information of all the insurance carriers. All quotes are standardized to allow for straightforward comparability. Nearly all purchasers choose to get multiple quotes before completing a purchase. Four is a typical number of quotes for those making a single purchase, but ten is a typical number for people making multiple purchases. Some of the variations that can be tested using multiple quotes include single versus joint life, joint life switching which spouse is primary, joint life with different percentages to the survivor, premium amounts, and the date when the annuity income will commence. Pricing is provided in real time. The competitive quote process is designed to be transparent and it includes comparable product features from different carriers and parallel information, offering a form of structural guidance. By including not only the income that can be provided but also the financial rating of the carriers, the approach highlights the importance of the insurance company's financial status.

Suitability reviews and guidance

As part of the purchase of an immediate annuity contract, the purchaser must complete a suitability form. While the specific forms may differ by insurer, data required include information to determine suitability. According to the NAIC: '"Suitability information" means information that is reasonably appropriate to determine the suitability of a recommendation, including age, annual income, financial situation and needs, financial experience and objectives, intended use of the annuity, financial time horizon, existing assets, liquidity needs and net worth, risk tolerance and tax status' (NAIC, 2010: 4). While this process is designed to provide consumer protection, it can be viewed as guidance as well and each insurer has forms and specific definitions of financial information to be reported.

The institutional purchasing platform includes suitability review as part of the purchase process, and a checklist is used for a systematic approach. Examples of flags that would prompt further review, and in some cases, a confirmation contact with the applicant for the annuity include: relatively large annuity purchase compared to assets, a single life annuity without refund or a certain period, a purchaser over age 80 or younger than age 59.5, and insufficient financial information on the suitability form. After the reviewer looks at the financial situation and reasons for purchase, there may be a follow-up contact if required.[7] The suitability review process serves to confirm that the buyer understands their purchase decision and that the sale is appropriate. An interview with a reviewer indicates that buyers rarely change their minds as part of the suitability process.

Experience with guidance models

Many facilitators are salaried employees of program partners, and Hueler has licensed employees who can answer questions for purchasers, partner employees, or advisors. In some situations, the facilitators initiate the process of securing a bid, and make a purchase; in others, they simply answer questions. Experience has shown that the conversation is a very important element in influencing purchase activity. Thus, 72 percent of the purchases in our analysis occurred via facilitators and advisors; the remaining 28 percent of the purchases occurred online, but here too, some people also ask questions after contacting their program partner's help center. Very few individuals buy an annuity without a conversation—probably fewer than 10 percent of purchasers—and many people request multiple bids and multiple purchases.

In the past, the decision about whether to purchase lifetime income annuities in an employer-sponsored arrangement assumed purchase would occur just when the employee was retiring, and it was presented as an all-or-nothing decision. Yet this approach does not conform well to peoples' preferred decision-making approach. In our experience, 70 percent of the annuity purchases were made by individuals who identify themselves as already retired. People prefer to make annuity purchases over a longer time period, since moving into retirement can require a period of transition and adjustment. Some need time to see how much they will be spending and how much more regular income they need; others seek to work part-time and it may take time to see how this affects their needs. Others change their living arrangements and housing. It also makes sense to phase purchases over time in order to diversify interest rate risk. As a consequence, offering an immediate annuity purchase as an irrevocable decision and an all-or-nothing option is likely to be rejected. The institutional choice platform is one alternative for moving away from the old unsuccessful delivery model.[8]

Immediate annuity buyers

An analysis of purchases drawn from the Hueler platform database indicates that about two-thirds of the immediate annuity buyers are men. The most common age for purchase is in the 60s (56 percent) but some purchasers are as young as age 50 and others as old as 85. Thirty-two percent are aged 70+, including 8 percent who are aged 80+. Seven percent of the immediate annuity purchasers reporting their net worth on the coded sample of suitability forms indicated having a net worth of under $100,000; 27 percent indicated net worth of $500,000–$1,000,000; 21 percent had $1,000,000–$2,000,000; and 14 percent said they had over $2,000,000. While financial profile questions vary, they do not include home equity, and wealth data are self-reported. Sixty-eight percent of the purchases are from tax-qualified assets,[9] either IRAs or DC plans; 28 percent are from non-qualified assets; and 4 percent are exchanges under Section 1035 of the Internal Revenue Code.[10] Exchanges are existing annuity contracts—often variable annuities—that are exchanged for immediate annuities purchased through this platform. Some purchasers use a combination of qualified and non-qualified funds to purchase multiple annuities.

TABLE 7.5 Characteristics of single premium immediate annuities purchased: amounts of income purchased and annuity features chosen

Type of annuity	Percentage of total purchases (%)	Average monthly income purchased ($)	Percentage of total purchases with inflation protection or fixed annual increases (%)	Percentage purchased by male buyers (%)	Percentage purchased by female buyers (%)
Joint life					
With cash refund	7	900	10	78	22
Life only	14	973	8	75	25
With term certain	17	799	23	87	13
Total joint life	37			81	19
Single life					
With cash refund	9	789	10	53	47
Life only	28	803	18	51	49
With term certain	13	843	13	45	55
Total single life	50			50	50
Fixed period only	13	1,032	3	65	35
Total of all contracts	100		14	63	37

Source: Authors' analysis of data provided by the Hueler Companies.

Table 7.5 provides a closer look at annuity purchases. Structural guidance included in the system provides that in addition to the requested quote, at least one alternative quote is presented. Many immediate annuity buyers (50 percent) purchase single life annuities; another third (37 percent) buy joint life annuities; and 13 percent buy period certain annuities. Only 14 percent of those buying immediate annuities purchase products with inflation protection, either consumer price index (CPI)-linked or annual percentage increases. We also see that men and women select different types of annuities: 81 percent of the joint life annuities are purchased by males, compared to only 50 percent of the single life annuities. It is likely that in married couples, the husband would be designated as the purchaser more often than the wife.

While the amount of income purchased averages over $850 per month, many purchases are for smaller amounts: 11 percent bought less than $200 monthly; 18 percent bought $200–$399 per month; and 22 percent $400–$599. Fifty percent purchased less than $600 per month, 22 percent from $600 to $999, and 28 percent more than $1,000 in monthly income. Women purchased lower amounts, averaging $110,000 of premium versus $156,000 for males. While the vast majority of buyers make a single purchase at a time, some do make multiple purchases (however, the purchase

The Role of Guidance in the Annuity Decision-Making Process   139

data shown here are based on single purchases; multiple purchases are not aggregated).

Timeline from quotes to purchase

Whereas a DB plan election must be made within a specified time window and the price of various options is part of the DB plan design, the annuity purchase process is very different when individuals utilize the institutional platform.[11] The buyer can choose when to purchase, what to buy, and can make the decision over a long period of time. People can buy annuities with different features and monthly income benefits, and they can obtain multiple contracts. In our experience, many buyers secure multiple quotes; though 78 percent of purchases are completed within four weeks of the initial quotation, some people take as long as two years to move from the initial quote to purchase.

Competition, issuer selection, and fee disclosure considerations

On the institutional platform, competitive bidding is used for all annuity quotations. Experience reviewing quote data shows that, at any given point in time, different individual issuers will be competitive for different quotation scenarios, and quote results also change over time. Differentials between results for individual quotation scenarios may be due to insurance carrier views of specific annuity features, demographics, underlying pricing assumptions, market conditions, and timing.

Our analysis of several thousand annuity quotes indicates that, on average, the difference in monthly income between the high and low quote averages 8 percent; in some instances, it may be as much as 20 percent though spreads greater than 15 percent are rare. Our analysis also examined individual issuers' positions on annuity quotes relative to peer companies, illustrated in Figure 7.1. Here we report a sample of fifty individual quotations, each with a $100,000 annuity purchase price; one specific insurance carrier's quote position is plotted against multiple peer companies across different annuity types over a twelve-month period. Each vertical line in the figure represents the range of the high to low annuity quotes across the various providers for each annuity quotation scenario. The box represents the same individual insurance carrier across each quote scenario. In the period shown, this carrier had the high result for some quotes and the low result for others; it was in the middle range for the remaining cases. Similar results have been found consistently over time. The size of the spread between the high and low quote varied by scenario.

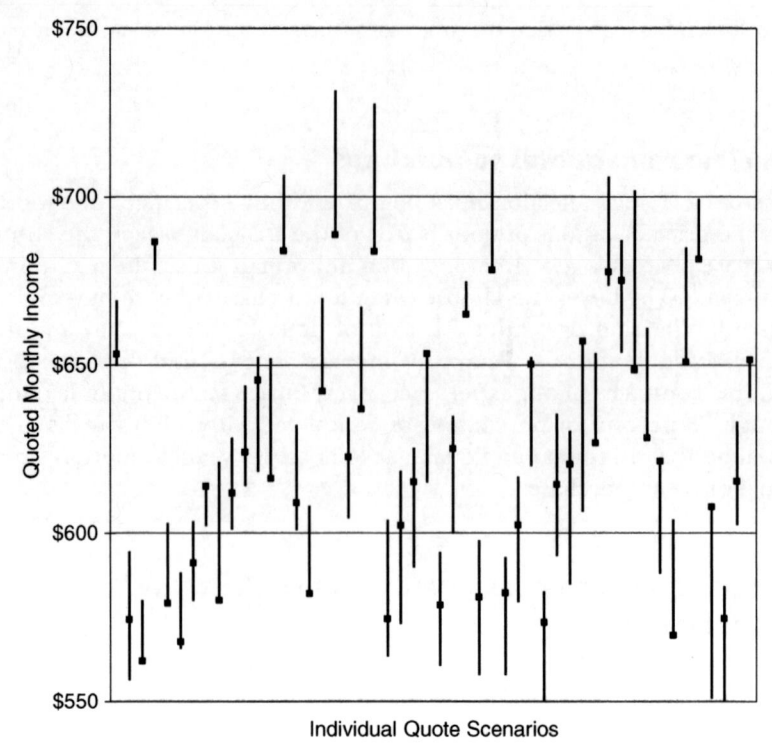

140 The Market for Retirement Financial Advice

Figure 7.1 Annuity quotes for a $100,000 deposit over one year
Source: Authors' analysis of data provide by the Hueler Companies.

To put results in context, the spreads are not as large as those found in the United Kingdom (Reyes and Stewart, 2008).

Handling questions and concerns

Some program partners have support staff to answer questions and assist with the purchase process, while others directly approach Hueler Companies staff. Some common questions are about process: How to access the live quotes and what happens during the quote/purchase process? Another common question is 'How much should I annuitize?' Individuals who ask this question are directed to the 'income gap' calculator at the website that helps them consider other sources of income and categories of typical expenses, and the difference between essential and discretionary expenses is also explained. Another common question is whether there are any fees involved in the program. The institutional platform embeds a flat

The Role of Guidance in the Annuity Decision-Making Process 141

one-time transaction fee in quotes for all purchases. Fees are fully disclosed to the individuals before and after purchase, which may generate additional questions (as this differs from other annuity delivery models). Buyers also often ask questions about providing survivor benefits and inflation protection.

Other commonly asked questions are about insurance companies and include how many insurance companies are available to choose from. This number can be as many as ten, depending on the annuity features requested and the program partners to which they are linked. Buyers also commonly ask how insurance companies are chosen and what the differences are between companies. They are directed to the location on the website that provides information about the companies used and their financial conditions, including ratings from Moody's, Standard & Poor's, and A. M. Best. Some annuity buyers as well as program partners are very aware of the issue of insurer insolvency and ask about this issue. Some buyers split the purchase between multiple insurance carriers to diversify insurance carrier risk. Plan sponsors who offer access to any form of annuity product or platform whether or not it includes competitive bidding are generally concerned about appropriate oversight with regard to the financial stability of any participating insurance company.

International comparisons

To illustrate two alternative approaches to the purchase of annuities by older individuals, we next discuss briefly the experiences of Chile and the United Kingdom.

The Chilean experience

Chile has had a national mandatory DC pension system since 1981, and retirees have the choice of taking 'programmed' or phased withdrawals, or buying an annuity. Workers' assets are accumulated in private pension funds, Administradoras de Fondos de Pensiones (AFPs), which also provide the programmed withdrawals; workers may not take lump sums from these accounts. Insurers compete to provide quotes for annuities, and persons whose accounts are less than the amount needed to provide the minimum benefit guarantee cannot purchase annuities. Currently, most Chilean retirees have elected annuity payments (Ruiz and Mitchell, 2012).

To address concerns about the cost and expenses of annuities, a government-sponsored competitive bidding computer-based system named SCOMP was introduced in 2004 to improve competitiveness and transparency, and to better meet participant needs. SCOMP annuity quotations can be solicited directly by individuals, or an insurance broker can generate these on the retiree's behalf. If an individual purchases an annuity directly via the computer there is no intermediation fee; if a broker is used, an intermediation fee of up to 2.5 percent can be charged (Reyes and Stewart, 2008). Members can request up to three quotes with or without the assistance of brokers or sales agents, from all competing insurers. Upon receipt, the member can accept one of the quotes, request additional offers, or rebid the account.

The Chilean system differs from the institutional platform described above in that it is connected to a mandatory government DC program. By contrast, our institutional platform is linked to a number of pension entities but it is up to plan participants to seek quotes. Once a quote is requested, competitive information is automatically provided for all carriers participating in the program. Moreover, in our institutional platform, there is a fully disclosed one-time transaction fee determined by the service level and program partner, and no further intermediation fees or commissions are paid. Where an advisor is used, the one-time transaction fee is typically the lowest fee available, because the individual then pays the advisor an out-of-pocket fee; the advisor is hired by and represents the individual.

In Chile, although 34 percent of the participants who enter the system do so directly via the Internet, only 12 percent finalize the process without paying a commission. In addition, only a small fraction of the participants use the option to secure a competitive bid (Reyes and Stewart, 2008). Therefore, in Chile and in the Income Solutions® platform, most participants seek and use active guidance and support. With the institutional platform, competitive bidding is automatic, but in Chile it is not, and its use is limited.

The experience in Chile also demonstrates that incentives matter. Where brokers were involved in the process of reviewing annuities, 75 percent of the individuals got the best (highest) payout. Only 43 percent did so when the retirees used the AFP for advice, and only 3 percent when a life insurer was consulted, perhaps because brokers had an incentive to capture customers once contacted. The AFPs participate actively during the accumulation phase but receive no payments for giving advice about payout products (Ruiz and Mitchell, 2012).

Lessons from the United Kingdom

In the past it was possible for retirees to take one-quarter of their accumulated pension wealth as a lump sum, whether from a DB or DC plan; the balance had to be annuitized by age 75. Individuals have had the right to shop around for an annuity through the Open Market Option (OMO) since 1978, but the majority still used their pension provider to supply their annuity despite the fact that they did not necessarily receive the best annuity rate. Indeed, the difference in income between the best OMO rate and the participant's existing pension provider could be as much as 30 percent, but only about one in three individuals switched to a new provider (Reyes and Stewart, 2008). Starting in 2002, pensioners had to be informed that they had the right to secure annuities from organizations other than their current pension providers, and those with higher incomes were more likely to switch. Twenty-six percent of people with monthly income from £250 to £499 went to the OMO, versus 67 percent of those with monthly incomes over £3800 (Reyes and Stewart, 2008).

The UK government has been working to improve the process with the Pensions Advisory Service, an independent voluntary organization that offers a Pensions Advisory Service (TPAS) online annuity planner. This planner assists individuals in selecting annuities and understanding prices. The planner and various information booklets are part of a larger Money Advice Service, a website organized by the government and financed by a levy on the financial services industry. The planner discusses issues such as single life versus joint, survivor income, inflation protection, and death benefits, thus providing a type of structural guidance (Reyes and Stewart, 2008; Money Advice Service, 2012).

Observations

While Chile and the United Kingdom focus heavily on lifetime income, in the United States program architecture is the main way that plan sponsors drive enrollment, saving, and investment choices. Of course, the United States differs from these other countries by providing significant inflation-adjusted monthly income from the national Social Security system, while the United Kingdom and Chile have mandatory DC plans.

Another factor worth highlighting is the role of competitive bidding. As shown by Hackethal and Inderst (2013), research on the effectiveness of financial advice calls for greater transparency with regard to outcomes, and supports the value of competitive bidding. As we have noted above, when bids are compared over a period of time, who offers the best bid varies over time and by quote scenario. Without a process to facilitate private-sector competition, people tend to remain with their existing providers even if they could substantially improve their monthly income amount and ultimate income sufficiency. Moreover, since many purchasers want multiple quotes before completing a purchase, having the product comparisons available on the Internet is useful. Nevertheless, a lifetime income product purchase decision is complex, so for most people it requires additional support or guidance.

Another factor is that most of the US annuity buyers (61 percent in our data) on our platform use one-quarter of their financial wealth or less when they annuitize. Thus, buyers appear to be thinking about the purchase as part of a portfolio, implying that the all-or-nothing traditional approach is unlikely to attract many buyers. In Chile, by contrast, people annuitize more because there is a much smaller safety net, compared to the United States. In other words, the commonly accepted belief that annuities are not an attractive way to provide plan distributions is probably flawed, since this conclusion does not recognize the significant deterrents that poor framing, constrained delivery, and lack of guidance often place in the way of annuitization.

Conclusion

Guaranteed lifetime income is an important part of retirement security, but in the United States, Social Security does not provide a sufficient single source of lifetime income for many retirees. When a retirement plan does not provide lifetime income, steps can be taken to boost guaranteed retirement income flows. The institutional purchasing platform described here offers a real-world model that brings together transparency, competition, and guidance in the annuity purchasing process. Structural guidance is a critical component to a system that works well, but it is insufficient: also needed are personal conversations to enhance the chances that people will annuitize a portion of their assets.

Taking advantage of institutional purchasing and structural guidance, the benefits of group pricing and an informed purchasing process can be provided to individuals served by plan sponsors, administrators, advisors, and financial services organizations. Purchasers are more comfortable and more likely to buy when they have active guidance; that is, someone with whom they can discuss the purchase decision and who can help them understand the relevant issues. Competitive pricing can yield higher monthly income amounts.

While annuitization of retirement assets may not suit everyone, it is important to have access to a fair presentation of payout options which include annuities. Further work is needed to better understand the choices made about managing resources in retirement, the barriers to considering guaranteed lifetime income, the influence of key parties, and the policies and programs that help individuals make the best decisions. Moreover, annuities often receive bad press related to their costs, complicated features, and provider risk. Unfortunately, immediate annuities offering lifetime income are often confused with more complex investment-focused variable annuity products. Another barrier is that financial advice sometimes emanates from sources whose revenue would be reduced if their advisees were to annuitize. In addition, some employers who do seek better financial outcomes for their retirees are still reluctant to get involved in the post-retirement period, due to concerns about fiduciary and legal liability. Further research is needed to determine where conflicts of interest or mixed messages impede actions that are in the best interests of participants with regard to lifetime income.

Appendix: Eight case studies

Case studies and analysis of purchases help explain what happens in the purchase process, based on our experience with the institutional platform.

Buyer A offers an example of a sophisticated purchaser. Buyer A was a female working with a financial advisor, who bought twelve separate annuity contracts, four per year for three consecutive years. Multiple carriers were used, diversifying carrier risk. The transactions were executed by the advisor and the quotes secured by the advisor. These were single life annuities, with inflation indexing in most and some variation in the features. Funds were withdrawn from an IRA and the amount of the premium paid per purchase ($10,000) was the same. Purchasing over time diversifies interest rate risk and allowed the buyer to get accustomed to the annuity. The buyer was at the age of 66 in the first year, and she purchased a total of $575 per month in additional income. Twenty-two competitive price quotes were secured during the process.

Buyer B, a male aged 62 and the joint annuitant a female aged 59, offers another example of a sophisticated purchasing strategy. This purchaser bought from three different insurance carriers at a single point in time, paying a premium of $50,000 per carrier for a purchase of $904 of monthly income. All purchases were from qualified plan funds from a DC plan with the same plan design for each: joint life with 50 percent benefit to the survivor and a ten-year certain benefit. Four quotes were requested within a six-month period from the date of first quote to the purchase date.

Buyer C, a couple, bought five annuity contracts using multiple carriers with a mix of qualified and non-qualified funds; they also bought both single life and joint life policies with a cash refund. Fewer than three weeks transpired from the initial quote to the purchase date, and fifty-one quotes were secured for many different annuity feature combinations.

Buyer D was a retiree aged 85, with a 67-year-old joint annuitant. He bought two contracts about five months apart. His first purchase was made with the help of a facilitator who requested the quote and executed the purchase. The second was made by the individual. Two different insurance carriers were used. The first purchase was for a joint annuity with 100 percent to the survivor and a term certain, and the second for a single life with term certain. Four quotes were secured and the first purchase was made the same week as the first quote. The premium was $250,000 for the first purchase and $175,000 for the second; the income stream purchased was $1,481 per month in the first purchase and $1,516 in the second.

Buyer E bought a five-year term certain annuity; he was a 61-year-old male using $70,000 of qualified plan funds to purchase $1,200 of monthly income. Nine quotes were obtained and four months passed from the first quote to the purchase. Possible reasons for the purchase of a five-year term certain annuity include a bridge to social security benefits, a desire to defer social security claiming, financing of college expenses, or providing more income to pay off a mortgage.

Buyer F was an 84-year-old female who used $150,000 to purchase $1,653 of monthly lifetime income using non-qualified funds; no refund features were purchased. A facilitator aided in the purchase. Eight quotations were secured, and it took five weeks from the first quotation to the purchase. Purchases by annuitants in their 80s are typically supported by facilitators, often use non-qualified assets, and receive additional scrutiny relative to suitability.

Buyer G was a male aged 65 and female aged 64 who made four purchases using four insurance carriers. A three-week period passed from first quote to final purchase, and thirty quotes were secured involving various combinations of annuity features including a mix of joint life with 100 percent survivor income and single life income; term certain periods of fifteen to twenty years were included. Purchases were made from qualified plan funds, and a facilitator secured the quotes. Total purchase price was more than $500,000 which amounted to less than a third of total liquid net worth. The individual diversified carrier risk by selecting different insurers.

Buyer H was a member of a couple where the wife was much younger: the husband was aged 66 at the time of the first purchase, and the wife was aged 46. The couple made purchases a year apart and bought six contracts, with a premium of $35,000 per contract; they elected a joint and 100 percent survivor benefit with inflation indexing. IRA funds were used, and two weeks elapsed between the time of the first quote and the first purchase. A total of nine quotes were secured and there was an advisor involved.

Endnotes

1. Advisors are individuals providing financial advice to clients. Advice providers are firms that provide advice to employee benefit plan sponsors and administrators, often using an automated platform. Their programs may include call centers and individuals who have conversations with users.
2. Advanced life deferred annuities are annuity contracts that provide for deferral to some advanced age, such as 85, with no death benefit if death occurs earlier. They provide a way to insure the longevity risk starting at the advanced age at moderate cost. Until now, the tax regulations were a barrier to use this type of annuity in tax-deferred retirement funds.
3. A rollover provision allows an amount for a DC plan to be transferred to a DB plan and lifetime income is then provided by the DB plan. In effect, the retiree is buying the annuity from the DB plan.
4. In addition, IRA balances may later be used to purchase individual annuities, but this information is not tracked so we cannot determine how many DC account balances are ultimately converted to annuities (Wray, 2008).
5. The projection could be for any form of structured income in retirement and need not be for lifetime income.
6. Relatively few advisors have taken this route to date; 75 percent of financial planners said they always or frequently advocate systematic withdrawals for income generation, 38 percent always or frequently advocate the time-segmentation approach, and 33 percent of planners always or frequently advocate the essential versus discretionary approach (Guyton, 2011).
7. As an example of a response to a review question from a facilitator, we have the following: 'The buyer has confirmed that he has sufficient funds to cover basic and emergency expenses and that he is not using more than 50 percent of his stated net worth to purchase the annuity.' Examples of review questions that life-only buyers are asked to confirm might be that they understand that there is no benefit beyond their lifetime, and those who buy period certain annuities are asked to confirm that there is no benefit beyond the certain period.
8. Trial annuitization is another example of an alternative model designed to address some of these inherent drawbacks. Advocates of lifetime income alternatives have proposed the concept of trial annuitization, where assets might be annuitized for an initial fixed period; after that, the individual would have a choice to convert to a lifetime annuity or to take some other approach, including receiving a lump sum.
9. Qualified funds are funds in tax-preferred retirement savings accounts such as IRAs and 401(k) plans. The Internal Revenue Code sets limits on how much can be contributed to these funds, and how funds must be withdrawn. The tax treatment of annuities is different when purchased with qualified funds and non-qualified funds.

10. Under US tax law, Section 1035 of the Internal Revenue Code, holders of annuity contracts are allowed to exchange them for other annuity contracts without paying tax at the time of transfer.
11. For an illustrative set of case studies, see the Appendix.

References

Callan Investments Institute (2012). *2012 Defined Contribution Trends Survey*. San Francisco, CA: Callan Associates.

Council of Economic Advisers (2012). 'Supporting Retirement for American Families.' Washington, DC: CEA. February 2 <http://www.whitehouse.gov/sites/default/files/cea_retirement_report_01312012_final.pdf>.

Guyton, J. (2011). 'Special Report: Retirement Income Planning: Study Suggests Link Between Planner Retirement Advice and Client Life Style Changes,' *Journal of Financial Planning*, 24(12): 28–32.

Hackethal, A., and R. Inderst (2013). 'How to Make the Market for Financial Advice Work,' in O. S. Mitchell and K. Smetters, eds., *The Market for Retirement Financial Advice*. Oxford, UK: Oxford University Press, pp. 213–28.

Hueler, K. (2012). 'PSCA Adds Hueler Income Solutions® as a Member Benefit,' *Defined Contribution Insights*, 60(1): 17.

Institutional Retirement Income Council (2011). *Types of Institutional Retirement Income Products*. Iselin, NJ: Institutional Retirement Income Council. http://www.iricouncil.org/types

Iwry, J. Mark, and J. A. Turner (2009). *Automatic Annuitization: New Behavioral Strategies for Expanding Lifetime Income in 401(k)s*. Washington, DC: Retirement Security Project. http://www.brookings.edu/~/media/Files/rc/papers/2009/07_annuitization_iwry/07_annuitization_iwry.pdf

Money Advice Service (2012). *Pensions and Retirement*. London, UK: Money Advice Service. https://www.moneyadviceservice.org.uk/en/categories/pensions-and-retirement

National Association of Insurance Commissioners (NAIC) (2010). *Revised Suitability in Annuity Transactions Model Regulation Executive Summary*. Kansas City, MO: NAIC. http://www.naic.org/documents/committees_a_suitability_reg_guidance.pdf

Rappaport, A. M. (2011). 'Retirement Security in the New Economy, Developing New Paradigms for the Payout Period,' in Society of Actuaries, eds. *Retirement Security in the New Economy: Paradigm Shifts, New Approaches and Holistic Strategies*. Schaumburg, IL: Society of Actuaries. http://www.soa.org/library/monographs/retirement-systems/retirement-security/mono-2011-mrs12-rappaport-paper.aspx

Reyes, G., and F. Stewart (2008). 'Transparency and Competition in the Choice of Pension Products: The Chilean and UK Experience,' Working Paper No. 7. Paris, France: International Organization of Pension Supervisors (OIPS).

Ruiz, J., and O. S. Mitchell (2012). 'Pension Payouts in Chile: Past, Present, and Future Prospects,' in O. S. Mitchell, J. Piggott, and N. Takayama, eds., *Securing Lifelong Retirement Income: Global Annuity Markets and Policy*. Oxford, UK: Oxford University Press, pp. 106–30.

Turner, J. A., and D. M. Muir (2013). 'The Market for Financial Advisers,' in O. S. Mitchell and K. Smetters, eds., *The Market for Retirement Financial Advice.* Oxford, UK: Oxford University Press, pp. 13–45.

United States Department of the Treasury (2012). *Treasury Fact Sheet: Helping American Families Achieve Retirement Security by Expanding Lifetime Income Choices.* Washington, DC: US GPO. http://www.treasury.gov/press-center/press-releases/Documents/020212%20Retirement%20Security%20Factsheet.pdf

United States Senate (2011). *Background on the Lifetime Income Disclosure Act (S.267).* Washington, DC: US GPO. http://bingaman.senate.gov/upload/Lifetime_Disclosure_Act.pdf

Wray, D. (2008). *Testimony before the ERISA Advisory Council Working Group Working Group on Spend Down of Defined Contribution Assets at Retirement.* Washington, DC: ERISA Advisory Council, US Department of Labor.

Part II
Measuring Performance and Impact

Chapter 8
Evaluating the Impact of Financial Planners

Cathleen D. Zick and Robert N. Mayer

Do professional financial planners improve their clients' financial well-being? The answer to this question is more important today than it was twenty-five years ago, because individuals now must shoulder increasing responsibility for their financial planning, and financial markets have become more complicated and volatile. As evidence of these trends, there were approximately 34 million shareholder accounts in the United States in 1985, and investors had their choice of 1,528 mutual funds. By 2010, there were 292 million shareholder accounts and 7,581 mutual funds (ICI, 2011).[1] Given the information and choice burdens of managing one's financial affairs, it is not surprising that roughly one-third of households report consulting a professional financial planner to help with saving, investments, and insurance (SunAmerica Financial Group, 2011; Twigg, 2011; Turner and Muir, 2013). But the challenges for consumers do not end here, because there are many different types of financial planners and a growing variety of titles, credentials, and certifications.[2]

Despite the importance of knowing about the conditions under which financial planners benefit their clients, to date only a handful of studies have evaluated the impact of financial planners. Moreover, prior studies are often plagued by design features that limit confidence in their conclusions. In this chapter, we detail 'best practice' approaches that can help an evaluator draw confident conclusions regarding whether financial planners improve their clients' financial well-being. We review existing literature in light of these best practices, and we provide an example of how the choice of evaluation design can affect a study's conclusions using the 2007 Survey of Consumer Finances (SCF).

Evaluation designs

A good evaluation of the impact of consulting with a professional financial planner involves insuring that three aspects of the study are sound: (*a*) the measurement of advice-seeking and its consequences, (*b*) the applicability of the evaluation's results to other settings, and (c) the confidence that observed relationships between seeking professional guidance and financial outcomes[3] are real (Langbein and Felbinger, 2006). We discuss each of these in turn as they apply to the evaluation of professional financial planner consultations.

Are the right concepts being measured?

At first blush, it may seem that it is simple to measure whether someone has sought out a professional financial planner. Yet in practice, this is complicated. For instance, the researcher must decide whether consultation with an Accredited Financial Counselor or Certified Financial Planner should count the same as a session with a bank customer service specialist. Decisions must be made regarding whether to differentiate a commission-based planner from a fee-only planner, and whether a one-time consultation should count the same as repeated consultations. Likewise, the researcher must make decisions about what types of time frames (e.g., one year, ten years) should matter for planning sessions. Resolution of these conceptual issues has practical implications regarding how contact with a professional financial planner is to be measured.

In prior studies, researchers have often relied on a single dichotomous self-reported question about use of financial planners, broadly defined. Yet four studies are notable for improving on this typical approach. First, research in Germany has relied on brokerage houses and banks to measure use of professional financial advice (Bluethgen et al., 2008; Gerhardt and Hackethal, 2009; Hackethal et al., 2012; Hackethal and Inderst, 2013). Presumably these organizational records are more accurate than self-reports. Second, one of these German studies has compared the results of using an independent financial advisor to those from using a bank-affiliated advisor (Hackethal et al., 2012). The results of these studies are mixed. One concluded that financial advisors aid in diversification and matching actual investments with the contents of a predefined, ideal portfolio; the other study found little evidence that working with a professional financial advisor was beneficial to clients.

A 2010 Canadian study took advantage of longitudinal data to more precisely measure contact with a financial planner (IFIC, 2010). Specifically, consumers were asked in 2005 and 2009 whether they used a financial advisor. The empirical analysis compared those people who said yes in both years to those who said no in both years. This procedure has the advantage of eliminating people who had not consulted an advisor recently, as well as those who only recently began to work with one. That study revealed that advised households had higher investable assets in 2009 than non-advised households. This result held within each of five household income groupings, and the difference was more dramatic for households making less than $100,000 per year compared to those earning more than this amount.

Despite the promising measurement practices of the studies just cited, existing research still does not do justice to the wide range of financial planners and the many factors that might differentiate their impacts on customers. The existing literature also fails to capture the nature of the planner–client relationship, especially its duration and the frequency of consultations. An equally thorny issue relates to the choice of measured outcomes. These should capture what financial planners are supposed to accomplish, but analysts disagree on this point. For instance, Collins (2010) distinguishes four roles that financial planners can play: technical expert, transactional agent, counselor, and coach. Each implies different criteria according to which the performance of a planner could be judged.

To give a flavor of the conceptual issues involved in selecting relevant outcomes, one should ask whether the benefits of using a planner are best measured in terms of dollars (e.g., account growth), time (e.g., time saved in the planning process), or psychological states (e.g., retirement confidence, peace of mind). Moreover, within financial results, it is unclear if a 'good' planner would be expected to help a person 'beat the market,' or help someone avoid major mistakes (e.g., by acting as a human 'circuit breaker' against behavioral biases). For example, Hackethal et al. (2012) conclude that planners play the role of 'babysitter,' that is, someone who allows competent people to use their time in other pursuits, as opposed to 'psychiatrists' (our term, not theirs) who provide the experience, expertise, and perspective that a consumer lacks.

If the benefits of working with a financial planner are primarily financial in nature, a stringent standard would be to generate higher risk-adjusted rates of return or greater wealth in the long run. Yet most researchers do not have the luxury of measuring exposure to financial advice at one point in time and account balances at a much later point in time. Moreover, in cross-sectional analyses, there is a danger of misinterpreting associations between using a financial planner and having greater than average wealth, since planners may help people become wealthier, but wealthier people may also have a greater propensity to seek financial advice.

Given the difficulty of using financial results (e.g., portfolio performance) as a measure of a planner's potential value, many studies focus on 'process' factors that planners can influence in the short run (e.g., taking particular planning actions, diversifying investments, or setting aside an emergency fund). The implicit assumption is that consistently following the recommended financial planning process steps will improve long-term financial outcomes. Our own research finds that the act of estimating retirement financial needs is indeed associated with the accumulation of more retirement assets (Marsden et al., 2011). Yet evidence is scarce regarding the impact on wealth of planning steps such as setting goals and specific objectives, creating and implementing a financial plan, and monitoring results (Certified Financial Planner Board of Standards, 2009).

Partially because it is relatively easy to measure and partially because it is under the immediate control of clients and their advisors, diversification is the most common measure employed in studies of the impact of financial planners. Both diversification across and within asset classes can be examined. Bluethgen et al. (2008) do a particularly good job of measuring multiple aspects of diversification, including the use of mutual funds, geographical diversity of equity assets (versus home bias), and portfolio volatility.

Lacking a single conceptual way to measure the impact of financial planners, analysts often adopt a pragmatic stance. That is, they measure multiple outcomes, some of which cover long-term investment performance. Most studies, however, focus on short-term results or controllable elements of the financial planning process.[4]

Will the results be applicable to other settings?

If the results of an evaluation are not generalizable to other settings, then they provide only limited insights about the effectiveness of financial planners. Two evaluation considerations are particularly relevant when assessing the generalizability of a study's design.

First, it is important to define the population of interest. A researcher may want to know the effectiveness of professional financial planners with respect to a relatively homogeneous group, such as individuals who work for the same employer or are customers at the same financial institution. Alternatively, a researcher may be interested in assessing the impact of professional financial planners on the general population or targeted subgroups (e.g., young adults, middle income households). The population of interest drives decisions about who should be in the study and how results can be extrapolated. For example, the findings from a study on individuals who invested their money with financial institution X should not be extrapolated to the population at large, as it may be that factors (e.g., education level) that led people to invest their money in institution X also influenced how they acted when given professional financial advice.

In practice, virtually all existing studies examining the potential effects of financial planners use idiosyncratic samples. First, one focuses on people who visited the website of a large financial services company (ING, 2010). Another US-based study examines only people with employer-provided 401(k) plans (Charles Schwab, 2007). A third uses survey data in which all of the respondents worked for one single US employer (Marsden et al., 2011). The most nationally representative survey relies on US data from the RAND American Life Panel (Hung and Yoong, 2013).[5] A study conducted in the Netherlands analyzes data from a single medium-sized bank (Kramer, 2012). Several German studies rely on data from a single online brokerage company and/or a single bank (Bluethgen et al., 2008; Jansen et al., 2008; Gerhardt and Hackethal, 2009; Hackethal et al., 2012; Hackethal and Inderst, 2013).

Second, once the population of interest has been determined, the researcher must decide whether data will be gathered from everyone or from a subset of the population. Cost considerations usually lead the evaluator to opt for a sample, but in such instances, every effort must be made to insure that the sample selected is representative of the population of interest. There is a well-established literature on how best to generate appropriate samples (Scheaffer et al., 2012) and insure reasonable survey cooperation rates (Groves and Couper, 1998). But, even if the overall sample does reflect the larger population of interest, item-specific non-response to questions can still create problems in representativeness, particularly in the case of potentially sensitive questions about financial matters (Riphahn and Serfling, 2003, 2005). Imputation methods can be used to deal with such non-response, but these are very technically sophisticated (Kennickell, 1998, 2011).

Are the observed relationships credible between professional financial consultation and the subsequent outcomes?

Evaluations of the impact of professional financial planners should seek to establish causality, meaning that the professional consultation led to improved financial practices and financial outcomes. Financial practices, such as goal setting and portfolio diversification, and financial outcomes, such as net financial holdings, are likely influenced by a myriad factors including economy-wide fluctuations in financial markets, individual life cycle stage, household income, risk tolerance, and random chance, as well as whether individuals have sought the counsel of professional financial planners. The evaluator wants to know the effect of seeking professional financial advice on the outcomes of interest, net of other random and systematic elements.

Random influences can be routinely controlled by imposing standard statistical testing techniques.[6] By contrast, netting out the effects of other systematic elements on financial outcomes is more complicated. Even studies using large samples can yield unconvincing results if they do not

158 The Market for Retirement Financial Advice

use the proper study design. Thus, simply comparing the financial well-being of people who use and do not use financial planners does not prove causality. For example, several industry-sponsored studies have concluded that professional financial planners are highly beneficial (Charles Schwab, 2007; FPA/Ameriprise, 2008; ING, 2010). One study claims (FPA/Ameriprise, 2008: 1): 'Consumer confidence is near historic lows, yet one group is feeling optimistic and on track to meet their financial goals including retirement—people in a comprehensive financial planning relationship.' Such simple comparisons, at a single point in time, without other controls, are not scientifically valid.

Drawing conclusions regarding causality is best done using a sophisticated evaluation design called a randomized field experiment (RFE). In an RFE, individuals are randomly assigned to treatment and control groups. Data on the financial variables of interest (e.g., financial plan development, implementation, and wealth) should be gathered for members of both groups at the outset. Then those assigned to the treatment group would be exposed to a professional financial planner's advice (i.e., the treatment). Depending on how professional financial planning is measured, the treatment could include a range of activities (e.g., goal setting, determination of risk tolerance, account diversification recommendations), dissemination modes (e.g., face to face, online), and one or several exposures. After an appropriate lapse of time (e.g., six months, one year, five years), data on the financial variables of interest would be remeasured and the change in the financial variables for the treatment group would be compared to the change for the control group. Statistically significant differences in the treatment group's financial outcomes when compared to the control group would be evidence of the impact of professional financial planning. Figure 8.1 depicts the structure of a well-designed RFE.[7]

Comparison of the treatment group's outcomes to those of a control group insures that the evaluator can net out systematic factors affecting both groups. For example, historical events like the 2008 Great Recession should affect both groups equally. Likewise, if the study involves a significant follow-up period, the comparison to a control group insures that life stage changes in financial outcomes are netted out. For instance, by comparing the changes in the treatment group to those experienced by the control group, the evaluator would net out any changes in financial outcomes that are attributable to some households moving in to the empty nest stage when resources may be redirected from child-related expenditures toward investments. Finally, the inclusion of a control group surveyed twice insures that the evaluator can net out any effects of sensitizing participants to the purpose of the study. That is, if participants become aware of the importance of financial planning as a result of the baseline data collection, this can be netted out from the analysis by comparing

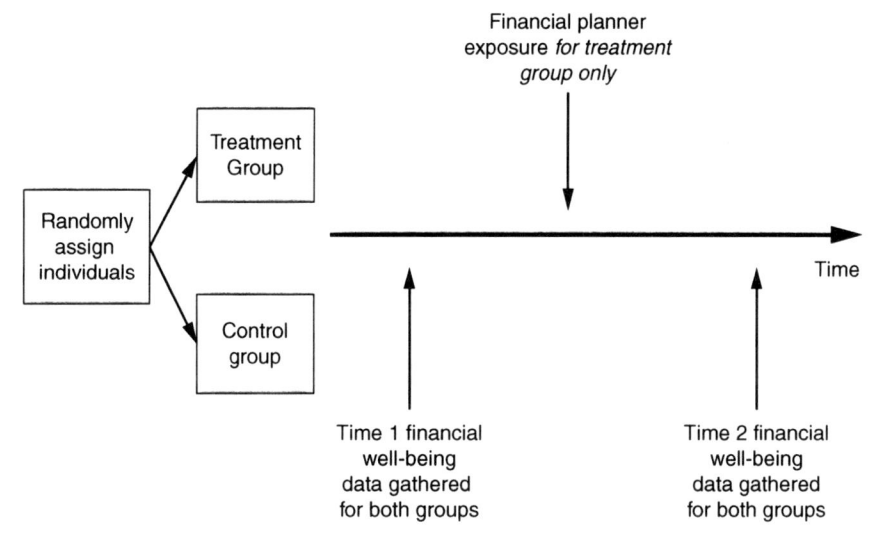

Figure 8.1 Randomized field experiment to assess the impact of consulting a professional financial planner

Source: Authors' analysis, adapted from Langbein and Felbinger (2006).

changes in the treatment group's financial outcomes to the changes in the control group's financial outcomes.

Random assignment to the treatment and control groups insures that when comparisons across the two groups are made that the evaluator will not have results that are confounded by the possibility of more motivated or more capable individuals self-selecting into the group that receives professional financial planning. Nor will the evaluator have to adjust for the possibility that one group contains more high- or low-income individuals that could affect financial comparisons.

For these reasons, RFEs are the 'gold standard' for assessing the causal relationship between an intervention such as meeting with a professional financial planner and one or more outcomes. Yet since these are typically very expensive to implement and require extensive planning, they are rarely carried out in practice. Instead, study designs most often used to assess how professional financial planners affect financial well-being involve some sort of non-experimental research design.

Non-experiments take one of two approaches. One approach simply compares the outcome variables of interest for a single group of individuals before and after the exposure to the treatment. In such a setting, individuals serve as their own controls. For instance, financial wealth levels prior to meeting with a professional financial planner might be compared to peoples' financial wealth one year later. A handful of studies to date incorporate such a before-and-after comparison, including a study by Gerhardt and Hackethal (2009), who analyze almost 600 German investors who had previously directed their own accounts but recently consulted an advisor. The researchers reported that switching to working with an adviser triggered higher trading activity, most likely as part of restructuring portfolios. Newly advised clients also increased their diversification and engaged in less risky trading.

Another analysis by Bhattacharya et al. (2012) found some minor benefits in terms of account diversification and performance from consulting a professional financial advisor, but in that study, subjects were a very idiosyncratic group. The authors examined the less than 5 percent of people who responded affirmatively to an opportunity to work with an advisor. As a result, these subjects represent a strongly self-selected group. Even then, most advised clients failed to follow the recommendations of the bank-provided advisors. Horn et al. (2009) also used the passage of time to compare advised and non-advised investors before and after a change in the tax laws relevant to investing. They noted that advised investors were less likely to fall victim to the new rules, but the authors could not rule out the possibility that people who were less prone to making tax errors were also more likely to choose to work with a financial planner.

A second non-experimental approach dominates existing research. Here, outcomes of interest are measured at a single point in time for two different sets of individuals, where one group has been exposed to the treatment, while the other has not. In our context, this might involve using cross-sectional survey data in which all respondents report on their financial wealth, but some respondents indicate that they have met with a financial planner while others say they did not.

Both non-experimental approaches make use of comparisons with control groups, but the absence of random assignment calls into question whether the two groups are similar on all relevant dimensions except for the treatment. As a result, analysts cannot rely on simple comparisons of means. Rather, researchers must control for variables that capture other systematic processes unrelated to the treatment that may affect the outcomes of interest. For instance, in the case of financial outcomes, these might include measures of education, household structure, and life cycle stage (to name a few). Omission of these potentially important covariates can lead to biased estimates of the causal relationship between professional financial planning and financial outcomes.

The absence of random assignment in non-experimental evaluations also creates concern about possible reverse causation, which could arise if people who seek professional financial planning do so because they have greater financial wealth initially. Alternatively, people with low levels of assets (or who experienced a recent drop) might seek professional help as a means of offsetting their past decisions. In either situation, uncertainty about the causal direction of the relationship between exposure to professional financial planning and financial outcomes leads to concerns about whether the estimate of the treatment effect on the outcome of interest may be biased.

Also, in the non-experimental evaluation design, confidence regarding estimated causal relationships requires the elimination of omitted variables and reverse causality bias. In essence, the evaluator must attempt to compensate for non-random assignment through the use of statistical modeling. When evaluating the impact of professional financial planning, confidence that the estimated relationship is truly causal is a function of two things: (*a*) the inclusion of covariates in the model that adequately capture the influence of other variables affecting financial well-being, and (*b*) the statistical allowance for the simultaneous relationship between seeking professional planning and financial well-being. A pioneering study in this field by Bluethgen et al. (2008) uses multiple regression analysis to examine the association between using a bank-based financial advisor and financial account characteristics. The authors control for a variety of individual attributes, including the investor's age, income, and risk attitude. The authors report that using an advisor appears to promote not only greater account diversification and closer adherence to predefined model portfolios but also higher expenses. Nevertheless, this study did not control for possible reverse causation.

An important methodological step forward was taken by Hackethal et al. (2012), who employed an instrumental variable approach to predict use of a financial advisor. First, they used regional-level data to approximate the geographic concentration of financial information, which they viewed as a substitute for the use of a professional financial planner. They then used the predicted likelihood of using an advisor in an analysis of various investor practices and portfolio outcomes. The authors uncovered little evidence that use of a financial professional was beneficial to clients.

Hung and Yoong (2013) set out to replicate the instrumental variable approach, but they elected to use two measures of financial literacy to help control for possible reverse causation between investor outcomes and use of an advisor. Their logic was that financial literacy could be a substitute or complement for advice and thus influenced the likelihood of seeking it. Therefore, to the extent that financial literacy helps drive the decision of whether to seek advice, controlling for literacy would help separate the impact of advice from the likelihood of seeking it. Hung and Yoong analyzed a variety of investment account features (account contributions and withdrawals, asset allocations, and variable investment 'mistakes'). They concluded that advice had little apparent influence. If anything, they found evidence of reverse causation, namely, that people who experienced declines in their account balances turned to advisors.

Research by Gerhardt and Hackethal (2009) exemplifies an alternative to the instrumental variables when identifying the influence of advisors on their clients. Rather than controlling on predicted use of financial advisors, these authors use a propensity score approach by which they statistically construct pairs of research subjects matched according to all observable characteristics except their reported use of a financial advisor. This procedure approximates random assignment in a true experimental design and thereby makes it less plausible that differences in investor outcomes are a function of anything other than use or non-use of professional advice, including differences in wealth. Using this approach, they found little evidence that professional advisors promoted better investment practices and outcomes for their clients.

A US-based study of employees of a large state university also used a propensity score approach, with mixed results (Marsden et al., 2011). Working with an advisor was linked to several important financial planning activities, including goal setting, calculation of retirement needs, retirement account diversification, use of supplemental retirement accounts, accumulation of emergency funds, positive behavioral responses to the recent economic crisis, and retirement confidence. Use of a financial advisor was not related, though, to self-reported retirement savings or short-term growth in retirement account asset values.

Two studies that most closely approximate the ideals of an RFE are a study by Kramer (2012) in the Netherlands, and a study by Hung and Yoong (2013) in the United States. The Dutch study is notable for its use of both cross-time and cross-group comparisons. Thus, Kramer compared the portfolios of previously self-directed investors after switching to being advised. Because this switch is relatively rare in real-world settings, the author analyzed only 228 investors during a four-year period (2003–7). Within a month of consulting an advisor, client portfolios not only evidenced extensive turnover in existing assets but investors also added capital to their accounts. To put these account changes into meaningful perspective, the author employed a matched-pair research design based on propensity scores. A final nicety of this study is the separation of the sample into larger and smaller investors, to account for the possibility that advisors put more effort into larger portfolios. In addition, the short-term effect of working with an advisor was an increase in account diversification, especially a rise in the use of stock mutual funds within the equity portion of the accounts. The author also compared the portfolio returns of early and late switchers over the 2003–7 period, finding that the accounts of early switchers performed slightly worse than late switchers. This result is apparently due to shifts from equities to bonds rather than differential performance of equity accounts. Despite the use of comparisons across time and investor group, this study did not account for the possibility of self-selection, namely, that people who switched from being self-directed to working with an advisor may have had characteristics that also influenced the outcome variables of interest.

Hung and Yoong's analysis (2013) is the only one to date to employ random assignment of subjects. Unfortunately for our purposes, that study examined the impact of printed advice rather than interaction with advisers, and people allocated funds to hypothetical portfolios, not actual accounts. People were assigned to three groups: participants in the control group received information on fund expenses and past returns only, and the default treatment group automatically received advice on their allocation choices. This advice was based on a model of optimal portfolio allocation and was provided as (*a*) information only or (*b*) information plus feedback on chosen allocations. Finally, participants in the affirmative decision treatment group chose whether to receive investment advice. (There were also low and high return variations.) In a nutshell, the results for the default advice group approximated those of the control group, but the choices of people who deliberately chose advice were superior. Members of the latter group were less likely to make two serious investment mistakes: under-diversification and investing too conservatively. While random assignment should account for the possible effects of other participant characteristics, the authors reported that the findings were robust to multiple regressions that include experimental group membership along with a variety of covariate measures, including financial literacy.

In summary, recent scholarship has employed a variety of methodological techniques to explore the impact of professional financial planners on clients. The best models reduce the likelihood that observed connections are due to unmeasured variables or reverse causation. Absent a randomized experimental design, the use of propensity scores may be the best available method. To date, studies using propensity scores have been confined to investors with a relationship to a single bank, brokerage, or employer. In addition, these research subjects have tended to be wealthier than their respective national populations. Our use of propensity scoring below extends this line of research to a national sample, including individuals who fall below a country's median income level.

Analyzing a national dataset

Measuring how much professional financial planners improve their clients' financial well-being is facilitated using data from the 2007 Survey of Consumer Finances (SCF), to demonstrate how evaluator choices can influence

164 The Market for Retirement Financial Advice

conclusions drawn from an evaluation. The SCF is a triennial survey sponsored by the Board of Governors of the US Federal Reserve and conducted by the National Opinion Research Center. It utilizes a dual-frame sample design with one frame focused on securing a sample that is representative of all US households while the other frame seeks to secure a sample of wealthy US households. In the 2007 SCF, there were 2,915 households in the former category, and 1,507 in the latter category (Kennickell, 2009).[8]

Measuring concepts in the SCF

National surveys like the SCF have the advantage of including questions that have been tested for both measurement validity and reliability. Nevertheless, a researcher using the SCF may not always find that questions asked reflect all dimensions of the underlying concept that he would like to measure. Such is the case with regard to the measurement of professional financial planning, since the SCF includes a single question regarding information sources used when making savings and investment decisions. The SCF question reads as follows:

What sources of information do you (and your family) use to make decisions about saving and investments? Do you call around, read newspapers, magazines, material you get in the mail, use information from television, radio, the Internet or advertisements? Do you get advice from a friend, relative, lawyer, accountant, banker, broker, or financial planner? Or do you do something else?

Respondents can give multiple answers to the above questions. Here we code respondents who included 'financial planner' among their sources of information as consulting a professional financial planner. These households are used as our treatment group, while those who did not list 'financial planner' among their sources of information constitute the control group.

The SCF contains a great deal of detail regarding household financial holdings, allowing us several choices for how we measure financial outcomes. Here we select three: total household financial wealth, the proportion of all financial assets in equities, and diversification of financial assets as measured by the number of asset categories with positive balances that a household has. These three measures reflect elements of both financial plan implementation and outcomes, though they only implicitly measure the steps taken in developing a financial plan.

Generalizing to a population

In the analyses below, we focus on households with working-age adults in the bottom 99 percent of the income distribution. To this end, we restrict the SCF sample to households where the head (defined as males in married couple households by SCF convention) is between the ages of 18 and 64. We also eliminate households with annual incomes of $425,000 or more, as this is the approximate threshold for the top 1 percent that year (Luhby, 2011). To illustrate how the choice of target populations can affect conclusions drawn from an evaluation study, we divide the sample by median household income in 2007 and re-estimate our models for each subgroup.

As noted earlier, survey respondents are sometimes hesitant to answer what they perceive to be sensitive financial questions, so SCF staffers have developed imputation algorithms to deal with missing values. Imputations are generated five separate times for each missing value and stored in five replicates for each record. The replicates not only provide greater precision for the estimation of missing values, but their use also requires that researchers use programming macros to compute correct standard errors (Kennickell, 2009). To keep our analyses manageable, we follow the simpler strategy of undertaking separate estimation for each of the five implicate datasets (Hogarth et al., 2004). Our results do not differ markedly across the five implicate datasets, so we present estimates for dataset three here.[9]

Insuring that observed relationships are credible

In what follows, we review three sets of estimates for the relationship between consulting a financial planner and our outcomes of interest, using the SCF. Bivariate estimates, presented first, do neither control for the influence of socio-demographic and economic factors that might affect the three financial outcomes of interest, nor do they allow for potential simultaneity of financial outcomes and seeking counsel from a professional financial planner. Second, we report ordinary least squares estimates that remove the systematic influence of socio-demographic and economic factors. Last, we report propensity score estimates that net out the socio-demographic and economic influences and also adjust for the potential simultaneity.

Descriptive information for the three outcome measures appears in Table 8.1, separately for households that do consult professional financial planners and those who do not. Here all observed mean differences are statistically significant ($p < 0.05$): households that consult professional financial planners hold significantly more financial wealth, have a larger fraction of their wealth in stock equity, and have greater diversification of assets when compared to those households that do not consult professional financial planners. This holds both for the full SCF sample, and for the two income-stratified subsamples. In other words, using only bivariate

TABLE 8.1 Weighted means and *t*-tests for financial outcome variables

	Full sample (N = 2,881)		<Median income (N = 1,350)		≥Median income (N = 1,531)	
	Consults planner (N= 696)	Does not consult planner (N= 2,185)	Consults planner (N= 178)	Does not consult planner (N= 1,172)	Consults planner (N= 518)	Does not consult planner (N= 1,013)
Total financial wealth ($)	228,123	89,189	79,145	23,746	302,286	178,626
t-test	7.86**		2.84**		4.55**	
Proportion in equity (0–1.0)	0.35	0.21	0.24	0.12	0.41	0.33
t-test	10.44**		5.69**		4.62**	
Number of asset categories (1–8)	2.86	2.00	2.22	1.50	3.18	2.70
t-test	15.22**		8.84**		7.38**	

Note: **$p < 0.05$.
Source: Authors' calculations from the 2007 Survey of Consumer Finances.

comparisons, it appears that professional financial planners do help households adopt sound financial planning principles and create more financial wealth.

The conclusion above must be tempered by the recognition that other systematic processes affect the decisions households might make regarding stock equity, portfolio diversification, and ultimately, financial wealth accumulation. For example, individuals who are more highly educated are more likely to understand the importance of asset diversification. Likewise, those who have minor children in the home may find it more challenging to build financial wealth because of the need to spend income on child-related goods and services. To capture the impact of consulting with a professional financial planner while also simultaneously accounting for these other socio-demographic and economic processes that affect a household's financial interests, we utilize multivariate (OLS) regressions (independent variables are defined in Appendix Table 8.A1).

Tables 8.2–8.4 report our multivariate OLS estimates for the three outcomes of interest, for both the full sample and the income-stratified subsamples. Several features of these results relative to the bivariate results are worth noting. Strikingly, the estimated impact of consulting with a professional financial planner declines by more than 50 percent for each of the three outcomes. In the case of the full sample, for example, the estimate of a financial planner's contribution to total financial wealth falls from $138,934 (bivariate) to $66,182 (OLS), controlling for the socio-demographic and

Evaluating the Impact of Financial Planners 167

TABLE 8.A1 Weighted means for ordinary least squares regression covariates

Variable name	Definition	Full sample	<Median income	≥Median income
Age	Age of the household head measured in years (head defined by SCF to be the husband in married couple households)	43.03	41.21	45.04
Education	Head's education measured by years of formal schooling (head defined by SCF to be the husband in married couple households)	13.50	12.63	14.46
Female	Interviews are done with the person in the household who self-identifies as the most knowledgeable about financial matters (1 = female, 0 = male)	0.54	0.58	0.50
Marital status	1 = Household head is currently married, 0 = otherwise	0.61	0.42	0.81
Number of children	Number of minor children in the home	1.01	0.97	1.06
Non-Hispanic Black	1 = Non-Hispanic Black household head, 0 = otherwise	0.14	0.19	0.09
Hispanic	1 = Hispanic household head, 0 = otherwise	0.11	0.14	0.07
Wage income	Annual wage income measured in $10,000s	5.34	2.18	8.83
DC pension plan	1 = Head and/or spouse have a DC pension plan with current employer(s), 0 = otherwise	0.42	0.23	0.62
DB pension plan	1 = Head and/or spouse have a DB pension plan with current employer(s), 0 = otherwise	0.22	0.13	0.32
DC and DB pension plan	1 = Head and spouse have both DC and DB pension plans with current employer(s), 0 = otherwise	0.11	0.03	0.20

Source: Authors' calculations from the 2007 Survey of Consumer Finance.

economic factors hypothesized to affect financial wealth. Correspondingly, the stock equity effect falls from 14 to 6 percent, while the diversification effect falls from 86 to 39 percent.

Comparisons across the income-stratified subsamples also reveal sizable differences in the estimated financial planner effects. In the case of total financial wealth, the estimates indicate that consulting a financial planner appears to boost higher-income households' financial wealth by $76,739, while such consultation has a smaller effect on lower-income households' financial wealth, raising it by $39,488 holding other factors constant. Financial planner consultation appears to have a larger marginal effect on the fraction of wealth held in stock equity for lower-income households (7 percent) compared to higher-income households (4 percent). Likewise,

TABLE 8.2 Ordinary least squares parameter estimates of total financial wealth[a]

Independent variables	Full sample Coefficient	<Median income Coefficient	≥Median income Coefficient
Consults financial planner	66,182.00 (3.88**)	39,488.00 (1.99**)	76,739.00 (3.01**)
Age[b]	6,385.75 (10.53**)	1,927.39 (3.31**)	11,561.00 (9.80**)
Age-squared[b]	243.44 (4.64**)	42.83 (0.90)	359.69 (3.15**)
Education	17,676.00 (5.71**)	6,207.86 (2.12**)	35,708.00 (5.96**)
Female	−39,569.00 (−2.85**)	−10,725.00 (−0.77)	−46,341.00 (−1.95)
Marital Status	−3,468.22 (−0.22)	12,196.00 (0.81)	−28,962.00 (−0.92)
Number of children	5,722.47 (0.91)	1,402.57 (0.24)	6,209.15 (0.54)
Non-Hispanic Black[c]	−39,352.00 (−1.97)	−17,310.00 (−0.99)	−98,753.00 (−2.38**)
Hispanic[c]	−4,305.89 (−0.19)	−11,112.00 (−0.53)	−12,559.00 (−0.28)
Wage income ($10,000s)	190.71 (11.75**)	28.22 (0.60)	172.97 (7.73**)
DC pension plan	−8,600.09 (−0.50)	22,238.00 (1.23)	−10,173.00 (−0.34)
DB pension plan	−60,088.00 (−2.53**)	12,093.00 (0.51)	−96,691.00 (−2.32**)
DC and DB pension plan	12,344.00 (0.37)	−20,118.00 (−0.42)	20,132.00 (0.39)
Adjusted-R^2	0.15	0.02	0.16
F-statistic	39.55**	2.61**	23.24

[a] Regressions use SCF final weights.
[b] Age centered on the mean age of the household heads so as to avoid multicollinearity between age and age-squared (Glantz and Slinker, 1990).
[c] The omitted racial/ethnic category in this sequence of dummy variables is households where the head is non-Black and non-Hispanic.
Notes: t-statistics in parentheses. **$p < 0.05$.
Source: Authors' calculations from the 2007 Survey of Consumer Finances.

the marginal diversification effects are larger for lower-income households (43 percent) than higher-income households (32 percent). Thus, the OLS models provide a more nuanced picture of professional financial planners' impacts compared to the bivariate results. While still statistically significant, the planner effects are more modest for all three outcomes and the effects also vary markedly by income group. These findings illustrate the importance of controlling for other factors

Evaluating the Impact of Financial Planners 169

TABLE 8.3 Ordinary least squares parameter estimates of proportion stock equity[a]

Independent variables	Full sample	<Median income	≥Median income
	Coefficient	Coefficient	Coefficient
Consults financial planner	0.06	0.07	0.04
	(4.69**)	(3.53**)	(2.76**)
Age[b]	0.00	0.00	0.00
	(5.09**)	(4.06**)	(3.19**)
Age-squared[b]	0.00	0.00	0.00
	(−2.53**)	(−0.11)	(−3.17**)
Education	0.02	0.01	0.02
	(6.82**)	(3.44**)	(4.28**)
Female	−0.04	−0.01	−0.06
	(−3.56**)	(−0.82)	(−4.12**)
Marital status	0.00	0.00	−0.03
	(0.06)	(−0.21)	(−1.40)
Number of children	−0.01	−0.01	−0.01
	(−2.64**)	(−2.29**)	(−1.77)
Non-Hispanic Black[c]	−0.07	−0.08	−0.05
	(−5.06**)	(−4.43**)	(−2.03**)
Hispanic[c]	−0.06	−0.06	−0.06
	(−3.30**)	(−2.69**)	(−2.20**)
Wage income ($10,000s)	0.01	0.01	0.00
	(5.90**)	(2.19**)	(3.09**)
DC pension plan	0.19	0.21	0.14
	(15.09**)	(11.71**)	(7.64**)
DB pension plan	0.00	−0.02	−0.01
	(0.17)	(−0.67)	(−0.28)
DC and DB pension plan	0.01	0.09	0.01
	(0.27)	(1.97)	(0.16)
Adjusted-R^2	0.27	0.22	0.14
F-statistic	81.43**	30.15**	20.02**

[a] Regressions use SCF final weights.

[b] Age centered on the mean age of the household heads so as to avoid multicollinearity between age and age-squared (Glantz and Slinker, 1990).

[c] The omitted racial/ethnic category in this sequence of dummy variables is households where the head is non-Black and non-Hispanic.

Notes: t-statistics in parentheses. **$p < 0.05$.

Source: Authors' calculations from the 2007 Survey of Consumer Finances.

that may influence financial outcomes, and also the relevance of focusing on the target population when selecting a sample for empirical work.

As noted above, OLS models do not incorporate a correction for reverse causation. Yet, the possibility exists, for example, that those with more financial wealth may be more motivated to seek professional advice in order to protect that wealth. In our data, statistical tests for reverse

TABLE 8.4 Ordinary least squares parameter estimates of the number of asset categories[a]

Independent variables	Full sample Coefficient	<Median income Coefficient	≥Median income Coefficient
Consults financial planner	0.39	0.43	0.32
	(8.34**)	(6.27**)	(5.26**)
Age[b]	0.02	0.02	0.02
	(12.42**)	(8.81**)	(7.54**)
Age-squared[b]	0.00	0.00	0.00
	(4.44**)	(4.46**)	(3.21**)
Education	0.12	0.09	0.11
	(14.33**)	(9.05**)	(7.86**)
Female	−0.04	0.02	−0.10
	(−1.00)	(0.45)	(−1.79)
Marital status	0.10	0.03	−0.11
	(2.41**)	(0.57)	(−1.51)
Number of children	0.01	0.01	0.02
	(0.34)	(0.35)	(0.58)
Non-Hispanic Black[c]	−0.33	−0.37	−0.12
	(−6.15**)	(−6.20**)	(−1.25)
Hispanic[c]	−0.31	−0.34	−0.28
	(−4.87**)	(−4.68**)	(−2.58**)
Wage income ($10,000s)	0.04	0.07	0.02
	(9.87**)	(4.24**)	(4.53**)
DC pension plan	0.80	0.91	0.53
	(17.26**)	(14.53**)	(7.52**)
DB pension plan	0.16	0.08	0.07
	(2.46**)	(0.93)	(0.65)
DC and DB pension plan	−0.20	−0.06	−0.12
	(−2.25**)	(−0.37)	(−0.95)
Adjusted-R^2	0.42	0.38	0.20
F-statistic	164.92	63.54**	30.84**

[a] Regressions use SCF final weights.
[b] Age centered on the mean age of the household heads so as to avoid multicollinearity between age and age-squared (Glantz and Slinker, 1990).
[c] The omitted racial/ethnic category in this sequence of dummy variables is households where the head is non-Black and non-Hispanic.
Notes: t-statistics in parentheses. **$p < 0.05$.
Source: Authors' calculations from the 2007 Survey of Consumer Finances.

causation (Baum et al., 2003) suggest that it exists.[10] Here we correct for this problem using a propensity score approach because, unlike structural equation modeling, the propensity score approach is not limited by the functional form that is chosen. It is also appealing because individuals in the treated sample who have no counterfactual in the control sample are dropped (Black and Smith, 2004; Gibson-Davis and Foster, 2006).[11]

In what follows, we develop a propensity score that adjusts for the bias caused by reverse causation by creating matches between members of the treatment and control groups rather than through a random assignment process used in true experiments (Rosenbaum and Rubin, 1983, 1984). We first estimate a logistic regression in which the dependent variable indicates whether the respondent consults with a financial planner. Independent variables in this equation include all factors that might affect the decision to meet with a financial planner, as well as those factors that might affect the substantive outcomes of interest (i.e., total financial wealth, proportion in stock equity, and diversification of assets). We use responses to attitudinal questions regarding financial risk, financial luck, spending, and retirement confidence as indicators of factors that affect only the likelihood of meeting with a financial planner. We also include the standard socio-demographic and economic variables described above as factors that could influence both the likelihood of consulting a financial planner and our substantive outcomes of interest. Using the first stage logit estimates (results presented in Appendix Table 8.A2), we generate predicted probabilities of meeting with a financial planner. These then are used to match treatment households to controls.[12]

Figure 8.2 compares the outcome of interest—the estimated incremental effect of consulting a financial planner on total financial wealth—across all three estimation approaches. Here we show that the bivariate model suggests that consultation with a professional financial planner is associated with significantly more financial wealth (for the full sample as well as both the lower- and higher-income subsamples). Adjusted for socio-demographic and economic characteristics, the OLS estimate of the net effect of consulting a professional financial planner is reduced. After using the propensity score adjustment, the impact of the professional financial planner on financial wealth becomes statistically insignificant (for the full and the two subsamples).

Turning to the proportion of total financial wealth held in stocks, Figure 8.3 again shows that simple bivariate comparisons provide the largest estimate of financial planner effects. Controlling for socio-demographic and economic covariates reduces the effect size. And adjusting for simultaneity reduces estimated effects even further (for both the full and the lower-income subsamples). Interestingly, now we see that consultation with a professional financial planner leads to a significantly higher equity proportion for lower-income households, but it has no significant effect for higher-income households.

Finally, Figure 8.4 shows how the estimates differ when the outcome of interest is the number of different financial assets held. Again, in all cases, the bivariate estimates of consulting a professional financial planner are largest, followed by the OLS estimates, and the propensity score estimates

TABLE 8.A2 Logistic regression parameter estimates of the first stage of the propensity score analysis: dependent variable is 'consults a financial planner'

Independent variables	Full sample			<Median income sample			≥Median income sample		
	Coefficient	Odds ratio	95% CI	Coefficient	Odds ratio	95% CI	Coefficient	Odds ratio	95% CI
Head age[a]	−0.02	0.98	0.98–0.99	−0.01	0.99	0.98–1.00	−0.02	0.98	0.97–0.99
Head age-squared[a]	0.00	1.00	1.00–1.00	0.00	1.00	1.00–1.00	0.00	1.00	1.00–1.00
Head education	−0.13	0.88	0.84–0.92	−0.13	0.88	0.81–0.95	−0.11	0.89	0.84–0.95
Female	−0.20	0.82	0.67–0.99	−0.16	0.85	0.60–1.20	−0.24	0.78	0.62–0.99
Marital status	−0.23	0.80	0.64–0.99	−0.13	0.88	0.61–1.27	−0.15	0.86	0.63–1.18
Number of children	0.01	1.01	0.93–1.11	0.07	1.07	0.91–1.26	−0.01	0.99	0.89–1.11
Non-Hispanic Black[b]	0.30	1.35	0.97–1.88	0.00	1.00	0.64–1.56	0.56	1.75	1.04–2.93
Hispanic[b]	0.22	1.25	0.84–1.86	0.06	1.06	0.57–1.97	0.23	1.26	0.74–2.13
Wage income ($10,000s)	−0.01	0.99	0.98–1.01	0.00	1.01	0.93–1.09	0.00	1.00	0.99–1.02
DC pension plan	−0.27	0.77	0.61–0.96	−0.15	0.86	0.56–1.32	−0.28	0.76	0.57–1.01
DB pension plan	−0.30	0.74	0.54–1.01	−0.33	0.72	0.43–1.21	−0.33	0.72	0.48–1.07
DC and DB pension plan	0.14	1.15	0.76–1.74	−0.25	0.78	0.30–2.04	0.24	1.27	0.77–2.09
Takes no financial risks (1 = yes)	1.03	2.81	2.17–3.66	0.78	2.17	1.51–3.13	1.24	3.45	2.30–5.18
Compared to others, lucky in financial affairs (1 = strongly agree or somewhat agree)	−0.33	0.72	0.58–0.89	−0.04	0.96	0.67–1.38	−0.46	0.63	0.48–0.83

When things increase in value, more likely to spend money (1 = strongly disagree or somewhat disagree)	−0.09	0.91	0.76–1.10	−0.39	0.67	0.47–0.96	0.03	1.03	0.82–1.29
Household retirement income will be enough to maintain standard of living, satisfactory, or very satisfactory (1 = yes)	−0.04	0.96	0.80–1.16	−0.35	0.71	0.50–0.99	0.11	1.12	0.89–1.41
In planning saving/spending, most important time horizon is 5+ years (1 = yes)	−0.27	0.76	0.63–0.92	−0.41	0.66	0.47–0.94	−0.16	0.85	0.68–1.07
χ^2	359.39**			89.51**			127.96**		

[a] Age centered on the mean age of the household heads so as to avoid multicollinearity between age and age-squared (Glantz and Slinker, 1990).
[b] The omitted racial/ethnic category in this sequence of dummy variables is households where the head is non-Black and non-Hispanic.
Note. **$p < 0.05$.

Source. Authors' calculations from the 2007 Survey of Consumer Finances.

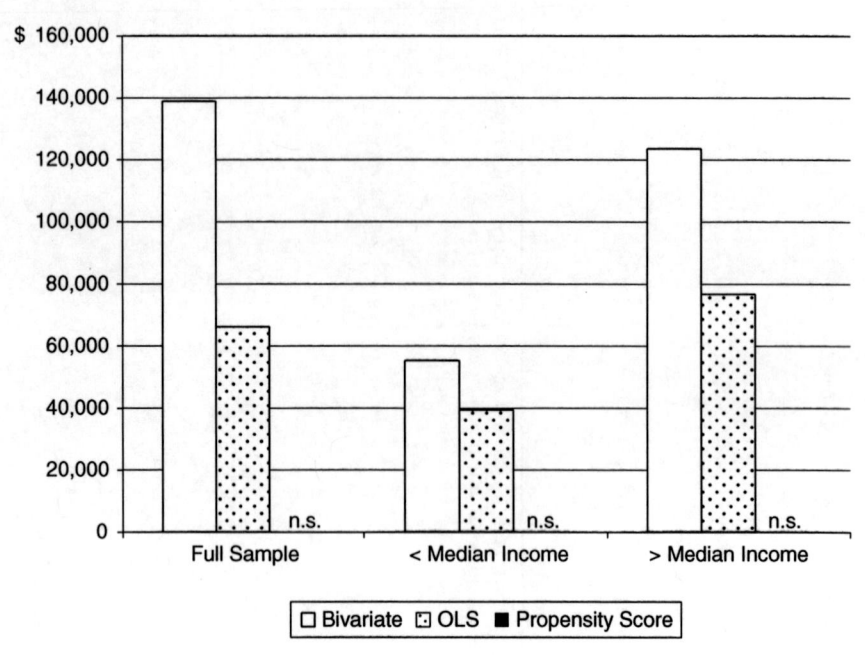

174 The Market for Retirement Financial Advice

Figure 8.2 Estimated incremental effect of consulting a financial planner on total financial wealth

Note: n.s. = not statistically significant at $p < 0.05$.

Source: Authors' calculations from the 2007 Survey of Consumer Finances (Kennickell, 2009).

are smallest. But, unlike the above, now we find that consulting a professional financial planner produces greater diversification.

Conclusion

This chapter describes how different methodologies can alter the estimated impact of financial professionals on advice recipients. We now know with reasonable certainty that simply comparing people who do and do not use professional financial advice paints an overly rosy picture of the benefits of working with a financial planner. More careful research that addresses self-selection, other confounding variables, and reverse causation shows smaller benefits of working with a financial planner. Moreover, the main effect is to enhance account diversification, as shown by our SCF analyses.

Yet knowledge of the impact of professional financial advice remains in its infancy, and future research can profitably proceed in three directions.

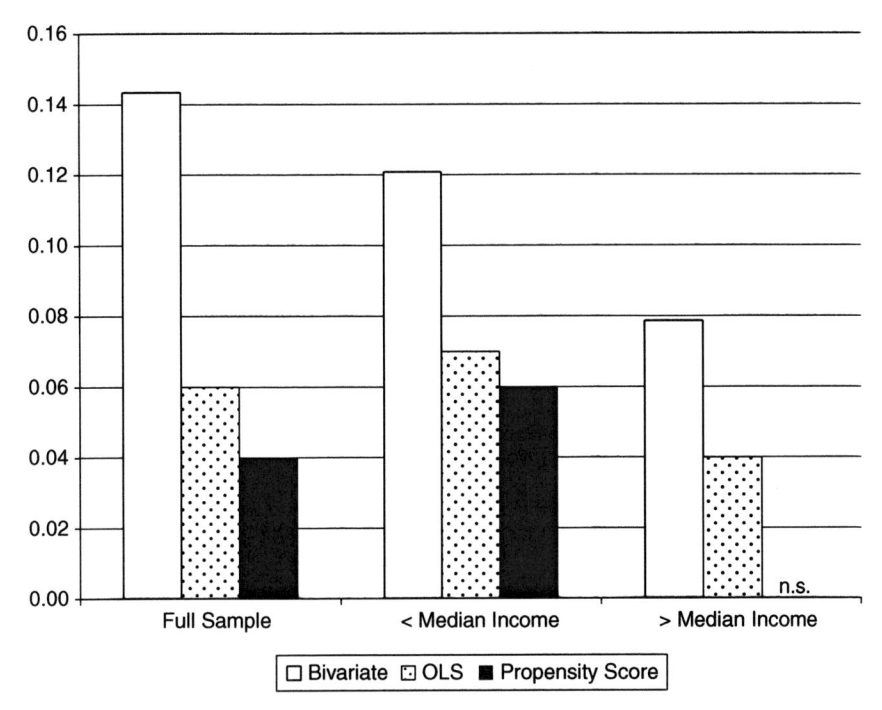

Figure 8.3 Estimated incremental effect of consulting a financial planner on proportion of total financial wealth held in stocks

Note: n.s. = not statistically significant at $p < 0.05$.

Source: Authors' calculations from the 2007 Survey of Consumer Finances (Kennickell, 2009).

First, to date no study has carefully distinguished different types of financial professionals, even though they vary enormously in expertise, access to investment products, and financial incentives. Some studies lump all types of financial planners into a single category, while others examine a single type of advisor employed by a single financial institution. Much remains to be learned about the impact of different types of financial professionals.

Second, structural equations and propensity score approaches are useful steps in learning more about the effects of professional financial advice, but these methods are no substitute for an RFE. Though these are expensive to conduct, RFEs eliminate the possibility of self-selection and reverse causation. Moreover, randomized experiments can recruit people who, under real-world conditions, would rarely elect to consult a financial planner but who might gain the most from professional advice—people with below-average incomes and/or in the early stages of their work life.

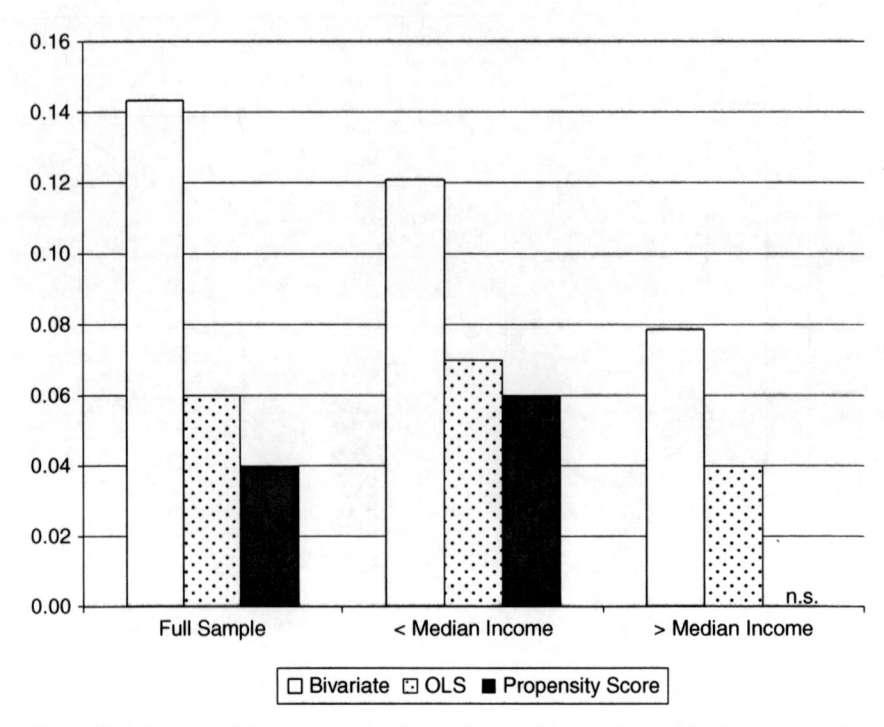

176 The Market for Retirement Financial Advice

Figure 8.4 Estimated incremental effect of consulting a financial planner on the number of different types of financial assets held

Note: n.s. = not statistically significant at $p < 0.05$.

Source: Authors' calculations from the 2007 Survey of Consumer Finances (Kennickell, 2009).

Third, in the future, we need studies of longer duration than those currently available. It is not surprising that the short-term effect of consulting a financial planner is to diversify a person's portfolio or rebalance it toward a particular risk profile. In light of the short-term and often ongoing financial costs of working with a financial professional, some may not find this compelling evidence of the value of professional advice. Results showing that advised investors feel more confident about their financial futures than do-it-yourself investors (as comforting as such findings may be to existing clients) are also unlikely to move people toward employing financial professionals. It would be more useful to demonstrate that working with an advisor or planner boosts long-term rates of return and levels of asset accumulation. Given short-term fluctuations in financial markets, what we need is evidence on account performance over the medium- or long-term, to allow planners and researchers alike to drop the word 'potential' in the phrase: 'potential benefits of professional financial advice.'

Endnotes

1. The growth in investor numbers and options has been fueled, in part, by the dramatic shift from defined benefit (DB) to defined contribution (DC) pension plans over the same time period. In 1985, 38 percent of Americans whose employer provided a pension plan were in a DB plan only, 35 percent were in a combination DB/DC plan, and 29 percent were in a DC 401(k) plan only. By 2008, those percentages had shifted to 7, 26, and 67 percent, respectively (EBRI, 2010: figure 2).
2. The Certified Financial Planning Board lists twenty-three different financial services credential designations (see http://www.cfp.net/learn/knowledge-base.asp?id=15).
3. Throughout this chapter we use the term 'financial outcomes' as a summary term for financial practices and wealth-related results that may be linked to seeking the counsel of a professional financial planner.
4. Once conceptual decisions about advising exposure and key outcomes are made, the next step is to insure that these measures are operationalized in ways that have little random measurement error. That is, the evaluator must insure that the data sources used (e.g., survey questions or administrative records) have minimal measurement error. Such measurement error may be particularly problematic in the case of surveys containing potentially complicated and/or sensitive financial questions. Fortunately, there is a literature that details the best practices for asking financial questions in a way that minimizes measurement reliability concerns (Avery et al., 1988; Juster and Smith, 1997; Kennickell and Starr-McCluer, 1997; Duncan and Petersen, 2001; Hurd et al., 2003).
5. Although the RAND American Life Panel survey is conducted via the Internet, the Panel has special arrangements to facilitate the participation of people with limited Internet access.
6. The influence of random elements can lead to erroneous conclusions in two ways. First, chance variation can lead to the conclusion that a professional financial planner had an impact on a financial outcome when s/he actually did not. The risk of making this error (i.e., Type I error) can be minimized by setting a low alpha level (i.e., <0.05) for statistical significance which will vary by sample size. Second, chance variation can lead to the conclusion that professional finance counsel had no impact on a financial outcome when it actually did (i.e., Type II error). The likelihood of making this second type of error is a function of the size of the sample, the magnitude of the effect size in the population associated with having sought professional financial counsel, and the type of statistical test used. Generally speaking, larger samples, larger effect sizes, and multivariate statistical tests all reduce the likelihood of making this second type of error.
7. In theory, RFEs should have four groups to control for measurement effects. In practice, this is very rarely done.

8. Sample weights are used when presenting descriptive statistics for the 2007 SCF because of the unusual sample design and to correct for systematic refusals to participate in the SCF. The decision to weight multivariate analyses is the subject of some debate in the literature (Lindamood et al., 2007); in the current chapter, no weights were used.
9. Other sets of estimates are available from the authors on request.
10. The test involves estimating the reduced form equation in which financial planner consultation is the dependent variable. The residuals from this equation are then included as an additional regressor in the structural equations estimating each of the three financial outcomes. The resulting Durbin-Wu-Hausman F-statistic generated from this second equation is a measure of endogeneity. For the current application, that F-statistic is 5.88 ($p = 0.02$) for total financial wealth, 15.37 ($p < 0.00$) for stock equity, and 42.85 ($p < 0.00$) for asset diversification, suggesting that there is ample evidence that consulting a financial planner and each of the three outcomes of interest are endogenous.
11. Rosenbaum and Rubin (1983, 1984) proposed the use of the propensity score method to address simultaneity problems by balancing members of a so-called treatment group (i.e., individuals who consult a financial planner) with specific members of a so-called control group (i.e., individuals who have NOT met with a financial planner) with regard to their covariates.
12. Several matching methods have been used in the literature (see Gibson-Davis and Foster, 2006). Given that there is no consensus on the best matching method, we use a radius caliper matching technique that makes use of all members of the control group within a 0.01 radius of the treatment observation. After the matching, t-tests are conducted to ascertain if statistically significant differences exist between the treatments and the controls.

References

Avery, R. B., G. E. Elliehausen, and A. B. Kennickell (1988). 'Measuring Wealth with Survey Data: An Evaluation of the 1983 Survey of Consumer Finances,' *Review of Income and Wealth*, 34(4): 339–69.

Baum, C. F., M. E. Schaffer, and S. Stillman (2003). 'Instrumental Variables and GMM: Estimation and Testing,' *The Stata Journal*, 3(1): 1–31.

Bhattacharya, U., A. Hackethal, S. Kaesler, B. Loos, and S. Meyer (2012). 'Is Unbiased Financial Advice to Retail Investors Sufficient? Answers from a Large Field Study,' *Review of Financial Studies*, 25(4): 975–1032.

Black, D. A., and J. A. Smith (2004). 'How Robust Is the Evidence on the Effects of College Quality? Evidence from Matching,' *Journal of Econometrics*, 121(1–2): 99–124.

Bluethgen, R., A. Gintschel, A. Hackethal, and A. Mueller (2008). 'Financial Advice and Individual Investors' Portfolios.' *Social Science Research Network.* http://papers.ssrn.com/sol3/papers.cfm?abstract_id=968197&download=yes

Certified Financial Planner (CFP) Board of Standards (2009). *What You Should Know About Financial Planning.* Washington, DC: CFP Board of Standards. http://www.cfp.net/Upload/Publications/187.pdf

Charles Schwab (2007). 'Press Release: New Schwab Data Indicates Use of Advice and Professionally-Managed Portfolios Results in Higher Rate of Return for 401(k) Participants,' San Francisco, CA, November 28.

Collins, J. M. (2010). 'A Review of Financial Advice Models and the Take-Up of Financial Advice,' Center for Financial Security Working Paper No. 10-5. Madison, WI: University of Wisconsin-Madison.

Duncan, G. J., and E. Petersen (2001). 'The Long and Short of Asking Questions About Income, Wealth, and Labor Supply,' *Social Science Research*, 30(2): 248.

Employee Benefit Research Institute (EBRI) (2010). *FAQs About Benefits—Retirement Issues.* Washington, DC: EBRI. http://www.ebri.org/publications/benfaq/index.cfm?fa=retfaq14

Federal Reserve System Board of Governors (2009). *Codebook for 2007 Survey of Consumer Finances.* Washington, DC: Federal Reserve System.

FPA/Ameriprise (2008). *Value of Financial Planning Study.* Washington, DC: FPA Press. http://www.ameriprise.com/global/sitelets/fpa/docs/fpa-study-final-report-2008.pdf

Gerhardt, R., and A. Hackethal (2009). 'The Influence of Financial Advisors on Household Portfolios: A Study on Private Investors Switching to Financial Advice,' *Social Science Research Network.* http://ssrn.com/abstract=1343607

Gibson-Davis, C., and E. M. Foster (2006). 'A Cautionary Tale: Using Propensity Scores to Estimate the Effect of Food Stamps on Food Insecurity,' *Social Service Review*, 80(1): 93–126.

Glantz, S. A., and B. K. Slinker (1990). *Primer of Applied Regression and Analysis of Variance.* New York: McGraw-Hill.

Groves, R. M., and M. P. Couper (1998). *Nonresponse in Household Interview Surveys.* New York: John Wiley & Sons, Inc.

Hackethal, A., and R. Inderst (2013). 'How to Make the Market for Financial Advice Work,' in O. S. Mitchell and K. Smetters, eds., *The Market for Retirement Financial Advice.* Oxford, UK: Oxford University Press, pp. 213–28.

Hackethal, A., M. Haliassos, and T. Jappelli (2012). 'Financial Advisors: A Case of Babysitters?' *Journal of Banking and Finance*, 36(2): 509–24.

Hogarth, J. M., C. E. Anguelov, and J. Lee (2004). 'Why Don't Households Have a Checking Account?' *Journal of Consumer Affairs*, 38(1): 1–34.

Horn, L., S. Meyer, and A. Hackethal (2009). 'Smart Investing and the Role of Financial Advice—Evidence from a Natural Experiment Using Data Around a Tax Law Change,' *Social Science Research Network.* http://ssrn.com/abstract=1343623

Hung, A. A., and J. K. Yoong (2013). 'Asking for Help: Survey and Experimental Evidence on Financial Advice and Behavior Change,' in O. S. Mitchell and K. Smetters, eds., *The Market for Retirement Financial Advice.* Oxford, UK: Oxford University Press, pp. 182–212.

Hurd, M., F. T. Juster, and J. P. Smith (2003). 'Enhancing the Quality of Data on Income: Recent Innovations from the HRS,' *Journal of Human Resources*, 38(3): 758–72.

ING Retirement Research Institute (2010). *Help Wanted.* New York: ING Retirement Research Institute. http://ing.us/rri/ing-studies/value-of-advice

Investment Company Institute (ICI) (2011). *2011 Investment Company Fact Book, 51st Edition.* Washington, DC: ICI. http://www.ici.org/pdf/2011_factbook.pdf

Investment Funds Institute of Canada (IFIC) (2010). *The Value of Advice: Report.* Toronto, ON: IFIC. https://www.ific.ca/Content/Document.aspx?id=5906

Jansen, C., R. Fischer, and A. Hackethal (2008). 'The Influence of Financial Advice on the Asset Allocation of Individual Investors,' *Social Science Research Network.* http://ssrn.com/abstract=1102092

Juster, F. T., and J. P. Smith (1997). 'Improving the Quality of Economic Data: Lessons from the HRS and AHEAD,' *Journal of the American Statistical Association*, 92(440): 1268–78.

Kennickell, A. B. (1998). 'Multiple Imputation in the Survey of Consumer Finances,' Federal Reserve Board Working Paper, September. Washington, DC: Federal Reserve Board.

—— (2009). 'Ponds and Streams: Wealth and Income in the U.S., 1989 to 2007,' Finance and Economics Discussion Series Working Paper 2009–13. Washington, DC: Federal Reserve Board.

—— (2011). 'Looking Again: Editing and Imputation of SCF Panel Data,' Federal Reserve Board Working Paper, August. Washington, DC: Federal Reserve Board.

—— M. Starr-McCluer (1997). 'Retrospective Reporting of Household Wealth: Evidence from the 1983–1989 Survey of Consumer Finances,' *Journal of Business and Economic Statistics*, 15(4): 452–63.

Kramer, M. (2012). 'Investment Advice and Individual Investor Portfolio Performance,' *Financial Management*, 41(2): 395–428.

Langbein, L., and C. L. Felbinger (2006). *Public Program Evaluation: A Statistical Guide*, New York: M.E. Sharpe.

Lindamood, S., S. D. Hanna, and L. A. N. Bi (2007). 'Using the Survey of Consumer Finances: Some Methodological Considerations and Issues,' *Journal of Consumer Affairs*, 41(2): 195–222.

Luhby, T. (2011). 'Who are the 1 Percent?' *CNN Money*. October 29.

Marsden, M., C. D. Zick, and R. N. Mayer (2011). 'The Value of Seeking Financial Advice,' *Journal of Family and Economic Issues*, 32(4): 625–43.

Riphahn, R. T., and O. Serfling (2003). 'Heterogeneity in Item Non-response on Income and Wealth Questions,' *Schmollers Jahrbuch: Zeitschrift fur Wirtschafts- und Sozialwissenschaften/Journal of Applied Social Science Studies*, 123(1): 95–107.

—— —— (2005). 'Item Non-response on Income and Wealth Questions,' *Empirical Economics*, 30(2): 521–38.

Rosenbaum, P. R., and D. B. Rubin (1983). 'The Central Role of the Propensity Score in Observational Studies for Causal Effects,' *Biometrika*, 70(1): 41–55.

—— —— (1984). 'Reducing Bias in Observational Studies Using Subclassification on the Propensity Score,' *Journal of the American Statistical Association*, 79(387): 516–24.

Scheaffer, R. L., W. Mendenhall III, R. L. Ott, and K. G. Gerow (2012). *Elementary Survey Sampling, Seventh Edition.* Boston, MA: Brooks/Cole.

SunAmerica Financial Group (2011). *The SunAmerica Retirement Re-Set Study.* Los Angeles, CA: SunAmerica Financial Group. http://retirementreset.com/

Turner, J. A., and D. M. Muir (2013). 'The Market for Financial Advisers,' in O. S. Mitchell and K. Smetters, eds., *The Market for Retirement Financial Advice.* Oxford, UK: Oxford University Press, pp. 13–45.

Twigg, M. (2011). *The Future of Retirement: Why Family Matters.* London, UK: HSBC. http://www.hsbc.com/1/PA_esf-ca-app-content/content/assets/retirement/111024_for6_family_pages.pdf

Chapter 9

Asking for Help: Survey and Experimental Evidence on Financial Advice and Behavior Change

Angela A. Hung and Joanne K. Yoong

As US policymakers focus on the difficult problem of increasing access to unbiased financial advice in the context of self-directed retirement plans, a key question is whether implementing potentially costly reforms and regulations is likely to bring about the desired changes in behavior. This chapter addresses two research questions: do individuals actually improve their financial behavior in response to advice? And, if policymakers could enhance the availability of neutral financial advice, would participants actually seek and implement the advice given?

We present two complementary observational and experimental analyses of investors and advice, relevant to 401(k) plans. In observational analyses, we observe actual investment outcomes from real planholders, but our inferences about the effect of advice are limited by two problems—self-selection into advice, and reverse causality—that are not mutually exclusive. In experimental analyses, we are restricted to hypothetical investment choices, but we can eliminate both selection and reverse causality. By comparing and contrasting our results, we are able to draw on implications from both approaches.

For policymakers, our lessons about advice are mixed. One key implication is that having employers offer advice as an elective and ensuring employees' active decision-making are likely to result in significant take-up and some improvement of financial outcomes. Moreover, employees with low financial literacy are more likely to take advantage of these programs. Yet going further, to make the provision of advisory services mandatory for every employee, may be extremely costly and achieve little behavioral change. Furthermore, in some situations, policymakers have recommended compulsory financial counseling as a remedy; our results suggest this may not work unless recipients are prepared to take the advice. In general, motivation is extremely challenging.

Background

Interactions between individual investors and financial advisors have changed considerably over the last few decades, as financial service providers have expanded their range of services and individuals have taken on greater responsibility for their own financial well-being. At year-end 2011, Americans held an estimated $9.4 trillion in employer-sponsored defined contribution (DC) plans and Individual Retirement Accounts (IRAs) (ICI, 2012). Yet research in behavioral finance suggests that when left to their own devices, investors often fail to make optimal investment decisions in their DC plans. Instead, they tend to use heuristics or simple decision rules to make their initial allocation decisions (Samuelson and Zeckhauser, 1988; Benartzi and Thaler, 2001; ICI, 2001; Hewitt Associates, 2004; Agnew and Szykman, 2005). Investing 'mistakes' and simple rules of thumb can have significant welfare implications, given that households may not invest according to optimal portfolio choice theory (Dominitz and Hung, 2008).[1] Some of these 'mistakes' may be attributed to individuals' lack of financial management skills: Lusardi and Mitchell (2006, 2007) argue that investing is a complex undertaking that requires consumers to gather, process, and project data on compound interest, risk diversification, and inflation, as well as to accumulate knowledge of the asset universe. Their findings suggest that most of the US population is not sufficiently financially literate to cope with the shifting burden of post-retirement planning to the individual.

In theory, financial advisors could ameliorate the negative consequences of differential financial literacy, improving returns and ensuring greater risk diversification among less sophisticated households (Hackethal et al., 2012; Hackethal and Inderst, 2013). Indeed, using advisors allows households to benefit from economies of scale in portfolio management and information acquisition, because advisors can spread these costs among their clients. But consumer advocates argue that investors who are unprepared to make sound decisions may also be most vulnerable to bad advice from affiliates of broker-dealers or investment companies who benefit from advising them to buy unsuitable products (Hung et al., 2008). Also, people who consult advisors but do not follow through might not benefit from good advice, as their knowledge may not translate into actual behavioral change.

Much attention has been paid to the pitfalls of bad investment advice. The theoretical and empirical economics research literature on investment advice has largely been concerned with moral hazard problems inherent in the advisor–advisee relationship (see, e.g., Liu, 2005; Inderst and Ottaviani, 2009; Yoong and Hung, 2009; Hackethal et al., 2012; Turner and Muir, 2013). Similarly, regulatory and legislative debate related to self-directed pension plans in the United States has focused on how best to mitigate the risk of exposing unsophisticated plan participants to manipulation while still allowing access to advice. The Pension Protection Act (PPA) of 2006 facilitated provision by granting exemptions to DC plan providers under level-fee compensation arrangements or for advice given by an unbiased computer model.

Nevertheless, and perhaps surprisingly, relatively little information exists about whether good investment advice actually works. Although regulators and legislators are deeply engaged in efforts to make financial advice more accessible to the everyday investor in a neutral setting, the practical benefit in terms of behavior change of achieving such a policy goal should not be regarded as a foregone conclusion. Indeed, there is remarkably little empirical evidence about individual responsiveness to financial advice outside an environment with moral hazard.

A long-standing literature on general advice-taking and receiving is rooted in psychology and organizational behavior. Findings on the propensity to seek advice are mixed and highly context dependent: studies find results that vary from resistance to advice-seeking, even if it is free (Gibbons, 2003), or nearly universal advice-seeking (Gino, 2008). Uncertainty about decisions, however, is found to predict advice-seeking (Gibbons et al., 2003). Although it is difficult to draw conclusions about when individuals seek advice, the research literature strongly suggests that people who do solicit advice are more likely to follow that advice, compared to those who receive unsolicited advice (Gibbons et al., 2003). Indeed, a robust finding is that individuals who receive advice by default tend to significantly discount it (Yaniv and Kleinberger, 2000; Yaniv, 2004a, 2004b; Bonaccio and Dalal, 2006). While explicitly solicited advice is perceived as helpful, unsolicited advice or imposed support is perceived as intrusive and can even lead to negative responses (Goldsmith and Fitch, 1997; Goldsmith, 2000; Deelstra et al., 2003). In a similar vein, Gino (2008) shows that individuals are significantly more receptive to advice they pay for, rather than advice they get for free.

Few empirical analyses specifically address the context of investment advice, particularly in a representative population. Much of the psychology-based evidence has been gathered in a laboratory using tasks unrelated to investment management. Moreover, it is difficult to extrapolate from the experimental laboratory-based literature on financial incentives, as the results are mixed: Sniezek and Van Swol (2001) and Sniezek et al. (2004) find that financial incentives decrease advice discounting, but, by contrast, Dalal (2001) finds the opposite. In the economics literature, evidence suggests that although investors often say they desire more advice, it is unclear how and when they implement the advice given (Helman et al., 2007). Furthermore, since investors actively choose whether to seek advice, correlations between actual behavior and advice may be the result of self-selection: people particularly prone to certain types of investing behavior may also be more likely to seek out advisors. Hackethal et al. (2012) find that self-selection largely explains better outcomes for advisees in the context of German internet brokerage accounts, and they suggest a theory of 'babysitters,' in which wealthy individuals outsource their financial management to others. Yet those online brokerage clients are likely to represent a population with experience and objectives that differ from the average US DC planholder. Kramer (2012) also finds that portfolio allocations of Dutch investors vary with advice, but performance does not. While some behavior in 401(k) plans such as trading activity has been found to be correlated with advice (Agnew, 2006), a causal relationship has not yet been well established.

Study setting

The primary data collection instrument for our investment behavior analyses was a survey administered to 2,224 members of the RAND American Life Panel (ALP).[2] Our behavior survey was administered as wave MS73 of the ALP between May 5, 2009, and June 22, 2009. For a subset of 1,467 individuals, we can match our behavior survey to a previous module on financial literacy used to compute an index of measured financial literacy as well as an index of self-assessed financial literacy. The first index is computed from respondents' answers to questions related to basic numeracy skills and knowledge of investments, retirement plans, and insurance, while the second is based on respondents' own judgments about their abilities. Details of the construction of the indexes can be found in Hung et al. (2009).

Individuals from our panel who reported being enrolled in a current employer's DC plan were asked whether they had consulted a financial advisor for individual recommendations regarding their DC plan. Table 9.1 shows the descriptive statistics of sample size and weighted demographic composition for this group of 618 individuals.

The propensity to seek advice

In 2008, 18 percent[3] of employees in our sample with DC plans consulted an advisor. The breakdown by demographic composition shows that proportionally, more women and minorities consulted an advisor in 2008 regarding their DC plan. Older, more educated and wealthier individuals were also more likely to have consulted an advisor. We estimate a linear probability (LP) model with reported advice-seeking in 2008 as the binary outcome variable. In the LP model, the coefficients may be interpreted as the best linear predictors (BLP) of changes in the probability of the outcome associated with a unit change of each regressor.[4] Column 1 of

TABLE 9.1 Summary statistics: American Life Panel (ALP) data

	Number of responses
Total ALP sample	2,224
Retired	498
Self-employed	185
Unemployed	287
Employer offers no retirement plan	293
Employer offers no DC plan or unknown	209
Employee is ineligible for plan	43
Employee is eligible but not enrolled	86
Missing/inconsistent status	5
Final sample: currently enrolled in DC	618

	Weighted %
Female	48.7
College degree	45.7
Married	65.4
Age ≤45	41.2
Annual family income (AFI) <$50,000	23.1
Black or Hispanic	18.7

Note: The sample consists of respondents to our ALP module who are current participants in DC plans (see text).

Source: Authors' computations; see text.

Table 9.2 shows that while the regression coefficients mirror the pattern observed in the summary statistics, among the various demographic characteristics, there are few statistically significant individual predictors of actual reported advice-seeking in 2008 apart from marital status.

The relationship between advice and reported DC plan behavior

Most DC planholders continued actively making contributions to their plans in 2008, and slightly more than half of plan assets were held in stock. But a large fraction of respondent portfolios featured at least one common investment mistake. Although respondents report that they most value advice for investing purposes, use of an advisor was not strongly related to investment portfolio quality.

When asked about the value of advice in a DC plan setting, most respondents (57 percent) placed the highest value on advice related to asset allocation. About one-third considered setting overall contribution goals most valuable, while only about one-quarter placed similar value on advice related to future planning such as tax and estate planning or decumulation.

Asking for Help 187

TABLE 9.2 Ordinary least squares estimates of the determinants of the propensity to seek advice

	(1)	(2)	(3)	(4)
Married	0.087**	0.036	0.035	0.071*
	(0.044)	(0.050)	(0.048)	(0.042)
Female	0.062	0.067	0.064	0.066
	(0.044)	(0.051)	(0.050)	(0.043)
Age <40	−0.020	0.059	0.059	−0.004
	(0.044)	(0.056)	(0.056)	(0.042)
AFI <$50,000	−0.039	−0.027	−0.029	−0.024
	(0.051)	(0.065)	(0.068)	(0.050)
Black or Hispanic	0.073	−0.014	−0.015	0.064
	(0.079)	(0.077)	(0.077)	(0.076)
College degree	0.024	0.012	0.015	0.012
	(0.043)	(0.051)	(0.047)	(0.043)
Measured financial literacy		−0.003		
		(0.034)		
Self-assessed financial literacy			−0.008	
			(0.033)	
Net plan losses (2008)				0.132**
				(0.055)
Constant	0.085*	0.108*	0.130	
	(0.048)	(0.056)	(0.113)	
N	590	450	450	590
R^2	0.02	0.01	0.01	0.04

Note: Standard errors are in parentheses. Statistical significance of differences are within the two categories, where * indicates significant at the 10 percent level, ** is significant at 5 percent, and *** is significant at 1 percent. See Table 9.1.

Source: Authors' calculations using the American Life Panel 2009; see text.

This suggests that many respondents look to advisors for specific tasks related to investment management, rather than larger retirement plan management issues. We therefore focus primarily on asset allocations throughout this work and also describe contributions behavior briefly below.

Table 9.3 shows that on average, 55 percent of DC plan assets are held in stock, 20 percent in bonds, and 20 percent in money market funds, with the remaining 4 percent in other assets. Women, Blacks, and Hispanics hold less stock, as do the less educated, older, and less wealthy respondents. Following Mottola and Utkus (2009), we diagnose portfolio 'mistakes' based on commonly accepted principles of investment. These 'mistakes' are defined as follows: (*a*) holding a zero balance in equities, (*b*) holding an equity balance of less than 40 percent (overly conservative), (*c*) holding more than 95 percent equity (overly aggressive), and (*d*) holding a portfolio that is 100 percent in a single asset class (under-diversified). More than half (56 percent) of respondents' portfolios are characterized by these

TABLE 9.3 Portfolio allocation patterns of current defined contribution (DC) planholders

	Panel A. Portfolio characteristics				
	Stocks (%)	Bonds (%)	Money market (%)	Other (%)	N
Male	60.0	18.0	19.1	2.9	503
Female	49.9	24.1	21.8	4.2	503
No college degree	52.3	21.4	22.8	3.5	503
College degree	58.5	20.4	17.6	3.6	503
Age <45	59.1	19.6	17.8	3.4	503
Age ≥45	52.4	21.8	22.2	3.6	503
AFI <$50,000	48.5	19.2	28.1	4.1	503
AFI ≥$50,000	56.8	21.3	18.5	3.4	503
Black or Hispanic	52.0	16.8	28.2	3.0	503
Total	55.2	20.9	20.4	3.5	503
No advisor	55.5	20.4	20.4	3.7	478
Advisor	52.5	24.0	20.0	2.6	478

	Panel B. 'Mistakes' in reported portfolio allocations				
	Zero equity (%)	Under diversified (%)	Too aggressive (%)	Too conservative (%)	N
Male	6.4	25.6	22.9	26.2	503
Female	12.4	30.1	20.7	42.2	503
No college degree	11.4	34.0	24.8	40.1	503
College degree	6.8	20.5	18.4	26.7	503
Age <45	6.5	26.5	22.9	31.3	503
Age ≥45	11.3	28.6	21.1	35.7	503
AFI <$50,000	13.1	27.7	17.5	40.9	503
AFI ≥$50,000	8.3	27.7	22.9	32.1	503
Black or Hispanic	8.2	29.6	25.1	43.0	503
Total	9.3	27.7	21.8	33.9	503
No advisor	9.2	27.3	22.1	33.9	478
Advisor	7.8	23.6	17.1	36.6	478

Note: See Table 9.1.

Source: Authors' computations using the American Life Panel 2009.

'mistakes.' Women tend to be more conservative, holding less equity, and they tend to be less well diversified. Indeed, more than 12 percent of female respondents hold no equity at all. Similarly, older, less wealthy, and less educated individuals hold no stocks, precluding longer-term asset growth. Table 9.3 also shows that individuals who use advisors invest less in stocks and more in bonds, and they also hold fewer assets outside the category of stocks, bonds, and money market funds. They tend not to be very aggressive, and they are less or equally likely to hold zero equities. Also, they are prone to being too conservative.

To examine the magnitude and significance of differences while controlling for potential demographic effects, we use ordinary least squares (OLS) regression to estimate a set of equations of the form:

$$Y_i = \alpha + \beta \text{ advice}_i + X_i'\delta + \epsilon \tag{9.1}$$

using alternative behaviors of interest as the outcome variables Y. In addition to a vector of demographic characteristics, X, we now include an indicator for advice as an explanatory variable. When the behavior of interest is a binary variable, the results are interpreted as an LP model, as before.

The multivariate regression (Table 9.4) yields results very similar to the trends in the summary tables, consistent with the finding that these demographic characteristics do not generally predict actual reported advice-seeking in 2008. Advice is not statistically significantly predictive of allocation levels or investment 'mistakes' within portfolios.

Contributions behavior also shows a mixed relationship to advice. In this sample, 88 percent of respondents eligible to contribute to their DC plan in 2007 and 2008 reported making a contribution and the average percentage contribution is above 7 percent, although this average is skewed by a small number of extremely high reported percentages. The median and modal value of the distribution is 5 percent. Twenty-two percent of respondents reported increasing their contributions since 2007, and 80 percent of those who were offered an employer match met the match amount. On the other hand, 9 percent reported either decreasing or stopping contributions in 2008, and 9.6 percent took an early withdrawal.[5] Both simple tabulations of the data and similar multivariate regression analysis reveal that individuals with advisors were somewhat more likely to make contributions in 2007 and 2008, and to meet their employer match. However, the data also show that those who received advice were more likely to have reduced their 2008 contribution relative to 2007.[6]

Does self-selection on financial literacy explain the advice–behavior relationship?

Researchers have argued that financial literacy is a key unobservable characteristic that often complicates analyses of advice, and vice versa. Theoretical arguments about the relationship between advice and behavior go in both directions. If financial literacy substitutes for advice and the least financially literate are more likely to take up advice, differences in observed behavior may understate the positive impact of advice. Conversely, if the

TABLE 9.4 Ordinary least squares parameter estimates

Panel A. Empirical determinants of portfolio allocations by DC planholders

	(1) Stocks	(2) Bonds	(3) Money market	(4) Other
Consulted advisor in 2008	−2.226	4.233	−0.772	−1.234
	(5.424)	(3.311)	(3.840)	(1.190)
Married	3.065	−4.002	1.211	−0.274
	(5.469)	(3.871)	(4.839)	(1.461)
Female	−6.666	4.352	1.387	0.927
	(4.572)	(2.860)	(3.638)	(1.341)
Age <45	6.027	−1.365	−4.697	0.035
	(4.107)	(2.554)	(3.193)	(1.279)
AFI <$50,000	−2.846	−3.752	6.939	−0.340
	(5.437)	(3.610)	(5.080)	(1.703)
Black or Hispanic	−4.578	−6.041	10.673**	−0.055
	(6.070)	(3.739)	(5.364)	(2.028)
College degree	7.021*	−1.205	−5.999*	0.183
	(4.201)	(2.842)	(3.569)	(1.393)
Constant	51.766***	23.732***	21.045***	3.456*
	(7.254)	(5.134)	(6.423)	(1.852)
N	478	478	478	478
R^2	0.05	0.03	0.05	0.00

Panel B. 'Mistakes' in reported portfolio allocations

	(1) Zero equity	(2) Under-diversified	(3) Too aggressive	(4) Too conservative
Consulted advisor in 2008	−0.012	−0.041	−0.057	0.007
	(0.037)	(0.071)	(0.072)	(0.079)
Married	−0.015	0.030	0.038	−0.038
	(0.051)	(0.074)	(0.069)	(0.072)
Female	0.041	0.075	0.023	0.136**
	(0.037)	(0.062)	(0.061)	(0.061)
Age <45	−0.049	−0.010	0.025	−0.029
	(0.031)	(0.055)	(0.054)	(0.059)
AFI <$50,000	0.021	−0.005	−0.028	0.011
	(0.056)	(0.073)	(0.064)	(0.078)
Black or Hispanic	−0.051	−0.036	0.022	0.129
	(0.045)	(0.081)	(0.081)	(0.099)
College degree	−0.027	−0.101*	−0.047	−0.165***
	(0.036)	(0.058)	(0.055)	(0.058)
Constant	0.120*	0.277***	0.200**	0.373***
	(0.063)	(0.103)	(0.100)	(0.084)
N	478	478	478	478
R^2	0.02	0.02	0.01	0.06

Note: See Table 9.2.

Source: Authors' computations, using the American Life Panel 2009.

most financially literate are more likely to take up advice, as proposed by Hackethal et al. (2012), differences in observed behavior may overstate this impact. Controlling for selection on observables using only formal education and experience as proxy variables for financial literacy may not adequately resolve this problem, as Dominitz et al. (2008) show that financial literacy has strong effects independent of both. Hackethal et al. (2012) go further by using an instrumental variables strategy to overcome this issue. In our study, we use measures of financial literacy to explicitly control for selection of this type, which is a major advantage. Our results suggest that self-selection on financial literacy plays no significant role.

To illustrate this, we first re-estimate the LP model from Table 9.2, but now we add financial literacy as an additional regressor (albeit on the smaller sample for which the financial literacy measure is available). Results in Table 9.5 provide no evidence of positive selection on financial literacy. Although having lower financial literacy is somewhat related to advice-seeking, the estimated relationship is very small and not significantly predictive. This is true of both measured financial literacy and self-assessed financial literacy. Further non-parametric analysis using a Lowess curve smoother shows a somewhat negative relationship between measured financial literacy and advice-seeking but the result is highly skewed by a few outliers; there is no discernible trend in the relationship between self-assessed financial literacy and advice-seeking. Consistent with this, re-estimating Equation (9.1) while controlling for financial literacy[7] in the regressions of behavioral outcomes on advice has little effect on the estimated coefficients, be they reported allocations or investment mistakes. Again, this result is robust to the use of both measured financial literacy and self-assessed financial literacy.

Discussion: potential reverse causality and selection on other unobservables

Our results show that although individuals believe that advice is important for investing, there appears to be no systematic, statistically significant relationship between advice and observed investment behavior. Moreover, individuals who consulted advisors were more likely to have reduced their contribution levels and were also more likely to continue making contributions. This apparently contradictory pattern of behavior suggests the presence of reverse causality: individuals who experienced unusual stress and negative plan performance may have turned to advisors.

To explore this possibility, we also examined year-end plan balances in 2008 as well as net changes in plan balances between 2007 and 2008. Our

TABLE 9.5 Portfolio allocations and financial literacy: ordinary least squares estimates for current DC planholders

Panel A. Reported portfolio allocations and financial literacy (current DC planholders)

	(1) Stocks	(2) Bonds	(3) Money market	(4) Other
Demographic controls only				
Consulted advisor in 2008	0.692	2.285	−2.519	−0.016
	(6.948)	(4.125)	(4.808)	(0.045)
Financial literacy controls:				
Specification I:				
Consulted advisor in 2008	0.639	2.285	−2.463	0.639
	(6.938)	(4.122)	(4.790)	(6.938)
Measured financial literacy	−1.313	0.004	1.379	−1.313
	(3.773)	(2.486)	(3.531)	(3.773)
Specification II:				
Consulted advisor in 2008	0.756	2.299	−2.567	−0.017
	(6.920)	(4.096)	(4.797)	(0.045)
Self-assessed financial literacy	1.086	0.245	−0.807	−0.010
	(3.365)	(2.008)	(2.487)	(0.025)

Panel B. 'Mistakes' in reported portfolio allocations and financial literacy

	(1) Zero equity	(2) Under-diversified	(3) Too aggressive	(4) Too conservative
Demographic controls only				
Consulted advisor in 2008	−0.016	−0.025	−0.024	−0.027
	(0.045)	(0.088)	(0.090)	(0.094)
Financial literacy controls:				
Specification I:				
Consulted advisor in 2008	−0.015	−0.027	−0.028	−0.028
	(0.045)	(0.088)	(0.089)	(0.094)
Measured financial literacy	0.039	−0.055	−0.103**	−0.024
	(0.037)	(0.053)	(0.046)	(0.050)
Specification II:				
Consulted advisor in 2008	−0.017	−0.027	−0.026	−0.029
	(0.045)	(0.086)	(0.088)	(0.094)
Self-assessed financial literacy	−0.010	−0.046	−0.035	−0.033
	(0.025)	(0.045)	(0.046)	(0.041)
N	360	360	360	360

Note: Other demographic controls are also included but estimates not shown. See also Table 9.2.
Source: Authors' calculations from the American Life Panel 2009.

Asking for Help

results (not detailed here) show that, indeed, individuals who experienced net plan losses were more likely to consult advisors, but that even accounting for financial literacy and income levels, consulting an advisor in 2008 had a marginally significant and positive effect on overall plan balances (and the point estimate is sizable). This reinforces the possibility that seeking advice may actually ultimately help in preserving wealth, but negative events tend to influence advice-seeking (rather than vice versa).

Another complication in establishing causality between advice and behavior is the possibility of selection on a wide variety of unobservable factors other than financial literacy. ALP respondents report diverse reasons for not consulting an advisor (individuals were allowed to indicate only one response). Thirty-seven percent of individuals felt they could make their own decisions (in other words, saw themselves as financially literate enough to forego advice), while 39 percent also cited the availability of various substitutes for professional advice, either from friends or family or other sources such as the Internet. A significant minority (one-quarter) did not do so because of financial constraints. This heterogeneity is consistent with our previous results, in which financial literacy (or the lack thereof) is correlated with advice-seeking but not an overwhelmingly dominant explanatory factor.

Experimental evidence on advice and behavior

In the case of survey data, it is not possible for us to rule out either reverse causality or selection on unobservables.[8] Without a plausibly exogenous and predictive source of variation in advice-seeking and given the issues described above, we cannot cleanly identify the causal impact of receiving advice on behavior. We therefore turn to an experimental analysis of advice and behavior. Given the focus on investment advice uncovered in the survey data, our experiment was designed to test the effect of receiving investment advice on portfolio allocation. While we are restricted to an analysis of hypothetical outcomes, we do have two key advantages: the advice provided is uniform, and reverse causality cannot arise. We designed a multi-stage randomized experiment in which participants were presented with a hypothetical portfolio allocation task. Participants were presented with six investment options: a money market fund, a bond market index fund, an S&P 500 index fund, a small cap value index fund, a REIT index fund, and a global equity index fund. Participants received basic information on the funds, namely fees and returns, and were then allocated a hypothetical portfolio among the funds.

Choice treatment: defaults and affirmative decisions

Participants were randomly assigned to either a control group or one of two experimental conditions. In all conditions, participants were informed that they would be asked to allocate an investment portfolio. The control group received no further information or support before performing the task. In one treatment, which we termed the *default treatment*, all participants received advice regarding optimal portfolio allocation. In the other treatment, the *affirmative decision treatment*, participants were given a choice and received advice only if they asked for it. These experiments were designed to allow us to study the effects of solicited versus unsolicited advice as well as self-selection into advice.

Financial environment treatment: low/high past returns

Previous research has shown that individual investor responses are very sensitive to reported past performance (Sirri and Tufano, 1998; Zheng, 1999). To see whether advice can mitigate this sensitivity, we varied the historical returns shown in the portfolio allocation task. For a randomly selected half of all respondents (the *low-returns treatment*), we presented returns for the various asset classes representative of typical fund performance over the last year, while in the other half (the *high-returns treatment*), we presented returns representative of performance over the last five years, which were significantly less negative.

Advice presentation

We presented advice about normatively desirable investing rules first proposed by Mottola and Utkus (2009). These rules are based on commonly accepted principles of investment as follows: (*a*) a zero balance in equities is not recommended, (*b*) an equity balance of less than 40 percent is considered overly conservative, (*c*) holding more than 95 percent equity is considered overly aggressive, and (*d*) a portfolio that is 100 percent in a single asset class may be under-diversified. In this analysis, we focus on the general results of advice, rather than the format, although we note that half the participants who received advice (whether by default or by choice) randomly received the *rules treatment*, in which participants were presented with the set of simple investing rules or guidelines in table form. The remaining half was assigned to the *portfolio checkup treatment*. We designed an interactive mechanism that provided feedback to participants after they enter a suggested allocation. A Portfolio Checkup Tool evaluates the allocation and compares it to the set of rules. A 'Green' signal was given if the portfolio did not violate any guidelines, while a 'Yellow' or 'Red' signal was given if the portfolio's allocation went against less or more stringent rules. Figure 9.1 shows samples of the task description for the control group and treatment groups.

Experimental sample and summary statistics

All 2,224 panel members of the ALP, regardless of plan status, were invited to participate in the experiment; 2,070 respondents completed the experiment. Table 9.6 shows the sample after accounting for missing responses, as well as the demographic composition for the final sample. Note that for the experimental analyses, we do not apply population weights to the analyses. Figure 9.2 shows a full schematic representation of the randomized experiment and probability of assignment for each treatment group.[9] For the present analysis, we focus attention on the choice treatments,[10] and a discussion of the other randomized treatments is held for future work. As a check on the randomization, we tabulated the number of individuals and summary statistics for the sample of the choice treatment groups, to identify any remaining differences across groups that need to be acknowledged and accounted for in later analysis. Results suggest that the randomization achieves a reasonable balance across the treatment groups in terms of observables, with two possible exceptions: firstly, a skew toward younger individuals in the 'affirmative decision' treatment versus the 'default' treatment and second, a skew toward DC plan enrollees in the control treatment versus the advice treatments. We therefore include appropriate demographic controls in our multivariate regression analysis.

Who chooses advice? Self-selection and financial literacy

About 65 percent of individuals in the 'affirmative decision' treatment group elected to receive advice. Accordingly, two observations are worth noting: first, not all individuals chose to receive advice and second, individuals did not appear to be randomly choosing to receive advice or not (as 50 percent lies outside the 95 percent confidence interval). The relative demographic composition of those who did solicit advice is quite different from those who did not. In the 'affirmative decision' treatment, there were clear and significant differences along age and wealth—those who chose advice were more likely to be older and wealthier than those who did not. For the subsample with financial literacy data, we also test for differences on financial literacy. Unlike the observational data, however, the bottom panel of Table 9.6 also shows strong evidence of selection on financial literacy. Those who chose advice were significantly less financially literate.

196 The Market for Retirement Financial Advice

In this section, we have some questions for you about possible investments in mutual funds. A mutual fund is a form of investment that pools money from many investors and invests their money in stocks, bonds, and/or other securities.

Suppose you were offered the following selection of mutual funds for investing your money in a retirement savings account(s). Below is a table that provides a brief description of the mutual funds, showing the annual fee charged by each fund and the annual rate of return on each fund over the past 5 years.
Suppose you have six options in which to invest.

Fund Choices	Fees	5 Year Return
Money Market Fund	0.21%	3.28%
Total Bond Market Index Fund	0.20%	4.56%
S&P 500 Index Fund	0.18%	-2.29%
Small Cap Value Index Fund	0.23%	-0.76%
REIT Index Fund	0.21%	0.77%
Global Equity Index Fund	0.72%	-0.24%

On the next screen, we'll ask you what percentage of your money you would like to allocate to each fund. Would you like to get some general advice while making these choices?
○ Yes
○ No

Please indicate the percentage of your portfolio that you would like to hold in each of the following funds.

My Portfolio Choices	%	Fees	5 Year Return
Money Market Fund		0.21%	3.28%
Total Bond Market Index Fund		0.20%	4.56%
S&P 500 Index Fund		0.18%	-2.29%
Small Cap Value Index Fund		0.23%	-0.76%
REIT Index Fund		0.21%	0.77%
Global Equity Index Fund		0.72%	-0.24%
% Total			

General Advice for Investing
1) A zero balance in equities is not recommended.
2) An equity balance of less than 40% is considered overly conservative.
3) Holding more than 95% equity is considered overly aggressive.
4) A portfolio that is 100% in a single asset class may be underdiversified.

When you're satisfied with your final choices click "Next" to move on.

Figure 9.1 Survey questions of ALP modules: Panel A. Screen shot of task description: high returns + affirmative decision advice treatment; Panel B. Screen shot of task: rules treatment; Panel C. Screen shot of task: portfolio checkup treatment

Source: RAND American Life Panel.

Asking for Help 197

Please indicate the percentage of your portfolio that you would like to hold in each of the following funds. Then click the "Evaluate my portfolio allocation" button and we'll then give you some feedback on your choices based on standard financial advice.

My Portfolio Choices	%	Fees	5 Year Return
Money Market Fund	100	0.21%	3.28%
Total Bond Market Index Fund	0	0.20%	4.56%
S&P 500 Index Fund	0	0.18%	-2.29%
Small Cap Value Index Fund	0	0.23%	-0.76%
REIT Index Fund	0	0.21%	0.77%
Global Equity Index Fund	0	0.72%	-0.24%

Based on your choices, the Portfolio Checkup Tool suggests

Portfolio Checkup Tool
You have zero equities in your portfolio - research suggests most people benefit from holding some equity allocation

If you want to change your choices you can update your allocations before submitting your final answer. Click the "Evaluate my portfolio allocation" button to get new feedback from the Portfolio Checkup Tool. When you are finished, click "Next" to move on.

Figure 9.1 Continued

Interestingly, the difference is more statistically significant for self-assessed financial literacy, rather than measured financial literacy.

Table 9.7 reports the determinants of the probability of advice-seeking for the 'affirmative decision' group estimated using the LP model used in Table 9.2. Column 1 includes as regressors the demographic characteristics from the survey data analysis, as well as an indicator for having a DC plan and an indicator for being in the low-returns treatment as these may independently affect the propensity to seek advice. Columns 2 and 3 add the financial literacy measures. Our results show that the age effect on the propensity to seek advice becomes insignificant once we account for financial literacy, but the wealth effect remains significant. This is remarkable, as the advice is free and the incentives for the hypothetical task have no relationship to actual wealth. We also note that financial literacy is strongly significant (regardless of whether measured or self-assessed financial literacy is used) regardless of the other demographic controls. Nevertheless, the relatively low fit indicates that a large amount of the variation in advice-seeking in the experiment is still not explained by observable characteristics, even with the inclusion of the financial literacy measures.

TABLE 9.6 Summary statistics on the ALP experimental sample

	Unweighted %
Married	66.5
Female	57.3
Age <45	31.8
AFI <$50,000	39.2
Black or Hispanic	9.5
College degree	45.2
Currently enrolled in employer DC plan	29.0

	Affirmative decision: chose advice (%)	N	Affirmative decision: chose no advice (%)	N	t-test of equality (p-value)	Default group (unsolicited advice) (%)	N
Married	70.26	548	65.76	295	0.18	65.29	801
Female	59.49	548	54.58	295	0.17	57.80	801
Age <45	30.66	548	40.68	295	0.00***	30.34	801
AFI <$50,000	33.39	548	42.71	295	0.01**	41.32	801
Black or Hispanic	8.94	548	10.17	295	0.56	10.36	801
College degree	45.26	548	43.73	295	0.67	46.82	801
Currently enrolled in employer DC plan	31.39	548	27.46	295	0.24	26.09	801
Measured financial literacy	0.23	406	0.36	178	0.09*	0.24	569
Self-assessed financial literacy	2.64	406	2.99	178	0.00***	2.66	569

Note: See Table 9.2.
Source: Authors' calculations using the American Life Panel 2009. See text.

The impact of advice on behavior

Having established that in the absence of reverse causality and financial constraints, negative self-selection on financial literacy is likely to occur, we next move on to analyze the impact of advice on investment behavior. Our next goals are to (*a*) establish whether advice itself has an effect, (*b*) understand if investors are likely to behave differently toward advice when it is presented as an affirmative choice rather than as a default, and (*c*) gain insight into the relative importance of selection versus the actual impact of advice in observed real-world behavior, where advice is typically a choice variable. These questions are of first-order importance when considering the likely impact of policy alternatives such as making advice more freely available, or instituting compulsory financial counseling.

Asking for Help 199

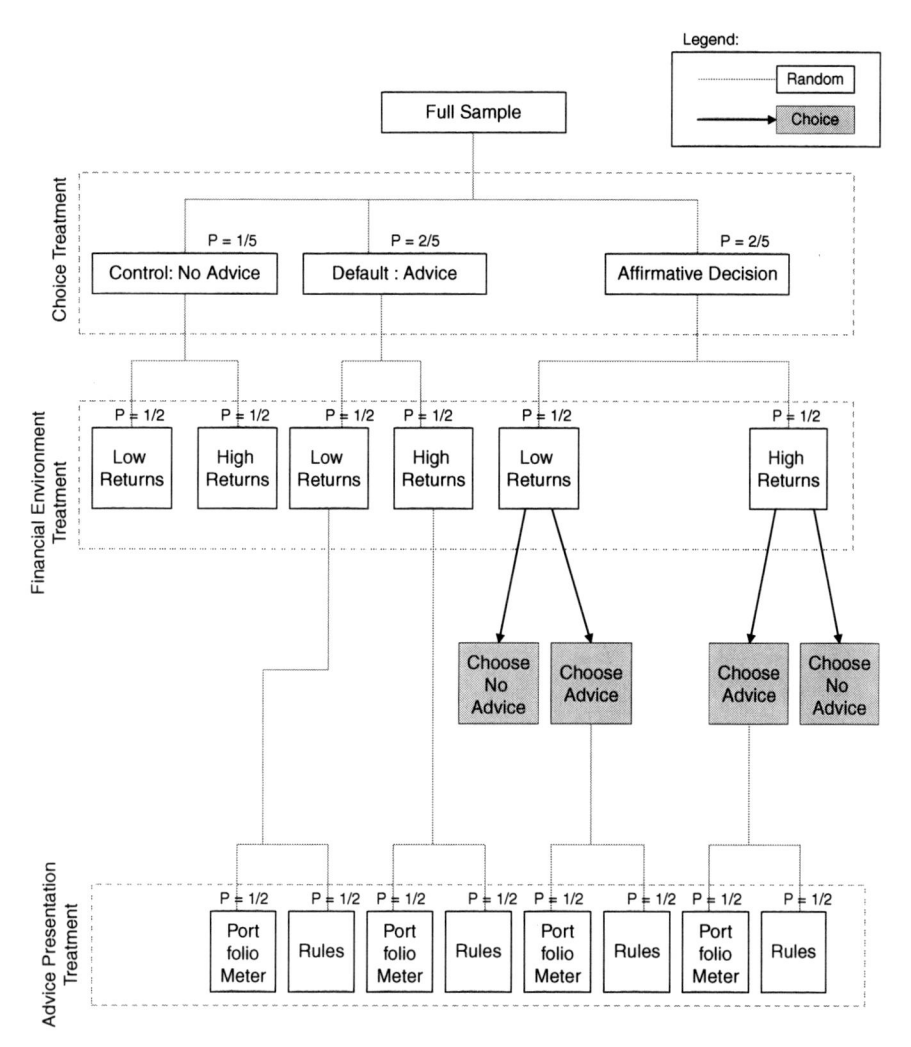

Figure 9.2 Experimental design schematic
Source: Authors' formulation; see text.

The average effect of default versus optional advice on behavior

With the randomized controlled trial design, we obtain unbiased estimates of the effects of a treatment by simply comparing mean outcomes of interest between treatment and control groups. We first describe respondents' portfolio allocations as well as the investment 'mistakes' explicitly addressed by the rules, comparing both the default treatment group

TABLE 9.7 Determinants of the propensity to seek advice: affirmative decision treatment (ordinary least squares estimates)

	(1)	(2)	(3)
Married	0.030	0.008	0.017
	(0.038)	(0.045)	(0.045)
Female	0.065*	0.025	−0.007
	(0.034)	(0.041)	(0.041)
Age <45	−0.104***	−0.031	−0.038
	(0.035)	(0.046)	(0.045)
AFI <$50,000	−0.077**	−0.092*	−0.092**
	(0.039)	(0.047)	(0.046)
Black or Hispanic	0.010	−0.020	−0.016
	(0.058)	(0.071)	(0.071)
College degree	−0.005	−0.057	−0.025
	(0.034)	(0.043)	(0.042)
Has DC plan	0.036	0.054	0.064
	(0.037)	(0.043)	(0.042)
Low-returns treatment	−0.007	0.032	0.029
	(0.033)	(0.038)	(0.038)
Measured financial literacy index		−0.045*	
		(0.027)	
Self-assessed financial literacy index			−0.089***
			(0.022)
Constant	0.650***	0.723***	0.952***
	(0.053)	(0.061)	(0.084)
N	843	584	584
R^2	0.02	0.02	0.05

Note: See Table 9.2.

Source: Authors' calculations using the American Life Panel 2009. See text.

(with unsolicited advice) and the affirmative decision group (where advice is optional), to the control group (with no advice). For each treatment group, we test the hypotheses that the group sample means are equal to the sample mean of the control (i.e., there is zero treatment effect for that group). Note that for the affirmative decision group, the mean includes outcomes for individuals who both chose and did not choose advice. The difference between treatment and control thus reflects the overall effect of being administered the affirmative decision treatment, regardless of the actual choice.

Table 9.8 shows clearly that the mean values of all outcomes for the default group are not significantly different from the control group. Unsolicited advice, it appears, may have no effect on behavior. In the affirmative decision group, on the other hand, we find that respondents are significantly less likely to commit two 'mistakes'—under-diversification and being too conservative. This implies that the affirmative decision

TABLE 9.8 Experimental results: comparisons of means

	Sample means		t-test of equality of means (p-value)		
	Control (no advice %)	Default group (unsolicited advice %)	Affirmative decision group (optional advice %)	Default = control	Affirmative decision = control
% Allocation					
Stocks	25.6	25.2	28.1	0.81	0.12
Bonds	29.9	29.9	29.3	0.97	0.65
Money market	38.2	39.2	37.1	0.54	0.48
Other	5.9	5.7	5.5	0.31	0.17
Mistakes					
Zero equity	37.6	37.1	34.1	0.87	0.22
Under-diversified	13.2	10.4	9.6	0.14	0.06*
Too aggressive	1.4	1.5	1.7	0.90	0.73
Too conservative	65.5	65.3	59.6	0.94	0.04**

	Sample means		t-test of equality of means (p-value)		
	Chose advice (%)	Did not choose advice (%)	Chose advice = did not choose advice	Chose advice = default	Did not choose advice = control
% Allocation					
Stocks	29.5	25.5	0.04**	0.00***	0.96
Bonds	29.8	28.4	0.36	0.96	0.40
Money market	34.5	41.9	0.00***	0.00***	0.11
Other	6.2	4.3	0.00***	0.28	0.00***
Mistakes					
Zero equity	27.6	46.1	0.00***	0.00***	0.02**
Under-diversified	4.4	19.3	0.00***	0.00***	0.02**
Too aggressive	1.1	2.7	0.08	0.53	0.21
Too conservative	56.2	65.8	0.01**	0.00***	0.94

Note: See Table 9.2.
Source: Authors' calculations using the American Life Panel 2009. See text.

treatment has a positive average effect on behavior for the group as a whole.

In light of the slightly differing demographic composition between the treatment groups, we run an OLS regression on the whole sample to estimate the following equation:

$$Y_i = \alpha + \beta_d \text{ default}_i + \beta_a \text{ affirmative}_i + X_i'\delta + \varepsilon, \qquad (9.2)$$

where 'default' and 'affirmative' are now treatment dummies, and we control for the observables vector X. In the terminology of program evaluation, we can think of the default experimental group as being enrolled in a compulsory program of free advice, and the affirmative decision group as a group which is enrolled in a program which simply offers advice for free. The β coefficients give the treatment effects of being exposed to the program, or the *intent-to-treat* estimate (which for mandatory, full-compliance programs similar to the default treatment is the same as the actual program effect).

Table 9.9 shows the results on portfolio quality using the 'mistake' indicators as outcome variables. The default treatment has no significant effect,

TABLE 9.9 Intent-to-treat effects on portfolio quality: all choice treatments (ordinary least squares estimates)

	(1) Zero equity	(2) Under- diversified	(3) Too aggressive	(4) Too conservative
Default treatment	−0.000	−0.026	0.002	−0.002
	(0.029)	(0.018)	(0.007)	(0.028)
Affirmative decision treatment	−0.030	−0.034*	0.002	−0.056**
	(0.028)	(0.018)	(0.007)	(0.028)
Married	−0.012	0.001	−0.003	0.005
	(0.024)	(0.015)	(0.006)	(0.024)
Female	0.072***	−0.002	−0.005	0.100***
	(0.021)	(0.014)	(0.006)	(0.021)
Age <45	−0.044*	0.000	0.014**	−0.096***
	(0.023)	(0.015)	(0.006)	(0.023)
AFI <$50,000	0.062**	0.010	−0.008	0.049**
	(0.024)	(0.016)	(0.006)	(0.024)
Black or Hispanic	−0.064*	−0.012	−0.007	−0.032
	(0.036)	(0.024)	(0.009)	(0.036)
College degree	−0.070***	−0.027*	−0.006	−0.041*
	(0.022)	(0.014)	(0.006)	(0.022)
Has DC plan	−0.058***	0.042***	0.008	−0.102***
	(0.021)	(0.014)	(0.005)	(0.021)
Low-returns treatment	−0.001	0.028*	0.016***	−0.060**
	(0.024)	(0.015)	(0.006)	(0.024)
Constant	0.394***	0.112***	0.012	0.694***
	(0.039)	(0.025)	(0.010)	(0.039)
N	2,070	2,070	2,070	2,070
R^2	0.03	0.01	0.01	0.05

Note: See Table 9.2.
Source: Authors' calculations using the American Life Panel 2009. See text.

while the previously noted affirmative decision treatment effects are robust to the inclusion of the demographic controls as well as controls for DC plan ownership and the low-returns treatment. For the subsample of individuals with financial literacy data, we also re-estimate Equation (9.2) using both measured and self-assessed financial literacy measures. When we control for financial literacy, we find that the overall effects in the affirmative decision are reduced, but there is still a positive and significant effect in reducing over-conservatism. More generally, in line with the message of the advice, we find that individuals who follow advice should allocate a significant part of their portfolio to stocks, but not more than 95 percent. Additional regression analysis shows there is no significant average effect on stockholding in either treatment, although the point estimates are consistently positive for the affirmative decision treatment and negative for the default treatment, whether or not we control for financial literacy.[11]

These results establish that unsolicited advice has no average effect, but that offering advice as a choice may indeed positively affect overall investment behavior. In the default treatment group, we explore the possibility of heterogeneous treatment effects that might justify the provision of advice even when it is not asked for. In the affirmative decision group, we next turn to the estimation of the actual effects of treatment on the treated, and analyze the implications of self-selection on other unobservable characteristics.

Are there heterogeneous treatment effects in the default treatment group?
Although in the default group, we find no strong average effects, it is reasonable to speculate that perhaps there are smaller subgroups of interest that do respond to such unsolicited advice and that may be targeted separately. In particular, policymakers may consider targeting such interventions to groups of individuals that have lower skills. One conclusion from the survey results might well be that, since the less financially literate are not seeking out advice on their own for reasons that may include financial constraints, and may also be prone to making mistakes, giving free advice as a default may help them. Our results show some support for this idea, but the evidence is not strong.

We focus on individuals in the default and control groups and we re-estimate Equation (9.2) with the default treatment dummy interacted with a measure that reflects skill levels (college education, age, or the financial literacy measures). In this specification, a significant coefficient on the interaction term suggests a differential (additive) treatment effect for that group. For this analysis, we characterize individuals who lie below the median value for each financial index as having 'low financial literacy' in order to generate an indicator of low financial literacy. Results show no clear trends: there are statistically significant differential impacts for the young or the less financially literate, although the point estimates suggest that giving out advice has a salutary impact on the less-financially literate respondents across all the portfolio quality metrics. Overall, however, in the default group, there is no overwhelming compelling case for making free counseling compulsory (we note however other studies, such as Hastings and Mitchell (2011), suggest that altering the format of advice can make a difference in low-literacy groups: the interactive portfolio meter treatment can have a greater effect than the non-interactive rules treatment).

Treatment effects vs. selection in the affirmative decision group

Within the affirmative decision group, we find extremely large behavioral differences between those who choose to receive advice and those who do not, implying that both treatment effects and selection are present. Our previous results rule out the most immediately intuitive type of selection, positive selection on financial literacy. Instead, the findings point to self-selection on other unobservables such as motivation or interest. At the same time, in line with the intent-to-treat analysis above, we also find positive average treatment effects on the treated—the advice itself does alter the behavior of the recipients. Yet the magnitude of the actual impact is small relative to the difference due to self-selection on unobservables, which serves as a cautionary note for those evaluating such programs with observational data alone.

Returning to the main results in Table 9.8, we find that recipients and non-recipients in the affirmative decision group differ significantly with respect to portfolio allocation and portfolio quality. On all four quality metrics, advice recipients perform significantly better than non-recipients: they are less likely to hold zero equity, be under-diversified, or rated as too conservative. Recipients are also not simply increasing risk exposure across the board, as they are also less likely to be too aggressive. While advice recipients in the affirmative decision group outperform advice recipients in the default group, those who do not receive advice do worse or no different compared to the control group (who also received no advice). The latter observation implies that some of these differences may be due to self-selection along some dimension that also influences task performance.

One way to explain the better performance by advice recipients might be that individuals who are more financially literate are also more likely to seek advice, but our earlier analysis shows that advice recipients self-select negatively on financial literacy. In the absence of any advice effect, if financial literacy was the primary source of selection, we would expect advice recipients to perform worse, not better, on the task. We therefore re-estimate Equation (9.1) using only the affirmative decision treatment group with a control vector that includes and excludes financial literacy measures. For portfolio quality metrics, we find a large significant association between better performance and advice, which is robust to the vector of regular demographics as well as the inclusion of either measure of financial literacy (Table 9.10).

If we assume that this set of controls resolves the selection problem, our estimates would imply very large effects of advice on behavior. Thus, individuals who choose to receive advice are about 18–25 percent less likely to have zero equities in their portfolios, or to be under-diversified. They are also about 10 percent less likely to be over-conservative, a result which contrasts dramatically to the zero effect of delivering the same advice automatically. However, we cannot rule out selection on other unobservable characteristics. To try to understand how much of this association is likely due to selection effects, we next estimate the average impact of treatment on the treated and compare it to these differences in behavior.

We note that the analysis in the preceding section implies that the advice does indeed have an effect, although it remains to be seen whether this effect can explain the whole observed difference. If advice had no impact

TABLE 9.10 Portfolio quality, advice, and financial literacy: affirmative decision treatment (ordinary least squares estimates)

	(1) Zero equity	(2) Under-diversified	(3) Too aggressive	(4) Too conservative
Demographic controls only				
Chose advice	−0.227***	−0.169***	−0.022**	−0.108**
	(0.041)	(0.025)	(0.010)	(0.043)
Financial literacy added:				
Specification I:				
Chose advice	−0.237***	−0.174***	−0.022**	−0.118***
	(0.041)	(0.025)	(0.011)	(0.043)
Measured financial literacy	−0.089***	−0.047***	0.003	−0.095***
	(0.027)	(0.016)	(0.007)	(0.028)
Specification II:				
Chose advice	−0.262***	−0.182***	−0.020*	−0.139***
	(0.041)	(0.025)	(0.011)	(0.043)
Self-assessed financial	−0.112***	−0.041***	0.006	−0.100***
literacy	(0.022)	(0.013)	(0.006)	(0.023)
N	584	584	584	584

Note: Other demographics from Table 9.9 included but not shown. See Table 9.2.

Source: Authors' calculations using the American Life Panel 2009. See text.

on behavior for anyone in both groups but simply acted as a sorting device, we would expect *on average* behavior in both the (randomly assigned) affirmative decision and control groups to be equal. Yet the significant intent-to-treat effect implies that, on average, the affirmative decision group is either less or equally likely to commit mistakes than the control group.

The intent-to-treat estimate is simply the average effect of treatment for the whole affirmative decision group; it therefore pools together both individuals who received and did not receive advice. We are interested in the average effect of treatment on the treated, or the effect of advice on those who actually took it up. An estimate of the average effect of treatment on the treated is simply the intent-to-treat estimate divided by the actual take-up rate, or, in this case, the average treatment effect for the whole affirmative decision group, divided by the fraction of respondents in the group who chose advice. In a multivariate regression framework, this is equivalent to re-estimating Equation (9.1) using instrumental variables regression on both treatment and controls, where assignment to the treatment group is the instrumental variable.

Results in Table 9.11 (with and without financial literacy) are relatively modest. In this case, an individual who chooses advice is 8–9 percent less

TABLE 9.11 Estimates of the average effect of treatment on those treated on portfolio quality and financial literacy: affirmative decision treatment vs. controls (IV regression: instrument for advice = assignment to affirmative decision treatment)

	(1) Zero equity	(2) Under-diversified	(3) Too aggressive	(4) Too conservative
Demographic controls only				
Chose advice	−0.055	−0.036	−0.002	−0.092*
	(0.047)	(0.029)	(0.012)	(0.048)
Financial literacy added:				
Specification I:				
Chose advice	−0.058	−0.038	−0.002	−0.095**
	(0.047)	(0.029)	(0.012)	(0.047)
Measured financial literacy	−0.099***	−0.049***	−0.003	−0.120***
	(0.022)	(0.014)	(0.006)	(0.022)
Specification II:				
Chose advice	−0.047	−0.033	−0.002	−0.083*
	(0.046)	(0.029)	(0.012)	(0.047)
Self-assessed financial literacy	−0.101***	−0.036***	0.006	−0.105***
	(0.018)	(0.011)	(0.005)	(0.018)
N	897	897	897	897

Note: Other demographics in Table 9.9 included but not shown. See Table 9.2.
Source: Authors' calculations using the American Life Panel 2009. See text.

likely to be over-conservative, but other effects are far more muted: the effects on under-diversification range from being 5 percent less likely to nothing significant across the various specifications. Compared to the estimates in Table 9.10, the magnitude of the actual treatment effects suggests that a sizable part of the gap between advice recipients and non-recipients is due to self-selection, and that this selection occurs on performance-related unobservables other than financial literacy.

Conclusion

Using experimental methods to try to better understand the causal relationship between advice and behavior, we report on a hypothetical choice experiment in which participants are asked to perform a portfolio allocation task. This means we can only analyze hypothetical outcomes rather than real plan outcomes, but there are several advantages to the experimental analysis. First, the advice provided is completely uniform in content. Second, the issue of reverse causality does not arise. Respondents are randomly assigned to one of three study arms. The first arm is a *control* group, in which the task is presented to respondents without any advice. Respondents in the second arm, the *default treatment* group, all receive the same financial advice. In the third arm, the *affirmative decision* group, respondents are given the choice of whether to receive the advice. Only those who choose advice receive it. Comparing the three groups allows us to study the effects of advice given as matter of course, versus the effects of advice given as a result of requiring an active rather than a passive decision.

Results demonstrate that unsolicited advice has no effect on investment behavior: in terms of behavioral outcomes, individuals who are simply given advice disregard it almost completely. When advice is optional, individuals with low financial literacy are more likely to seek it out. In spite of this negative selection on ability, individuals who actively solicit advice do perform better. Solicited advice thus appears to have more of an effect than unsolicited advice, although the magnitude of self-selection effects can overshadow actual treatment effects.

In some situations, policymakers may find mandatory counseling an attractive remedy. Our results suggest this is not likely to work, however, if the target population is not inherently prepared to take advice, even if it is truly lacking necessary skills. We do know that when employers offer advice as an elective benefit and ensuring employees' active decision-making, this can result in significant take-up and some improvement of financial outcomes, and employees with low financial literacy are more likely to take advantage of these programs. At the same time, policymakers should be realistic about the effects of such programs. One cannot overestimate the impact of voluntary advice programs, since observed differences between recipients and non-recipients are likely to be influenced by selection. Ex-post evaluations are particularly likely to be subject to such biases, even when researchers have access to data on seemingly key variables such as financial skills and education.

Our findings point to a challenging problem. Building financial literacy can improve outcomes, but other unobservable factors such as inherent motivation are also highly performance-relevant and do not appear to be not perfectly correlated with financial ability. Hence, if motivation and other underlying factors remain unaffected, increased advice and other support tools may not only raise average outcomes but also increase the disparities between individuals who are self-motivated and those who are not. Accordingly, transitioning from knowledge to actual behavior change requires advice and educational materials designed to engage rather than simply inform the consumer. Future work will investigate whether an engaging presentation format in addition to knowledge content can independently promote behavioral change.

This research was supported by funds from the US Department of Labor (DOL) and the National Institute on Aging (NIA) via the RAND Roybal Center for Financial Decision Making. The authors thank Jeff Dominitz, Prakash Kannan, Arie Kapteyn, Annamaria Lusardi, Erik Meijer, and Kata Mihaly for related work and insightful discussion, Alice Beckman for research assistance, and Natalia Weil for editorial assistance. The findings and conclusions expressed are solely those of the authors and do not represent the views of DOL, NIA, any agency of the federal government, or the RAND Corporation. The authors are responsible for all errors and omissions.

Endnotes

1. Their approach is similar in spirit to Calvet et al. (2007), who assess the welfare costs of household investment 'mistakes' in Sweden, focusing on under-diversification of risky assets and non-participation in risky asset markets.
2. The ALP is an Internet panel of respondents aged 18 and over. Respondents in the panel either use their own computer to log on to the Internet or a Web TV, which allows them to access the Internet using their television and a telephone line. The technology allows respondents who did not have previous Internet access to participate in the panel. ALP members are recruited from among individuals aged 18 and older who respond to the monthly Survey of Consumers conducted by the University of Michigan's Survey Research Center. The monthly survey produces, among other measures, the widely used Index of Consumer Sentiment and Index of Consumer Expectations. On joining, respondents to the

ALP complete a separate survey about individual demographic, work history, and other household information, which they are prompted to update each time they log in to a new module. This provides a series of self-reported demographic characteristics of interest, including birth date, gender, education, ethnicity, occupation, state of residence, and income. The ALP population as a whole tends to have more education and income than the broader US population; there are two main reasons for this sample selection. First, the Michigan respondents tend to have more education than the population at large, as described by Census data. Second, the great majority of ALP members have their own Internet access. Americans with Internet access tend to have more education and income than the broader population. As such, for survey data analysis, we apply population weights to all survey response. For the experimental data analysis, the data remain unweighted.
3. It should be noted that twenty-five respondents were erroneously omitted from the survey sample for the question about advice received in 2008; in addition, three individuals gave no response. The maximum and minimum possible bounds for the true full-sample statistic are 17–22 percent, computed using the extreme assumptions of 0–100 percent take-up for the omitted group. We note that the low overall use of advice for the rest of the sample suggests that the true sample mean is likely to be at the lower end of this range.
4. Throughout this chapter, we use linear probability models for simplicity. In robustness checks, probit regressions delivered qualitatively and quantitatively similar results.
5. We also note that of the forty-one individuals reporting making early withdrawals, seven did not report their contributions activity. However, only two individuals reported also stopping their contributions, and five individuals made lower contributions. On the other hand, twenty-three individuals report continuing the same (positive) average contribution from the previous year, and five people actually increased their contribution.
6. As individuals with missing data were in the group reporting early withdrawals, the latter statistics are the most sensitive to assumptions about the missing values. In the sample without missing data, individuals with advice were more likely to report early withdrawals. Assuming the upper bound of one for all missing, this is clearly even more pronounced; assuming a lower bound of zero for all missing, we find that, unsurprisingly, this result is reversed. While no conclusive inference can be made, given that prevalence of advice in the group of early withdrawals without missing data is close to the sample average, true early withdrawal behavior is not likely to be very different across those with and without advisors.
7. A detailed analysis of the impact of financial literacy itself on these and other related outcomes is found in Hung et al. (2009).
8. In their study of German investors, Hackethal et al. (2012) used an instrumental variables strategy to identify the impact of advice, employing regional statistics for number of bank branches per capita, voter participation, log income, and

fraction of population with a college degree as instruments for use of a financial advisor. As ALP respondents report their current state of residence, we collected analogous data for the United States and replicated this strategy using state-level averages for the number of financial advisors per capita in 2005–6, log 2006 median income, the fraction of population above age 25 with a college degree in 2009, and voter participation rates for the 2008 general election. However, the first-stage regression (not reported here) with these instruments is extremely weak (F-statistic < 2). We conclude that in the United States, unlike Germany, local geographical variation in the supply of advisors is not a strong predictor for advice-seeking, and that instrumental variables regression is not a valid strategy.

9. We drop 16 observations in which the individuals did not complete the survey and a further 138 responses which were missing or invalid. Cross-tabulations and chi-squared tests indicate that the missing responses are not correlated with the choice treatments.

10. The randomization for the other treatments is conducted orthogonally, and so it should not affect the results of the analysis which essentially compares means across this set of randomized treatments.

11. A Kolmogorov–Smirnov test of equality of distributions does not reject the null of no difference between default and control ($p = 0.996$). It also does not reject the null of no difference between affirmative decision and control ($p = 0.144$), but this result is considerably more marginal. As an aside, both financial literacy measures strongly and significantly predict behavior independent of the treatments, in a direction consistent with the advice: the more literate are more likely to hold stock and less likely to commit mistakes.

References

Agnew, J. (2006). 'Personalized Retirement Advice and Managed Accounts: Who Uses Them and How Does Advice Affect Behavior in 401(k) Plans?' CRR No. WP2006–9. Chestnut Hill, MA: Center for Retirement Research at Boston College.

——L. R. Szykman (2005). 'Asset Allocation and Information Overload: The Influence of Information Display, Asset Choice, and Investor Experience,' *Journal of Behavioral Finance*, 6(2): 57–70.

Benartzi, S., and R. Thaler (2001). 'Naive Diversification Strategies in Defined Contribution Saving Plans,' *American Economic Review*, 91(1): 79–98.

Bonaccio, S., and R. S. Dalal (2006). 'Advice Taking and Decision-making: An Integrative Literature Review, and Implications for the Organizational Sciences,' *Organizational Behavior and Human Decision Processes*, 101(2006): 127–51.

Calvet, L. E., J. Y. Campbell, and P. Sodini (2007) 'Down or Out: Assessing the Welfare Costs of Household Investment Mistakes,' *Journal of Political Economy*, 115: 707–47.

Dalal, R. S. (2001). *The Effect of Expert Advice and Financial Incentives on Cooperation.* Unpublished Master's Thesis. Champaign, IL: University of Illinois at Urbana-Champaign.

Deelstra, J. T., M. C. W. Peeters, W. B. Schaufeli, W. Stroebe, F. R. H. Zijlstra, and L. P. van Doornen (2003). 'Receiving Instrumental Support at Work: When Help Is Not Welcome,' *Journal of Applied Psychology*, 88(2): 324–31.

Dominitz, J., and A. A. Hung (2008). 'Retirement Savings Portfolio Management, Simulation Evidence on Alternative Behavioral Strategies,' *Journal of Financial Transformation*, 24: 161–72.

—— J. K. Yoong (2008). 'How Do Mutual Funds Fees Affect Investor Choices? Evidence from Survey Experiments,' RAND Working Paper No. WR-653. Santa Monica, CA: RAND Corporation.

Gibbons, A. M. (2003). *Alternative Forms of Advice in Natural Decision Settings,* Unpublished Master's Thesis. Champaign, IL: University of Illinois at Urbana-Champaign.

—— J. A. Sniezek, and R. S. Dalal (2003). 'Antecedents and Consequences of Unsolicited Versus Explicitly Solicited Advice,' in Symposium presented at the annual meeting of the *Society for Judgment and Decision Making*. Vancouver, BC: Symposium in Honor of Janet Sniezek.

Gino, F. (2008). 'Do We Listen to Advice Just Because We Paid for it? The Impact of Advice Cost on Its Use,' *Organizational Behavior and Human Decision Processes*, 107 (2): 234–45.

Goldsmith, D. J. (2000). 'Soliciting Advice: The Role of Sequential Placement in Mitigating Face Threat,' *Communications Monographs*, 67(1): 1–19.

—— K. Fitch (1997). 'The Normative Context of Advice as Social Support,' *Human Communication Research*, 23(4): 454–76.

Hackethal, A., and R. Inderst (2013). 'How to Make the Market for Financial Advice Work,' in O. S. Mitchell and K. Smetters, eds., *The Market for Retirement Financial Advice.* Oxford, UK: Oxford University Press, pp. 213–28.

—— M. Haliassos, and T. Jappelli (2012). 'Financial Advisors: A Case of Babysitters?' *Journal of Banking and Finance*, 36(2): 509–24.

Hastings, J. S., and O. S. Mitchell (2011). 'How Financial Literacy and Impatience Shape Retirement Wealth and Investment Behaviors.' NBER Working Paper 16740. Cambridge, MA: National Bureau of Economic Research.

Helman, R., J. VanDerhei, and C. Copeland (2007). 'The Retirement System in Transition: The 2007 Retirement Confidence Survey,' EBRI Issue Brief No. 304, April.

Hewitt Associates (2004). 'Press Release: Hewitt Study Shows US Employees Sluggish in Interacting with 401k Plans: Research Shows Poor 401k Saving and Investing Habits Despite Improved Economy,' May 24.

Hung, A. A., N. Clancy, J. Dominitz, E. Talley, C. Berrebi, and F. Suvankulov (2008). 'Investor and Industry Perspectives on Investment Advisers and Broker-Dealers,' RAND Technical Report No. TR-556-SEC. Santa Monica, CA: RAND Corporation.

—— E. Meijer, K. Mihaly, and J. K. Yoong (2009). 'Building Up, Spending Down: Financial Literacy, Retirement Savings Management, and Decumulation,' RAND Working Paper No. WR-712. Santa Monica, CA: RAND Corporation.

Inderst, R., and M. Ottaviani (2009). 'Misselling Through Agents,' *American Economic Review*, 99(3): 883–908.

Investment Company Institute (ICI) (2001). 'Redemption Activity of Mutual Fund Owners,' Investment Company Institute Research in Brief, 10(1). Washington, DC: ICI. http://www.ici.org/pdf/fm-v10n1.pdf

—— (2012). *Retirement Assets Total $18.9 Trillion in First Quarter 2012.* Washington, DC: ICI. http://www.ici.org/research/retirement/retirement/ret_12_q1

Kramer, M. M. (2012). 'Financial Advice and Individual Investor Portfolio Performance,' *Financial Management*, 41(2): 395–428.

Liu, W.-L. (2005). 'Motivating and Compensating Investment Advisors,' *Journal of Business*, 78(6): 2317–50.

Lusardi, A., and O. S. Mitchell (2006). 'Financial Literacy and Planning: Implications for Retirement Wellbeing,' Pension Research Council Working Paper 2006–01. Philadelphia, PA: Pension Research Council.

—— (2007). 'Baby Boomer Retirement Security: The Roles of Planning, Financial Literacy, and Housing Wealth,' *Journal of Monetary Economics*, 54(1): 205–24.

Mottola, G. R., and S. P. Utkus (2009). 'Red, Yellow, and Green: Measuring the Quality of 401(k) Portfolio Choices,' in A. Lusardi, ed., *Overcoming the Saving Slump: How to Increase the Effectiveness of Financial Education and Saving Programs.* Chicago, IL: University of Chicago Press, pp. 119–39.

Samuelson, W., and R. Zeckhauser (1988). 'Status Quo Bias in Individual Decision Making,' *Journal of Risk and Uncertainty*, 1: 7–59.

Sirri, E. R., and P. Tufano (1998). 'Costly Search and Mutual Fund Flows,' *Journal of Finance*, 53: 1589–622.

Sniezek, J. A., and L. M. Van Swol (2001). 'Trust, Confidence, and Expertise in a Judge–Advisor System,' *Organizational Behavior and Human Decision Processes*, 84(2): 288–307.

—— G. E. Schrah, and R. S. Dalal (2004). 'Improving Judgment with Prepaid Expert Advice,' *Journal of Behavioral Decision Making*, 17(3): 173–90.

Turner, J. A., and D. M. Muir (2013). 'The Market for Financial Advisers,' in O. S. Mitchell and K. Smetters, eds., *The Market for Retirement Financial Advice.* Oxford, UK: Oxford University Press, pp. 13–45.

Yaniv, I. (2004a). 'The Benefit of Additional Opinions,' *Current Directions in Psychological Science*, 13(2): 75–8.

—— (2004b). 'Receiving Other People's Advice: Influence and Benefit,' *Organizational Behavior and Human Decision Processes*, 93(2004): 1–13.

—— E. Kleinberger (2000). 'Advice Taking in Decision Making: Egocentric Discounting and Reputation Formation,' *Organizational Behavior and Human Decision Processes*, 83(2): 260–81.

Yoong, J. K., and A. A. Hung (2009). 'Self-dealing and Compensation for Financial Advisors,' RAND Working Paper. Santa Monica, CA: RAND Corporation.

Zheng, L. (1999). 'Is Money Smart? A Study of Mutual Fund Investors' Fund Selection Ability,' *Journal of Finance*, 54: 901–33.

Chapter 10
How to Make the Market for Financial Advice Work

Andreas Hackethal and Roman Inderst

The regulation of the financial industry is changing rapidly. In order to effect far-reaching protection of retail financial consumers, the newly created Financial Stability Board in Europe has made several proposals to advance consumer finance protection, including the establishment of a dedicated consumer protection authority (FSB, 2011). Such an authority has also been newly created in the United States, in the form of the Consumer Financial Protection Bureau operating since July 2011. In the United Kingdom, the former Financial *Services* Authority will be replaced by a Financial *Conduct* Authority (FSA, 2011). A key motivation behind these changes is that the system of *financial advice* is seen to be profoundly deficient. Rather than helping consumers by bridging gaps in knowledge and facilitating transactions, professional financial advice stands accused of helping to exploit consumers' lack of financial literacy and inexperience. In its blueprint for a new architecture of financial regulation, the US Department of the Treasury (2009: 68) has put this as follows:

Impartial advice represents one of the most important financial services consumers can receive [...] Mortgage brokers often advertise their trustworthiness as advisors on difficult mortgage decisions. When these intermediaries accept side payments from product providers, they can compromise their ability to be impartial. Consumers, however, may retain faith that the intermediary is working for them and placing their interests above his or her own, even if the conflict of interest is disclosed. Accordingly, in some cases consumers may reasonably but mistakenly rely on advice from conflicted intermediaries.

This conjecture of a malfunctioning and therefore welfare-impairing market for financial advice is echoed by the European Commission's (EC, 2011: 27) recast proposal for a directive on markets in financial instruments (MiFID II):

The continuous relevance of personal recommendations for clients and the increasing complexity of services and instruments require enhancing the conduct of business obligations in order to strengthen the protection of investors. [...] In order to give all relevant information to investors, it is appropriate to require investment firms providing investment advice to clarify the basis of the advice they provide, notably the range of products they consider in providing personal recommendations to clients, whether they provide investment advice on an independent basis and whether they provide the clients with the on-going assessment of the suitability of the financial instruments recommended to them. [...] In order to strengthen the protection of investors and increase clarity to clients as to the service they receive, it is appropriate to further restrict the possibility for firms to accept or receive inducements from third parties, and particularly from issuers or product providers, when providing the service of investment advice on an independent basis and the service of portfolio management.

In this chapter, we contend that financial advice is key to improving the quality of investment decisions of retail investors. As consumers often have deficient financial literacy or may be prone to make systematic errors, well-informed and unbiased financial advice has an important role to play. Here, we discuss this with particular attention to retail investment services. Recent survey evidence shows that retail investors typically turn to and receive professional advice. While this may complement the knowledge of more educated consumers, we show that the impact of advice may be particularly large for less-knowledgeable consumers.

But do consumers make the right use of financial advice? We argue that this may often not be the case. One reason is that—as suggested in the preceding quotes—they may fail to understand the underlying inherent conflicts of interest. We discuss empirical and theoretical papers that show how such a system of biased advice may persist in the marketplace. But we also show that consumers may wrongly use even unbiased advice.

Throughout this chapter we focus on advice given specifically to particular consumers, rather than being provided generically, for example, through investment newsletters or analyst reports. Also, for the present discussion, we refer to financial advice or a financial advisor, without singling out particular roles and professions and thereby the particular legal obligations that would apply to each. Accordingly, general remarks about the role and scope of financial advice should apply equally to dedicated investment advisors or broker-dealers whose advice is legally considered to be 'solely incidental' to their business.[1]

The financial investment problem

One reason why the decision problem of retail investors is complex is simply the staggering number of different products.

Complexity of investment decision and systematic errors

Lack of transparency allows for significant price dispersion even for relatively simple products, such as S&P 500 index funds.[2] Moreover, many retail investment products are quite complex, involving derivative structures or various *hidden* costs that an investor must carefully add up and compare before making a decision. Another reason for complexity is the very nature of household investment decisions. Theory posits that investors maximize subjective expected utility under a life-time budget constraint, given stochastic labor income and asset returns (Campbell and Viceira, 2002). Investors should formulate dynamic optimal plans for consumption and portfolio composition, but in practice the optimization problem is far from easy. Little is known about how consumers actually search for investment products, and the realization of state variables relevant for optimal portfolio composition. Several recent studies suggest, however, that consumers seem to conduct only a very limited search, often collecting information only from a single source.[3] One would suspect that this involves their most trusted financial advisor. To what extent the presence of the advisor then stimulates information acquisition, or whether it instead stalls this process, has unfortunately not yet been the subject of research.

When making investment decisions in practice, the informed consumer should consider a number of different steps. He would first assess his personal balance sheet to determine how much he is already exposed to different classes of risk and to what extent he can afford to save and invest for the long term. This then feeds into his risk tolerance and his investment horizon. The next step is to save and invest optimally across different asset classes, thereby achieving diversification as well as an optimal trade-off between expected return, risk, and illiquidity. It then remains to pick individual securities and to undertake the respective transactions. Over time, the investor will also need to review his decisions in light of shocks, and he should also potentially readjust his decisions.

The academic literature has suggested numerous instances how at least some consumers are prone to make systematic errors along this process.[4] The key obstacles to making good decisions include unstable or undefined preferences, heuristic decision-making (narrow) framing or unsuitable anchoring of expectations, inertia and procrastination, overconfidence, and choice and information overload.[5] Moreover, systematic errors may stem from misconceptions about how financial products or financial markets work—or from a failure to adequately conceive risk. This is where professional advice can have a major role to play. Advisors should improve the quality of investor decisions along the five steps of the generic investment process sketched out above. At its best, this process will match people with their optimal portfolios throughout time.[6]

Consumers' financial capability

Financial capability refers to the knowledge and skills to make financial (investment) decisions to promote a consumer's interests. Several recent studies suggest that many households do not possess a sufficient level of financial capability, given the complexity of the decisions they face.[7] Surveys suggest that many adults lack even basic knowledge of financial products and concepts, such as inflation or risk, essential to make well-informed and self-directed decisions, and to validate the recommendations.

This lack of knowledge is clearly not uniform across the whole population: better-educated households (as well as wealthier ones) tend to be more capable, while very young adults show a particular lack of knowledge. It is at best unclear whether gaps in financial capability can be overcome by better financial education. Some studies based on, for instance, the provision of financial literacy courses in high schools or within employer-sponsored programs, have suggested that any benefits may be short lived, but others come to the opposite conclusion.[8] If this is the case, then this clearly strengthens the importance of professional financial advice.

The unfulfilled promise of advice

There is considerable scope for professional financial advice to help consumers make better decisions, and retail financial consumers do frequently seek and receive advice. In a large online survey among recent purchasers of investment products in Europe, nearly 80 percent made their purchase in a face-to-face setting, mostly with an employee of the investment provider or a professional advisor (Chater et al., 2010).[9] Almost 60 percent reported that their choice was directly influenced by the advisor. The size of the US market for financial planning and advice was estimated to be almost $44 billion in 2011.[10]

Several studies have documented that the probability of seeking financial advice increases with age, education, financial literacy, wealth, and income.[11] Moreover, women are more likely to seek advice than men. Older and more educated people are presumably more confident and able to combine different views than younger people, and higher wealth or income warrants greater search costs and comes with greater opportunity cost of time. Women may be less overconfident than men and therefore place higher weight on the opinion of an advisor. Even if less sophisticated consumers seek little advice, those that do might nevertheless tend to rely on just a single source of advice. For instance, Hackethal et al. (2010) report that less-knowledgeable advisory customers of a large German bank relied more on the financial advice received than most financially skilled customers, which then translated into significant differences in investment and trading behavior between the two groups. In fact, customers who relied heavily on the specific advisor assigned to them tended to have over 20 percent higher turnover in their financial assets, after controlling for a number of characteristics such as portfolio value and general education. Hence, these accounts generated higher bank revenues than customers who adhered less closely to advisor recommendations. In European survey data, Georgarakos and Inderst (2010) show that trust in financial advice was a significant determinant of the willingness to hold risky assets among less educated households or households who found financial decisions more complex, and to a much lesser degree for more educated and more confident households.[12] Taken together, these studies suggest heterogeneity of financial consumers, one group relying strongly on recommendations of a trusted financial advisor, and another which makes self-determined decisions.

While financial advice can play an important role in consumer investment decisions, in some cases consumers may not benefit from the relationship. For instance, they might have better diversified portfolios, but these portfolios may not have lower turnover or higher performance (Hackethal et al., 2012). One reason is that advice may not be disinterested and consumers fail to adequately take this into account. A well-functioning market of financial advice would ensure that the self-interest of advisors is sufficiently aligned with that of their customers. Often, the compensation of financial intermediaries creates distorted incentives, as it rather aligns the interests of a particular 'high-fee' product provider with those of the 'advisor-salesman.' Yet consumers may often be ignorant about such payments, or they may not become salient at the time of purchase.

The US Federal Trade Commission's staff report (Lacko and Pappalardo, 2007) on disclosure rules for mortgage brokers suggests that many individuals view such brokers as trusted advisors who shop for the best loans for their clients. In a survey of recent purchasers of financial products, Chater et al. (2010) find that most respondents are largely ignorant of conflicts of interest. More than half of all respondents believed that financial advisors or the staff of a tied provider gave fully independent advice or information. Studies of investors' reactions to analysts' recommendations also suggest that at least some investors are naïve about analysts' incentives.[13] In addition, experimental evidence suggests that some subjects are willing to follow advice rather blindly.[14] When consumers are insufficiently wary about conflicts of interest, there is scope for financial advice to generate consumer detriment, rather than helping them with their decisions. With respect to investment services, consumers might then inadvertently purchase products with excessive fees or churn their portfolios too often.

Self-interested financial advice may also risk aggravating systematic mistakes that some consumers are prone to make. Mullainathan et al. (2010) used mystery shopping in the United States to test how investment advisors reacted to consumers at their first encounter. Results showed that, at a first meeting, investment advisors seemed not to risk arguing against potential customers' misperceptions. Rather than mitigating potential errors, they could even amplify biases and misperceptions.

We summarize this discussion by illustrating how advice can help or harm retail investors by either bridging or exploiting ignorance, and through either mitigating or exploiting systematic errors. There are four possible configurations in the market for financial advice, depending on (*a*) whether conflicts of interest exist between adviser and customer; and (*b*) different customer characteristics (see Table 10.1). Situations 1 and 2 describe the possible configurations when the interests are aligned between adviser and customer. Situation 3 probably has different policy implications than 4. Situation 3 calls for more transparency on the effective cost of advice, whereas Situation 4 rather calls for better information on the outcome of investment and advisor activity over time.

Yet, even unbiased professional advice may fail to create benefits when consumers do not make appropriate use of advice or when they simply do not adhere to the recommendations. A consumer who expects a financial advisor to provide him with 'tips on hot stocks' may turn away from the advisor who, instead, educates him about the benefits of diversification. As yet, there is only limited evidence about how consumers actually make use of financial advice.[15] In a randomized field experiment with a large brokerage, Bhattacharya et al. (2012*a*) found that investors whose portfolio structure and trading behavior suggested that they were in the greatest need for financial advice were, in fact, least likely to obtain it. And investors who obtained advice hardly followed the recommendations. Moreover, adherence to these recommendations would have significantly improved portfolio efficiency, compared to what investors actually achieved after

TABLE 10.1 Four possible configurations in the market for financial advice

	Consumer with limited financial capability	Consumer with systematic misperceptions
Interests between advisor and consumer aligned	(1) Advisor bridges knowledge gap (products, providers, fees, etc.)	(2) Advisor educates consumer about systematic errors (home bias, overconfidence, etc.)
Conflict of interest between advisor and consumer	(3) Advisor hides fees or risks	(4) Advisor exploits misperceptions (portfolio churning, attention-driven trading, etc.)

Source: Authors' tabulations.

receiving the advice. This suggests that advice can, in principle, improve retail investor decision-making, though demand-side obstacles must be overcome to reap the potential benefits from advice.

Some obstacles include overconfidence regarding one's own financial capabilities relative to advisor capabilities, general distrust in the quality of advice resulting in only selective adherence, or ignorance of portfolio selection in conjunction with unavailability of information to accurately assess the expected benefits from following the advice. A straightforward policy implication of the low adherence to good advice is that policies focusing on the supply side of the market for financial advice and, in particular, on the inputs to an organization of advice might reduce the occurrence of situations of Types 3 and 4 in Table 10.1, yet then might not be sufficient to significantly increase consumer benefits from advice even in situations of Types 1 and 2. How can consumers find out ex post facto whether and to what extent conflicts of interests (ex ante disclosed) translate into impaired welfare? How can consumers assess whether the improvements in decision-making from unconflicted advice cover the cost of advice? How can consumers compare proven quality of advice among different conflicted or unconflicted suppliers? Answers to these questions demand further research.

Possibly useful policy responses might put consumers into a position to, first, assess their own needs for advice and, second, to anticipate the expected outcomes of advice from different suppliers. In the next section, we discuss current regulatory approaches and possible alternatives.

How to enhance the market for financial advice

Several policies can seek to reduce the need for financial advice, for instance, by improving the quality of information that consumers can gather and digest themselves. Standards for mandatory disclosure, such as key product documents, also fall into this category. Moreover, professional advice also becomes less of a necessity when products themselves become simpler. Policies that grant preferred tax status (say for retirement accounts) to only a preapproved range of savings and investment products would also meet this aim. Yet even simple financial products which most financial economists would judge to be beneficial for retail investors by construction could lose their built-in benefits in the hands of the average consumer.

As an example, Bhattacharya et al. (2012*b*) analyze what happens when retail investors replace single stocks and actively managed mutual funds with low-cost index-linked instruments such as exchange-traded funds and index funds. They report that the positive effects from better portfolio diversification are fully offset by negative abnormal returns from increased factor timing activity. As discussed previously, consumer education would further reduce the need for professional advice, though some studies suggest that the impact might be short lived. The gap between existing financial literacy levels in the population and what is needed in light of the growing complexity of financial decision-making might simply be too large to be bridged by (costly) training measures.

An alternative approach to improve the quality of financial advice is to give advisors appropriate incentives to provide unbiased advice. The evidence cited above suggests that some consumers may fail to rightly anticipate that advisors receive contingent payments or, if that is disclosed, the incentive conflicts that such payments may engender are not salient at the time of purchase. Such naïveté can lead to an outcome where consumers mostly or exclusively pay indirectly for advice, through markups on product prices that are passed on to advisors through commissions, rather than through a direct fee for advice (Inderst and Ottaviani, 2012a). Individual firms may also have insufficient incentives to explain the resulting biases and implement a system that does not compromise the efficiency of the advice, as consumers' inflated beliefs through biased advice tend to relax competition.

If such a description applies to particular products or channels of distribution, mandatory disclosure of conflicts of interest would seem warranted. Moreover, the experimental evidence in Chater et al.'s report (2010) suggests that such disclosure must be in a format such that it acts as a strong 'eye-opener'—and even then it may not prove sufficiently salient. However, when transparency succeeds, this can also have unwanted consequences. Loewenstein et al. (2011) show that, under disclosure, advisors seem to feel more comfortable giving biased advice, and advisees seem to adhere more to the advice given to avoid signaling outright distrust in the advisor. This may not be the case with a cap or even a ban on certain contingent fees, though these could also lead to market distortions. In particular, when consumers are wary about the implications that contingent payments can have on the services that advisors perform, interfering with the structure and level of these payments may lead to inefficiencies. Commissions and other performance-based sales inducements may serve important functions, for example, as they steer advice to the most efficient product or generate incentives for customer acquisition and information gathering.[16]

Accordingly, policymakers would do well to establish to what extent different groups of consumers are unaware of the prevailing inducement structure and the implied conflicts of interest, or whether they fail to distinguish between advice given by professionals with vastly different fiduciary responsibilities. Next, it must be asked whether mandatory disclosure would backfire, such as benefitting arrangements where conflicts of interest are less visible (e.g., through vertical integration). Certain arrangements may also prove to be efficient in a second-best sense, for example, if they solve agency problems in a setting where the agent performs different tasks and advises on the products of multiple providers.[17]

Creating transparency in the market for advice

How can a consumer who receives investment advice assess whether the advice received was good or poor? Very sophisticated consumers might be able to do so almost immediately, through validating an advisor's recommendation or even probing him with their own questions. For such consumers, of course, the advisor will only be one source of information, or they may merely be interested in having a facilitator for their transactions. Instead, less financially sophisticated consumers may have to look at the outcome of advice to judge how good it was. Yet for many financial products this may be far in the future. There may also be little that can be done to correct an initially bad decision, for example, in the case of certain life insurance policies that can only be redeemed at a high cost. If the investment is in marketable securities, consumers can, in principle, regularly observe the outcome of their decisions and can adjust them by changing their portfolio allocations.

At least in principle, consumers could then also establish whether a recommended investment yielded a high or low return, or even how volatile its market price was over, say, the last year. They could then establish whether the investment indeed proved to be as risky as indicated in a recommendation and whether, say, compared to a benchmark, the earned return net of costs was commensurate with the risk. Note that an advisor need not be a talented 'stock-picker' but he may be able to create 'alpha' for the consumer simply by avoiding fees and assessing the relative riskiness of particular products.

So much for what is possible in principle! In reality, however, most retail investors lack the information that would be necessary even for assessing the riskiness of their current portfolios—and even when they can learn such information, they may not be able to process it appropriately. Koestner (2012) analyzes individual trading behavior of some 20,000 self-directed retail investors over a period of eight years, to measure whether investors who do not quit trading altogether learn from past mistakes. He finds that under-diversification and the disposition effect do not abate as investors gain trading experience.[18] More trading experience is associated with less future portfolio turnover, driving down transaction costs and raising net returns over time. Transaction costs are possibly more salient to retail investors than idiosyncratic risk share and timing patterns in round-trip transactions. These findings suggest that retail investors will improve risk management only if they obtain salient information on the risk and return profile of their portfolios.

Figure 10.1 suggests that (portfolio) risk management can offer substantial potential for improvement. The left panel shows average actual portfolio risk for self-directed customers of Financial Institution 1 (a German online brokerage firm). When opening an investment account with this brokerage, each customer reports the desired risk level for his portfolio, where Category 1 denotes very low risk and Category 5 denotes very high risk. It is clear that there is no monotonic relation between the clients' desired risk category and actual portfolio return variation. Customers who stated that they preferred very low risk levels achieved actual portfolio risk comparable to investors who stated they had very high risk tolerance.

Financial Institution 1 did not report past portfolio risk nor past portfolio returns to its customers; the same is true for most German retail financial institutions. This implies that customers will likely have difficulty verifying whether actual portfolio risk was commensurate with their desired levels, and whether actual portfolio returns were in line with benchmark returns. In other words, the two key measures, risk and return, are not readily available to consumers when deciding whether to seek advice or switch advisors. The right panel of Figure 10.1 shows how portfolio risk targeted by individual investors (A = low risk, E = high risk) and actual portfolio risk (standard deviation of actual portfolio returns of these investors) compare to each other under a specific advisory model offered by Financial Institution 2 (and examined by Bhattacharya et al., 2012a). The advisors of Financial Institution 2 determine target risk categories together with their clients and then recommend portfolios that match these risk preferences. In principle, a financial institution could report matches ex post, in order to demonstrate the high quality of its advisory services with regard to portfolio risk management.

We have also conducted an online survey of consumer preferences regarding investment advice, where we find that an advisor's proven ability to manage portfolio risk according to target risk is the number one criterion when selecting advisors. We also tested alternative ways to measure and report portfolio risk, and we concluded that the ordering of retail portfolios according to historical riskiness was hardly affected by the choice of specific risk measure. Furthermore, we found that risk reporting to consumers must be as simple as possible (e.g., a scale from 1 to 10 that maps standard deviations of portfolio returns) and highly standardized in order to be meaningful. These results are incorporated into a recent report to the German Department of Consumer Protection, which has recommended enhancing market transparency by giving retail investors legal right to

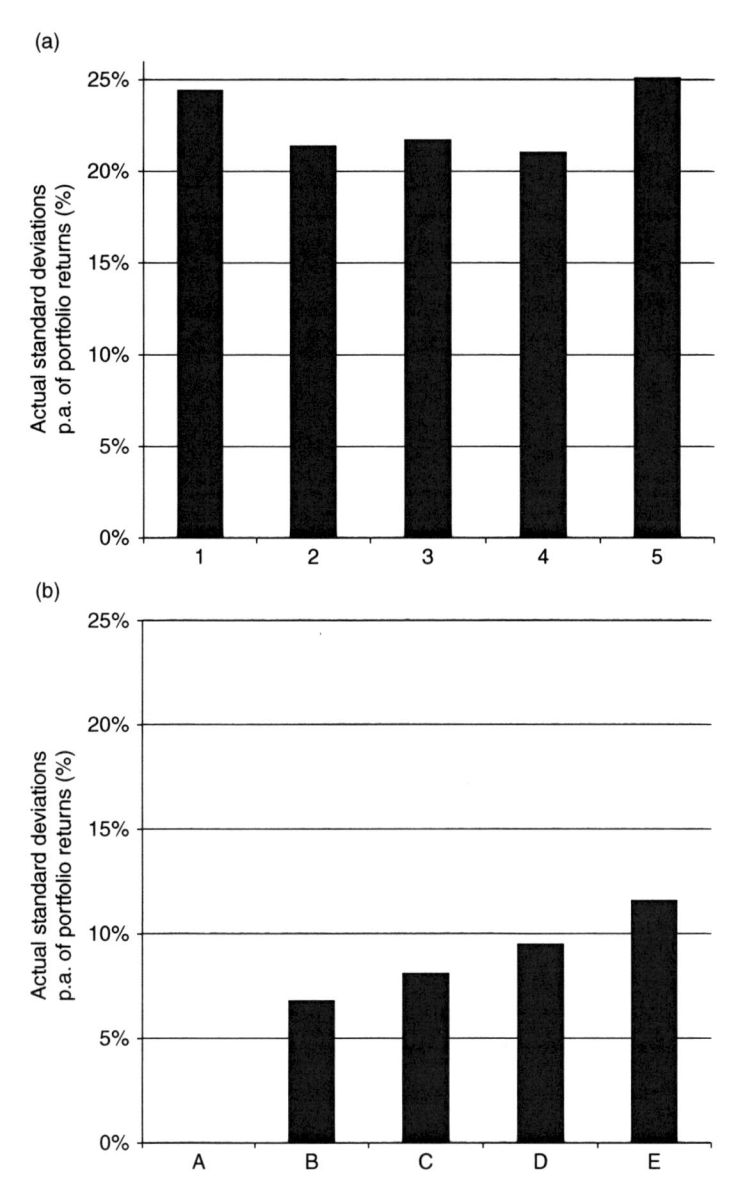

Figure 10.1 Comparison of stated risk preferences and average actual portfolio risk. Panel A: Risk categories for target portfolio risk (Financial Institution 1); Panel B: Risk categories for target portfolio risk (Financial Institution 2)

Notes: Panel A shows average annual standard deviations of portfolio returns for approximately 14,000 self-directed clients of Financial Institution 1 for the time period January 2007 to December 2008. Panel B shows average annual standard deviations of returns of portfolios recommended to some 400 advisory clients of Financial Institution 2 for the time period May 2009 to April 2010. The ordinal categories on the horizontal axis in each panel indicate the preferred risk levels as stated by the clients. Portfolios in Category 1 (A) are typically referred to as 'conservative' portfolios and those from Category 5 (E) are typically referred to as 'speculative' portfolios. Reading example: The portfolio returns of self-directed clients of Financial Institution 1 who reported ex ante that they target risk level 2 ('moderate risk') had an average standard deviation p.a. of 21.5 percent in 2007 and 2008.

Source: Authors' calculations.

obtain (at reasonable cost) their own detailed portfolios and transaction data in a unified electronic format that would allow third-party intermediaries to calculate standard measures for past portfolio risk and return, and to compare those to appropriate benchmarks (Hackethal and Inderst, 2011). While such a policy intervention would only target consumers already sophisticated enough to see the potential benefits of having such measures at their disposal, it could generate a much-needed stimulus in the market for financial advice simply by generating the potential for better transparency.

Conclusion

Our review of the marketplace for financial advice informs policy discussion of how to make this market work better. Most consumers are not well prepared to make complex financial decisions, so professional financial advice is likely to be a promising remedy. In practice, professional advice is widespread, yet the welfare impacts of such advice appear to be neutral, at best. For policymakers, the main problem seems to be advisor incentive schemes coupled with opaque product information. Yet pure supply side measures and mandatory disclosure of conflicts of interest are insufficient to ensure stronger competition for high-quality advice, as well as better adherence to good advice. Instead, more transparency is needed regarding the outcomes rather than the inputs of advisor recommendations. Easy-to-digest reports on one's own portfolio risk and return profile, in conjunction with a standardized categorization of past return variation, might induce advisors and consumers to pay more attention to individual target risk and actual portfolio risk. Such outcome transparency would allow advisors to demonstrate their abilities to meet their main value-added task, namely matching portfolios with consumer preferences.

Endnotes

1. In fact, consumers may not adequately distinguish between these different sources of advice, despite the different fiduciary duties that are imposed (Hung et al., 2008).
2. See, e.g., Hortaçsu and Syverson (2004).
3. The most comprehensive survey studies of this are Chater et al. (2010) and Eurobarometer (EC, 2012) (with a European focus).

4. For an authoritative survey on the field of behavioral finance, see Barberis and Thaler (2003). Chater et al. (2010) offer a more policy-oriented overview, applied to retail investment services.
5. For a survey, see Barber and Odean (2011).
6. Kahneman (2011) distinguishes in his stylized description of human decision-making between an automatic, fast, and emotional System 1 that generates intuition, and an effortful, slow, and somewhat lazy System 2 that processes information more thoroughly than System 1 to either endorse ('rationalize') or refute ('disbelieve') intuition. Systematic errors in decision-making can therefore be the result of incorrect intuition unfettered by System 2 or they can be the result of interventions by an unskilled System 2 (see next section). Kahneman proposes two complementary instruments to improve individual decision-making. The first is to involve others to exert better control over one's own System 1 and at the same time to enhance the capabilities of one's own System 2. The second instrument is to establish a general but distinctive vocabulary that aids in identifying and overcoming judgment errors. Professional financial advice can be viewed as a variant of Instrument 1. At the end of Section 4, we propose a variant of Instrument 2, namely a standardized vocabulary to better deal with desired and actual portfolio risk.
7. See Lusardi and Mitchell (2007).
8. The UK's Personal Finance Research Center has recently carried out a study on these evaluations (FSA, 2008). On the other hand, Lusardi and Mitchell (2007) find a positive impact of financial education in school a decade beyond graduation.
9. Across European countries and across products the source of advice varies considerably, with bank employees playing a key role in many continental European countries.
10. See www.ibisworld.com/industry/default.aspx?indid=1316. See also Turner and Muir (2013).
11. See Hackethal et al. (2012) and Van Rooij et al. (2011).
12. Interestingly, for more educated consumers—and for consumers who consider financial decisions to be less complex—it is their confidence in consumer protection that is a key determinant of their willingness to hold risky assets. For less educated consumers—and for consumers who consider financial decisions to be more complex—trust in consumer protection matters less.
13. See Hung et al. (2008).
14. Even when subjects are informed about a conflict of interest, this knowledge does not seem to always make them sufficiently wary (cf. the various experiments discussed in Chater et al., 2010).
15. See other chapters: Hung and Yoong (2013); Finke (2013); Turner and Muir (2013); and Zick and Mayer (2013).
16. Inderst and Ottaviani (2009, 2011) introduce such multiple tasks into models of advice.

17. Inderst and Ottaviani (2012b) introduce a simple mode of advice and provide a detailed formal discussion of mandatory disclosure policies.
18. Seru et al. (2010) also show that learning effects are small after controlling for investor attrition.

References

Barber, B. M., and T. Odean (2011). 'The Behavior of Individual Investors,' SSRN Working Paper, No. 1872211. http://papers.ssrn.com/sol3/papers.cfm?abstract_id=1872211

Barberis, N., and R. Thaler (2003). 'A Survey of Behavioral Finance,' in G. Constantinides, M. Harris, and R. Stulz, eds., *Handbook of the Economics of Finance*, Vol. 1. Amsterdam, The Netherlands: North-Holland, pp. 1053–128.

Bhattacharya, U., A. Hackethal, S. Kaesler, B. Loos, and S. Meyer (2012a). 'Is Unbiased Financial Advice to Retail Investors Sufficient? Answers from a Large Field Study,' *Review of Financial Studies*, 24: 975–1032.

——— (2012b). 'Passive Aggressive: Index-Linked Securities and Individual Investors,' SSRN Working Paper, No. 2022442. http://papers.ssrn.com/sol3/papers.cfm?abstract_id=2022442

Campbell, J. Y., and L. Viceira (2002). *Strategic Asset Allocation—Portfolio Choice for Long-Term Investors*. New York: Oxford University Press.

Chater, N., S. Huck, and R. Inderst (2010). *Consumer Decision-Making in Retail Investment Services: A Behavioral Economics Perspective*. Report to the European Commission Directorate-General Health and Consumers (SANCO). Brussels, Belgium: SANCO.

Department of the Treasury (Treasury) (2009). *Financing Regulatory Reform—A New Foundation: Rebuilding Financial Supervision and Regulation*. June: 68. Washington, DC: Department of the Treasury.

European Commission (EC) (2011). *2011/0298 Proposal for a Directive of the European Parliament and of the Council on Markets in Financial Instruments Repealing Directive 2004/39/EC (MiFID II)*. Brussels, Belgium: EC Directorate-General Internal Market and Services.

——— (2012). *Special Eurobarometer on Retail Financial Services*. Brussels, Belgium: EC Directorate-General Internal Market and Services.

Financial Services Authority (FSA) (2008). 'Evidence of Impact: An Overview of Financial Education Evaluations,' *Consumer Research*, 68 (July): 1–87. London, UK: FSA.

——— (2011). *The Financial Conduct Authority: Approach to Regulation*. London, UK: FSA.

Financial Stability Board (FSB) (2011). *Consumer Finance Protection with Particular Focus on Credit*. Report to G20 Leaders. Basel, Switzerland: FSB.

Finke, M. (2013). 'Financial Advice: Does It Make a Difference?' in O. S. Mitchell and K. Smetters, eds., *The Market for Retirement Financial Advice*. Oxford, UK: Oxford University Press, pp. 229–48.

Georgarakos, D., and R. Inderst (2010). 'Financial Advice and Stock Market Participation,' SSRN Working Paper No. 1641302. http://papers.ssrn.com/sol3/papers.cfm?abstract_id=1641302

Hackethal, A., and R. Inderst (2011). *Messung des Kundennutzens der Anlageberatung.* Report to the German Ministry of Consumer Affairs (BMELV). Berlin, Germany: BMELV.

—— S. Meyer (2010). 'Trading on Advice,' SSRN Working Paper No. 1701777. http://papers.ssrn.com/sol3/papers.cfm?abstract_id=1701777

—— M. Haliassos, and T. Jappelli (2012). 'Financial Advisors: A Case of Babysitters?' *Journal of Banking and Finance*, 36: 509–24.

Hortaçsu, A., and C. Syverson (2004). 'Product Differentiation, Search Costs, and Competition in the Mutual Fund Industry: A Case Study of S&P 500 Index Funds,' *Quarterly Journal of Economics*, 119: 403–56.

Hung, A. A., and J. K. Yoong (2013). 'Asking for Help: Survey and Experimental Evidence on Financial Advice and Behavior Change,' in O. S. Mitchell and K. Smetters, eds., *The Market for Retirement Financial Advice.* Oxford, UK: Oxford University Press, pp. 182–212.

—— C. Noreen, J. Dominitz, E. Talley, C. Berrebi, and F. Suvankulov (2008). *Investor and Industry Perspectives on Investment Advisers and Broker-Dealers*, Technical Report. Santa Monica, CA: RAND Institute for Civil Justice.

Inderst, R., and M. Ottaviani (2009). 'Misselling through Agents,' *American Economic Review*, 99: 883–908.

Inderst, R., and M. Ottaviani (2011). 'Competition through Commissions and Kickbacks,' *American Economic Review*, 102(2): 780–809.

—— (2012a). 'How (Not) to Pay for Advice: A Framework for Consumer Financial Protection,' *Journal of Financial Economics*, 105(2): 393–411.

—— (2012b). 'Financial Advice,' *Journal of Economic Literature*, 50(2): 494–512.

Kahneman, D. (2011). *Thinking, Fast and Slow.* London, UK: Allen Lane.

Koestner, M. (2012). *Essays in Household Investment Behavior.* Ph.D. Thesis. Goethe University Frankfurt, Germany.

Lacko, J. M., and J. N. Pappalardo (2007). *Improving Consumer Mortgage Disclosures: An Empirical Assessment of Current and Prototype Disclosure Forms*, Federal Trade Commission (FTC) Bureau of Economics Staff Report. Washington, DC: FTC.

Loewenstein, G., D. Cain, and S. Sah (2011). 'The Limits of Transparency: Pitfalls and Potential of Disclosing Conflicts of Interest,' *American Economic Review*, 101: 423–28.

Lusardi, A., and O. S. Mitchell (2007). 'Financial Literacy and Retirement Preparedness: Evidence and Implications for Financial Education,' *Business Economics*, 42: 35–44.

Mullainathan, A., M. Nöth, and A. Schoar (2010). 'The Market for Financial Advice: An Audit Study,' NBER Working Paper No. 17929. Cambridge, MA: National Bureau of Economic Research.

Seru, A., T. Shumwayand, and N. Stoffman (2010). 'Learning by Trading,' *Review of Financial Studies*, 23: 705–39.

Turner, J. A., and D. M. Muir (2013). 'The Market for Financial Advisers,' in O. S. Mitchell and K. Smetters, eds., *The Market for Retirement Financial Advice*. Oxford, UK: Oxford University Press, pp. 13–45.

van Rooij, M., A. Lusardi, and R. Alessie (2011). 'Financial Literacy and Stock Market Participation,' *Journal of Financial Economics*, 101(2): 449–72.

Zick, C. D., and R. N. Mayer (2013). 'Evaluating the Impact of Financial Planners,' in O. S. Mitchell and K. Smetters, eds., *The Market for Retirement Financial Advice*. Oxford, UK: Oxford University Press, pp. 153–81.

Chapter 11

Financial Advice: Does It Make a Difference?

Michael Finke

Households are faced with substantial responsibility for funding retirement through an increasingly complex mix of financial instruments. Making these difficult choices on their own requires investments in specific finance-related human capital that may be neither efficient for households nor for society. Given the large potential loss in welfare from poor financial decisions, renting the expertise of financial professionals may be even more useful than seeking the services of an attorney or an accountant.

Economics suggests that a household will hire a financial adviser if the expected increase in discounted lifetime utility from receiving professional advice exceeds the expected discounted cost of fees and expenses levied by the adviser. A rational household would recognize the benefit of hiring someone with financial expertise to develop a plan to invest in an efficient portfolio, make appropriate use of risk management products, distribute financial resources optimally across the life cycle, and develop a tax-minimizing bequest strategy.

Nevertheless, despite ample evidence of poor financial decisions by households, only about one in five relies on the advice of a financial professional in the United States (Elmerick et al., 2002). While it is remarkable that so few households are willing to pay for some financial help, it is also remarkable that so many households do hire a professional despite understanding little about the magnitude of the difference between informed and uninformed consumption, and often very little about how much it costs to receive the financial advice. Efforts to estimate the benefit of advice have not shown conclusively that consumers benefit from hiring a financial advisor (e.g., Hackethal and Inderst, 2013). This could be attributed to opaque and non-salient pricing of financial advising services and conflicts of interest within the industry.

Problems with pricing and the measurable benefit of financial advice may be traced to the emergence of the profession from a business that is primarily concerned with marketing financial products (Turner and Muir, 2013). The Securities Exchange Act of 1934 that regulates the conduct of broker-dealers assumes that the advice given by registered representatives is incidental to the sale of financial products. Customers (not clients) are assumed to seek out the services of a representative in order to facilitate the purchase of financial products such as a mutual fund or annuity. The representative recommends a product that falls within the bounds of suitability. Each party willingly participates in the transaction and presumably is made better off from trade. Unfortunately, one party (the customer) is at an informational disadvantage and may not even recognize that the advice is solely incidental to the sale of the financial product.

There are predictable costs that arise when consumers hire an agent to act on their behalf. As is well known, the principal and agent both seek to maximize their own welfare, which leads to a conflict when the interests of principal and agent are not aligned. Lusardi and Mitchell (2008) review a number of studies that document the low level of financial literacy in the United States. A principal (household) who knows little about financial markets will have difficulty assessing the quality of financial advice. This imbalance of financial knowledge between household and adviser thus can lead to difficulty assessing service quality before and even after purchase.

This chapter reviews the literature describing the value added from professional advice. The potential welfare gains from increased reliance on expert financial advice are significant, and there is some evidence that financial advisers help households make better financial decisions. Nevertheless, the results are generally mixed, and the outcomes may be worse when there are conflicts of interest resulting from adviser compensation incentives. In the absence of sound and consistent regulation of financial advisers, some households may be harmed by the use of an advisor who uses product pricing that is shrouded (not readily perceived by the consumer) and has informational advantages to extract wealth from clients. A lack of educational standards, reliable quality certifications, and consistent regulation to reduce conflicts of interest all prevent the financial advice profession from achieving the quality of other, similar advice professions.

Who receives professional financial advice?

Campbell (2006) documents numerous examples of household financial decision-making that are far from theoretically efficient (normatively optimal). Half of all households do not own equity, despite high historical returns and significantly reduced information and transaction costs. When they do invest in stocks, households tend to purchase more when stock prices are high and do not properly diversify their portfolios. Consumers also borrow at high interest rates while simultaneously holding liquid assets with little or no yield. Many do not refinance when they should and choose mortgage instruments that are inappropriate. Tax complexity leads to additional inefficient asset location outcomes. Few households annuitize at retirement despite obvious gains from mortality credits and protection against outliving assets. There is no doubt that household welfare could be improved through expert advice.

Wealth is far and away the strongest predictor of using a financial planner, followed by high income, a college degree, and self-employment (Finke et al., 2011). Respondents indicate that the most common reason they chose a financial adviser was a major life event such as the receipt of an inheritance or the sale of a business (ICI, 2007). Nevertheless, financial advice is not solely demand-driven. Advisers market their services to clients who have the greatest investible wealth because most compensation models for financial advisers provide an incentive to target wealthy clients. One reason for this is because there are often fixed costs associated with locating new clients, meeting with them to assess their goals and establish trust, and developing initial financial plans or product strategies. Since both commission compensation and asset under management fees rise with investible wealth, advisors are likely to earn more per unit of effort with wealthier clients.

Conversely, since the receipt of financial advice involves significant fixed costs even when free—for example, the time spent meeting with the advisor as well as evaluating and implementing advice—households with lower wealth may estimate that the benefit from improved investing is not worth the indirect costs. When free independent expert investment advice was offered to 8,000 randomly selected customers of a brokerage in Germany, only 5 percent of those were willing to accept it (Bhattacharya et al., 2012). Since the advice was offered at no cost to a random sample, preferences for receiving professional financial advice were free of supply bias. Higher wealth was strongly related to the probability of opting to receive financial advice. Greater financial sophistication among customers who accepted the financial advice suggests that those who anticipated gains from better informed financial decisions motivated the demand for professional advice.

The National Longitudinal Survey of Youth 1979 cohort asked respondents whether they consulted a financial planner when preparing for retirement. By the time of the 2008 survey, respondents were in their late 40s at the peak saving period of their life cycles. Table 11.1 shows the percentage of respondents by income, wealth, and cognitive ability quintiles, as well as by level of education and by respondent self-esteem (which may impact help-seeking behavior). Clearly, the use of a financial planner rises dramatically with wealth and income: nearly ten times the percentage of respondents in the top income and wealth quintile consulted a financial planner compared to the bottom income quintile. Only 10 percent of high school-educated respondents consulted a financial planner, more than one in

232 The Market for Retirement Financial Advice

TABLE 11.1 Household characteristics and retirement planning (%)

Household characteristics	Consulted a financial planner	Calculated retirement needs	Used a computer program	Read magazines or books
Income				
Lowest	4.0	10.2	2.5	14.1
Quintile 2	8.7	15.5	5.8	21.4
Quintile 3	15.5	24.4	11.9	32.6
Quintile 4	21.3	28.3	15.6	38.8
Highest	37.0	43.7	27.7	53.8
Net worth				
Lowest	5.4	10.8	3.6	15.8
Quintile 2	7.1	14.4	5.5	21.3
Quintile 3	12.0	19.8	8.8	28.9
Quintile 4	22.8	29.6	14.5	38.1
Highest	38.2	46.1	29.5	54.4
Education				
Less than high school	2.1	10.6	1.6	6.6
High school	10.2	17.1	6.3	21.7
Some college	18.5	25.1	13.5	37.6
College	33.4	41.5	25.6	51.3
Graduate	35.9	42.4	27.8	55.1
Renter	8.2	14.2	6.0	20.0
Homeowner	21.2	31.3	16.3	37.9
Cognitive ability				
Lowest	5.7	12.8	4.1	15.3
Quintile 2	11.5	17.1	7.4	25.7
Quintile 3	17.9	24.0	10.4	33.9
Quintile 4	21.7	31.6	15.8	39.3
Highest	34.1	39.7	27.3	50.7
Self-esteem				
Lowest	7.7	13.9	5.9	19.4
Quintile 2	15.7	22.6	11.9	29.8
Quintile 3	17.4	23.5	11.1	30.9
Quintile 4	20.1	29.0	15.3	36.8
Highest	25.7	31.9	17.5	41.0

Source: Author's computations from the National Longitudinal Survey of Youth (NLSY79) 2008 data.

three respondents with a college education did. Over one-third (34 percent) of respondents with the highest cognitive ability scores (measured as teenagers) used a financial planner, versus 6 percent of those in the lowest cognitive ability quintile. Respondents with higher self-esteem were also more likely to seek professional advice. In summary, those most likely to seek advice are not those who are most prone to make financial mistakes. Rather, they are most aware of the potential benefits from advice and have sufficient wealth to justify the psychic and time costs of seeing an adviser. People more likely to seek professional advice are also more likely to self-educate by seeking retirement-related information from books and computer programs.

The fact that professional financial advice is sought by households with more financial resources to manage is likely driven both by greater demand among the wealthy and by greater supply of planning services to them from advisers whose compensation increases with investible assets. These results provide evidence that financial sophistication increases demand for professional advice. The least sophisticated may have difficulty envisioning the benefit of seeking information or professional assistance without a clear understanding of the difference between their current and ideal financial situations.

Benefits from financial advice

Studies documenting the impact of financial advisers on household investment outcomes suffer, to some degree, from an inability to differentiate advisers according to their costs and ability to provide value. For instance, a study of German investors by Bluethgen et al. (2008) showed that investors who received advice had higher quality, more diversified portfolios, and also paid higher fees on their investments. It is possible that these fees provided compensation to the adviser for the benefits derived from improved investment efficiency. Kramer (2012) similarly found no evidence of portfolio performance differences between self-directed and professionally advised accounts, but did report that advised accounts were better diversified. Hackethal et al. (2011) indicated that German bank customers who used a commission-compensated financial adviser had lower performing portfolios net of costs, perhaps attributable to adviser incentives to increase turnover. Since many who used advisers had greater financial experience, the authors raised the possibility that advisers were like babysitters—they allowed otherwise high-quality 'parents' to buy a poorer-quality substitute for their costly time. It is also possible that advisors recommend more efficient investment choices that clients do not follow (Hackethal and Inderst, 2013).

Hung and Yoong (2013) reported that respondents who received unsolicited financial advice did not improve their investment behavior, while respondents who chose financial advice when it was optional did enhance their financial outcomes. The authors noted that offering financial advice as an employee benefit would help primarily the three-quarters of employees who indicated that they would use the advice if provided. It is possible that in order for advice to be effective, a client must be motivated to seek it out. This may also explain why the free advice provided to bank customers in Bhattacharya et al.'s study (2012) seemed to have little impact on financial performance.

Neuroscience theory has recently been used to help explain how the process of developing a financial plan can motivate a household to make welfare-maximizing decisions they otherwise would have avoided (James, 2011). Financial decisions made in the present can compromise long-run goals, because present thinking tends to be more emotional and less calculated. This occurs because rational, deliberate thinking occurs in the human cortex and we spend much of our daily lives using the emotional mammalian (limbic) brain. Reactions to risk or to the pain of resisting temptation are limbic responses that people attempt to control through cognitive effort. McClure et al. (2004) show through brain imaging that the limbic brain is primarily involved in short-run decisions, while long-run decision-making is conducted in the cortex. These findings can help explain why many households believe they should save more for retirement, but they are also unwilling to take time in the present to increase their contributions to their 401(k).

In such a setting, using a financial adviser has two benefits. One is that by simply sitting down, articulating goals, and developing a financial plan, a household is forced to apply a cooler, more rational decision-making process to help it make better decisions that involve intertemporal trade-offs. The second is that, by delegating some financial decisions to another person, such decisions are now distanced from the client's emotions. Emotions such as loss aversion are associated with limbic responses. If a client feels an emotional response to a market decline, an adviser can remind the client to focus on his long-term investment policy—allowing him to control emotions by literally providing a 'voice of reason.'

Loss aversion can also help explain why investors appear to do a poor job of market timing. Friesen and Sapp (2007) find that sentiment-driven flows into equity funds following an increase in equity valuations, and away from equity funds following a bear market, resulted in an annual underperformance of 1.56 percent per year. Withdrawals from equity funds were particularly harmful, causing an average loss of 15 basis points per month. There was a 233 percent increase in the number of defined contribution participants who sold 100 percent of their equity investments during the great recession of 2007 and 2008 (Mottola and Utkus, 2009). Winchester et al. (2011) used a survey that asked respondents receiving comprehensive advice (common among fee-based investment advisers) whether they shifted their portfolio toward cash during the financial crisis. A prudent adviser would have suggested either maintaining the current portfolio or rebalancing away from cash following an equity market decline. The authors found that the strongest predictor of not shifting into cash was

Financial Advice: Does It Make a Difference? 235

whether the investor had a written financial plan. This suggests that comprehensive planning, which often includes an investment policy statement, can help reduce sentiment-driven flights to safety by individual investors. Shapira and Venezia (2001) also reported that professional managers were less susceptible to behavioral biases, such as the disposition effect, and that individuals can reduce losses from behavioral investment mistakes by delegating some decision-making to professional advisers.

Table 11.2 shows results from multivariate analyses in order to estimate the independent impact of using a financial planner on household financial outcomes. The nationally representative data include nearly 5,000 households between the age of 42 and 49 with balance sheet information measured in 2007. We examined net worth, wealth held in sheltered retirement accounts, ownership of an Individual Retirement Account (IRA), and whether the respondent had calculated the amount of money needed to save for retirement. These are related to demographic and socioeconomic controls[1] as well as an indicator of whether the respondent consulted a financial planner in preparing for retirement.

The evidence shows that consulting a financial planner is positively related to net worth and retirement wealth even when controlling for income, education, and cognitive ability. Those who have consulted a financial planner were five times more likely to have calculated their retirement needs. Although it is possible that financial planners are more attracted to households that have accumulated greater assets, the strong impact of the financial planner variable on sheltered retirement saving and ownership of an IRA suggests that the use of planners may be responsible for the positive financial outcomes. As noted by James (2011), the financial planning process often involves encouraging clients to engage in intertemporal decisions that they would otherwise avoid. In other words, the financial planning process can force households to acknowledge tradeoffs between present consumption and future goals, and the use of a planner appears to help clients select investment vehicles (such as tax-sheltered accounts) that are best suited to meet these goals.

Incentives and investment advice

Mutual funds with lower expense ratios consistently underperform mutual funds with higher expenses, since there is little evidence that fund managers are generally able to achieve returns exceeding index benchmarks (Fama and French, 2010). Despite this inverse relation between fund fees

TABLE 11.2 Financial planner regressions

Household characteristics	Net worth[a]	Retirement wealth[b]	Own IRA[c]	Calculated retirement needs[d]
Financial planner	0.449***	1.190***	2.133***	6.038***
Log(Income)	1.591***	1.803***	1.430***	1.458***
Log(Net worth)	–	–	1.184***	1.023*
Education (reference < high school)				
High school	0.109	0.920***	2.703*	1.117
Some college	0.008	1.036***	2.689*	1.139
College	−0.089	1.386***	2.979**	1.235
Graduate school	−0.242	1.531***	3.266**	1.221
Male	0.025	−0.557***	0.811**	1.04
Married	0.314**	0.585***	0.895	0.770**
Children	−0.039	0.177	1.005	0.935
IQ	0.014***	0.047***	1.028***	1.010***
Age (reference 43–44) (years)				
45–46	−0.006	0.0900	0.996	1.088
47–48	−0.064	−0.006	1.019	1.214*
49–51	−0.062	0.145	1.230*	1.201*
Own home	3.222***	1.539***	1.387**	1.376***
Own business	0.298	−0.277	1.602***	1.123
Inheritance	0.435***	0.146	1.388***	0.995
Divorced	−0.052	−0.580***	0.832	0.837
Working spouse	−0.028	0.849***	0.83	0.875
Region (reference South)				
North	−0.089	0.643***	1.356***	0.893
Northeast	0.085	0.605***	1.420***	0.808***
West	0.199	−0.122	1.213*	1.081
Sample size (N)	4,987	4,987	4,962	4,970
Adj. R^2	0.4354	0.3396	0.3002	0.2575

[a] This regression models the predictors of log household net worth.
[b] This regression models the predictors of assets held in all tax-sheltered retirement accounts.
[c] This regression models the predictors of holding any money in an IRA, Keogh, variable annuity, or other tax-advantaged account.
[d] This regression models the predictors of having calculated retirement income needs in retirement.

Note: ***, **, and * indicates significance at the 0.01, 0.05, and 0.10 levels, respectively.

Source: National Longitudinal Survey of Youth (NLSY79) 2008 data.

and performance, only 14.5 percent of equity mutual fund assets were invested in lower-fee index funds in 2010 (ICI, 2011). One explanation for this pattern is that higher-fee funds provide compensation for both fund management and investment advice. Investors seeking advising services buy a product that combines advice with mutual funds, providing the adviser with indirect compensation for the added-value portfolio recommendations. In a competitive market, variation in fund fees may reflect the value of add-on advising services (Coates and Hubbard, 2007).

Another explanation for the persistence of high fund fees may be that the market for mutual funds is segmented by consumer sophistication, where higher-fee funds may cater to less-sophisticated investors through financial adviser intermediaries, and lower-fee funds cater to more sophisticated investors through a direct-sales channel. Del Guercio et al. (2010) report that mutual fund families tend to focus on catering either to direct channel investors who are more sensitive to performance, or to broker channel investors who value brokerage in-kind services above fund performance. For example, direct channel mutual funds devote more resources to hiring better quality fund managers to attract assets from investors who primarily search for investment returns. The difference in investor clientele may explain why Bergstresser et al. (2009) find that mutual funds recommended by brokers tend to underperform on a risk-adjusted basis. Those authors conclude that such underperformance provides evidence that professional financial advisers do not add value in terms of investment selection. Nevertheless, professionals may still be providing value through services incidental to the recommendation of mutual funds.

According to the Investment Company Institute (ICI, 2007), the primary reason households seek financial advice through brokers who sell mutual fund investments is to draw from their expertise in asset allocation and investment options. Most financial advisers, whether they provide advising through a broker-dealer, an insurance company, bank, or other financial institution, obtain compensation through product commissions or a combination of commissions and fees (Turner and Muir, 2013). Commissions are often subtracted from the value of the financial product immediately after purchase, resulting in an immediate negative return on the value of the investment. For example, a household investing $20,000 in Class A mutual fund shares with a 5 percent front-end load pays $1,000 in commissions, leaving a balance of $19,000. Since no-load substitutes are readily available, this short-term loss in wealth must be compensated by a long-run gain in household satisfaction from the use of an adviser. Financial advisers who are compensated through commissions often justify the commissions as payment for the value of their advising services. Nevertheless, such advice must be incidental to the sale of the financial product to their customers according to the Securities Exchange Act.

An important attribute of mutual fund adviser compensation is that it often goes unrecognized by fund investors. The most opaque form of compensation is not front-end loads, but recurring 12b-1 fees that provide a trail of compensation to the broker paid for by the investor and disclosed only as part of the total fund expense ratio in the fund prospectus. This form of compensation accounts for the popularity of fund shares classes

(Class C) which involve adviser compensation that is more difficult to assess than the decrease in net asset value when an investor buys front-end load (Class A) shares. Such fees were originally framed as marketing and distribution expenses when they were authorized by the Securities and Exchange Commission (SEC) in 1980, but they have been transformed over time into a broader form of compensation. Evidence of the importance of shrouded mutual fund fees comes from industry resistance to the SEC's proposal to improve fee salience (ICI, 2010). Gabaix and Laibson (2006) present a model where product attributes are shrouded in order to segment the market between naïve consumers, who are unable to detect differences in the shrouded attribute, and sophisticated consumers who are aware of the attribute. Fees that are automatically deducted are attractive to sellers because they often go unrecognized by consumers (are less salient), reducing consumer sensitivity to pricing (Finkelstein, 2009). In one interesting case, a regulatory change in India briefly allowed closed-end funds formed within a twenty-two-month period to shroud expenses by amortizing their cost over time in a manner similar to 12b-1 fees. Anagol and Kim (2012) find that forty-five closed-end funds were initiated during this brief period, compared to just two closed-end funds in the previous sixty-six months and none after the period ended. These funds captured half a billion dollars in excess fees during this brief period, presumably because the shrouded fees made the funds appear more attractive to unsophisticated investors.

Compensation and agency costs

Agency costs occur in any transaction where a principal hires an agent to act on its behalf. Although advice relationships may not involve the actual delegation of decision-making to the agent, the agent's superior information creates an opportunity to provide advice leading to decisions that can favor the advisor's interests over the client's. Financial advice resembles a credence good because it is often impossible for the consumer to judge the quality of the recommendation, for example investment in a mutual fund, even after purchase. To do so would require the human capital needed to assess relative fund performance—a skill that most consumers lack (Beshears et al., 2011). When an advisor receives greater compensation from recommending an underperforming fund, he may do so to the extent that his recommendation is not constrained by regulation or by the possibility of losing future business.

An omniscient and selfless advisor would provide a set of recommendations that maximize the client's expected welfare. Yet, it is neither practical nor economically efficient to expect that a financial adviser will always act entirely in the interest of the client. Jensen and Meckling (1976) identify the means through which principals can seek to minimize the costs of delegating advice. First, people can monitor advisers by periodically assessing the quality of their advice. Yet, most consumers lack the financial knowledge to monitor effectively so the monitoring may be most efficiently delegated to an impartial expert acting on behalf of investors (e.g., through the SEC or the Financial Industry Regulatory Authority (FINRA)). Second, advisers can restrict their own capacity to make self-serving recommendations through bonding. For instance, advisers who obtain the Certified Financial Planner professional designation must maintain a fiduciary duty toward their clients. By obtaining a designation that voluntarily restricts the adviser's ability to extract rents from a client, an agent provides a signal of reduced agency costs in order to increase demand for his services. Third, the principal and agent can create a contract to align the interests of the client with the adviser. The most common contracts in the financial advice industry are product commissions, fees levied as a percentage of assets under management, a combination of commissions and asset fees, and a fee-for-service model where advisers are compensated for creating a plan or by the hour. The most common forms of compensation for broker-dealers are commissions or a combination of commission and fees, and assets under management fees dominate other forms of compensation among investment advisers (Dean and Finke, 2011).

The regulation of investment advisers as fiduciaries provides a bonding mechanism enforced by a government entity that can efficiently monitor excessive rent-seeking behavior. FINRA regulates advisers based on a standard of suitability. Suitability provides constraints on adviser behaviors that are much more explicit than the fiduciary bonding mechanism provided through regulation by the SEC. However, advisers who are constrained by rules have an incentive to maximize rent-seeking behavior within the boundaries of those rules to the extent that doing so is in the best interest of the agent.

As previously mentioned, many consumers have little understanding of how much they pay for financial advice or the potential conflicts of interest related to adviser compensation (Hung et al., 2008). Commission compensation is generally opaque since many investors are unaware of how much they pay for investment loads, and disclosure does not appear to alleviate this confusion (Beshears et al., 2011). In a market where price is less visible, advisers have an incentive to maximize commission compensation constrained by suitability requirements and the risk of losing future revenues from the client through excess rent extraction. As an example, commissions for mutual funds often decrease on a sliding scale of breakpoints, where larger amounts invested result in a lower commission applied to all invested funds. An adviser hoping to maximize commissions could allocate an investor's wealth across funds within a family in order to maximize commissions, a possibility that motivated the SEC to create a task force to eliminate the practice (NASD, 2003).

The financial advice profession often does not meet the same standards of other professions due to the co-mingling of advice with product, which creates potential conflicts of interest (Frankel, 2010). Of course, agency costs will always exist in any market where a consumer must delegate decision-making control to an expert; many financial advisers are not held to a legal standard that requires them to make recommendations that are in the best interest of the client, unlike most advice professionals. Many of these advisers, who need only recommend products that are potentially suitable to the household, use professional titles (financial consultant, financial planner) that are similar or identical to the titles used by advisers who are regulated as fiduciaries. Most who use an adviser, even the more educated and wealthy, are not able to differentiate between the two (Hung and Yoong, 2013).

Commission compensation incentivizes an adviser to sell financial products but does not provide incentives to invest passively. In fact, Mullainathan et al. (2012) report that financial advisers often encourage clients to engage in return-chasing behavior, possibly to increase the frequency of trades in a manner that takes advantage of (rather than discourages) the behavioral instinct to focus too much on investments with high recent returns. These high sentiment investments are then likely to underperform subsequently (Frazzini and Lamont, 2006). Indeed, Bullard et al. (2008) find that investors who bought mutual funds through a broker channel underperformed no-load investors by 150 basis points, primarily because of poor investment timing. Anagol et al. (2012) also found that commission advisers did not de-bias behavioral clients when it was not in their best interest to do so.

A market with naïve consumers and shrouded pricing creates an opportunity for commission advisers to recommend products that maximize commissions at the expense of consumer welfare. For instance, in India, Anagol et al. (2012) found that insurance agents routinely recommended inferior products to less knowledgeable customers, while simultaneously recommending more suitable products to more sophisticated customers. When given a choice between recommending more competitive products that required price disclosure, and more expensive products that did not, insurance agents recommended the latter. This tendency to recommend inferior products with opaque pricing may be even more acute in a competitive marketplace if consumers are unable to detect the cost of the commission product. Agents who recommend lower-cost, lower-commission products will ultimately be forced out of business by agents recommending less suitable, higher-commission products who are able to use the excess revenues to increase marketing expenses, rent better placed office suites, and hire more talented employees.

Among those who charge fees for financial planning services, 97 percent base their fee amount on assets under management (Hung et al., 2008), a practice that may lead advisers who charge fees to prefer higher-wealth clients. Dean and Finke (2011) explore SEC compensation disclosures among the 7,043 registered investment advisers in the United States and found that those who charged commission compensation were more likely to cater to lower net worth clients and were more likely to provide financial planning services.

Fees may also reduce the focus on short-term advising services by creating an incentive to establish a long-run advising relationship. For example, Finke et al. (2009) found that households that used financial planners (who are often investment advisors compensated primarily by asset fees) were far more likely to have adequate life insurance coverage than households who obtain financial advice from brokers. If brokers were primarily concerned with receiving compensation from the initial sale of investment products, they have little incentive to provide more comprehensive financial advising services. However, fee compensation is not free of potential agency costs (Robinson, 2007). Advisers are not able to receive compensation from non-investible assets, so they may be more likely to recommend the liquidation of assets such as investment real estate or business equity. They may also be less likely to recommend annuitization since this would reduce the amount of invested assets. Fee compensation may also create a disincentive to reduce debt in an investor's portfolio since this would require a reduction in assets. There also appears to be surprisingly little price competition among investment advisors (Hung et al., 2008). This may be because asset-based fees are analogous to income taxes, which are less salient to taxpayers, while fixed and hourly fees more closely resemble property taxes, which taxpayers seem to care much more about because the amount paid is more readily apparent (Cabral and Hoxby, 2011).

Potential regulatory alternatives

One way of reducing increased agency costs that arise from commission compensation might be to eliminate commissions and apply a uniform fiduciary standard among financial advisers. To this end, the UK Financial Services Authority (FSA) has proposed eliminating commission compensation on retail investment products in 2013 (FSA, 2011). The FSA has argued that commissions can produce incentives to withhold information or take advantage of the information imbalance to sell products with a low likelihood of being declared unsuitable by regulators. Australia's Future of Financial Advice Committee has also recommended eliminating commissions and applying a fiduciary standard of care to investment advisers. Finke and Langdon (2012) explore differences in US state common law standards for broker-dealers to compare non-fiduciary to strict fiduciary states. They find no evidence that stricter fiduciary standards reduce the number of registered representatives within these states, or negatively impact representatives' ability to recommend commission products or provide services to lower-wealth clients. A universal fiduciary standard could reduce incentives to recommend suitable products that are nonetheless inferior to other available products. It could also reduce consumer confusion about the unequal application of fiduciary standards between brokers and investment advisers.

Surveys in the United States and in Australia suggest that most respondents would prefer commissions over fees when paying for financial products, and that the amount they would be willing to pay for financial plans is generally much lower than the amount advisers commonly receive (e.g., Australian School of Business, 2010; Ody, 2011). This is consistent with evidence that mutual fund investors appear to reward funds with more opaque expenses, despite strong evidence that opacity is negatively related to performance (Edelin et al., 2012). Disclosure increases competitiveness and efficiency, but less sophisticated consumers gravitate toward products with opaque pricing. This demand for inferior products with shrouded prices may be caused by an underestimation of the actual cost in the absence of full information. In a model of naïve and sophisticated financial consumers with hidden sales incentives, Inderst and Ottaviani (2011) find that naïve households will likely be exploited while sophisticated investors may benefit from broker incentives that increase efficiency in response to market pressures (much like dealer kickbacks on slow-selling cars allow dealers to negotiate lower prices). There is little evidence, however, of many sophisticated consumers who are able to perceive advice conflicts of interest (Hung et al., 2008).

Of course, it is also possible that fewer average investors would be served by advisers if they were unwilling to pay market prices for expert financial advice. Preference for commission compensation may persist if consumers assume that the prices they pay for advice are much below the full price. This leads to the counterintuitive conclusion that many households would be unwilling to pay for advice if they knew the cost might actually benefit from shrouded pricing.

In addition to differences in compensation and regulation among financial advisers, there may be important differences in financial planning knowledge that bias estimates of the value added from financial advice. Education ranges from a university degree in financial planning that includes specific instruction in investments, tax, retirement, estate, and insurance topic areas, to a brief proprietary training session focused on product characteristics and suitability requirements. Registered representatives of broker-dealers must pass a 7-hour Series 7 examination through FINRA that primarily tests product knowledge and regulation. Registered investment advisers generally must pass a 3-hour Investment Adviser Competency Exam that also emphasizes knowledge of securities and regulation. The Certified Financial Planner examination is a two-day examination that includes topic areas focused on knowledge specifically related to providing comprehensive financial advice. Certifications can provide a quality signal, but only if unqualified advisers are unable to obtain the certification. A proliferation of certifications within the financial advice industry means that consumers are often unable to determine which are credible quality signals. To some degree, household financial advice suffers from inconsistency because it has not developed as a science-based profession with uniform best practices and quality standards.

Age and financial advice

The most frequent reason given for not seeking professional advice among respondents aged 60 or over is an unwillingness to hand over control of investment decisions (ICI, 2007). The percentage of households under age 45 unwilling to delegate control over investments (57 percent) was much lower than households aged 60 or older (82 percent). The second most frequent reason driving the decision to avoid professional advice among respondents in the oldest age group is the belief that they have all the knowledge they need to invest on their own (ICI, 2007). The percentage was again higher than among younger age groups.

This pattern is confounded by the fact that efficient processing of mental stimuli and the ability to place it into context, or fluid intelligence, peaks in young adulthood. Problem solving involving a combination of knowledge and experience (crystallized intelligence) peaks around age 60 (McArdle et al., 2002). Financial decisions require some mathematical skill, but they primarily involve the ability to process complex information and place it into context in a manner consistent with other decision-making domains that require crystallized intelligence. For example, taking a sheltered investment portfolio and turning wealth into an income stream during retirement require knowledge of available financial instruments including annuities and traditional investment products, an understanding of complex and constantly changing tax laws, and knowledge of investment and economic theory. A study of credit decisions found that credit making decision quality peaked in the mid-50s and declined in a manner similar to the observed decline in crystallized intelligence (Agarwal et al., 2009).

The Baby Boom cohort is the first having to deal with turning 401(k) and IRA assets into consumption during retirement, and its ability to make welfare-maximizing choices is likely to decline as the group ages. Finke et al. (2011) show that basic financial literacy skills decline by about 2 percent each year after age 60. The decline is consistent among all decision-making domains, including insurance, investments, credit, and basic literacy, and the decline occurs even among the most educated and financially sophisticated respondents. Somewhat ironically, although financial decision-making abilities decline throughout old age, confidence in financial decisions does not. Finke et al. (2011) find that confidence increases significantly in old age, though more educated respondents are less (over)confident in their financial decision-making abilities. Overconfidence in financial abilities may explain why fewer respondents aged 60 and older believe they would benefit from expert financial advice (ICI, 2007).

This decline in competency with tasks requiring fluid intelligence suggests that older households are able to modify behavior to avoid mistakes. Thus, aging erodes our ability to process and react to visual stimuli while driving, though the decline is so slight that many older drivers do not perceive it. The good news is that, when confronted with objective evidence of diminished driving skills, subjects subsequently changed their driving patterns by driving during low-traffic times and avoiding complex intersections (Holland and Rabbitt, 1992). By acknowledging an inevitable decline in financial decision-making ability, older households may be more willing to delegate financial decisions to an expert or to choose investments that are easier to manage such as annuities or automatically rebalancing mutual funds.

Conclusion

There is ample evidence that households who lack the financial knowledge needed to make efficient choices in an increasingly complex financial marketplace. Financial advice professionals can substitute for costly and inefficient investment in finance-related human capital by households, if the expected benefits from better decisions exceed the costs of advice. Yet financial advisers are often compensated through opaque commissions and non-salient fees. Accordingly, the benefits from advice are fraught with potential conflicts of interest.

For these reasons, a financial advice market that functions well is needed to arm a new generation of consumers tasked with increased responsibility for funding retirement with the information needed to make efficient choices. Ensuring that consumers have access to well-educated financial advisers whose job is to make recommendations in the best interest of the consumers seems a logical solution to this consumer information problem. There is evidence that consumers who seek advice from fiduciary planners who provide comprehensive advising services are much better off than those who do not receive advice. Yet even the most sophisticated consumers are sometimes unable to identify which advisers are most likely to provide good advice, due to a patchwork of adviser regulations and the customer's inability to recognize genuine quality signals.

Equity markets in countries with greater investor protections are healthier because stock owners have reason to believe that managers will look out for their interests despite significant information asymmetries (La Porta et al., 1998). It is likely that the health of the financial advice market in the future will depend on whether consumers are confident that the advice professionals they hire are people whose recommendations they can trust. Other countries are closer to the adoption of consumer protections on advice compensation and fiduciary regulation. In the United States, an early version of the 2010 Dodd-Frank Act would have applied fiduciary standards to all financial advice professionals. Some who benefit from non-fiduciary regulatory standards would oppose this legislation, but like equity and insurance markets characterized by information asymmetry, increased consumer protections can engender trust and increase demand for a much-needed service.

Endnote

1. Net worth and income are log transformed and negative values are set equal to one prior to transformation.

References

Agarwal, S., J. C. Driscoll, X. Gabaix, and D. Laibson (2009). 'The Age of Reason: Financial Decisions over the Life-cycle and Implications for Regulation,' *Brookings Papers on Economic Activity*, Fall: 51–117.

Anagol, S., S. Cole, and S. Sarkar (2012). 'Understanding the Incentives of Commissions Motivated Agents: Theory and Evidence from the Indian Life Insurance Market,' Harvard Business School (HBS) Finance Working Paper No. 12-055. Boston, MA: HBS.

—— H. Kim (2012). 'The Impact of Shrouded Fees: Evidence from a Natural Experiment in the Indian Mutual Funds Market,' *American Economic Review*, 102 (1): 576–93.

Australian School of Business (2010). 'Financial Planning: What is the Right Price for Advice?' *Knowledge@Australian School of Business.* http://knowledge.asb.unsw.edu.au/article.cfm?articleid=1150

Bergstresser, D., J. Chalmers, and P. Tufano (2009). 'Assessing the Costs and Benefits of Brokers in the Mutual Fund Industry,' *Review of Financial Studies*, 22(10): 4129–56.

Beshears, J., J. Choi, D. Laibson, and B. Madrian (2011). 'How Does Simplified Disclosure Affect Individuals' Mutual Fund Choices?' in D. A. Wise, ed., *Explorations in the Economics of Aging.* Chicago: University of Chicago Press, pp. 75–96.

Bhattacharya, U., A. Hackethal, S. Kaesler, B. Loos, and S. Meyer (2012). 'Is Unbiased Financial Advice to Retail Investors Sufficient? Answers from a Large Field Study,' *Review of Financial Studies*, 25: 975–1032.

Bluethgen, R., A. Gintschel, A. Hackethal, and A. Mueller (2008). 'Financial Advice and Individual Investor's Portfolios,' Working Paper. http://ssrn.com/abstract=968197

Bullard, M., G. C. Friesen, and T. Sapp (2008). 'Investor Timing and Fund Distribution Channels,' Working Paper. http://ssrn.com/abstract=1070545

Cabral, M., and C. Hoxby (2011). 'The Hated Property Tax: Salience, Tax Rates, and Tax Revolts,' Unpublished manuscript. http://economics.stanford.edu/seminars/hated-property-tax-salience-tax-rates-and-tax-revolts

Campbell, J. (2006). 'Household Finance,' *Journal of Finance*, 61(4): 1553–604.

Coates IV, J. C., and R. G. Hubbard (2007). 'Competition in the Mutual Fund Industry: Evidence and Implication for Policy,' *Journal of Corporate Law*, 33: 151–222.

Dean, L., and M. S. Finke (2011). 'Compensation and Client Wealth Among U.S. Investment Advisors,' Working Paper. http://ssrn.com/abstract=1802628

Del Guercio, D., J. Reuter, and P. A. Tkac (2010). 'Broker Incentives and Mutual Fund Market Segmentation,' NBER Working Paper No. 16312. Cambridge, MA: National Bureau of Economic Research.

Edelin, R. M., R. B. Evans, and K. B. Kadlec (2012). 'Disclosure and Agency Conflict: Evidence from Mutual Fund Commission Bundling,' *Journal of Financial Economics*, 103(2): 308–26.

Elmerick, S., C. Montalto, and J. Fox (2002). 'Use of Financial Planners by US Households,' *Financial Services Review*, 11: 217–31.

Fama, E., and K. French (2010). 'Luck versus Skill in the Cross-section of Mutual Fund Returns,' *Journal of Finance*, 65(5): 1915–47.

Financial Services Authority (FSA) (2011). 'Product Intervention,' Discussion Paper DP11/1 (January 2011). http://www.fsa.gov.uk/pubs/discussion/dp11_01.pdf

Finke, M. S., and T. P. Langdon (2012). 'The Impact of the Broker-Dealer Fiduciary Standard on Financial Advice,' Working Paper. http://ssrn.com/abstract=2019090

—— S. J. Huston, and W. Waller (2009). 'Do Contracts Impact Comprehensive Financial Advice?' *Financial Services Review*, 18: 177–93.

—— —— D. Winchester (2011). 'Financial Advice: Who Pays?' *Financial Counseling and Planning*, 22(1): 18–26.

—— J. S. Howe, and S. J. Huston (2011). 'Old Age and the Decline in Financial Literacy,' Working Paper. http://ssrn.com/abstract=1948627

Finkelstein, A. (2009). 'EZ-Tax: Tax Salience and Tax Rates,' *Quarterly Journal of Economics*, 124(3): 969–1010.

Frankel, T. (2010). 'Fiduciary Duties of Brokers-Advisers-Financial Planners and Money Managers,' Boston University (BU) Law Working Paper No. 09-36. Boston, MA: BU.

Frazzini, A., and O. Lamont (2006). 'Dumb Money: Mutual Fund Flows and the Cross-section of Stock Returns,' *Journal of Financial Economics*, 88(2): 299–322.

Friesen, G. C., and T. Sapp (2007). 'Mutual Fund Flows and Investor Returns: An Empirical Examination of Fund Investors Timing Ability,' *Journal of Banking and Finance*, 31(9): 2796–816.

Gabaix, X., and D. Laibson (2006). 'Shrouded Attributes, Consumer Myopia, and Information Suppression in Competitive Markets,' *Quarterly Journal of Economics*, 121(2): 505–40.

Hackethal, A., and R. Inderst (2013). 'How to Make the Market for Financial Advice Work,' in O. S. Mitchell and K. Smetters, eds., *The Market for Retirement Financial Advice*. Oxford, UK: Oxford University Press.

—— M. Haliassos, and T. Jappelli (2011). 'Financial Advisors: A Case of Babysitters,' CSEF Working Paper No. 219. Naples, Italy: Centre for Studies in Economics and Finance, University of Naples.

Holland, C. A., and P. M. A. Rabbitt (1992). 'People's Awareness of their Age-related Sensory and Cognitive Deficits and the Implications for Road Safety,' *Applied Cognitive Psychology*, 6(3): 217–31.

Hung, A. A., and J. K. Yoong (2013). 'Asking for Help: Survey and Experimental Evidence on Financial Advice and Behavior Change,' in O. S. Mitchell and K. Smetters, eds., *The Market for Retirement Financial Advice*. Oxford, UK: Oxford University Press, pp. 182–212.

—— N. Clancy, J. Dominitz, E. Talley, C. Berrebi, and F. Suvankulov (2008). 'Investor and Industry Perspectives on Investment Advisers and Broker-Dealers,' RAND Institute for Civil Justice Technical Report for the Securities and Exchange Commission. Santa Monica, CA: RAND.

Inderst, R., and M. Ottaviani (2011). 'How (Not) to Pay for Advice: A Framework for Consumer Financial Protection,' Working Paper. http://www.kellogg.northwestern.edu/faculty/ottaviani/homepage/Papers/pay%20for%20advice.pdf

Investment Company Institute (ICI) (2007). 'Why Do Mutual Fund Investors Use Professional Financial Advisors?' *Research Fundamentals*, 16(1): 1–8.

—— (2010). 'Investment Company Institute Cost-Benefit Analysis of SEC Rule 12b-1 Reform Proposal.' Washington, DC: ICI. http://www.ici.org/pdf/10_12b1_sec_cba.pdf

—— (2011). 'Recent Mutual Fund Trends,' *2011 Investment Company Fact Book*. Washington, DC: ICI. http://www.icifactbook.org/fb_ch2.html

James, R. (2011). 'Applying Neuroscience to Financial Planning Practice: A Framework and Review,' *Journal of Personal Finance*, 10(2): 10–65.

Jensen, M. C., and W. H. Meckling (1976). 'Theory of the Firm: Managerial Behavior, Agency Costs, and Ownership Structure,' *Journal of Financial Economics*, 3: 305–60.

Kramer, M. M. (2012). 'Financial Advice and Individual Investor Portfolio Performance,' *Financial Management*, 41(2): 395–428. Summer.

La Porta, R., F. Lopez-de-Silanes, A. Shleifer, and R. W. Vishny (1998). 'Law and Finance,' *Journal of Political Economy*, 106(6): 1113–55.

Lusardi, A., and O. S. Mitchell (2008) 'How Much Do People Know About Economics and Finance? Financial Illiteracy and the Importance of Financial Education,' *University of Michigan Retirement Research Center Policy Brief*, No. 5. Ann Arbor, MI: MRRC.

McArdle, J. J., E. Ferrer-Caja, F. Hamagami, and R. Woodcock (2002). 'Comparative Longitudinal Structural Analyses of the Growth and Decline of Multiple Intellectual Abilities over the Life Span,' *Developmental Psychology*, 38(1): 115–42.

McClure, S. M., D. I. Laibson, G. Loewenstein, and J. D. Cohen (2004). 'Separate Neural Systems Value Immediate and Delayed Monetary Rewards,' *Science*, 306: 503–7.

Mottola, G., and S. P. Utkus (2009). 'Flight to Safety? Market Volatility and Target-Date Funds,' *Research Note*. Valley Forge, PA: Vanguard. https://institutional.vanguard.com/iam/pdf/BBBBBBMZ.pdf?cbdForceDomain=false

Mullainathan, S., M. Nöth, and A. Schoar (2012). 'The Market for Financial Advice: An Audit Study,' NBER Working Paper No. 17929. Cambridge, MA: National Bureau of Economic Research.

National Association of Securities Dealers (NASD) (2003). 'Report of the Joint NASD/Industry Task Force on Breakpoints.' Washington, DC: FINRA. http://www.finra.org/Industry/Issues/Breakpoints/P006422

Ody, E. (2011). 'Investors Prefer Commissions to Account Fees, Cerulli Study Says,' *Bloomberg.com*, June 7. http://www.bloomberg.com/news/2011-06-07/investors-prefer-commissions-to-account-fees-study-says-1-.html

Robinson, J. H. (2007). 'Who's the Fairest of Them All? A Comparative Analysis of Advisor Compensation Models,' *Journal of Financial Planning*, 20(5): 56–65.

Shapira, Z., and I. Venezia (2001). 'Patterns of Behavior of Professionally Managed and Independent Investors,' *Journal of Banking and Finance*, 25: 1573–87.

Turner, J. A., and D. M. Muir (2013). 'The Market for Financial Advisers,' in O. S. Mitchell and K. Smetters, eds., *The Market for Retirement Financial Advice*. Oxford, UK: Oxford University Press, pp. 13–45.

Winchester, D. D., S. J. Huston, and M. S. Finke (2011). 'Investor Prudence and the Role of Financial Advice,' *Journal of Financial Services Professionals*, 65(4): 43–51.

Chapter 12

When, Why, and How Do Mutual Fund Investors Use Financial Advisers?

Sarah A. Holden

More than four in ten US households owned mutual funds in May 2011, and about half of mutual fund-owning households indicated they have ongoing advisory relationships (Bogdan et al., 2011). Almost four in ten US households owned Individual Retirement Accounts (IRAs), with nearly six in ten IRA-owning households holding mutual funds in their IRAs.[1] About half of US households owned defined contribution (DC) plan accounts, with more than half of DC account-owning households holding mutual funds in their DC accounts.[2] These investing households held their mutual funds using a variety of channels, in many instances seeking the assistance of financial professionals when investing. Using survey information on mutual fund-owning households, this chapter explores when, why, and how mutual fund investors use financial advisers; the interactions of the investors with their advisers; and whether certain mutual fund-owning households are more likely than others to seek financial advice.

In what follows, the first section briefly summarizes prior research on the role of financial advice and financial literacy. The next section highlights key results from an in-depth survey of mutual fund investors regarding their interactions with financial advisers, along with results from other surveys on the use of financial advisers for specific retirement-related decisions. Subsequently, interactions between the investor and the adviser are explored, because this relationship is complex and collaborative, involving give and take in the decision-making process. Another set of recent survey results explore whether mutual fund-owning households with ongoing advisory relationships differ in significant demographic and financial ways from mutual fund-owning households without these relationships. Conclusions follow.

A brief overview of prior research on the role of financial advice

Two strands of literature discuss investors and the factors that influence investor portfolios, apart from risk preferences. One focuses on the role of financial literacy (and financial education) in influencing household investing experiences. A key finding from that literature is that households with higher levels of financial literacy tend to be more engaged in the stock market. For example, van Rooij et al. (2011) find that individuals with low financial literacy are significantly less likely to invest in stocks. In addition, Collins (2010) reports that customers with lower levels of financial literacy are less likely to obtain advice.[3]

A second research strand focuses on the role of financial advisers, seeking to quantify the impact of financial advice, determine what types of investors seek financial advice, and measure the impact of investment advice on their portfolios. For example, Hung and Yoong (2013) provide experimental evidence that individuals who choose to receive advice improve their investment performance. They also conclude that individuals with lower financial literacy are more likely to take advantage of financial advice programs offered by employers. Hackethal and Inderst (2013) argue that financial advice is key to improving investment outcomes, particularly among less-knowledgeable investors. However, they caution that the functioning of the market for financial advice needs to be improved. Another study analyzes data from a German retail bank and finds that 'financial advice enhances portfolio diversification' and 'makes investor portfolios more congruent with predefined model portfolios' (Bluethgen et al., 2008: 2 and abstract). This literature examines rates of return, conflicts of interest, and whether the provision of advice makes the investor better off.

One difficulty with these exercises is that the adviser–investor relationship is complex. In addition, there are many qualitative and non-quantifiable factors that come into play, which might not be captured by a rate of return analysis. In what follows, we extend the second research strand by exploring what types of mutual fund investors obtain financial advice and what they gain from it.

When, why, and how mutual fund investors seek financial advice?

In 2006, the Investment Company Institute (ICI) undertook a household survey to explore in detail when, why, and how mutual fund-owning households engage or do not engage with professional financial advisers.[4]

When, Why, and How Do Investors Use Advisers? 251

This telephone survey asked individuals owning mutual funds outside of employer-sponsored retirement plans whether they had ongoing relationships with professional financial advisers. Respondents with such relationships were then asked detailed questions about the timing of seeking financial advice, their reasons for seeking financial advice, and the multiple services obtained. Respondents without such relationships were asked why they did not obtain financial advice.

When mutual fund investors seek financial advice?

Mutual fund investors tend to first seek professional financial advice during their prime earning and saving years (i.e., in their late 20s to early 50s). As shown in Figure 12.1, almost one-third of mutual fund shareholders with ongoing advisory relationships indicated they first sought financial investment advice between the ages of 25 and 34, and one-quarter indicated they did so between the ages of 35 and 44. About one-fifth first sought financial

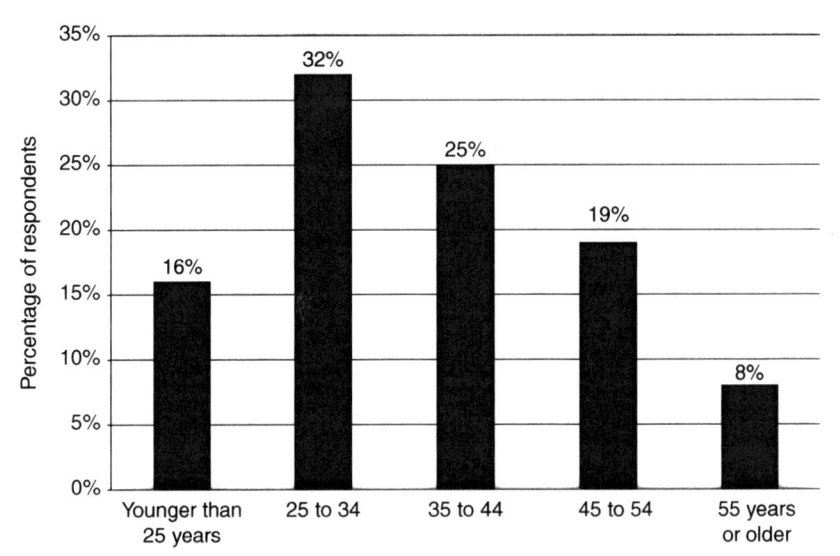

Age of head of household when the household first sought professional investment advice	Percentage of respondents
Younger than 25 years	16%
25 to 34	32%
35 to 44	25%
45 to 54	19%
55 years or older	8%

Figure 12.1 Majority of mutual fund investors initially seek professional investment advice during their peak earning and saving years

Notes: The sample is 602 US households owning mutual funds outside workplace retirement plans and with ongoing relationships with professional financial advisers. The survey was conducted between late July 2006 and September 2006.

Source: ICI Mutual Fund Shareholder Financial Advice Survey; see Schrass and Bogdan (2012).

advice between the ages of 45 and 54. Thus, it appears that changing needs and goals along the lifecycle often prompt mutual fund investors to seek financial advice.

In addition, a particular event can trigger mutual fund investors to seek professional investment advice, as shown in Table 12.1. For some shareholders (27 percent), the trigger event is an inheritance or a lump-sum distribution from a workplace retirement plan. Also, 46 percent of shareholders who first sought advice when they were in their mid-50s or older indicated they had received lump sums, compared with about one-fifth of those who were in their late 20s through their early 40s when they initially sought advice.

Another event triggering demand for advice is retirement; that is, many consult professional advisers when they contemplate the distribution decisions for their DC plan assets. Sabelhaus et al. (2008) find that, among retiring DC account-owning households with distribution choices in their DC plans, 42 percent consulted professional financial advisers obtained on

TABLE 12.1 Achieving specific financial goals often prompts mutual fund investors to seek professional investment advice

Percentage of respondents with ongoing advisory relationships indicating each reason

	All respondents with ongoing advisory relationships	\multicolumn{5}{c}{Age at which respondent initially sought professional investment advice}
		Younger than 25 years	25–34	35–44	45–54	55 years or older
Had a trigger event	48	53	46	40	56	57
Received a lump sum through an inheritance, retirement, or job change	27	38	18	21	37	46
Had a change in household composition, such as a change in marital status, birth of a child, and death of a spouse or partner	21	15	28	19	19	11
Wanted to address a specific financial goal, such as saving to pay for retirement or education	40	33	42	50	34	26
Some other reason[a]	12	14	12	10	10	17

Notes: The sample is 602 US households owning mutual funds outside workplace retirement plans and with ongoing relationships with professional financial advisers. The survey was conducted between late July 2006 and September 2006. [a] Other reasons include seemed like a good idea, family or friends suggested it, and wanted to purchase stocks.

Source: ICI Mutual Fund Shareholder Financial Advice Survey; see Schrass and Bogdan (2012).

their own, and 13 percent consulted with professional financial advisers provided by their employers.[5] In addition, Holden and Schrass (2011), using the 2011 ICI IRA Owners Survey, find that 52 percent of traditional IRA-owning households taking withdrawals from their traditional IRAs consulted a financial adviser to calculate the distribution amount.[6] Furthermore, they find that 62 percent of traditional IRA-owning households who had a strategy to manage income and assets in retirement indicated a professional financial adviser helped them form the strategy.

In addition to inheritances and lump-sum distributions, another trigger event that often causes individuals to seek financial advice is a change in the composition of their household, such as getting married, having a child, or losing a spouse or partner. Twenty-one percent of mutual fund investors with ongoing advisory relationships indicated that a change in the makeup of their households triggered the need for professional financial advice (see Table 12.1). Finally, 40 percent of mutual fund investors with ongoing advisory relationships first sought professional investment advice to address a specific financial goal, rather than in response to a trigger event. Those who first sought financial advice in their late 30s to early 40s were most likely to do so to address a specific financial goal. Among this age group, half indicated they initially obtained professional financial advice because they wanted to begin saving for retirement, their children's education, or some other specific goal.

Why mutual fund investors obtain financial advice?

Mutual fund investors turn to advisers for financial expertise on multiple topics. For example, nearly three-quarters of mutual fund investors with ongoing advisory relationships indicated they wanted help with asset allocation (see Figure 12.2). Nearly three-quarters indicated they wanted a financial professional to explain various investment options to them. In addition, as Leonard-Chambers and Bogdan (2007) report, 38 percent of mutual fund investors with ongoing advisory relationships indicated they did not want to make their own investment decisions, and 44 percent indicated they did not have time to make their own investment decisions. By contrast, the majority of mutual fund investors lacking ongoing advisory relationships indicated they were more 'hands-on' with respect to asset allocation; 66 percent indicated they wanted to be in control of their own investments and 64 percent indicated they had access to all of the resources needed to invest on their own (see Figure 12.2). In addition, among those not using financial advisers, 56 percent said they knew enough to make their own investment decisions, and 44 percent indicated they enjoyed investing on their own (Leonard-Chambers and Bogdan, 2007).

254 The Market for Retirement Financial Advice

Percentage of respondents <u>with</u> ongoing advisory relationships indicating each is a "major" reason for using advisers, 2006

Want help with asset allocation — 74%

Want a financial professional to explain various investment options — 73%

Percentage of respondents <u>without</u> ongoing advisory relationships indicating each is a "major" reason for <u>not</u> using advisers, 2006

Want to be in control of own investments — 66%

Have access to all the resources needed to invest on own — 64%

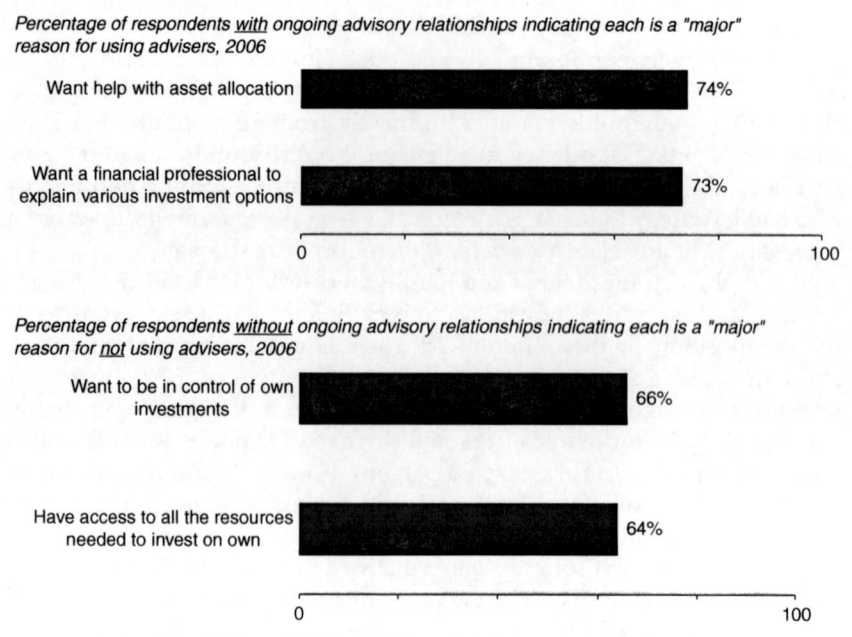

Age of head of household when the household first sought professional investment advice

Figure 12.2 Mutual fund investors and help with asset allocation

Notes: The sample is 1,003 US households owning mutual funds outside workplace retirement plans, of which 602 had ongoing relationships with professional financial advisers and 401 were without ongoing advisory relationships. The survey was conducted between late July 2006 and September 2006. Multiple responses are included.

Source: ICI Mutual Fund Shareholder Financial Advice Survey; see Schrass and Bogdan (2012).

Mutual fund investors also seek advice regarding their financial planning beyond asset allocation or specific investment decisions. For example, as Figure 12.3 highlights, 71 percent of mutual fund investors with ongoing advisory relationships said they seek help making sense of their total financial picture. Seventy-one percent indicated they wanted to be sure they were saving enough to reach their financial goals, and 65 percent indicated their advisers helped to make sure their estates were in order.

How mutual fund investors interact with financial advisers?

The relationship between the investor and the financial adviser involves some give and take, as well as trust. Indeed, as Table 12.2 indicates, one-quarter of mutual fund investors with ongoing advisory relationships always conducted their own research to evaluate or confirm the investment advice they received from their (primary) adviser, and an additional 43 percent

When, Why, and How Do Investors Use Advisers? 255

Percentage of respondents with ongoing advisory relationships indicating each is a "major" reason for using advisers, 2006

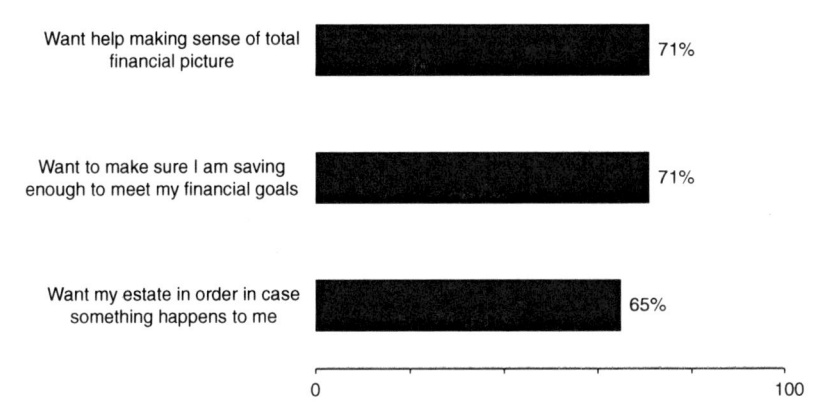

- Want help making sense of total financial picture: 71%
- Want to make sure I am saving enough to meet my financial goals: 71%
- Want my estate in order in case something happens to me: 65%

Figure 12.3 Mutual fund investors and help with financial planning

Notes: The sample is 602 US households owning mutual funds outside workplace retirement plans and with ongoing relationships with professional financial advisers. The survey was conducted between late July 2006 and September 2006. Multiple responses are included.

Source: ICI Mutual Fund Shareholder Financial Advice Survey; see Schrass and Bogdan (2012).

indicated that they 'sometimes' conducted their own research. Another 22 percent said that they rarely conducted their own research, and only 10 percent never conducted their own research. When it comes to following the investment advice, 36 percent indicated they always followed the investment advice from their (primary) adviser, and another 60 percent indicated they sometimes followed the advice.

Mutual fund investors with ongoing advisory relationships are roughly evenly split into three camps of investors: delegators, collaborators, and leaders. Thirty-eight percent indicated they delegated all decision-making to the financial adviser or the financial adviser took the lead in decision-making (see Table 12.3). Another 34 percent indicated that the investor and adviser usually made decisions together, while another 29 percent indicated the investor usually took the lead in investment decision-making. These groups do differ somewhat by demographic and financial characteristics. For example, investors with a high school degree or less were much more likely to delegate decision-making or let the adviser take the lead, compared with those with more education. Investor-lead decision-making tends to fall with age: 36 percent of mutual fund investors younger than 35 and with ongoing advisory relationships indicated they took the lead in investment decision-making, while only 22 percent of those 65 or older indicated they took the lead. Lower-income mutual fund investors also were more likely to delegate, while those with higher-income were more

TABLE 12.2 Mutual fund investors and research and investment advice

Respondents with ongoing advisory relationships; percentage in each row		How often do you conduct your own investment research to evaluate or confirm the investment advice you receive from your (primary) investment adviser?				
		Always (row %)	Sometimes (row %)	Rarely (row %)	Never (row %)	All
How often do you follow the investment advice you receive from your (primary) investment adviser?	Always	19	37	26	18	100
	Sometimes	28	49	20	3	100
	Rarely[a]	40	20	25	15	100
	Never[a]	17	33	0	50	100
	All	25	43	22	10	100

Respondents with ongoing advisory relationships; percentage of total		How often do you conduct your own investment research to evaluate or confirm the investment advice you receive from your (primary) investment adviser?				
		Always	Sometimes	Rarely	Never	All
How often do you follow the investment advice you receive from your (primary) investment adviser?	Always	7	13	9	7	36
	Sometimes	17	29	12	2	60
	Rarely[a]	1	1	1	1	3
	Never[a]	<0.5	<0.5	0	1	1
	All	25	43	22	10	100

[a] There is an extremely small sample size in this row.
Notes: The sample is 602 US households owning mutual funds outside workplace retirement plans and with ongoing relationships with professional financial advisers. The survey was conducted between late July 2006 and September 2006.
Source: ICI Mutual Fund Shareholder Financial Advice Survey.

likely to take the lead. Mutual fund investors willing to take substantial financial risk were most likely to say they took the lead in decision-making, while those willing to take below-average risk were least likely.

Which mutual fund-owning households tend to use financial advisers?

Each spring, ICI's Annual Mutual Fund Shareholder Tracking Survey asks mutual fund-owning households about their interactions with financial advisers as part of a battery of questions regarding the household's saving and investing in mutual funds. The May 2011 survey covered 4,216 US households, of which, 44 percent, or 1,859 held mutual funds.[7] This

TABLE 12.3 Investor/adviser split of decision-making

Mutual fund investors with ongoing advisory relationships; percentage of row agreeing with the statement

	Delegate all decision-making or adviser takes the lead	You and your adviser usually make decisions together	You usually take the lead in investment decision-making
Marital status			
Married or living with a partner	36	33	31
Single	33	37	31
Divorced or separated	43	28	29
Widowed	48	39	13
Education level			
High school graduate or less	49	34	17
Some college or associate's degree	44	28	28
Completed four years of college	33	40	27
Some graduate school	42	19	39
Completed graduate school	33	36	31
Respondent age			
Younger than 35[a]	31	33	36
35–44	34	32	34
45–54	38	29	32
55–64	42	31	27
65 or older	36	41	22
Retirement status			
Retired from lifetime occupation	41	38	21
Not retired	36	32	33
Employment status			
Employed full-time	33	33	33
Employed part-time	39	33	28
Not currently employed	45	35	21
Total household income before taxes in 2005			
Less than $50,000	52	33	15
$50,000–$99,999	44	31	26
$100,000–$249,999	31	36	33
$250,000 or more	39	27	34
Sex			
Male	33	37	31
Female	41	32	27

(*Continued*)

TABLE 12.3 Continued

Mutual fund investors with ongoing advisory relationships; percentage of row agreeing with the statement

	Delegate all decision-making or adviser takes the lead	You and your adviser usually make decisions together	You usually take the lead in investment decision-making
Type of decision-maker			
Married/partner female sole decision-maker	42	24	35
Married/partner female co-decision-maker	39	32	30
Married/partner male sole decision-maker	33	28	39
Married/partner male co-decision-maker	32	46	21
Single female	33	33	33
Single male	30	50	20
Divorced/separated/ widowed female	48	37	16
Divorced/separated/ widowed male	37	21	42
Willingness to take financial risk			
Not willing to take any financial risk	36	32	32
Willing to take below-average financial risk	58	23	20
Willing to take average financial risk	37	37	26
Willing to take above-average financial risk	34	34	32
Willing to take substantial financial risk	29	26	45
All	38	34	29

[a] There is an extremely small sample size in this row.

Notes: The sample is 602 US households owning mutual funds outside workplace retirement plans and with ongoing relationships with professional financial advisers. The survey was conducted between late July 2006 and September 2006. Row percentages may not add to 100 percent because of rounding.

Source: ICI Mutual Fund Shareholder Financial Advice Survey; see Schrass and Bogdan (2012).

When, Why, and How Do Investors Use Advisers? 259

section first summarizes the channels through which mutual fund-owning households own mutual funds, and then presents tabulations to discern demographic and financial differences between mutual fund-owning households who have ongoing advisory relationships and those who do not. Finally, multivariate analysis explores which variables appear to be related to ongoing financial adviser use.

Mutual fund investors purchase funds through a variety of channels

Of the 52.3 million US households owning mutual funds in 2011, half indicated they had ongoing advisory relationships with investment professionals. As Figure 12.4 demonstrates, 69 percent of mutual fund-owning households held mutual funds through their employer-sponsored retirement plans, 68 percent held mutual funds outside of employer-sponsored retirement plans, and 37 percent held mutual funds both inside and outside such plans (Schrass and Bogdan, 2012). Mutual funds purchased outside employer-sponsored retirement plans usually are obtained through

Percentage of US households owning mutual funds, May 2011
Owned mutual funds outside employer-sponsored retirement plans (68%)

- Inside employer-sponsored retirement plans: 69%
- Full-service broker: 31%
- Independent financial planner: 27%
- Bank or savings institution representative: 18%
- Insurance agent: 9%
- Fund company directly: 23%
- Discount broker: 16%

Sales force (54%)

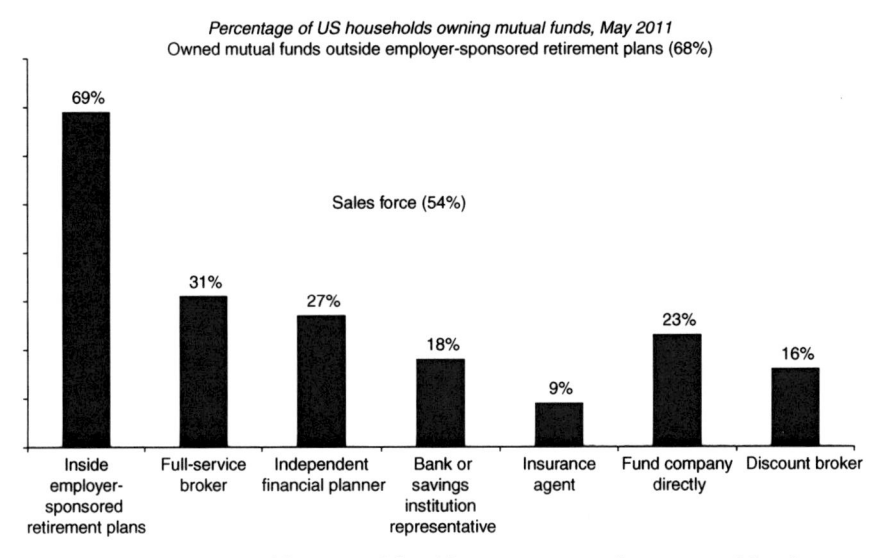

Figure 12.4 Sources used by mutual fund investors to purchase mutual funds

Notes: Multiple responses are included. The sample is 1,859 US households owning mutual funds in May 2011.

Source: 2011 ICI Annual Mutual Fund Shareholder Tracking Survey; see Schrass and Bogdan (2012).

260 The Market for Retirement Financial Advice

two channels: the sales force and the direct market approach. Fifty-four percent of mutual fund-owning households purchased them through the sales force channel, which includes registered investment advisers, full-service brokers, independent financial planners, bank or savings institution representatives, and insurance agents. About one-third (32 percent) owned funds purchased from the fund company directly or through a discount broker (the direct market channel). About half (52 percent) of mutual fund-owning households held funds purchased through one source type, about one-third (35 percent) owned funds through two source types, and the remaining 13 percent held funds through all three source types (see Figure 12.5).[8] Nevertheless, nearly one-third of (32 percent) mutual fund-owning households owned funds only through employer-sponsored

- 32% Inside employer-sponsored retirement plan[a]
- 15%
- 15% Investment professionals[b]
- 13%
- 11%
- 6%
- 2% Fund companies, fund supermarkets, or discount brokers

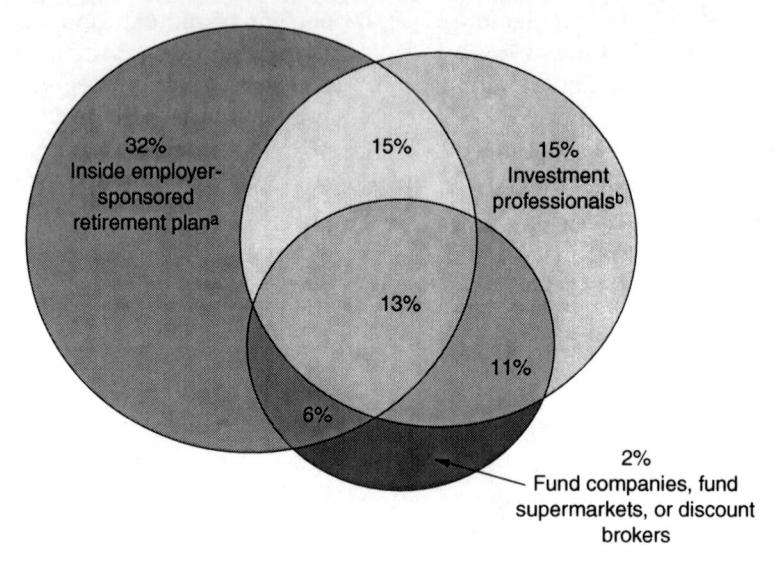

Figure 12.5 Nearly half of mutual fund-owning households held shares through multiple sources

Notes: Figure does not add to 100 percent because 6 percent of households owning mutual funds outside of employer-sponsored retirement plans did not indicate which source was used to purchase funds. Of this 6 percent, 3 percent owned funds both inside and outside employer-sponsored retirement plans and 3 percent owned funds only outside of employer-sponsored retirement plans. The sample is 1,859 US households owning mutual funds in May 2011.
[a]Employer-sponsored retirement plans include DC plans (401(k), 403(b), or 457 plans, Keoghs, and other DC plans without 401(k) features) and employer-sponsored IRAs (SEP IRAs, SAR-SEP IRAs, and SIMPLE IRAs). [b]Investment professionals include registered investment advisers, full-service brokers, independent financial planners, bank and savings institution representatives, insurance agents, and accountants.

Source: 2011 ICI Annual Mutual Fund Shareholder Tracking Survey; see Schrass and Bogdan (2012).

retirement plans, and 15 percent owned funds only through investment professionals outside of such plans.

Ownership patterns by purchase source vary with household age. Younger households were more likely to indicate that employer-sponsored retirement plans were the only channel through which they held mutual funds: indeed, 42 percent of those under age 50 indicated they held mutual funds only inside employer-sponsored retirement plans.[9] By contrast, households aged 50 or older were more likely to indicate mutual fund ownership outside of those plans, with 39 percent owning mutual funds only outside of such plans.[10] The differential pattern of mutual fund ownership outside employer-sponsored retirement plans among older households is in part due to the lifecycle progression through work, employer-sponsored retirement plan accumulations, change of job and retirement, and rollover of retirement plan assets to traditional IRAs, which fall into the 'outside' category.[11]

Characteristics of mutual fund-owning households by ongoing advisory relationship status

This section explores which mutual fund-owning households are more likely to have ongoing relationships with financial advisers, using the 2011 ICI Mutual Fund Shareholder Tracking Survey. Both cross tabulations and multivariate analysis are used to determine which demographic and financial characteristics appear to be correlated with ongoing advisory relationships.

About half of mutual fund-owning households indicated that they had ongoing advisory relationships in May 2011. Mutual fund-owning households with ongoing advisory relationships tended to be headed by slightly older individuals, with a median age of head of household of 53, compared with a median age of 47 among households without ongoing advisory relationships; they also were more likely to be married or widowed (see Table 12.4). Those with advisory relationships were more likely to be non-working retired and less likely to be employed, compared with households without advisory relationships.[12] Nevertheless, incomes between the two groups were very similar. Educational distributions also were similar between the two groups.

Conventional wisdom suggests that households with more financial assets would be more likely to use financial advisers than those with fewer assets, a supposition which is confirmed in the survey data. Median household financial assets for mutual fund-owning households with advisory relationships ($285,000) were more than double that of their peers without advisory relationships ($130,000; see Table 12.4). Mutual fund-owning

TABLE 12.4 Mutual fund investor head of household characteristics

Percentage of US households owning mutual funds by advisory relationship status, May 2011

	All mutual fund-owning households	With an ongoing relationship with adviser	Without an ongoing relationship with adviser
Age of household sole or co-decision-maker for saving and investing			
Younger than 35	16	10	20
35–44	21	18	24
45–54	24	24	26
55–64	21	26	16
65 or older	18	22	14
Median (years)	50	53	47
Mean (years)	50	53	48
Education level			
High school graduate or less	24	24	22
Some college or associate's degree	29	28	30
Completed four years of college	23	23	23
Some graduate school	6	6	6
Completed graduate school	18	19	19
Marital status			
Married or living with a partner	74	76	72
Single	10	9	12
Divorced or separated	9	7	12
Widowed	7	8	4
Household investment decision-maker			
Male is sole decision-maker	19	16	23
Female is sole decision-maker	19	17	21
Co-decision-makers	62	67	56
Memo: Household financial assets			
Total household financial assets (median)	$200,000	$285,000	$130,000
Mutual fund assets (median)	$120,000	$170,000	$85,000
Number of responding households	1,859	890	874

Source: 2011 ICI Annual Mutual Fund Shareholder Tracking Survey; see Schrass and Bogdan (2012).

households with ongoing advisory relationships also were more likely to have non-mutual fund investments.[13]

Ownership of employer-sponsored DC plan accounts was higher among mutual fund-owning households without advisory relationships, which would be expected given the limited role that advice plays in such plans and the fact that these households were more likely to indicate they held mutual funds only through such plans.[14] These ownership patterns likely also reflect their slightly younger age profile and the work-lifecycle phenomenon that does not yet have them to the rollover stage. In a similar vein, mutual fund-owning households with advisory relationships were more likely to report IRA ownership compared with those without advisory relationships.[15]

The median household mutual fund assets among mutual fund-owning households with advisory relationships ($170,000) were double that for mutual fund-owning households without advisory relationships ($85,000; see Table 12.4). They also tended to own more mutual funds and expressed higher confidence that mutual funds could help them meet their financial goals. The 2006 ICI Mutual Fund Shareholder Financial Advice Survey shows that mutual fund investors using professional financial advisers were less engaged with the Internet than those not obtaining financial advice.[16] Similarly, in May 2011, the ICI Annual Mutual Fund Shareholder Tracking Survey data show that, although mutual fund-owning households with advisory relationships were roughly similar to households without advisory relationships in terms of much of their Internet access and activity, they differed in at least one significant dimension: only 14 percent of mutual fund-owning households with Internet access and ongoing advisory relationships had bought or sold investments online, compared with 24 percent of those with Internet access but no ongoing advisory relationships.

Multivariate analysis

A probit analysis helps confirm that many of the patterns evident in the cross tabulations also are statistically significant in a multivariate analysis. Table 12.5 presents the variables included in the regression analysis and Table 12.6 reports the regression results. The dependent variable is a 0-1 dummy for the ongoing relationship with a financial adviser.

Higher household financial assets tend to be significantly positively related to the probability that the household had ongoing financial advice. For example, mutual fund-owning households with financial assets of $250,000 or more have a significantly higher probability of having an ongoing advisory relationship than those with less than $10,000 in financial assets (see Table 12.6). Those with a head of household who has completed graduate school had a significantly lower probability of having an ongoing advisory relationship than those with high school or less education, although the distribution of educational attainment is similar between the two groups (see Table 12.4). Willingness to take any amount of risk is positively correlated with having an ongoing advisory relationship, although not all risk categories are statistically significant (see Table 12.6).[17] Mutual fund-owning households who use the Internet for financial purposes have a

TABLE 12.5 Variables used in probit regression model

Variable name	Variable description
finadv	1 if respondent has ongoing advisory relationship, 0 if not
age	Head of household age
age2	Head of household age squared
hh_income1	Household income < $25,000 (omitted)
hh_income2	$25,000 ≤ household income < $35,000
hh_income3	$35,000 ≤ household income < $50,000
hh_income4	$50,000 ≤ household income < $75,000
hh_income5	$75,000 ≤ household income < $100,000
hh_income6	$100,000 ≤ household income < $149,000
hh_income7	$150,000 ≤ household income < $250,000
hh_income8	Household income ≥ $250,000
hh_finassets1	Household financial assets < $10,000 (omitted)
hh_finassets2	$10,000 ≤ household financial assets < $30,000
hh_finassets3	$30,000 ≤ household financial assets < $50,000
hh_finassets4	$50,000 ≤ household financial assets < $75,000
hh_finassets5	$75,000 ≤ household financial assets < $100,000
hh_finassets6	$100,000 ≤ household financial assets < $250,000
hh_finassets7	Household financial assets ≥ $250,000
education1	High school graduate or less (omitted)
education2	Some college or associate's degree
education3	Completed four years of college
education4	Some graduate school
education5	Completed graduate school
risk1	Not willing to take any financial risk (omitted)
risk2	Willing to take below-average financial risk
risk3	Willing to take average financial risk
risk4	Willing to take above-average financial risk
risk5	Willing to take substantial financial risk
dm_female	1 if the sole or co-decision-maker is female; 0 if the sole or co-decision-maker is male
int_fin	Used Internet for financial purpose
own_dc	Own DC account
own_ira	Own IRA
confidence1	Not at all confident that mutual funds are an investment that can help the household meet financial goals (omitted)
confidence2	Not very confident that mutual funds are an investment that can help the household meet financial goals
confidence3	Somewhat confident that mutual funds are an investment that can help the household meet financial goals
confidence4	Very confident that mutual funds are an investment that can help the household meet financial goals

Source: 2011 ICI Annual Mutual Fund Shareholder Tracking Survey; see Schrass and Bogdan (2012).

TABLE 12.6 Probability mutual fund investor has ongoing advisory relationship

Variable	Finadv = Estimate	Standard error	z	P > z	Significance	Mean	Average marginal effects Coefficient	Standard error	z
intercept	−1.8729	0.6066	−3.09	0.002	***				
age	0.0277	0.0186	1.49	0.135		55.952	0.0100	0.0067	1.5
age2	−0.0002	0.0002	−1.29	0.197		3330.55	−0.0001	0.0001	−1.29
hh_income2	0.0775	0.2299	0.34	0.736		0.0740	0.0265	0.0784	0.34
hh_income3	0.1068	0.2192	0.49	0.626		0.1033	0.0364	0.0746	0.49
hh_income4	0.0485	0.2072	0.23	0.815		0.2213	0.0170	0.0724	0.23
hh_income5	0.1567	0.2164	0.72	0.469		0.1912	0.0561	0.0771	0.73
hh_income6	0.0398	0.2240	0.18	0.859		0.1993	0.0146	0.0820	0.18
hh_income7	0.0679	0.2383	0.28	0.776		0.1221	0.0247	0.0866	0.29
hh_income8	0.1068	0.2792	0.38	0.702		0.0407	0.0370	0.0961	0.39
hh_finassets2	0.6217	0.3253	1.91	0.056	*	0.0578	0.1815	0.1093	1.66
hh_finassets3	0.4116	0.3461	1.19	0.234		0.0423	0.1150	0.1083	1.06
hh_finassets4	0.9974	0.3247	3.07	0.002	***	0.0667	0.3254	0.1172	2.78
hh_finassets5	0.6053	0.3416	1.77	0.076	*	0.0448	0.1891	0.1210	1.56
hh_finassets6	0.9341	0.3058	3.05	0.002	***	0.2449	0.3129	0.1057	2.96
hh_finassets7	1.1584	0.3125	3.71	0	***	0.5183	0.4034	0.0985	4.1
education2	−0.1703	0.1369	−1.24	0.213		0.2897	−0.0598	0.0481	−1.24
education3	−0.1854	0.1471	−1.26	0.207		0.2433	−0.0658	0.0524	−1.26
education4	−0.2913	0.1806	−1.61	0.107		0.0830	−0.1023	0.0637	−1.61
education5	−0.2698	0.1470	−1.84	0.066	*	0.2685	−0.0968	0.0528	−1.83
risk2	0.3456	0.1797	1.92	0.054	*	0.0960	0.1226	0.0629	1.95
risk3	0.3291	0.1456	2.26	0.024	**	0.4939	0.1184	0.0520	2.28

(*Continued*)

TABLE 12.6 Continued

Variable	Estimate	Standard error	z	P > z	Significance	Mean	Coefficient	Standard error	z
risk4	0.1520	0.1562	0.97	0.331		0.2832	0.0559	0.0575	0.97
risk5	0.5083	0.2332	2.18	0.029	**	0.0407	0.1798	0.0799	2.25
dm_female	0.1062	0.0782	1.36	0.174		0.4475	0.0383	0.0281	1.36
int_fin	−0.2919	0.1048	−2.79	0.005	***	0.7852	−0.1047	0.0368	−2.85
own_dc	−0.3169	0.0971	−3.26	0.001	***	0.7413	−0.1144	0.0345	−3.32
own_ira	0.3330	0.0876	3.8	0	***	0.7217	0.1228	0.0324	3.79
confidence2	−0.2874	0.2055	−1.4	0.162		0.1082	−0.1020	0.0714	−1.43
confidence3	0.1725	0.1781	0.97	0.333		0.6013	0.0632	0.0651	0.97
confidence4	0.3127	0.1893	1.65	0.099	*	0.2417	0.1147	0.0682	1.68

Notes: Regression was run on an unweighted sample of 1,229 mutual fund-owning households. Pseudo-R^2 is 0.0846.
*Significant at the 90% confidence level;
**significant at the 95% confidence level;
***significant at the 99% confidence level.

Source: 2011 ICI Annual Mutual Fund Shareholder Tracking Survey; see Schrass and Bogdan (2012).

lower probability of obtaining ongoing financial advice, consistent with the 2006 advice survey results and the tabulations of the May 2011 survey data.

Also, bearing out the cross tabulations, IRA ownership increases the probability of the mutual fund investor having an ongoing advisory relationship, and DC account ownership decreases the probability of having an ongoing advisory relationship (see Table 12.6). These variables are highly significant and their interaction with ongoing advisory relationships makes intuitive sense: financial advice is more readily available outside of employer-sponsored retirement plans, and rollover activity, which is common throughout people's working lives, generates traditional IRAs, which are considered to be outside employer-sponsored plans.

Finally, mutual fund investors agreeing that they are 'very confident' that mutual funds can help them meet their financial goals have a higher probability of having ongoing advisory relationships than do mutual fund investors who are not at all confident (see Table 12.6). This result is consistent with the 2006 advice survey's finding that mutual fund investors often seek professional financial advice to achieve peace of mind and grow their assets.[18]

Conclusion

About half of mutual fund-owning households report they have ongoing financial advisory relationships. They seek professional financial advice for a variety of reasons going much beyond the selection and purchase of specific mutual funds. Many seek financial advice as the result of a trigger event, such as the receipt of a lump sum through inheritance, retirement, or job change, or a change in household composition, while others seek financial advice to address a specific financial goal, such as saving for retirement or education. Mutual fund investors typically receive multiple services and choose to work with financial advisers because advisers have expertise in areas they themselves do not.

The advisory relationship is complex and involves a range of give and take in the decision-making process. Mutual fund investors with ongoing advisory relationships were roughly evenly split into three camps of investors with respect to decision-making: delegators or adviser taking the lead (38 percent), collaborators (34 percent), and investors taking the lead (29 percent). Mutual fund-owning households with ongoing advisory relationships tend to have higher household financial assets and higher confidence that mutual funds can help them meet their goals. Use of the Internet for financial purposes—which perhaps indicates a more self-help investor—is negatively correlated with the use of ongoing financial advice.

268 The Market for Retirement Financial Advice

The author thanks Steven Bass, Michael Bogdan, and Daniel Schrass for their expert research assistance with this chapter.

Endnotes

1. In May 2011, 38.8 percent of US households owned IRAs and 22.7 percent of US households owned mutual funds in IRAs. See Holden and Schrass (2011) and Bogdan et al. (2011). These statistics are tabulations from the May 2011 ICI Annual Mutual Fund Shareholder Tracking Survey.
2. In May 2011, 51.1 percent of US households owned DC plan accounts and 29.1 percent of US households owned mutual funds in DC plan accounts. These statistics are tabulations from the May 2011 ICI Annual Mutual Fund Shareholder Tracking Survey.
3. Other research concludes from an analysis of a sample of German investors that 'investors who most need the financial advice are least likely to obtain it' (Bhattacharya et al., 2011: 4).
4. The ICI Mutual Fund Shareholder Financial Advice Survey sample consisted of 1,003 households owning mutual funds outside of employer-sponsored retirement plans. Of those households, 60 percent, or 602 respondents, currently had ongoing advisory relationships; 13 percent, or 131 respondents, had used one-time advice; 18 percent, or 176 respondents, had never used advisers; and the remaining 9 percent, or 94 respondents, were currently not using advisers. This telephone survey was fielded from late July 2006 through September 2006 to a random selection of households from telephone exchanges with median household incomes of $75,000 or more. For additional analysis of the ICI Mutual Fund Shareholder Financial Advice Survey, see Leonard-Chambers and Bogdan (2007).
5. Multiple responses are included, and about two-thirds of respondents indicated they consulted multiple sources of information and advice. Fifty-six percent of respondents with a choice of distribution option indicated they consulted with family or peers, and 46 percent consulted employer-provided resources (including professional financial advisers, seminars, workshops, online retirement software, and printed materials). The ICI Defined Contribution Plan Distribution Decision Survey was a phone–mail–phone survey to a random sample from an age-targeted sample and from a retirement-targeted sample, fielded from October 2007 through December 2007. The survey identified 1,187 recently retired individuals with DC accounts, of which 876 agreed to complete the mail survey, of which 659 did the follow-up phone survey. In the final analysis, 608 respondents completed the survey. See Sabelhaus et al. (2008) for additional results from the survey.

When, Why, and How Do Investors Use Advisers? 269

6. The 2011 ICI IRA Owners Survey was a random digit dial telephone survey, fielded in May 2011, with 2,300 IRA-owning households completing the survey. See Holden and Schrass (2011) for additional detail.
7. The 2011 ICI Annual Mutual Fund Shareholder Tracking Survey was a random digit dial telephone survey fielded in May 2011. See Bogdan et al. (2011) and Schrass and Bogdan (2012) for additional detail and survey results.
8. This statistic counts the number of different source types. Mutual fund-owning households may use multiple firms within a given source type.
9. In May 2011, 42 percent of mutual fund-owning households younger than 50 held mutual funds only inside employer-sponsored retirement plans; 10 percent held mutual funds only through investment professionals; and 2 percent held mutual funds only through fund companies, fund supermarkets, or discount brokers. Fourteen percent held mutual funds inside employer-sponsored retirement plans and through investment professionals; 7 percent held mutual funds through investment professionals and fund companies, fund supermarkets, or discount brokers; and 7 percent held mutual funds inside employer-sponsored retirement plans and through fund companies, fund supermarkets, or discount brokers. Twelve percent owned funds through all three channels. The remaining 6 percent owned mutual funds outside of employer-sponsored retirement plans but did not specify the source. Of this 6 percent, 3 percent owned funds both inside and outside employer-sponsored retirement plans and 3 percent owned funds only outside of employer-sponsored retirement plans. These results are based on a sample 896 mutual fund-owning households headed by an individual younger than 50. Data are from the 2011 ICI Annual Mutual Fund Shareholder Tracking Survey and notes from Figure 12.5 apply.
10. In May 2011, 23 percent of mutual fund-owning households aged 50 or older held mutual funds only inside employer-sponsored retirement plans; 19 percent held mutual funds only through investment professionals; and 3 percent held mutual funds only through fund companies, fund supermarkets, or discount brokers. Seventeen percent held mutual funds inside employer-sponsored retirement plans and through investment professionals; 15 percent held mutual funds through investment professionals and fund companies, fund supermarkets, or discount brokers; and 6 percent held mutual funds inside employer-sponsored retirement plans and through fund companies, fund supermarkets, or discount brokers. Thirteen percent owned funds through all three channels. The remaining 4 percent owned mutual funds outside of employer-sponsored retirement plans but did not specify the source. Of this 4 percent, 2 percent owned funds both inside and outside employer-sponsored retirement plans and 2 percent owned funds only outside of employer-sponsored retirement plans. These results are based on a sample 963 mutual fund-owning households headed by an individual aged 50 or older. Data are from the 2011 ICI Annual Mutual Fund Shareholder Tracking Survey and notes from Figure 12.5 apply.

11. For discussion of the role of rollovers and IRAs in the process of planning for retirement, see Sabelhaus and Schrass (2009), Holden et al. (2010), and Holden and Schrass (2011).
12. Over half (58 percent) of mutual fund-owning households with advisory relationships were employed full-time, compared with 68 percent of households without ongoing advisory relationships. Twenty-six percent of mutual fund-owning households with advisory relationships were non-working retired, compared with 16 percent of households without ongoing advisory relationships. These results are from tabulations of the May 2011 ICI Annual Mutual Fund Shareholder Tracking Survey.
13. This result is from tabulations of the May 2011 ICI Annual Mutual Fund Shareholder Tracking Survey.
14. In May 2011, 82 percent of mutual fund-owning households without advisory relationships had DC plan accounts compared with 73 percent of mutual fund-owning households with advisory relationships. In addition, 42 percent of mutual fund-owning households without advisory relationships held mutual funds only through employer-sponsored retirement plans, compared with 17 percent of mutual fund-owning households with advisory relationships. These results are from tabulations of the May 2011 ICI Annual Mutual Fund Shareholder Tracking Survey.
15. Nearly three-quarters (74 percent) of mutual fund-owning households with advisory relationships owned traditional or Roth IRAs, compared with about half (51 percent) of mutual fund-owning households without advisory relationships. Such IRAs are considered investments outside of employer-sponsored retirement plans, and mutual fund-owning households with advisory relationships were more likely to report mutual fund ownership outside such plans; 38 percent of mutual fund-owning households with ongoing advisory relationships owned mutual funds only outside employer-sponsored retirement plans, compared with 26 percent of those without ongoing advice. In addition, 45 percent of mutual fund-owning households with ongoing advisory relationships owned mutual funds both inside and outside employer-sponsored retirement plans, compared with 32 percent of those without ongoing advice. (Households with advisory relationships also were more likely to report employer-sponsored IRA ownership.) These results are from tabulations of the May 2011 ICI Annual Mutual Fund Shareholder Tracking Survey.
16. Logit analysis of the 2006 advice survey data finds that mutual fund investors who do not go online for investment information are nearly twice as likely to have ongoing advisory relationships compared with those who do go online for investment information (Leonard-Chambers and Bogdan, 2007: 7).
17. Mutual fund-owning households without ongoing advisory relationships were more likely to indicate that they were unwilling to take any financial risk than those with ongoing advisory relationships.

18. In the 2006 advice survey, 76 percent of mutual fund investors with ongoing advisory relationships indicated a major reason for using a professional adviser was to have a better chance of growing their money with the adviser than on their own. Three-quarters agreed 'wanting peace of mind about investments' was a major reason to seek professional advice. For additional information on this survey, see endnote 4 in this chapter and Leonard-Chambers and Bogdan (2007).

References

Bhattacharya, U., A. Hackethal, S. Kaesler, B. Loos, and S. Meyer (2012). 'Is Unbiased Financial Advice to Retail Investors Sufficient? Answers from a Large Field Study,' *Review of Financial Studies*, 25(4): 975–1032.

Bluethgen, R., A. Gintschel, A. Hackethal, and A. Müller (2008). 'Financial Advice and Individual Investors' Portfolios,' SSRN Working Paper No. 968197. http://papers.ssrn.com/sol3/papers.cfm?abstract_id=968197

Bogdan, M., S. Holden, and D. Schrass (2011). 'Ownership of Mutual Funds, Shareholder Sentiment, and Use of the Internet, 2011,' *ICI Research Perspective*, 17(5). www.ici.org/pdf/per17-05.pdf

Collins, J. M. (2010). 'A Review of Financial Advice Models and the Take-Up of Financial Advice,' Center for Financial Security Working Paper No. 10-5. Madison, WI: University of Wisconsin-Madison.

Hackethal, A., and R. Inderst (2013). 'How to Make the Market for Financial Advice Work,' in O. S. Mitchell and K. Smetters, eds., *The Market for Retirement Financial Advice*. Oxford, UK: Oxford University Press, pp. 213–28.

Holden, S., and D. Schrass (2011). 'The Role of IRAs in U.S. Households' Saving for Retirement, 2011,' *ICI Research Perspective*, 17(8). www.ici.org/pdf/per17-08.pdf

—— J. Sabelhaus, and S. Bass (2010). *The IRA Investor Profile: Traditional IRA Investors' Rollover Activity, 2007 and 2008*. Washington, DC: Investment Company Institute; and New York, NY: Securities Industry and Financial Markets Association. www.ici.org/pdf/rpt_10_ira_rollovers.pdf

Hung, A. A., and J. K. Yoong (2013). 'Asking for Help: Survey and Experimental Evidence on Financial Advice and Behavior Change,' in O. S. Mitchell and K. Smetters, eds., *The Market for Retirement Financial Advice*. Oxford, UK: Oxford University Press, pp. 182–212.

Leonard-Chambers, V., and M. Bogdan (2007). 'Why Do Mutual Fund Investors Use Professional Financial Advisers?' *ICI Research Fundamentals*, 16(1). www.ici.org/pdf/fm-v16n1.pdf

Sabelhaus, J., and D. Schrass (2009). 'The Evolving Role of IRAs in U.S. Retirement Planning,' *ICI Research Perspective*, 15(3). www.ici.org/pdf/per15-03.pdf

—— M. Bogdan, and S. Holden (2008). 'Defined Contribution Plan Distribution Choices at Retirement: A Survey of Employees Retiring Between 2002 and 2007,' *Investment Company Institute Research Series*. Washington, DC: Investment Company Institute. www.ici.org/pdf/rpt_08_dcdd.pdf

Schrass, D., and M. Bogdan (2012). 'Profile of Mutual Fund Shareholders, 2011,' *ICI Research Report*. Washington, DC: Investment Company Institute. www.ici.org/pdf/rpt_12_profiles.pdf

van Rooij, M., A. Lusardi, and R. Alessie (2011). 'Financial Literacy and Stock Market Participation,' *Journal of Financial Economics, Elsevier*, 101(2): 449–72.

Part III
Market and Regulatory Considerations

Chapter 13
Harmonizing the Regulation of Financial Advisers

Arthur B. Laby

Financial services professionals who advise individuals about securities, such as stocks, bonds, or mutual funds, are generally either broker-dealers or investment advisers, titles that have little meaning to ordinary investors (RAND Report, 2008; SEC Staff, 2011*b*; Hung and Yoong, 2013). Although brokers and advisers historically provided distinct services, the roles they serve today are often similar or nearly identical. Regulation, however, has not kept pace with changes in the industry and brokers and advisers remain subject to separate regulatory regimes. The U.S. Securities and Exchange Commission (SEC) is now considering whether to harmonize the regulation of broker-dealers and investment advisers and place a fiduciary duty on brokers that give advice to retail customers. Under a fiduciary standard, brokers would be subject to a higher duty of care applicable to investment advisers. This chapter explores the debate over regulatory harmonization, places it in historical context, and discusses recent developments shaping its resolution.

We proceed by explaining how the debate over harmonization has migrated from the SEC to the courts, to Congress, and back to the SEC. First, we provide background information regarding harmonization, followed by a review of the historical context of the regulation of brokers and advisers, culminating in the SEC's adoption of an ill-fated rule under the Advisers Act to address harmonization-related concerns. Next, we explain the legal challenge to the rule mounted by the Financial Planning Association and the reasons the District of Columbia (DC) Circuit Court of Appeals vacated the rule. Then we turn to Congressional action, summarizing how the Dodd-Frank Wall Street Reform and Consumer Protection Act (Dodd-Frank Act) addressed regulatory harmonization and placed ultimate responsibility for the issue back on the SEC's shoulders. Subsequently, we discuss a 2011 SEC staff study mandated by the Dodd-Frank Act. Finally, we identify challenges facing the SEC as it pursues a path of harmonization.

Regulatory harmonization

Individual investors planning for a child's education, preparing for retirement, or just managing short-term savings, face a dizzying array of financial services providers eagerly seeking to gather more assets under their management. Banks, mutual funds, stockbrokers, investment advisers, insurance brokers, and financial planners of different stripes offer a wide variety of investment products and services, many of which are devilishly complex and beyond the understanding of average investors. In some cases, the roles performed by these service providers overlap. A financial planner who trades securities for a client, for example, must also be a broker-dealer. A securities salesman who also sells insurance policies is subject to the insurance-licensing regime in the state where he does business.

Labels used by financial services providers tend to confound investors. Many individuals and firms which call themselves 'financial advisers' may not be considered 'investment advisers' under the law; instead, they are regulated as broker-dealers. In addition, many brokers and advisers perform an identical function when they provide advice to individuals about securities. Under a philosophy of functional regulation, service providers performing the same role should be treated similarly. The federal securities laws, however, contain separate regulatory schemes, one for brokers and another for advisers, and the duties and obligations differ under each. This result—same function but different regulation—appears nonsensical, particularly when most people pay little attention to whether the individual sitting across the table recommending a stock or mutual fund is considered a broker or an adviser under the law.

What are the key differences between broker-dealer and investment adviser regulation? Brokers are regulated under a Depression-era law, the Securities Exchange Act of 1934, which defines brokers and dealers and requires their registration with the SEC (Securities Exchange Act, 1934: §15(a)). When providing advice to customers, brokers are subject to a 'suitability' standard; they must ensure that investments they recommend are suitable to a customer's investment needs (FINRA, 2012). The theory behind the suitability rule is that when a broker recommends a security, he is making an implied representation that the security is consistent with the investor's objectives and therefore a suitable investment (Hazen, 2009).

Investment advisers are financial services professionals devoted primarily to rendering advice. Advisers are subject to the Investment Advisers Act of 1940, which regulates persons who meet the definition of 'investment adviser' as defined by the Act. Under the Advisers Act, advisers are subject to a higher 'fiduciary' standard of care (*SEC v. Capital Gains Research Bureau*, 1963: 191–2). According to a fiduciary standard, an adviser's recommendation must not only be 'suitable,' it also must be in the client's 'best interest'

(*SEC v. Tambone*, 2008: 146). The adviser's best interest standard is analogous to a fiduciary's best interest standard in other areas, such as the law of trust or guardianship, and the duty has been called the 'highest known to the law' (*Donovan v. Bierwirth*, 1982: 272 n.8).

Over the last 15 years, the SEC has considered whether the bifurcated system of regulation for brokers and advisers should be revisited. During this period, regulators watched in disbelief as Bernard Madoff Investment Securities, which as of 2005 was both an investment adviser registered with the SEC and a broker-dealer registered with the SEC and the Financial Industry Regulatory Authority (FINRA), was exposed as a monumental Ponzi scheme, emphasizing the importance of vigorous regulation of financial services providers (Schapiro Statement, 2009). The courts and Congress have inserted themselves into the harmonization debate, and the Dodd-Frank Act required the SEC to further study the issue. The Act also authorized the SEC to harmonize the law but did not require new rules (Dodd-Frank, 2010: §913).

The decision regarding whether to harmonize regulation is critically important for the legal duties imposed on broker-dealer and investment adviser firms, as well as the hundreds of thousands of registered representatives who work for them, many of whom provide advice to retail customers (SEC Staff, 2011*b*). The decision also has important implications for brokers' business model, which is dependent in certain respects on application of the suitability standard as opposed to a fiduciary norm. Resolution of the debate is also pertinent to regulation of fiduciaries by the US Department of Labor (DOL) under the Employee Retirement Income Security Act (ERISA, 1974). As discussed below, the DOL has proposed a new definition of fiduciary under ERISA. Topics the SEC might address in new rules authorized by Dodd-Frank could apply to ERISA fiduciaries as well (EBSA, 2010).

Securities and Exchange Commission regulation
Historical development
Broker-dealers and investment advisers first faced federal regulation in the early part of the twentieth century when Congress enacted federal securities laws during the Great Depression. The Securities Act of 1933, a seminal securities statute passed as part of Franklin D. Roosevelt's First Hundred Days, required companies offering and selling securities to the public to register offerings with the government and provide detailed disclosure to the purchaser about the issuer and the securities to be sold. The Securities Act, however, did not regulate market professionals, such as brokers or advisers, in any detail.

Regulation of broker-dealers and the establishment of the SEC came one year later in the Securities Exchange Act of 1934. Leading up to passage of the Exchange Act, a bitter clash ensued between the Roosevelt Administration and the brokerage community over matters such as margin requirements, limitations on broker' activities, and the composition of the SEC itself. In the end, the Act was a product of political compromise after intensive lobbying not only by the New York Stock Exchange (NYSE), led by the infamous but formidable Richard Whitney, but also by dozens of local exchanges, which echoed Whitney's concerns. After months of negotiation, Congress passed the Exchange Act, which defined brokers and dealers, placed restrictions on their activities, and required their registration with the newly created SEC (Parrish, 1970; Seligman, 2003).

In 1938, after a scandal ensnaring the NYSE's Richard Whitney, Congress passed the Maloney Act as an amendment to the Exchange Act. The Maloney Act authorized the creation of the National Association of Securities Dealers (NASD) as a self-regulatory organization (SRO) for over-the-counter brokers and dealers (Maloney Act, 1938). Although the NASD played a salutary regulatory role, it also functioned as a powerful trade association and often opposed the SEC's initiatives (Seligman, 2003). The NASD's successor, FINRA, serves today as the SRO for broker-dealers, imposing detailed regulation and registration obligations on broker-dealer firms and their registered representatives. There are now approximately 5,100 broker-dealer firms and 600,000 registered representatives associated with those firms (SEC Staff, 2011b).

A statute dedicated to the regulation of investment advisers did not appear until 1940, when the last of the Depression-era securities laws were enacted. On the eve of America's entry into World War II, Congress passed the Investment Company Act, a voluminous statute regulating mutual funds. As Title 2 of the same bill, Congress passed the more modest Investment Advisers Act regulating investment advisers. Unlike the Exchange Act, the Advisers Act contained no reference to a self-regulatory structure for advisers, and no SRO for advisers exists today, although the topic is timely once again (SEC Staff, 2011a). The key provisions of the Advisers Act were a registration section, requiring certain advisers to register with the SEC, and an antifraud provision modeled after the Securities Act, which prohibited defrauding advisory clients or potential clients (Advisers Act, 1940: §§203, 206). SEC-registered investment advisers now number approximately 11,000; another 15,000 advisers are regulated by state authorities. There are approximately 275,000 investment adviser representatives associated with advisory firms (SEC Staff, 2011b).[1]

The Advisers Act's antifraud provision contained an important section affecting the business models of investment advisers. The provision severely restricted an adviser from engaging in principal transactions with advisory clients. A principal transaction occurs when an adviser, acting as a principal, buys securities from or sells securities to a client. Because principal trading presents a conflict of interest with one's client, the Advisers Act prohibited an adviser from engaging in such trading unless the adviser provided prior written disclosure to the client and obtained her consent on a trade-by-trade basis. When Congress adopted this provision, it clarified that the purpose was to reduce the chance that the adviser would dump a 'sour issue' on its own client (Schenker, 1940). Brokers faced no such restriction in the Exchange Act.

Brokers, who often advise their brokerage customers about securities, were excluded from coverage under the Advisers Act as long two conditions were met. Under the first condition, the broker's advice must be 'solely incidental to' brokerage services. (The phrase 'solely incidental' was not defined.) Under the second, the broker must receive no 'special compensation' for providing advice (Advisers Act, 1940: §202(a)(11)(C)). According to the Act's legislative history, the term 'special compensation' was shorthand for non-commission-based compensation (S. Rep. 76-1775, 1940: 22). Thus, as long as a broker could meet those two conditions—provide advice that is 'solely incidental' to brokerage and charge only commissions—the broker could provide investment advice but steer clear of regulation under the Advisers Act.

For decades, the division between brokers and advisers was fully functional for both regulators and the regulated. Brokers differentiated themselves from advisers by charging commissions. They were regulated under the Exchange Act and subject to a 'suitability' standard enforced by the SEC and the NASD, now FINRA. By contrast, advisers typically charged asset-based fees, such as 100 or 125 basis points, depending on the adviser, the client, and the amount of assets in the account. Advisers were regulated under the Advisers Act and subject to a stricter fiduciary standard of conduct enforced by the SEC. Brokers and advisers seemed to understand what the law required, depending on the type of account at issue, and the law worked fairly effectively and efficiently.

This quiescent state of affairs was disrupted in the 1970s and 1980s when the business model of established brokers came under attack. Deregulation of fixed commissions in 1975 squeezed the profits of many broker-dealers as discount brokers offered inexpensive execution options for customers who did not want to pay for full service brokerage. In addition, financial planning professionals began to offer comprehensive financial planning services to brokerage customers who were interested in advice not only about securities but also about other aspects of their financial lives, such as preparing a will, purchasing insurance, investing in a home, or establishing retirement or college savings accounts (Roper, 2011a). As indicated in

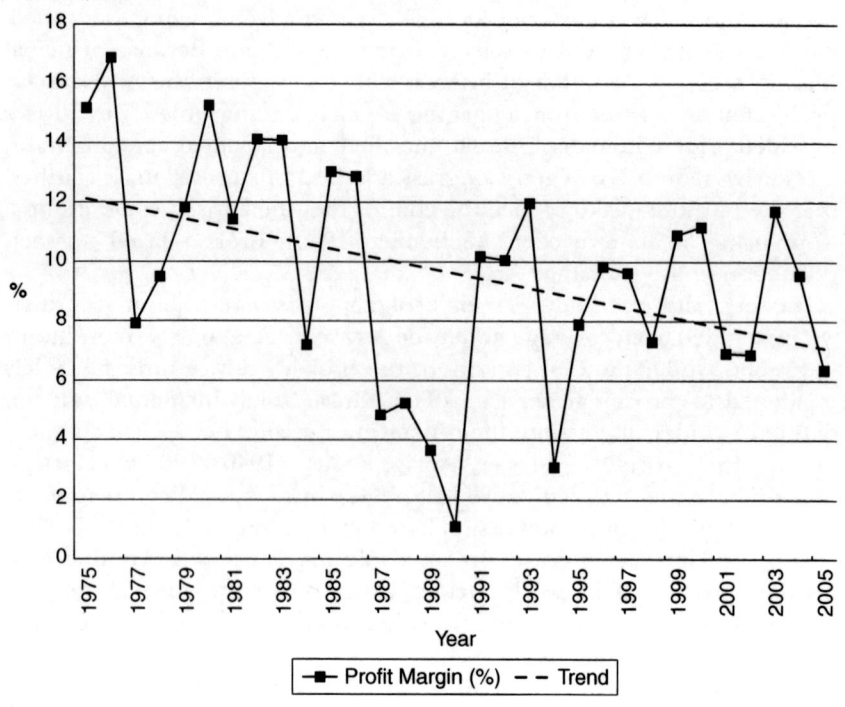

280 The Market for Retirement Financial Advice

Figure 13.1 Broker-dealers' profit margins (%) from 1975 to 2005

Note: Profit margin defined as the profitability ratio calculated as net income divided by revenues.

Source: SEC (1968–2006) (see Table 13.1).

Figure 13.1, the profitability of broker-dealers declined in the 30-year period beginning in 1975.

Brokers responded to the pressure on profitability in several ways. In the 1980s, some began to offer financial planning services to brokerage customers. In the 1990s, many brokers openly began to market themselves as advisers, even calling themselves financial consultants or financial advisers (Roper, 2011a). These brokers marketed their services based largely on trusted advice as opposed to the sale of particular products or traditional brokerage services such as trade execution, custody, recordkeeping, or hypothecation services. Also in the 1990s, to compete with the discount houses, some full service brokerage firms began to offer two tiers of services, one for full service brokerage customers and another for execution-only services (Gordon, 1999).

Finally, many brokers began to migrate from charging commission-based fees to asset-based compensation (White and Ramsey, 1999). This migration was a response, in part, to the publication of the Report of the Tully Committee, led by Daniel P. Tully, then Chairman and CEO of Merrill Lynch & Co. The Tully Committee, appointed to address the negative aspects of 'churning' in customer accounts, concluded that firms should base at least part of their compensation on the amount of assets held in a customer's account, regardless of whether any trading occurs (Tully Report, 1995). An asset-based fee, however, can lead to conflicts of interest as well. When charging an asset-based fee, the firm may pay too little attention to a customer, who must pay the fee regardless of effort expended by the firm, or the firm may fail to recommend that a customer remove assets from an account for the purchase of a product, such as life insurance, that would lower the amount of assets in the account and result in a lower fee for the firm. Nevertheless, after issuance of the Tully Report, many brokers began to charge asset-based fees not only because those fees reduced the risk of churning but also because asset-based fees ensured a constant stream of income for the firm.

The shift from brokers providing traditional brokerage services, such as securities execution, to the provision and marketing of advice, cast doubt on brokers' reliance on the statutory exclusion in the Advisers Act discussed above. If a broker held himself out as a financial adviser, could that broker maintain that his advice was still solely incidental to brokerage? This apprehension was heightened for brokers who charged an asset-based fee. As mentioned, charging any fee other than a commission could disqualify a broker from relying on the exclusion. In addition, introduction of a two-tier fee structure could trigger application of the Advisers Act because regulators could attribute a portion of the higher tier compensation (the difference between the two fees) to investment advice (SEC, 1999). Compensation attributable to advice could be considered 'special compensation' under the Advisers Act, preventing application of the exclusion.

Advisers Act Rule 202(a)(11)-1

By the late 1990s, brokers grew concerned that, as a result of changing their method of compensation, they would become subject to Advisers Act regulation in addition to regulation already imposed under the Exchange Act. In their effort to quell additional regulation, brokers made a policy argument based on a philosophy of functionality. If their activities had not changed, they reasoned, why should they become subject to an additional layer of supervision merely by virtue of offering investors alternative fee structures, particularly when regulators themselves encouraged brokers to adopt those very fee structures to address the pernicious abuse of churning (Gottlieb, 2005)? The SEC agreed in principle with this reasoning and, in 1999, proposed a rule that would allow brokers to charge non-commission-based compensation and still avail themselves of the brokers' exclusion in the Advisers Act (SEC, 1999).

The proposed rule was entitled *Certain Broker-Dealers Deemed Not To Be Investment Advisers*. Under the rule, a broker-dealer who provided investment advice would be excluded from the definition of adviser, regardless of how the broker was compensated, as long as three conditions were met. First, the advice had to be solely incidental to brokerage services. This condition reaffirmed the statutory condition discussed above. Second, the advice had to be non-discretionary. Under this condition, the Commission was stating for the first time that discretionary advisory services could no longer be considered 'solely incidental to' brokerage.[2] Third, the broker had to disclose to its customer that the account was a brokerage account. The last condition was intended to put the customer on notice that although s/he is receiving investment advice, the advice is coming from a broker, not an adviser and, as a result, s/he is not entitled to the statutory protections of the Advisers Act (SEC, 1999).

The Commission received over 1,700 comment letters on the proposal. As expected, brokers generally supported the rule while advisers assailed the initiative for harming investor protection, providing a marketing advantage to brokers over advisers, promoting investor confusion regarding the law, and sending mixed messages regarding functional regulation (Thompson, 2000). The advisers complained that the SEC failed to recognize that the nature of brokers' services changed sharply since 1940 when the Advisers Act was first enacted, and that advice, far from being incidental to brokerage, was now a critical component of brokers' business activities (Thompson, 2000).

The SEC did not act on the rule proposal for several years. In 2004, the Financial Planning Association (FPA), a membership organization for personal financial planning professionals, filed a petition for review of the 1999 proposal. One month later, the SEC reopened the comment period on the proposal, noting that the FPA had raised additional comments (SEC, 2004). In January 2005, the SEC re-proposed the rule in its entirety, making few changes from the original (SEC, 2005*a*). Later in 2005, the SEC adopted the rule as final (SEC, 2005*b*).

When the SEC adopted the rule, it recognized that it did not address some of the troublesome issues raised by the evolving nature of brokerage services. Presaging the difficult debate to come, the Commission, in its adopting release, instructed its staff to consider undertaking a detailed study, which would include the issue of whether broker-dealers who provide investment advice should be subject to fiduciary obligations normally imposed on advisers (SEC, 2005*b*). After the rule was passed, the FPA again petitioned the court for review. The court consolidated the two petitions and issued its decision in March 2007.

Financial Planning Association v. SEC

In its lawsuit, the FPA argued that the SEC exceeded its statutory authority in adopting Advisers Act rule 202(a)(11)-1 (*Financial Planning Ass'n v. SEC*, 2007: 483). In adopting the rule, the SEC relied on exemptive authority contained within the definition of investment adviser. This exemptive authority permits the SEC to exclude from the statute 'other persons not within the intent' of the statutory definition. The FPA argued that reliance on this provision was erroneous because Congress, in 1940, identified elsewhere in the statute the group of brokers it intended to exclude from the statute, namely those brokers whose advice was solely incidental to brokerage and who did not receive special compensation (i.e., non-commission compensation). The exemptive provision, the FPA argued, was inserted to allow the SEC to exclude a wholly different category of advisers from the Act; it was not meant to broaden a category of advisers Congress already addressed in another subsection (*Financial Planning Ass'n v. SEC*, 2007: 487).

Under US administrative law, if the terms of a statute unambiguously preclude an agency's interpretation, the court must reject that interpretation. If the terms are ambiguous, however, the court must defer to the agency's interpretation as long as it is reasonable (*Chevron v. NRDC*, 1984: 842–4). The DC Circuit Court agreed with the FPA that the exemptive provision was unambiguous and rejected the SEC's view. The court stated that the category of brokers the SEC wished to exempt, namely brokers who do charge 'special compensation,' were not *other persons* because the statute already addressed brokers as a category of persons.

Moreover, the court ruled that the SEC's proposed exclusion was not consistent with the intent of the Advisers Act. The statute's legislative history did not support an exclusion broader than the statute itself (*Financial Planning Ass'n v. SEC*, 2007: 488–9). A Senate report explained that brokers were excluded from the definition of adviser insofar as their advice was solely incidental to brokerage and they only charged commissions (S. Rep. 76-1775, 1940). Thus, by excluding brokers who charged other forms of compensation, the SEC's rule conflicted with the statute and legislative history (*Financial Planning Ass'n v. SEC*, 2007: 488). The court granted the FPA's petition and vacated the SEC's rule (*Financial Planning Ass'n v. SEC*, 2007: 493).

Judge Garland prepared a vigorous dissent, explaining that in addition to the ambiguity inherent in the words 'such other persons' and 'within the intent of this paragraph,' the exemptive authority contains a final clause: 'as the Commission may designate by rules.' This language authorizes the SEC, Garland wrote, to determine the intent of the paragraph. Judge Garland simply disagreed that the statute only allowed the SEC to exclude advisers other than those already addressed in the statute (*Financial Planning Ass'n v. SEC*, 2007: 495).

The dissent pointed out that the real ambiguity in the case is whether the authority to exclude 'other persons' means persons other than broker-dealers (the FPA's view) or persons other than the particular broker-dealers covered by the statute (the SEC's view). For the same reasons that Judge Garland found the terms of the exemptive provision ambiguous, he found the SEC's construction reasonable. There is nothing unreasonable about interpreting the words 'other persons' to include persons not actually excluded in the definition itself (*Financial Planning Ass'n v. SEC*, 2007: 498). Judge Garland then moved to the second step of the analysis under administrative law, namely deciding whether the agency's interpretation was reasonable and he found that it was (*Financial Planning Ass'n v. SEC*, 2007: 499–501).

The FPA also argued that the SEC failed to properly analyze the costs and benefits of the proposed rule (FPA, 2007a). According to the FPA, when counting benefits, the SEC took into consideration savings by brokers, who, under the rule, could avoid investment adviser regulation. When counting costs, however, the SEC failed to take into account costs that would be imposed on certain investors, who, under the rule, would not receive the benefits of the Advisers Act. In other words, if a benefit of the proposed rule were the resources a broker would save by omitting certain disclosures that were required under the Advisers Act, a concomitant cost of the proposed rule must be the harm imposed on investors who do not receive the disclosure. The SEC responded that it took into consideration costs such as investor confusion and differences in obligations that would follow from the rule (SEC, 2007). The FPA found this inadequate and repeated its earlier attack in subsequent briefing on the issue (FPA, 2007b).

Because the court decided the case on statutory authority grounds, it did not address the SEC's cost–benefit analysis. Developments since 2007, however, have placed examination of costs and benefits in the limelight, and the question of costs may determine whether the SEC will once again take up the mantle of harmonization. As discussed below, both industry participants and regulators are now focused primarily on the costs and benefits of additional rulemaking.

Congressional action

The court's decision in the *FPA* case failed to end the debate over the regulation of brokers and advisers; instead, it merely raised additional questions. With the SEC's rule now vacated by the court, lawyers and their brokerage clients puzzled over how to treat fee-based brokerage accounts, which were arguably no longer subject to a valid exclusion and, therefore, covered by the Advisers Act. Moreover, if fee-based brokerage accounts must be treated as advisory accounts, did that mean brokers had to follow the Advisers Act and the SEC rules adopted under the Act with respect to those accounts? If that were the case, the business model of broker-dealers, particularly the ability to enter into principal transactions with customers, would be in question.

One year after the *FPA* case was decided, the RAND Institute for Civil Justice released the SEC-sponsored study referenced in the release adopting the ill-fated rule. A key finding of the RAND Report was that survey respondents and focus group participants did not understand the distinctions between investment advisers and broker-dealers. Investors were confused by the titles these professionals use, the firms they work with, and the services they offer (RAND Report, 2008).

In 2009, the Obama Administration raised the issue of the regulation of brokers and advisers in a white paper on financial regulatory reform entitled *A New Foundation: Rebuilding Financial Supervision and Regulation.* The Administration wrote that, from an investor's perspective, advisers and brokers often provide identical services, yet they are regulated under different statutory frameworks (Treasury, 2009). Echoing the RAND Report, Treasury stated that investors are often confused about the differences between advisers and brokers. Treasury noted that brokers often provide investment advice to clients, and clients may rely on a trusted relationship with their broker. Nevertheless, the fiduciary responsibilities of advisers are not imposed on brokers. As a result, the Administration's position in 2009 was that new legislation should require broker-dealers who provide advice to have the same fiduciary duties as advisers.

The Obama Administration's approach to the problem was the reverse of the SEC's approach ten years earlier. In 1999, the SEC was inclined to liberalize the rules governing broker-dealers, broadening the scope of the brokers' exclusion in the Advisers Act, thereby making it easier for brokers to market and sell their advisory services without adhering to rules placed on investment advisers. By contrast, the Administration sought to tighten the rules governing brokers and treat brokers who provide advice more like investment advisers.

In that spirit, draft legislation prepared by the Senate Banking Committee took an aggressive position that did not prevail in the final bill. The draft language would have struck the broker-dealer exclusion in the Advisers Act in its entirety (Senate Banking Committee, 2009: §913). Under that approach, brokers who give advice would be subject to all regulations imposed on advisers, including the restrictions on principal trading discussed above. Such restrictions imposed on broker-dealers would jeopardize brokers' business model (Laby, 2010). Brokers often sell securities from their own accounts to customers, and they also buy securities for their own accounts from customers, either as a market maker in particular securities or as a market participant seeking to generate trading profits. Engaging in this trading activity is the very definition of dealer in the Exchange Act (Exchange Act, 1934: §3(a)(5)).

Resolving the issue of principal trading is one of the great difficulties in finding a way forward in achieving harmonization. On the one hand, any broker-dealer who provides advice should be required to act in the best interest of the client to whom the advice is given. On the other hand, imposing a fiduciary duty on dealers is inconsistent, or not completely consistent, with the dealer's role. A dealer's profit is earned to the detriment of his trading partner, the very person to whom the dealer would owe a fiduciary obligation. As Norman Poser and James Fanto have explained, when acting as a dealer and selling securities as principal, a broker-dealer firm may be tempted to purchase the securities for a customer's account at a price unduly favorable to the firm; or, when acting as a market maker, the firm may be tempted to unduly pressure a customer to buy securities in which the market maker has a position he would like to dispose of (Poser and Fanto, 2010). Perhaps the real problem is that firms are permitted to act as both brokers and dealers. If this role was split, a fiduciary duty could be imposed on brokers, who would act as agents for buyers and sellers, giving them advice and facilitating the purchase and sale of securities, but not on dealers, who would be permitted to trade with customers for the dealers' own accounts but refrain from providing advice.

In a largely forgotten chapter of the history of securities regulation, this very idea—segregating the roles of brokers and dealers—was discussed, debated, and ultimately abandoned during the dismal days of the Great Depression. When the Securities Exchange Act was debated in Congress, an initial bill included a provision prohibiting brokers from acting as dealers (H.R. 7852, 1934). John T. Flynn, a leading reformer at the time and member of the Senate Banking Committee staff, advocated this position in *The New Republic*: 'I lay it down as a truism that no man whose primary function is a fiduciary one—that of an agent—should be permitted to enter the market in which he appears as an agent for others and to trade in that market for himself' (Flynn, 1936). Proponents of segregation, however, could not overcome industry opposition. Congress struck the provision prohibiting brokers from acting as dealers and instructed the SEC to study the issue (S. Rep. No. 73–1455, 1934). Dealers, however, were not permitted to charge any price they could get away with; charging prices substantially apart from market prices was considered unreasonable and deemed illegal (Duker and Duker, 1939).

The conundrum of how to apply a fiduciary obligation to a dealer which trades with customers out of its own account continues to bedevil Congress and the SEC nearly eighty years later. In a legislative maneuver that parallels Congress' actions in 1934, Congress in 2010 similarly struck the draft provision of Dodd-Frank that would have eliminated the broker-dealer exclusion and which would have imposed a fiduciary duty on broker-dealers who give advice. Instead, as in 1934, Congress required the SEC to study the effectiveness of the existing standard of care for brokers, dealers, and investment advisers when providing advice (Dodd-Frank, 2010: §913(b)).

In addition to requiring a study, Congress authorized, but did not require, the SEC to impose a fiduciary duty on brokers who give advice. In Section 913 of Dodd-Frank, Congress included two rulemaking provisions. Section 913(f) authorizes the SEC to adopt a rule to 'address' the legal standards imposed on brokers and advisers when providing advice. In adopting rules under this section, the SEC must consider the findings, conclusions, and recommendations of the required study. This provision is quite general. The term 'address' is not defined and is arguably limited by existing federal securities laws. This provision does not explicitly hand the SEC the authority to raise the standard of care applicable to broker-dealers (Dodd-Frank, 2010).

The other provision, Section 913(g), is more specific. First, the subsection is entitled, 'Authority to Establish a Fiduciary Duty for Brokers and Dealers.' Second, the subsection amends both the Exchange Act and the Advisers Act to state that the SEC may adopt rules providing that the standard of conduct for brokers and advisers when providing personalized investment advice about securities to retail customers shall be to act in the best interest of the customer—a fiduciary standard. Subsection (g) also provides that the standard of conduct, if adopted, shall be 'no less stringent' than the standard currently applicable to advisers under Section 206 (1) and (2) of the Investment Advisers Act. It is well accepted that the standard applicable under Section 206(1) and (2) is a fiduciary standard (Laby, 2010).[3]

The SEC study on harmonization

The SEC staff published the study required by Dodd-Frank in January 2011.[4] The study contained two principal recommendations, one regarding a uniform fiduciary standard and one regarding regulatory harmonization. As to the first, the staff recommended that the Commission consider adopting a new rule to apply a fiduciary standard uniformly to broker-dealers and investment advisers when they provide personalized investment advice about securities to retail customers. Tracking the language of Section 913 of Dodd-Frank, the staff recommended that the

288 The Market for Retirement Financial Advice

fiduciary standard be no less stringent than the standard currently applied to investment advisers under Section 206(1) and (2) of the Advisers Act. According to the SEC staff, the standard of conduct for brokers, dealers, and investment advisers should be to act in the 'best interest' of the customer, without regard to the interests of the broker, dealer, or adviser.

The staff placed responsibility for ironing out the thorny details of implementing a fiduciary standard back on the Commission itself. According to the study, for example, the Commission must ultimately address how broker-dealers should fulfill their fiduciary obligation when engaging in principal trading (SEC Staff, 2011*b*). But such details of implementation are the heart of the problem. Most observers would likely agree that broker-dealers who give advice should owe a fiduciary duty to customers. There is far less agreement over how to implement this change.

Similarly, the staff postponed the difficult question of how to handle conflicts of interest. Should SEC rules prohibit conflicts, require firms to mitigate them, or impose disclosure and consent requirements? (SEC Staff, 2011*b*). Much like Congress declined to tackle the substantive issues and placed responsibility for deciding them on the SEC, the SEC shifted responsibility to its staff to address in the study, then the staff moved responsibility back to the Commission itself. It is no wonder that commentators have used the phrase 'hot potato' to describe the manner in which harmonization has been addressed inside the beltway in Washington (Green, 2011).

As to the second recommendation, harmonization of regulation, the staff suggested several areas where the regulation of brokers and advisers differs and could be brought into accord. Those topics include advertisements, use of solicitors, supervision, licensing and registration, and maintenance of books and records.

The future of harmonization

The future of regulatory harmonization for brokers and advisers will turn on choices and compromises largely unforeseen in 1999 when the SEC first proposed its rule to address fee-based brokerage accounts. The regulatory environment has evolved since the late 1990s. Since that time, investors have witnessed the bursting of the internet bubble in 2000, colossal corporate scandals in 2001 and 2002 such as the failures of Enron and WorldCom, the passage of the Sarbanes-Oxley Act of 2002, the Bernard Madoff Ponzi scheme uncovered in 2008, the financial crisis of 2008 and 2009, and, most recently, passage of the Dodd-Frank Act of 2010. The composition of the Commission has changed as well. Three SEC Chairmen have served between the tenure of Arthur Levitt, who was Chairman in 1999, and the confirmation of Chairman Mary L. Schapiro in 2009. No commissioner governing in 1999 serves today. Thus, the context in which regulators are addressing harmonization is very different from the context in which the SEC's rule was first proposed.

Priorities are different too. In order to gain an understanding of how harmonization might be resolved, one must examine new pressures bearing on the dispute. As a result, we now review three developments essential to understanding the debate over harmonization today. Each of these issues weighs on regulators as they attempt to fashion a solution that is the best for investors and for the markets. The issues are (*a*) whether regulators can quantify the costs of any new rule and satisfy demands for a robust economic analysis; (*b*) whether multiple regulators can work together to find consistent solutions; and (*c*) whether Congress should authorize an SRO for investment advisers akin to FINRA, the SRO for broker-dealers.

Economic justification

The fate of regulatory harmonization for brokers and advisers will likely turn on whether the SEC can justify the initiative in terms of costs and benefits. In their statement regarding the staff study, Commissioners Kathleen L. Casey and Troy A. Paredes criticized the outcome based on an insufficient analysis of the costs and benefits of imposing a uniform fiduciary duty (Casey and Paredes, 2011). They explained that the study failed to identify whether investors are harmed under one regulatory scheme as opposed to the other and accordingly, the staff lacked a basis to conclude that a uniform fiduciary standard would enhance investor protection. Casey and Paredes also called for an analytical and empirical foundation before rewriting the rules governing brokers and advisers. As possible areas of further research, they recommended analyzing investor returns under the two existing regimes, comparing security selections of brokers and advisers, surveying investors, and considering evidence regarding the ability of investors to bring legal claims. The statement by Casey and Paredes was published contemporaneously with the study in January 2011.

In April 2011, the views of Casey and Paredes regarding the necessity of economic analysis were corroborated and validated by a decision of the United States Court of Appeals for the DC Circuit, entitled *Business Roundtable v. SEC* (*Business Roundtable v. SEC*, 2011). In that case, the court overturned Securities Exchange Act Rule 14a-11, a controversial SEC rule, which required public companies to provide shareholders with information about their ability to vote for shareholder-nominated candidates for a board of directors. The basis for the court's decision was the

Commission's failure to adequately consider the rule's effect on efficiency, competition, and capital formation, which is required under the law. When the SEC adopted the rule, Commissioners Casey and Paredes dissented, faulting the SEC for failing to act on the basis of empirical data (Casey, 2010; Paredes, 2010).

In the *Business Roundtable* case, the court punctuated its prose with unblunted criticism of the agency. According to the court, the SEC failed 'once again' to assess the economic effects of a new rule—citing two other examples over the last several years when the same court struck down SEC rules on similar grounds. The court charged the SEC with 'inconsistently and opportunistically' framing the costs and benefits of the rule, with contradicting itself, and with failing to respond to problems raised by commenters (*Business Roundtable v. SEC*, 2011: 7). At one point, the court described an SEC argument regarding use of the rule by mutual funds as an 'unutterably mindless reason' for applying the rule to mutual funds (*Business Roundtable v. SEC*, 2011: 21).

The statements by Commissioners Casey and Paredes regarding the proxy access rule, married with the court's decision in the *Business Roundtable* case, now form the backdrop on which the regulatory harmonization initiative is being sketched. Although the January 2011 statement by Casey and Paredes regarding the SEC's harmonization study predated the *Business Roundtable* decision, once the decision was handed down, all eyes turned to these two commissioners as authoritative regarding the requisite economic analysis for a new SEC rule to withstand scrutiny by the courts. It did not take long for one member of Congress to connect the *Business Roundtable* case with the SEC's harmonization initiative. In a statement delivered at a Congressional hearing examining regulatory oversight of brokers and dealers, Representative Scott Garrett, Chairman of the Financial Services Subcommittee on Capital Markets and Government Sponsored Enterprises, referred to the SEC's loss on the proxy access rule. He then stated that until the SEC comes forward with a reason, backed up by data, that a uniform fiduciary standard is necessary, the rulemaking should not be under consideration (Garrett, 2011).

The SEC appears to be listening. In a letter to Representative Garrett, SEC Chairman Schapiro described steps the SEC staff is taking to understand available data and evidence as it relates to possible new rules governing brokers and advisers (Schapiro, 2012). Chairman Schapiro recognized the importance of gathering additional data and empirical analysis. She wrote that SEC staff economists were preparing a public request for information to obtain data regarding the market for retail financial advice and regulatory alternatives.

The controversy over the need for an economic analysis of any proposed rule and the ability to perform one is itself becoming politicized. Advocates of a unified fiduciary duty urged members of Congress not to get sidetracked by demands for an extensive economic justification before moving forward. In May 2011, the Consumer Federation of America, a long-time supporter of a unified fiduciary standard, wrote to key members of the House of Representatives asking that a few industry members intent on maintaining the status quo not be allowed to derail a process to provide needed protections to middle-income investors (Roper, 2011b). Notwithstanding these statements, there is little doubt based on recent developments, in particular the *Business Roundtable* decision, that the SEC is unlikely to propose a rule to harmonize the regulation of brokers and advisers absent sufficient economic analysis and data demonstrating that the benefits justify the costs or, at a minimum, that the relevant data are unavailable to make that determination.

Retirement plan advisers

In addition to the call for more robust empirical data and economic analysis before the adoption of a fiduciary standard, another development, which could affect any possible SEC rule, is the initiative by the DOL to redefine the term 'fiduciary' for purposes of ERISA (EBSA, 2010). The DOL has overlapping jurisdiction with the SEC because the DOL, under ERISA, regulates advice by financial services professionals to employee benefit plans, participants, and beneficiaries, with respect to plans sponsored by private-sector employers. The debate over the SEC's harmonization initiative parallels an equally vigorous debate over the DOL's initiative to redefine fiduciary as it relates to retirement accounts. Since a key aim of Section 913 of Dodd-Frank is to produce a unified standard governing those who provide individualized investment advice, it is ironic that another agency, the DOL, has proposed to expand the category of persons to whom the ERISA fiduciary standard would apply, including many of the same persons and firms subject to SEC regulation.

The current rule-defining fiduciary under ERISA was adopted in 1975. The rule established a five-part test for determining when an ERISA service provider becomes a fiduciary by virtue of providing advice to an ERISA plan. The five-part test for an adviser without discretionary control contains the following elements: the service provider must (a) render advice, (b) on a regular basis, (c) pursuant to mutual agreement, (d) where the advice will serve as the primary basis for investment decisions concerning plan assets, and (e) where the advice will be individualized pursuant to the particular needs of the plan (DOL, 2012). The DOL's proposal is intended to adapt the five-part test to current market conditions.

Under the proposed new definition, a service provider generally would become a fiduciary if it rendered investment advice for compensation, whether directly or indirectly, with respect to any plan assets and met one of four additional criteria (EBSA, 2010). The new rule would clarify that the term 'advice' would cover advice to a plan as well as to a plan beneficiary or participant (EBSA, 2010). As a result of the proposed changes, the definition would likely apply to many brokers and advisers who offer advice to clients holding Individual Retirement Accounts (IRAs). The definition is broader than the current rule in other respects as well. It requires neither that advice be provided on a regular basis nor that the parties have a mutual agreement that the advice will serve as a primary basis for the plan's investment decisions. These two criteria have kept the current definition narrow (EBSA, 2010).

Industry representatives are concerned about the divergent tracks followed by the SEC and the DOL. One set of concerns is practical. The DOL's definition of adviser is broader than the Advisers Act definition. It includes a person who provides an appraisal or a fairness opinion concerning the value of securities or other property, which is generally not covered in the Advisers Act (EBSA, 2010). Moreover, an SEC rule governing harmonization would affect services offered by ERISA fiduciaries, such as proprietary trading, compensation, and sales of proprietary products (Financial Services Roundtable, 2011).

Another set of concerns is structural. The SEC and the DOL approach fiduciary norms from different perspectives. According to the SEC, disclosure is often sufficient to address a conflict of interest. The US Supreme Court has written that the Advisers Act reflects a Congressional recognition to eliminate 'or at least to expose' an adviser's conflicts of interest (*SEC v. Capital Gains Research Bureau, Inc.*, 1963: 191). By contrast, the DOL appears to be expanding the definition of fiduciary and prohibiting certain compensatory practices (Financial Services Roundtable, 2011). Without agreement between the agencies, the SEC might permit conduct, if disclosed, that would be prohibited by the DOL. Some have argued that this difference in approach demonstrates the necessity for agreement or coordination (Financial Services Roundtable, 2011).

Dissatisfaction with the DOL's proposed rule prompted leading industry groups, including the American Bankers Association, the Financial Services Roundtable, and the Investment Company Institute, to ask members of Congress to urge the DOL to re-propose the rule and explain how it would be implemented in conjunction with a new SEC fiduciary standard (American Bankers Association, 2011).[5] Shortly after this request was sent, the DOL announced it would withdraw and re-propose the rule. Although the DOL had received significant input in the form of comment letters, hearings, and individual meetings, it stated that it could benefit from additional views (EBSA, 2011). Supporters of the DOL initiative predict that the DOL will not flag regarding this initiative and will propose and adopt an ambitious new rule (Toonkel and Barlyn, 2012).

Those who oppose a broad DOL rule raise cost considerations similar to concerns raised with regard to an SEC rule. A letter to DOL Secretary Solis from 53 members of Congress thanked the DOL for withdrawing the proposed rule and urged it to 'avoid costly new regulations that may reduce choice among qualified service providers and investment products' (Biggert, 2011). Similarly, the President of the National Association of Insurance and Financial Advisors (NAIFA) stated that the DOL should be 'wary of imposing an overly rigid fiduciary rule with unintended consequences that would raise costs and reduce access to advice for millions of middle class retirement savers' (Miller, 2011). To address cost considerations, the DOL has requested data from firms that would be affected by a new fiduciary standard. Industry groups, however, responded that they were unable to provide certain data due to confidentiality concerns, that the data would be costly to provide, and that the request was too broad. The requested data, they said, would not be useful in any case (Bleier et al., 2012). Barbara Roper of the Consumer Federation of America raised the temperature of the debate, asserting that the industry's opposition is ideological and not fact driven (Schoeff, 2012).

Phyllis Borzi, Assistant Director of the DOL's Employee Benefits Security Administration (EBSA), has stated that the laws must be updated to protect workers and retirees and that the new fiduciary standard must cover defined contribution plans such as 401(k) plans (Postal, 2012). The DOL, therefore, appears poised to pursue new rules to redefine 'fiduciary.' At the same time, the DOL is well aware of the SEC's initiatives. Regulators recognize the importance of information sharing and cooperation. When different regulators issue inconsistent positions, it can be just as frustrating for the regulators as it is for the regulated firms, since regulated entities often turn back to the regulators for relief or other assistance when the firms believe they are caught between inconsistent guidelines. Thus, although cooperation might slow the initiatives by both agencies, cooperation is likely to be an important theme before rules by the DOL or the SEC are finalized.

An SRO for investment advisers

In addition to the SEC and the DOL, another organization responsible for regulating investment professionals is FINRA, the SRO for broker-dealers. FINRA, however, does not regulate investment advisers. As discussed, in

1938, the Maloney Act amended the Exchange Act and authorized an SRO for brokers. The Advisers Act, passed just two years later, contained no parallel provision authorizing an SRO for advisers. Whether to place a fiduciary duty on brokers who provide advice is tied closely to an ongoing debate over whether to create an SRO for investment advisers. The SRO question has plagued the SEC for nearly 50 years and Congress once again raised the issue in Dodd-Frank.

In 1963, the SEC's Special Study of the Securities Markets recommended an SRO for advisers (SEC, 1963). The Study concluded that an SRO could 'formulate standards and educate the industry to a higher ethical plane,' and that an SRO would be 'highly desirable.' The Study's recommendation was that registered advisers, other than brokers, should be organized into an official SRO, which would adopt and enforce substantive rules. Alternatively, the Study concluded that the SEC should strengthen its direct regulation of advisers (SEC, 1963).

In 1989, due to growth in the adviser population, the SEC again proposed that Congress provide for the establishment of an SRO (Tittsworth, 2009). Then in 2008, in its blueprint for financial regulatory reform, the Treasury Department echoed these concerns stating that self-regulation by advisers would enhance investor protection and be more efficient than SEC oversight. Treasury recommended that advisers be subject to a self-regulatory scheme similar to the one for broker-dealers (Treasury, 2008). None of these recommendations has resulted in new legislation and the regulatory model has remained unchanged. Brokers are regulated and examined primarily by the NASD, now FINRA, as well as by the SEC; advisers are regulated by the SEC only.[6]

As the number of advisers has continued to grow, some have questioned whether the SEC is up to the task of adviser regulation, including undertaking inspections and examinations (Karmel, 2011). There are approximately 11,000 advisers registered with the SEC, although investor assets are highly concentrated in the top 1 percent of firms (Tittsworth, 2009).[7] This large number of advisers, in light of the relatively meager resources given to the SEC staff, means that advisers rarely undergo examination. In 2011, only 9 percent of registrants were subject to an SEC examination and, on average, SEC-registered advisers are examined once every 11 years. Because this situation appeared untenable, the Dodd-Frank Act required the SEC to address an SRO for advisers in a study, which was completed in January 2011.[8]

The study authors approached the issue in terms of resources and proposed three alternatives: (*a*) authorize the SEC to impose user fees on SEC-registered advisers to fund examinations, (*b*) authorize one or more SROs to examine SEC-registered advisers, or (*c*) authorize FINRA to examine dual registrants for compliance with the Advisers Act (SEC Staff,

2011a). Presumably each alternative would require legislation. Consistent with the second alternative, House Financial Services Committee Chairman Spencer Bachus prepared draft legislation that would allow for one or more groups to act as an SRO for advisers.

There is acute disagreement over establishing an SRO for advisers. Advocates point to additional resources for examinations and oversight; consistency between broker and adviser regulation; eliminating the redundancy of two regulatory bodies (FINRA and the SEC) overseeing brokers and advisers, especially a broker and adviser housed under one roof; and an SRO's ability to carry out prudential tasks, such as conducting inspections and examinations, because of a less adversarial relationship between FINRA and the brokerage industry (Ketchum, 2009; Karmel, 2011). Those in opposition point to an extra layer of bureaucracy and cost; conflicts of interest due to industry funding and influence; questions regarding the quality of SRO transparency, accountability, and oversight; historical differences between brokerage and advisory firms; and lack of fit between an SRO model of command-and-control regulation and a diverse adviser community with multifarious business models and a heterogeneous client base (Tittsworth, 2009).

If there is to be an SRO for advisers, FINRA is vying for the job. FINRA maintains it is 'uniquely positioned' to build a strong oversight program for advisers (Ketchum, 2009). Supporters argue this would be efficient because 88 percent of advisers are affiliated with a broker-dealer already overseen by FINRA. The adviser community strongly disagrees that FINRA should be its SRO. In a recent survey, 80 percent of advisers preferred SEC regulation to a FINRA-type SRO for advisers; this preference remained strong even when the cost of SEC oversight exceeded the cost of FINRA oversight (Boston Consulting Group, 2011). Advisers assert that there is a risk, based on FINRA's own statements, that FINRA would attempt simply to export its regulatory structure governing brokers to the world of investment advisers, ignoring the practices and culture of the advisory profession (Tittsworth, 2009).

If cost is a primary consideration, the best solution might not be an SRO. A recent study, sponsored by groups opposing an SRO, concluded that the cost of an SRO model ($550–$610 million annually) is twice as high as the cost to fund a robust SEC examination program ($240–$270 million annually). A new non-FINRA SRO would be even more expensive to administer, $610–$670 million annually (Boston Consulting Group, 2011). Regardless of the cost, resolution of the SRO issue is critical to the harmonization debate, especially if the SRO is to be FINRA, which has been regulating broker-dealers for many years, previously through the NASD, but has little or no experience regulating advisers.

Conclusion

Broker-dealers and investment advisers regularly provide advice and recommendations to investors who often know little about the stocks, bonds, and mutual funds in which they invest. Investors entrust these securities professionals with trillions of dollars of assets, and their futures often depend on the ability of these professionals to meet clients' needs. Notwithstanding the importance placed on financial advisers, most ordinary investors know little about the differences between them. Are they obliged to act in our best interest or merely to determine whether an investment is suitable? Are they selling securities from the firms' own accounts or pairing us with other traders in the market?

Since the 1930s, brokers and advisers have differentiated themselves largely by the way they were compensated. This difference, however, has eroded as brokers have begun to charge asset-based fees, and many brokers now hold themselves out as advisers, causing further confusion as to their roles and responsibilities. As a result, regulators are grappling with proposals to harmonize the regulation of brokers and advisers and place a uniform standard of care on both. Although few would disagree that a uniform standard is a good idea in principle, regulators also must guard against imposing new duties and obligations that would disrupt market liquidity.

The debate over harmonization has evolved since the late 1990s when the SEC first tackled the problem in its proposed rule. The SEC's approach began with a deregulatory philosophy, proposing to expand the brokers' exclusion in the Advisers Act. This initial attempt was vacated by the courts. Congress required further study in the Dodd-Frank Act, and, in its study, the SEC's position seems to have evolved to a more regulatory view, which would impose heightened duties on brokers. Three other developments have transformed the debate over harmonization. When fashioning a proposed rule, the SEC must now be sensitive to increased demands for an empirically based cost–benefit analysis to support the initiative. The SEC must work closely with the DOL, which is seeking to fashion a new fiduciary duty of its own. A DOL rule would likely be applicable to many firms regulated by the SEC. Finally, the SEC must be mindful of calls for an SRO for investment advisers, under which FINRA or a new SRO would be the first-line regulator of advisers, much like FINRA is for brokers. These three developments will shape the politics and the substance of the debate over harmonization in the months and years to come.

The author received helpful comments from Brian Baltz, Dana Muir, and John Turner. He is also grateful to David Clark and David Falk for excellent research assistance.

Harmonizing the Regulation of Financial Advisers   297

TABLE 13.1 Financial information for broker-dealers (1969–2010) [N]

Year		Pre-tax income ($ millions)	Total revenues ($ millions)	Profit margin (%)
2005	[A]	21,184.10	332,501.10	6.4
2004	[A]	23,188.90	242,929.60	9.5
2003	[A]	25,655.40	218,956.00	11.7
2002	[A]	15,262.00	221,811.00	6.9
2001	[A]	19,396.90	280,095.80	6.9
2000	[B]	39,103.30	349,493.30	11.2
1999	[B]	29,116.30	266,809.40	10.9
1998	[B]	17,184.20	234,964.40	7.3
1997	[B]	19,964.00	207,244.70	9.6
1996	[B]	16,978.50	172,411.50	9.8
1995	[C]	11,325.10	143,414.00	7.9
1994	[C]	3,492.20	112,758.10	3.1
1993	[C]	13,038.60	108,843.70	12.0
1992	[C]	9,116.60	90,584.00	10.1
1991	[D]	8,655.90	84,889.50	10.2
1990	[D]	790.10	71,356.20	1.1
1989	[D]	2,822.90	76,864.00	3.7
1988	[D]	3,477.30	66,100.40	5.3
1987	[E]	3,209.90	66,104.40	4.9
1986	[E]	8,301.20	64,423.80	12.9
1985	[E]	6,502.40	49,844.30	13.0
1984	[E]	2,856.60	39,607.10	7.2
1983	[F]	5,206.80	36,904.10	14.1
1982	[G]	4,073.00	28,801.00	14.1
1981	[H]	2,789.00	24,372.00	11.4
1980	[I]	3,053.00	19,984.00	15.3
1979	[J]	1,652.00	13,957.00	11.8
1978	[K]	1,072.00	11,273.00	9.5
1977	[L]	682.00	8,602.00	7.9
1976	[M]	1,505.00	8,915.00	16.9
1975	[M]	1,120.00	7,373.00	15.2

Notes:

[A]–[E] From 1989 to 2011, the SEC Annual Reports' Pre-tax Income and Total Revenue was consistently recorded for preceding years. However, in *all* Annual Reports, the most recent year (and in some cases, years) was a preliminary projection. Thus, all data from 1984 to 2010 was obtained from SEC Annual Reports in subsequent years where such data was not noted as a preliminary projection.

[E]–[M] From 1975 to 1984, reported data varied from yearly reports due to preliminary projections and revisions. Thus, data was obtained from the most recent SEC Annual Report available which reported the noted year's data.

[N] 'The Commission on June 28, 1968, adopted Rule 17a-10 under the Securities Exchange Act, which requires exchange members and broker-dealers to file annual income and expense reports with the Commission or with a registered self-regulatory organization which will transmit the reports to the Commission. The rule will become effective on January 1, 1969, and the first reports, which will be due in 1970, will cover the calendar year 1969.' See 34 SEC Annual Report 14–15 (1968).

(*Continued*)

TABLE 13.1 Continued

Sources:
[A] Selected SEC and Market Data: Fiscal 2006, Table 7: Unconsolidated Financial Information for Broker-Dealers, at 22 (available at http://sec.gov/about/secstats2006.pdf)
[B] SEC Annual Report: 2001, Table 5: Unconsolidated Financial Information for Broker-Dealers, at 159 (available at http://sec.gov/pdf/annrep01/ar01full.pdf)
[C] SEC Annual Report: 1997, Table 12: Unconsolidated Financial Information for Broker-Dealers, at 192 (available at http://sec.gov/about/annual_report/1997.pdf)
[D] SEC Annual Report: 1993, Table 12: Unconsolidated Financial Information for Broker-Dealers, at 134 (available at http://sec.gov/about/annual_report/1993.pdf)
[E] SEC Annual Report: 1989, Table 1: Unconsolidated Financial Information for Broker-Dealers, at 121 (available at http://sec.gov/about/annual_report/1989.pdf)
[F] SEC Annual Report: 1988, Table 1: Unconsolidated Financial Information for Broker-Dealers, at 131 (available at http://sec.gov/about/annual_report/1988.pdf)
[G] SEC Annual Report: 1987, Table 1: Unconsolidated Financial Information for Broker-Dealers, at 104 (available at http://sec.gov/about/annual_report/1987.pdf)
[H] SEC Annual Report: 1986, Table 1: Unconsolidated Financial Information for Broker-Dealers, at 107 (available at http://www.sec.gov/about/annual_report/1986.pdf)
[I] SEC Annual Report: 1985, Table 1: Unconsolidated Financial Information for Broker-Dealers, at 92 (available at http://www.sec.gov/about/annual_report/1985.pdf)
[J] SEC Annual Report: 1984, Table 1: Unconsolidated Financial Information for Broker-Dealers, at 84 (available at http://www.sec.gov/about/annual_report/1984.pdf)
[K] SEC Annual Report: 1983, Table 1: Unconsolidated Financial Information for Broker-Dealers, at 72 (available at http://www.sec.gov/about/annual_report/1983.pdf)
[L] SEC Annual Report: 1982, Table 1: Unconsolidated Financial Information for Broker-Dealers, at 74 (available at http://www.sec.gov/about/annual_report/1982.pdf)
[M] SEC Annual Report: 1981, Table 1: Financial Information for Broker-Dealers, at 98 (available at http://www.sec.gov/about/annual_report/1981.pdf)

Endnotes

1. Certain firms are dually registered as broker-dealers and investment advisers, and certain individuals are registered as both broker-dealer registered representatives and investment adviser representatives, leading to some overlap in the numbers.
2. Investment discretion is legal authority, similar to authority granted under a power of attorney, to trade on a customer's behalf without obtaining the customer's prior approval (Cox et al., 2009).
3. Section 913(g)(1) amends the Securities Exchange Act to permit the SEC to adopt rules providing that a broker-dealer must comply with the standard of care imposed on advisers under Section 211 of the Advisers Act. In addition, Section 913(g)(2) amends Section 211 of the Advisers Act to give the SEC authority to require that the standard of care for brokers, dealers, and advisers, is to act in their customers' 'best interest.' Section 913(g)(2) also amends Section 211 of the Advisers Act so that the new rules would provide that the

standard of conduct be no less stringent than the standard applicable to advisers under Section 206(1) and (2) of the Advisers Act.
4. The statute required the study to be conducted by the Commission. The January 2011 study was authored by the SEC staff, not the Commission itself, and the study contains a disclaimer stating that the Commission expressed no view regarding the analysis, findings, or conclusion.
5. The other signatories are the Association for Advanced Life Underwriting, the Financial Services Institute, the National Association for Fixed Annuities, the National Association of Insurance and Financial Advisors, the Securities Industry and Financial Markets Association, and the Insured Retirement Institute.
6. The states retain authority to regulate both brokers and advisers in some respects. The scope of state regulation is beyond the scope of this chapter.
7. As of 2008, fewer than 1 percent of advisory firms accounted for more than half of approximately $40 trillion in discretionary assets managed by these advisers (Tittsworth, 2009).
8. This study, issued under Section 914 of Dodd-Frank, should not be confused with the study on the issue of a fiduciary duty for brokers issued under Section 913 of the Act.

References

American Bankers Association, American Bankers Association, American Council of Life Insurers, Association for Advanced Life Underwriting, Financial Services Institute, Investment Company Institute, National Association for Fixed Annuities, National Association of Insurance and Financial Advisors, Securities Industry and Financial Markets Association, The Financial Services Roundtable, and The Insured Retirement Institute (2011). Letter from the American Bankers Association et al., to Phil Roe, Chairman of the Health, Labor, and Pensions Subcommittee. http://www.sifma.org/workarea/downloadasset.aspx?id=8589935364

Biggert, J., et al. (2011). Letter from 53 Representatives to Hilda Solis, Secretary, US Department of Labor. http://www.naifablog.com/2011/12/53-members-of-congress.html

Bleier, L. J., B. Tate, and C. Weatherford (2012). Letter to Joseph S. Piacentini, Director, The Office of Policy Research, Employee Benefits Security Administration, US Department of Labor. http://www.sifma.org/issues/item.aspx?id=8589937616

Boston Consulting Group (BCG Study) (2011). *Investment Adviser Oversight, Economic Analysis of Options.* Bethesda, MD: Boston Consulting Group. http://www.aicpa.org/interestareas/personalfinancialplanning/newsandpublications/insideinformation/downloadabledocuments/bcg%20ia%20oversight%20economic%20analysis_final_15dec2011.pdf

Business Roundtable v. SEC (2011). 647 F.3d 1144 (D.C. Cir.).

Casey, K. L. (2010). 'Statement at Open Meeting to Adopt Amendments Regarding Facilitating Shareholder Director Nominations' (Speech by SEC Commissioner). http://www.sec.gov/news/speech/2010/spch082510klc.htm

—— T. A. Paredes (2011). 'Statement Regarding Study on Investment Advisers and Broker-Dealers' (Statement by SEC Commissioners). http://www.sec.gov/news/speech/2011/spch012211klctap.htm

Chevron, U.S.A., Inc. v. Natural Resources Defense Council, Inc. (Chevron v. NRDC) (1984). 467 U.S. 837, 842–844.

Cox, J. D., R. W. Hillman, and D. C. Langevoort (2009). *Securities Regulation: Cases and Materials.* New York, NY: Aspen Publishers.

Department of Labor (DOL) (2012). Definition of 'Fiduciary,' 29 C.F.R. § 2510.3–21.

Department of Labor, Employee Benefits Security Administration (EBSA) (2010). Proposed Rule: Definition of the Term 'Fiduciary,' 75 Fed. Reg. 65,253, 65,277.

—— (2011). 'Press Release: US Labor Department's EBSA to Re-propose Rule on Definition of a Fiduciary,' Washington, DC: September 19. http://www.dol.gov/opa/media/press/ebsa/EBSA20111382.htm

Department of the Treasury (Treasury) (2008). *Blueprint for a Modernized Regulatory Structure.* Washington, DC: Department of Treasury. http://www.treasury.gov/press-center/press-releases/Documents/Blueprint.pdf

—— (2009). *Financial Regulatory Reform a New Foundation: Rebuilding Financial Supervision and Regulation.* Washington, DC: Department of Treasury. http://www.treasury.gov/initiatives/Documents/FinalReport_web.pdf

Dodd-Frank Wall Street Reform and Consumer Protection Act (Dodd-Frank) (2010). 12 U.S.C. § 5301 et seq.

Donovan v. Bierwirth (1982). 680 F.2d 263, 272 n.8 (2d Cir.).

Duker and Duker (1939). Exchange Act Release No. 2350, 6 SEC 386, 389.

Employee Retirement Income Security Act of 1974 (ERISA) (1974). 29 U.S.C § 1001 et seq.

Financial Industry Regulatory Authority (FINRA) (2012). Rule 2111. Suitability.

Financial Planning Association (FPA) (2007a). Opening Brief for the Petitioner, *Financial Planning Ass'n v. SEC,* 482 F.3d 481 (D.C. Cir. 2007) (Nos. 04-1242, 05–1145).

—— (2007b). Reply Brief for the Petitioner, at 28. *Financial Planning Ass'n v. S.E.C.,* 482 F.3d 481 (D.C. Cir. 2007). (Nos. 04-1242, 05-1145.)

Financial Planning Ass'n v. SEC (2007). 482 F.3d 481 (D.C. Cir.).

Financial Services Roundtable (2011). *Ensuring Appropriate Regulatory Oversight of Broker-Dealers and Legislative Proposals to Improve Investment Adviser Oversight: Hearing Before the Capital Markets and Government Sponsored Enterprises Subcommittee of Committee on Financial Services,* 112th Congress (statement of the Financial Services Roundtable).

Flynn, J. T. (1936). 'Other People's Money,' *The New Republic,* January 8: 253.

Garrett, S. (2011). 'Press Release: Garrett Chairs Hearing to Examine Oversight of Broker Dealers and Investment Advisors,' Washington, DC: September 13. http://garrett.house.gov/press-release/garrett-chairs-hearing-examine-oversight-broker-dealers-and-investment-advisors

Gordon, J. S. (1999). 'Manager's Journal: Merrill Lynch Once Led Wall Street. Now It's Catching Up,' *Wall Street Journal*, June 14.

Gottlieb, P. S. (2005). Letter from First Vice President and Assistant General Counsel, Private Client Counsel, Office of General Counsel, Merrill Lynch, Pierce, Fenner & Smith Inc., to Jonathan G. Katz, Secretary, Securities and Exchange Commission. http://www.sec.gov/rules/proposed/s72599/mlpfs020705.pdf

Green, J. J. (2011). 'SEC's Blass at IAA: Fiduciary Standard Will Only Be Toughened,' *AdvisorOne*. March 11 (quoting comments of attorney Michael Koffler).

Hazen, T. L. (2009). *The Law of Securities Regulation*. St. Paul, MN: Thomson Reuters.

H. R. 4441 (1990). 101st Cong., 2d Sess.

H. R. 7852 (1934). 73d Cong. § 10.

Hung, A., and J. Yoong (2013). 'Asking for Help: Survey and Experimental Evidence on Financial Advice and Behavior Change,' in O. S. Mitchell and K. Smetters, eds., *The Market for Retirement Financial Advice*. Oxford, UK: Oxford University Press, pp. 182–212.

—— N. Clancy, J. Dominitz, E. Talley, C. Berrebi, and F. Suvankulov (RAND Report) (2008). *Investor and Industry Perspectives on Investment Advisers and Broker-Dealers*. Washington, DC: RAND Institute for Civil Justice. http://www.sec.gov/news/press/2008/2008-1_randiabdreport.pdf

Investment Advisers Act (Advisers Act) (1940). 15 U.S.C. §80b-1 et seq. (1940).

Karmel, R. S. (2011). 'Should There Be an SRO for Investment Advisers?' *New York Law Journal*, June 16: 3.

Ketchum, R. G. (2009). *Enhancing Investor Protection and the Regulation of the Securities Markets—Part II: Hearing Before the Committee on Banking, Housing, and Urban Affairs, United States Senate*, 111th Congress (statement of Chairman and Chief Executive Officer, Financial Industry Regulatory Authority).

Laby, A. B. (2010). 'Reforming the Regulation of Broker-Dealers and Investment Advisers,' *The Business Lawyer*, 65(2): 395–440.

Maloney Act (1938). 15 U.S.C. § 78o-3.

Miller, R. (2011). '55 Members of Congress Tell DOL to Preserve Investors' Access to Financial Products and Services,' Blog post. December 5. http://www.naifa-blog.com/2011/12/53-members-of-congress.html

Paredes, T. A. (2010). 'Statement at Open Meeting to Adopt the Final Rule Regarding Facilitating Shareholder Director Nominations' (Speech by SEC Commissioner). http://www.sec.gov/news/speech/2010/spch082510tap.htm

Parrish, M. E. (1970). *Securities Regulation and the New Deal*. New Haven, CT: Yale University Press.

Poser, N. S., and J. A. Fanto (2010). *Broker Dealer Law and Regulation*. New York, NY: Aspen Publishers.

Postal, A. D. (2012). 'DOL Faces Bi-Partisan Pushback Against Proposed Fiduciary Standard,' National Underwriter Life & Health Magazine. March. http://www.lifehealthpro.com/2012/03/07/dol-faces-bi-partisan-pushback-against-proposed-fi

Roper, B. (2011a). *Ensuring Appropriate Regulatory Oversight of Broker-Dealers and Legislative Proposals to Improve Investment Adviser Oversight: Hearing Before the Capital Markets and Government Sponsored Enterprises Subcommittee of Committee on Financial*

302 The Market for Retirement Financial Advice

Services, 112th Congress (statement of Director of Investor Protection of the Consumer Federation of America).

Roper, B. (2011*b*). Letter from Barbara Roper, Director of Investor Protection of the Consumer Federation of America, to The Honorable Spencer Bachus, Chairman of the Financial Services Committee, et al. http://www.consumerfed.org/pdfs/CFA-fiduciary-consequences-letter-5-9-2011.pdf

S. Rep. No. 73-1455 (1934). 29–30.

S. Rep. No. 76-1775 (1940). 22.

Schapiro, M. L. (2009). 'Statement on the Release of the Executive Summary of the Inspector General's Report Regarding the Bernard Madoff Fraud' (Statement by SEC Chairman). http://www.sec.gov/news/speech/2009/spch090209mls-2.htm

—— (2012). Letter from SEC Chairman, to Scott Garrett, Chairman of the House Capital Markets Subcommittee. http://www.mfdf.org/images/uploads/blog_files/Garrett_1-10-12.pdf

Schenker, D. (1940). Investment Trusts and Investment Companies: Hearings on S. 3580 Before the Subcomm. of the S. Comm. on Banking and Currency, 76th Cong. 322 (1940) (statement of Chief Counsel, Securities and Exchange Commission). http://www.sechistorical.org/museum/papers/1940

Schoeff, M. (2012). 'Industry Stiffs DOL on Request for IRA Data in Fiduciary Analysis,' *InvestmentNews*. March 4.

Securities Exchange Act (Exchange Act) (1934). 15 U.S.C. § 78a et seq.

Securities and Exchange Commission (SEC) (1963). *Report of Special Study of Securities Markets*, H.R. Doc. No. 88-95, Pt. 1. Washington, DC: SEC.

—— (1968). *34th Annual Report of the Securities and Exchange Commission*. Washington, DC: SEC. http://www.sec.gov/about/annual_report/1968.pdf

—— (1981). *47th Annual Report of the Securities and Exchange Commission*. Washington, DC: SEC. http://www.sec.gov/about/annual_report/1981.pdf

—— (1982). *48th Annual Report of the Securities and Exchange Commission*. Washington, DC: SEC. http://www.sec.gov/about/annual_report/1982.pdf

—— (1983). *49th Annual Report, U.S. Securities and Exchange Commission*. Washington, DC: SEC. http://www.sec.gov/about/annual_report/1983.pdf

—— (1984). *50th Annual Report, Securities and Exchange Commission, 1984*. Washington, DC: SEC. http://www.sec.gov/about/annual_report/1984.pdf

—— (1985). *51st Annual Report, U.S. Securities and Exchange Commission*. Washington, DC: SEC. http://www.sec.gov/about/annual_report/1985.pdf

—— (1986). *Fifty-Second Annual Report*. http://www.sec.gov/about/annual_report/1986.pdf

—— (1987). *Fifty-Third Annual Report*. Washington, DC: SEC. http://www.sec.gov/about/annual_report/1987.pdf

—— (1988). *Fifty-Fourth Annual Report*. Washington, DC: SEC. http://www.sec.gov/about/annual_report/1988.pdf

—— (1989). *Fifty-Fifth Annual Report*. Washington, DC: SEC. http://www.sec.gov/about/annual_report/1989.pdf

—— (1993). *1993 Annual Report*. Washington, DC: SEC. http://sec.gov/about/annual_report/1993.pdf

—— (1997). *1997 Annual Report*. Washington, DC: SEC. http://sec.gov/about/annual_report/1997.pdf

—— (1999). Proposed Rule: Certain Broker-Dealers Deemed Not to Be Investment Advisers, Investment Advisers Act Release No. 1845. 64 Fed. Reg. 61,226.

—— (2001). *Annual Report*. Washington, DC: SEC. http://sec.gov/pdf/annrep01/ar01full.pdf

—— (2004). Proposed Rule: Certain Broker-Dealers Deemed Not to Be Investment Advisers, Investment Advisers Act Release No. 2278. 69 Fed. Reg. 51,620.

—— (2005a). Proposed Rule: Certain Broker-Dealers Deemed Not to Be Investment Advisers, Investment Advisers Act Release No. 2340. 70 Fed. Reg. 2716.

—— (2005b). Final Rule: Certain Broker-Dealers Deemed Not to be Investment Advisers, Investment Advisers Act Release No. 2376. 70 Fed. Reg. 20,424.

—— (2006). *Selected SEC and Market Data, Fiscal 2006*. Washington, DC: SEC. http://sec.gov/about/secstats2006.pdf

—— (2007). Brief for the Respondent. *Financial Planning Ass'n v. S.E.C.*, 482 F.3d 481 (D.C. Cir. 2007) (Nos. 04-1242, 05-1145).

Securities and Exchange Commission Staff (SEC Staff) (2011a). *Study on Enhancing Investment Adviser Examinations*. Washington, DC: SEC. http://www.sec.gov/news/studies/2011/914studyfinal.pdf

—— (2011b). *Study on Investment Advisers and Broker-Dealers*. Washington, DC: SEC. http://www.sec.gov/news/studies/2011/913studyfinal.pdf

SEC v. Capital Gains Research Bureau, Inc. (1963). 375 U.S. 180.

SEC v. Tambone (2008). 550 F.3d 106 (1st Cir.), affirmed in part and reversed in part, *SEC v. Tambone* (2010). 597 F.3d 436 (1st Cir.).

Seligman, J. (2003). *The Transformation of Wall Street: A History of the Securities and Exchange Commission and Modern Corporate Finance*. New York, NY: Aspen Publishers.

Senate Committee on Banking, Housing and Urban Affairs (Senate Banking Committee) (2009). Restoring American Financial Stability Act: Chairman's Mark Text. http://banking.senate.gov/public/_files/111609FullBillTextofTheRestoringAmericanFinancialStabilityActof2009.pdf

Thompson, D. R. (2000). Letter from Duane Thompson, Director of Governmental Relations for the Financial Planning Association, to Jonathan G. Katz, Secretary of the Securities and Exchange Commission. http://www.sec.gov/rules/proposed/s72599/thompso1.htm

Tittsworth, D. G. (2009). *Enhancing Investor Protection and the Regulation of the Securities Markets—Part II: Hearing Before the Committee on Banking, Housing, and Urban Affairs, United States Senate*, 111th Congress (statement of Executive Director and Executive Vice President of the Investment Adviser Association).

—— (2011). *Ensuring Appropriate Regulatory Oversight of Broker-Dealers and Legislative Proposals to Improve Investment Adviser Oversight: Hearing Before the Capital Markets and Government Sponsored Enterprises Subcommittee of Committee on Financial Services*, 112th Congress (statement of David G. Tittsworth, Executive Director and Executive Vice President of the Investment Adviser Association).

Toonkel, J., and S. Barlyn (2012). 'Exclusive: Debate over Labor Fiduciary Plan Likely to Drag,' *Reuters*. January 5. http://www.reuters.com/article/2012/01/05/us-fiduciary-plan-idUSTRE80428N20120105

Tully, D. P., T. E. O'Hara, W. E. Buffet, R. A. Mason, and S. L. Hayes III (Tully Report) (1995). *Report of the Committee on Compensation Practices.* Washington, DC: Committee on Compensation Practices. http://www.sec.gov/news/studies/bkrcomp.txt

White, J., and D. Ramsey (1999). 'A Belle Epoque for Wall Street?—Investing Will Benefit from Turn-of-the-Century Gains in Technology,' *Barrons.* October 18.

Chapter 14

Regulating Financial Planners: Assessing the Current System and Some Alternatives[1]

Jason Bromberg and Alicia P. Cackley

Consumers are increasingly turning to professionals who describe themselves as financial planners for assistance with a broad range of services (Turner and Muir, 2013). Although there is no statutory or unique definition of financial planning, it can be broadly defined as a systematic process that individuals use to develop and achieve their financial goals. Financial planning typically involves a variety of services including preparing financial plans for clients based on their financial circumstances and objectives, and making recommendations for specific actions clients may take. In many cases, financial planners also help implement these recommendations by, for example, providing insurance products, securities, or other investments, selecting the right balance of stocks and bonds for an investment portfolio, choosing among insurance products, and providing tax and estate planning. Some financial planning organizations have raised concerns that no single law governs providers of financial planning services, broadly describing this situation as a 'regulatory gap' (Financial Planning Coalition, 2009). There are also concerns that financial planners may have an inherent conflict of interest in recommending products they may stand to benefit from selling (GAO, 2010a). In addition, some believe consumers may be confused by the numerous titles and designations that financial planners can use (GAO, 2010a).

In this chapter, we first review US federal and state laws and regulations that apply to financial planners and their activities. Next we assess the comprehensiveness and effectiveness of the regulatory structure for financial planners, and we discuss some key consumer protection challenges—in particular, consumers' understanding of the applicable standard of care and the titles and designations that financial planners use. We conclude with a presentation of some of the advantages and disadvantages of four alternative approaches to the regulation of financial planners.

Financial planners are primarily regulated under investment adviser laws

While there is no specific direct regulation of 'financial planners' per se at the federal or state levels, the activities of financial planners in the United States are regulated under federal and state laws as well as by regulations governing investment advisers—that is, individuals or firms that provide investment advice about securities for compensation. The Securities and Exchange Commission (SEC) has issued guidance that broadly interprets the Investment Advisers Act of 1940 (Advisers Act) to apply to most financial planners, because the advisory services they offer clients typically include providing advice about securities for compensation. States take a similar approach on the application of investment adviser laws to financial planners and, as a result, they usually register and oversee financial planners as investment advisers.

The SEC and state securities departments share responsibility for the oversight of investment advisers in accordance with the Advisers Act. The SEC generally oversees investment advisor firms that manage $100 million or more in client assets, while the states oversee those that manage less. The SEC's supervision of investment adviser firms includes evaluating their compliance with federal securities laws by conducting examinations of firms—including reviewing disclosures made to customers—and investigating and imposing sanctions for violations of securities laws. According to SEC staff, in its examinations the agency takes specific steps to review the financial planning services of investment advisers (GAO, 2010a). For example, the SEC may review a sample of financial plans that the firm prepared for its customers, to check whether the firm's advice and investment recommendations are consistent with customers' goals, the contract with the firm, and the firm's disclosures. Yet the frequency with which the SEC conducts these examinations varies, largely because of resource constraints faced by the agency. GAO (2007) has noted that harmful practices could go undetected because investment adviser firms rated less risky are unlikely to undergo routine examinations within a reasonable period of time, if at all. More recently, the SEC stated in a staff report that, as a result of growth in the investment adviser industry and a reduction in SEC enforcement staff, the agency 'likely will not have sufficient capacity in the near or long term to conduct effective examinations of registered investment advisers with adequate frequency' (SEC, 2011a: 3–4).

State oversight of investment adviser firms generally includes activities similar to those undertaken by the SEC, including specific steps to review firm financial planning services. States generally register not just investment adviser firms but also investment adviser representatives—that is, individuals who provide investment advice and work for a state- or federally registered investment adviser firm.

Financial planners can also be subject to broker-dealer and insurance laws, and to marketing and disclosure rules

In addition to providing advisory services such as developing a financial plan, financial planners generally help clients implement their plans by making specific recommendations, and by selling securities, insurance products, and other investments. SEC data show that, as of October 2010, 19 percent of investment adviser firms that provided financial planning services also provided brokerage services, and 27 percent provided insurance (GAO, 2010*b*).

Broker-dealers

Financial planners that provide brokerage services such as buying or selling stocks, bonds, or mutual fund shares, are subject to broker-dealer regulation at the federal and state levels. At the federal level, the SEC oversees US broker-dealers, and the SEC's oversight is supplemented by self-regulatory organizations (SROs), including the Financial Industry Regulatory Authority (FINRA). State securities offices work in conjunction with the SEC and FINRA to regulate securities firms. Salespersons working for broker-dealers are subject to state registration requirements, including examinations. The SEC and SROs examined about half of broker-dealers in 2009, the most recent year for which these data are readily available.

Insurance agents

The states are generally responsible for regulating the business of insurance. Financial planners that sell insurance products, such as life insurance or annuities, must be licensed by the states to sell these products and are subject to state insurance regulation. Financial planners that sell variable insurance products, such as variable life insurance or variable annuities, are subject to both state insurance regulation and broker-dealer regulation, because these products are regulated as both securities and insurance products. Yet the GAO (2009) has reported that the effectiveness of market conduct regulation, such as examination of the sales practices and behavior of insurers, may be limited by a lack of reciprocity and uniformity, which may lead to uneven consumer protection across states. That is, the extent to which state regulators accept other states' regulatory actions may vary, and not all states have implemented the same, or substantially similar, regulatory standards or procedures.

Marketing and disclosures

The SEC and FINRA have regulations on advertising and standards of communication that apply to the strategies used by investment adviser firms and broker-dealers to market their financial planning services. In addition, the SEC and state securities agencies regulate information that investment advisers are required to disclose to their clients. In the Uniform Application for Investment Adviser Registration, known as Form ADV, regulators have typically required investment adviser firms to provide new and prospective clients with background information, such as the basis of the advisory fees, types of services provided (such as financial planning services), and other information.

Existing regulation covers most financial planning services

Although there is no single stand-alone regulatory body with oversight of financial planners in the United States, the regulatory structure for financial planners covers most activities in which they engage. As discussed above and summarized in Figure 14.1, a financial planner's primary activities are subject to regulation at the federal or state level primarily via regulation pertaining to investment advisers, broker-dealers, and insurance agents. In interviews with GAO in 2010, staff at the SEC, FINRA, state securities regulators, financial industry representatives, consumer groups, and academic and subject matter experts expressed a belief that, in general, the regulatory structure for financial planners was comprehensive. This was largely because, as noted earlier, the activities a financial planner normally engages in generally include advice related to securities, and such activities make financial planners subject to regulation under the Advisers Act. Providing financial planning services would be difficult without offering investment advice or considering securities, and holding even broad discussions of securities—for example, what proportion of a portfolio should be invested in stocks—would require registration as an investment adviser. In theory, a financial planner might offer only services that do not fall under existing regulatory regimes (e.g., advice on household budgeting) but this is likely rare and such a business model may be hard to sustain. Furthermore, to the extent that financial planners offer services

Regulating Financial Planners 309

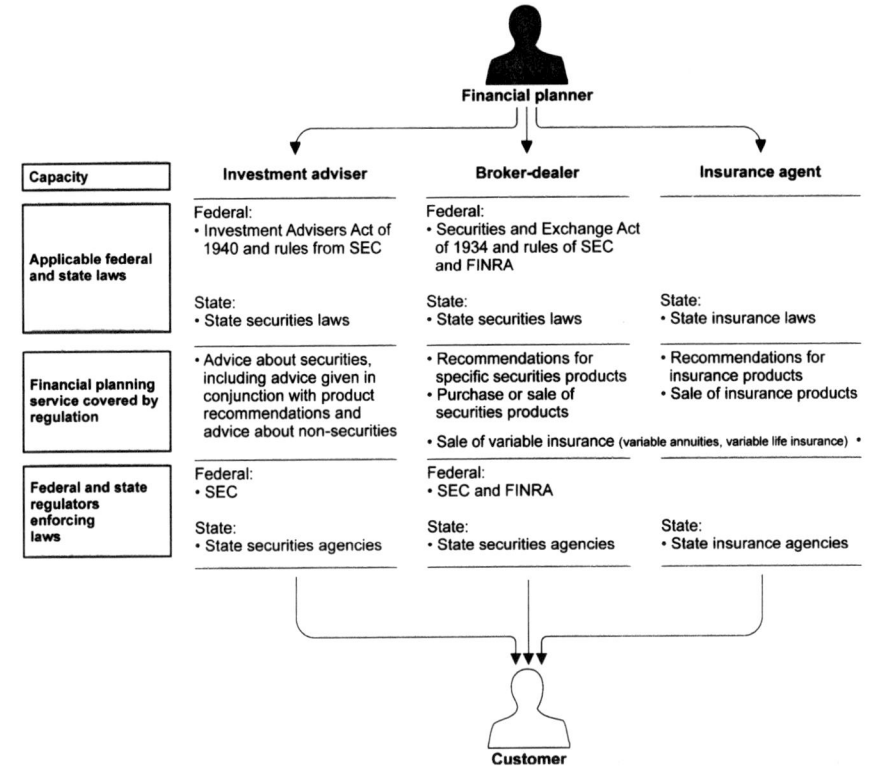

Figure 14.1 Summary of key statutes and regulations that can apply to financial planners

Source: GAO (2011).

Capacity	Investment adviser	Broker-dealer	Insurance agent
Applicable federal and state laws	Federal: • Investment Advisers Act of 1940 and rules from SEC State: • State securities laws	Federal: • Securities and Exchange Act of 1934 and rules of SEC and FINRA State: • State securities laws	State: • State insurance laws
Financial planning service covered by regulation	• Advice about securities, including advice given in conjunction with product recommendations and advice about non-securities	• Recommendations for specific securities products • Purchase or sale of securities products • Sale of variable insurance (variable annuities, variable life insurance)	• Recommendations for insurance products • Sale of insurance products
Federal and state regulators enforcing laws	Federal: • SEC State: • State securities agencies	Federal: • SEC and FINRA State: • State securities agencies	State: • State insurance agencies

that do not fall under such regulation, the Consumer Financial Protection Bureau potentially could have jurisdiction over such services.[2]

Some disagree that regulation of financial planners is as comprehensive as it should be. The Financial Planning Coalition (2009) contends that a regulatory gap exists because no single law governs the delivery of the broad array of financial advice to the public. The group posits that the provision of integrated financial advice is unregulated, including topics such as selecting and managing investments, income taxes, saving for college, home ownership, retirement, insurance, and estate planning. Instead, it argues that there is patchwork regulation of financial planning advice, and it sees as problematic having two sets of laws—one regulating the provision of investment advice, and the other regulating the sale of products. In addition, certain professionals (including attorneys, certified public accountants, broker-dealers, and teachers) who provide financial planning advice are exempt from regulation under the Advisers Act, if such advice is 'solely incidental' to their other business activities. According to an SEC staff interpretation, this exemption would not apply to individuals who held themselves out to the public as providing financial planning services, and it would apply only to individuals who provided specific investment advice in rare, isolated, and non-periodic instances. Banks and bank employees are also excluded from the Advisers Act and are subject to separate banking regulation.

While the regulatory structure for financial planners may be deemed comprehensive by many, enforcement of existing statute and regulation has been variable. As noted earlier, examination of SEC-supervised investment advisers is infrequent and market conduct regulation of insurers is inconsistent. Some industry representatives have argued that a better alternative to additional regulation of financial planners would be increased enforcement of existing law and regulation, particularly related to fraud and unfair trade practices (GAO, 2010a).

Consumers may not understand that financial planners have potential conflicts of interest when selling products

As illustrated in Figure 14.2, financial planners are subject to different standards of care in their capacities as investment advisers, broker-dealers, and insurance agents. We describe these in turn.

Fiduciary standard of care

Investment advisers are subject to a fiduciary standard of care: that is, they must act in their client's best interests, ensure that recommended investments are suitable for the client, and disclose to the client any material conflicts of interest. This fiduciary standard applies even when investment advisers provide advice or recommendations about products other than securities, such as insurance, in conjunction with advice about securities.

Suitability standard of care when recommending security products

FINRA regulation requires broker-dealers to adhere to a suitability standard when rendering investment recommendations. Hence, they must recommend only those securities that they reasonably believe are suitable for the customer. Unlike the fiduciary standard, suitability rules do not

Regulating Financial Planners 311

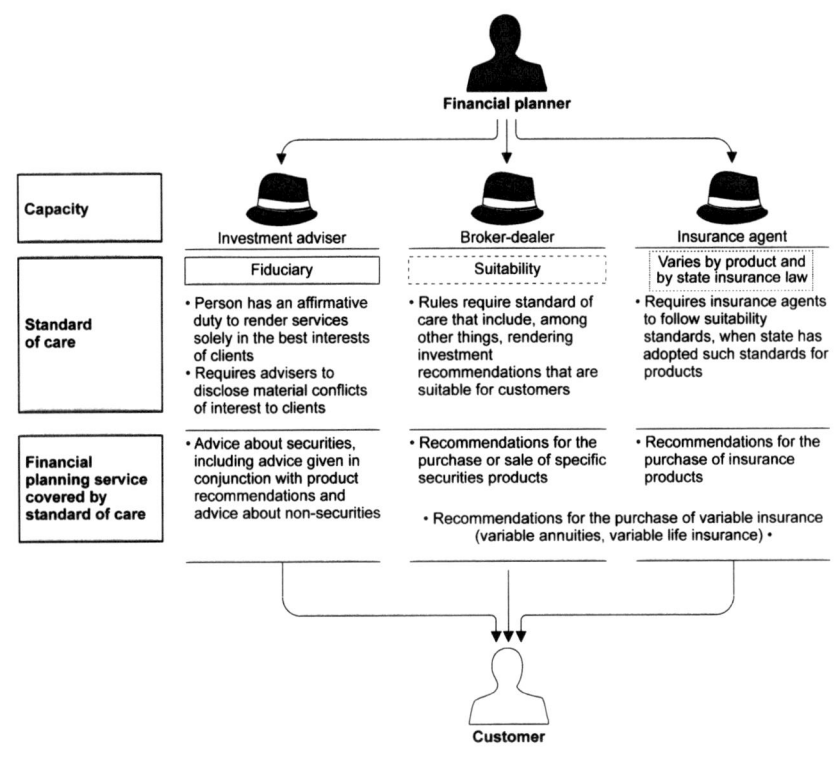

Figure 14.2 Differences in the standards of care required of financial planners
Source: GAO (2011).

Capacity	Investment adviser	Broker-dealer	Insurance agent
	Fiduciary	Suitability	Varies by product and by state insurance law
Standard of care	• Person has an affirmative duty to render services solely in the best interests of clients • Requires advisers to disclose material conflicts of interest to clients	• Rules require standard of care that include, among other things, rendering investment recommendations that are suitable for customers	• Requires insurance agents to follow suitability standards, when state has adopted such standards for products
Financial planning service covered by standard of care	• Advice about securities, including advice given in conjunction with product recommendations and advice about non-securities	• Recommendations for the purchase or sale of specific securities products • Recommendations for the purchase of variable insurance (variable annuities, variable life insurance) •	• Recommendations for the purchase of insurance products

necessarily require that the client's best interest be served. Up-front general disclosure of a broker-dealer's business activities and relationships that may cause conflicts of interest is not required, though broker-dealers are subject to many FINRA rules that require disclosure of conflicts in certain situations, even when those rules may not cover every possible conflict of interest, and disclosure may occur after conflicted advice has already been given.

Suitability standard of care when recommending insurance products

Standards of care for the recommendation and sale of insurance products vary by product and by state. For example, the National Association of Insurance Commissioners' model regulations on the suitability standard for annuity transactions (NAIC, 2010), adopted by some states but not others, require consideration of the insurance needs and financial objectives of the customer. Its model regulation for life insurance (NAIC, 2005) does not include a suitability requirement per se.

Conflicts of interest can exist when, for example, a financial services professional earns a commission on a product sold to a client. Under the fiduciary standard applicable to investment advisers, financial planners must mitigate potential conflicts of interest and disclose any that remain. But under a suitability standard applicable to broker-dealers, conflicts of interest may exist and generally may not need to be disclosed up-front. For example, financial planners functioning as broker-dealers may recommend a product that provides them with a higher commission than a similar product with a lower commission, as long as the product is suitable and the broker-dealer complies with other requirements. Because the same individual or firm can offer a variety of services to a client—a practice sometimes referred to as 'hat switching'—these services could be subject to different standards of care. This raises concerns that consumers may not fully understand which standard of care, if any, applies to a financial professional during a given transaction.

Financial services firms that provide financial planning argue that clients are sufficiently informed about the differing roles and accompanying standards of care that a firm representative may have. They note that when they provide both advisory and transactional services to the same customer, each service—such as planning, brokerage, or insurance sales—is accompanied by a separate contract or agreement with the customer. These agreements disclose that the firm's representatives have different obligations to the customer depending on their roles. Once a financial plan has been provided, some companies have customers sign an additional agreement stating that the financial planning relationship with the firm has ended. In addition, the SEC and FINRA have certain disclosure requirements designed to inform consumers of firms' conflicts of interest, compensation, business activities, and disciplinary information, all intended to help consumers evaluate investment advisers' integrity.

Nonetheless, the SEC (2011*b*) has observed that many investors find the standards of care confusing and do not appear to understand the differences between investment advisors and broker-dealers or the standards of care that apply to them. In the same way, the Financial Planning Association has noted how difficult it would be for an individual investor to discern when the adviser was acting in a fiduciary or a non-fiduciary capacity. Others have similarly found that consumers generally do not understand the distinction between a suitability and fiduciary standard of care, and when financial professionals are required or not required to put their client's interest ahead of their own (Hung et al., 2008; Infogroup, 2010; Hung and Yoong, 2013). In a staff report, SEC (2011*b*) has recommended a uniform fiduciary standard of care, whereby the standard of care for all brokers, dealers, and investment advisers, when providing investment advice about securities to retail customers, would be to act in the best interest of the customer without regard to their own financial or other interests.

Consumer confusion on standards of care may also be a source of concern with regard to the sale of some insurance products. A 2010 national survey of investors found that 60 percent mistakenly believed that insurance agents had a fiduciary duty to their clients (Infogroup, 2010). Some insurance products, such as annuities, are complex and can be difficult to understand, and annuity sales practices have drawn complaints from consumers and various regulatory actions from state regulators as well as SEC and FINRA for many years (CRS, 2010). Some states have requirements that insurance salespersons sell annuities only if the product is suitable for the customer, while others do not. Consumer groups and others have stated that high sales commissions on certain insurance products including annuities may provide salespersons with a substantial financial incentive to sell these products, which may or may not be in the consumer's best interest.

Consumers may be confused about financial planners' titles and designations

Individuals who provide financial planning services use a variety of titles when presenting themselves to the public, including financial planner, financial consultant, and financial adviser, among many others. FINRA has identified more than 100 professional designations, five of which include the term 'financial planner,' and 24 of which contain comparable terms such as financial consultant or counselor. Given the large number of designations for financial planners, consumers may have difficulty distinguishing among them, and even experienced investors are confused about the titles used by broker-dealers and investment advisers, including financial planner and financial adviser (Hung et al., 2008; Hung and Yoong, 2013). In consumer focus groups held by the SEC, participants were generally unclear about the distinctions among titles, including broker, investment adviser, and financial planner (Siegel & Gale LLC and Gelb Consulting Group, 2005). In addition, concerns have long existed that some financial professionals use titles suggesting that they provide financial planning services as a marketing tool, when in fact they are only selling products. The Financial Planning Coalition (2009) has noted that some individuals may hold themselves out as financial planners without meeting minimum training or ethical requirements.

Financial planners' professional designations are typically conferred by a professional or trade organization. These designations—such as Certified Financial Planner®, Chartered Financial Consultant®, or Personal Financial Specialist—may indicate that a planner has passed an examination, met certain educational requirements, or had related professional experience. Some of these designations require extensive classroom training and examination requirements and include codes of ethics with the ability to remove the designation in the event of violations (Turner and Muir, 2013). State securities regulators view certain designations as meeting or exceeding the registration requirements for investment adviser representatives and allow these professional designations to satisfy necessary competency requirements for prospective investment adviser representatives. Nevertheless, the criteria used by organizations granting professional designations for financial professionals vary greatly. Privately conferred designations range from those with rigorous competency, practice, and ethical standards and enforcement, to those that can be obtained with minimal effort and no ongoing evaluation. 'Senior-specific designations' that imply expertise or special training in advising elderly investors have received particular attention from state regulators of late, as a result of cases in which financial professionals targeted seniors by using such designations to wrongly imply they had a particular expertise for older investors (SEC et al., 2007). In response, some states now limit the use of senior-specific designations.

SEC-registered investment advisers must follow SEC regulations on advertising and other communications prohibiting false or misleading advertisements, and these regulations apply to investment advisers' marketing of financial planning services. FINRA regulations on standards for communication with the public similarly prohibit false, exaggerated, unwarranted, or misleading statements or claims by broker-dealers, and broker-dealer advertisements are subject to additional approval, filing, and recordkeeping requirements and review procedures. In addition, most states regulate the use of the title 'financial planner,' and state securities and insurance laws can apply to the misuse of this title and other titles. In many states, regulators can use unfair trade practice laws to prohibit insurance agents from holding themselves out as financial planners, when in fact they are purely engaged in the sale of life or annuity insurance products. But the effectiveness of the regulation of insurers' market conduct varies across states, and GAO (2010c) has noted inconsistencies in the state regulation of life settlements, a potentially high-risk transaction in which financial planners may participate.

Some stakeholders have recommended alternative approaches to the regulation of financial planners

Over the past few years, a number of stakeholders, including consumer groups, FINRA, and trade associations representing financial planners, securities firms, and insurance firms, have proposed different approaches to the regulation of financial planners. Following are four of the most prominent approaches, and some of their potential advantages and disadvantages.

Creation of a board to oversee financial planners

In 2009, the Financial Planning Coalition, comprised of the Certified Financial Planner Board of Standards, the Financial Planning Association, and the National Association of Personal Financial Advisors, proposed that Congress establish a professional standards-setting oversight board for financial planners (Financial Planning Coalition, 2009). The coalition's proposed legislation would establish federal regulation of financial planners by allowing the SEC to recognize a financial planner oversight board that would set professional standards for and oversee the activities of individual financial planners, although not financial planning firms. For example, such a board would have the authority to establish baseline competency standards in the areas of education, examination, and continuing education, and it would be required to establish ethical standards designed to prevent fraudulent and manipulative acts and practices. It would also have the authority to require registration or licensing of financial planners and to perform investigative and disciplinary actions. The Financial Planning Coalition contends that a potential advantage of this approach is that it would treat financial planning as a distinct profession and regulate across the full spectrum of activities in which financial planners may engage, including activities related to investments, taxes, education, retirement planning, estate planning, insurance, and household budgeting. A financial planning oversight board could also help ensure high standards and consistent regulation for all financial planners by establishing common standards for competency, professional practices, and ethics.

Nevertheless, many securities regulators and financial services trade associations believe that such a board would overlap with and in many ways duplicate existing state and federal regulations, which already cover virtually all of the products and services that a financial planner provides (GAO, 2010a). The board could also entail unnecessary additional financial costs and administrative burdens for the government and regulated entities. In addition, some opponents of this approach question whether 'financial planning' should be thought of as a distinct profession requiring its own regulatory structure, noting that financial planning is not easily defined and can span multiple professions including accounting, insurance, investment advice, and law.

Augmenting oversight of investment advisers with an SRO

Several proposals over the years have considered having FINRA or a newly created SRO supplement SEC oversight of investment advisers. These proposals date back to at least 1963, when the SEC recommended that all registered investment advisers be required to be members of an SRO. In 1986, the National Association of Securities Dealers, a predecessor to FINRA, explored the feasibility of examining the investment advisory activities of members who were also registered as investment advisers. The US House of Representatives passed a bill in 1993 that would have amended the Advisers Act to authorize the creation of an 'inspection only' SRO for investment advisers, although the bill did not become law. In 2011, the SEC (2011*b*) released a staff study recommending that Congress consider new approaches to address the SEC's insufficient resources for examining investment advisers. Among them were authorizing one or more SROs to examine all SEC-registered investment advisors, or authorizing FINRA to examine investment advisers dually registered as broker-dealers for compliance with the Adviser's Act.

According to FINRA, the primary advantage of augmenting investment adviser oversight with an SRO is that doing so would allow for more frequent examinations, given the limited resources of states and the SEC. The Financial Services Institute, an advocacy organization for independent broker-dealers and financial advisers, has stated that an industry-funded SRO with the resources necessary to appropriately supervise and examine all investment advisers would close the existing gap between the regulation of broker-dealers and investment advisers (GAO, 2010*a*). Yet some state securities regulators oppose adding an SRO component to the regulatory authority of investment advisers, believing that investment adviser regulation is a governmental function that should not be outsourced to a private, third-party organization lacking the objectivity, independence, expertise, and experience of a government regulator. Furthermore, SROs are less transparent than government regulators inasmuch as they are not subject to open records laws through which the investing public can obtain information. In addition, funding an SRO and complying with its rules could impose additional costs on firms.

Extending coverage of the fiduciary standard

As noted earlier, the SEC (2011*b*) recommended extending coverage of the fiduciary standard of care to all brokers, dealers, and investment advisers. Proponents of extending the fiduciary standard of care, including consumer groups, some financial planning groups, and some state regulators, generally maintain that consumers should be able to expect that financial professionals they work with will act in their best interests (GAO, 2010*a*). They say that a fiduciary standard is more protective of consumers' interests than a suitability standard, which requires only that a product be suitable for a consumer rather than in the consumer's best interest. In addition, extending a fiduciary standard could somewhat reduce consumer confusion about financial planners that are covered by the fiduciary standard in some capacities (such as providing investment advice) but not in others (such as selling a product).

Yet some participants in the insurance and broker-dealer industries still argue that the fiduciary standard of care is vague and undefined (GAO, 2010*a*). They say that replacing a suitability standard with a fiduciary standard could actually weaken consumer protections because the suitability of a product is easier to define and enforce. Opponents also have argued that complying with a fiduciary standard would increase compliance costs that in turn would be passed along to consumers or otherwise lead to fewer consumer choices (GAO, 2010*a*).

Clarifying financial planners' credentials and standards

The American College, a non-profit educational institution that confers several financial designations, has proposed clarifying the credentials and standards of financial professionals, including financial planners (GAO, 2010*a*). In particular, it has suggested creating a working group of existing academic and practice experts to establish voluntary credentialing standards for financial professionals. Clarifying the credentials and standards of financial professionals could conceivably take the form of prohibiting the use of certain designations or establishing minimum education, testing, or work experience requirements needed to obtain a designation. The American College suggests that greater oversight of such credentials and standards could provide a 'seal of approval' that would generally raise the quality and competence of financial professionals, including financial planners, help consumers distinguish among the various credentials, and screen out less-qualified or reputable players.

Yet the ultimate effectiveness of such an approach is not clear, because the extent to which consumers take designations into account when selecting or working with financial planners is unknown, as is the extent of the harm caused by misleading designations. In addition, implementation and ongoing monitoring of financial planners' credentials and standards could be challenging. Moreover, the issue of unclear designations has already been addressed to some extent—for example, as noted earlier, some states regulate the use of certain senior-specific designations and allow certain professional designations to satisfy necessary competency requirements for prospective investment adviser representatives. State securities regulators also have the authority to pursue the misleading use of credentials through their existing antifraud authority.

Conclusion

This chapter has argued that existing statutes and regulations appear to cover most, if not all, financial planning services in the United States, and individual financial planners nearly always fall under one or more regulatory regimes, depending on their activities. While no single law governs the broad array of activities in which financial planners may engage, an additional layer of regulation specific to financial planners may not be warranted at this time. At the same time, more robust enforcement of existing laws would strengthen oversight efforts.

Financial markets function best when consumers understand how financial providers and products work and know how to choose among them. Yet consumers may be unclear about standards of care that apply to financial professionals, particularly when the same individual or firm offers multiple services that have differing standards of care. As such, consumers may not always know whether and when a financial planner is required to serve their best interests. In addition, consumer confusion about standard of care remains a concern with regard to advice on, and sale of, insurance products, which is largely outside the jurisdiction of the SEC. Finally, we have seen that financial planners can adopt a variety of titles and designations that can imply different types of qualifications, yet consumers may not understand or distinguish among these designations, leaving them unable to properly assess the qualifications and expertise of financial planners. The SEC, FINRA, and state regulators have all taken actions in recent years to address this issue, but how successful they will be remains to be seen.

Endnotes

1. The present chapter draws heavily on the GAO's study (2011) on the regulation of financial planners.

2. The Consumer Financial Protection Bureau, created by the Dodd-Frank Wall Street Reform and Consumer Protection Act in 2010, regulates the offering and provision of consumer financial products or services under federal consumer financial laws. A financial product or service is defined in the act to include financial advisory services to consumers on individual financial matters, with the exception of advisory services related to securities regulated by the SEC or state securities regulators.

References

Congressional Research Service (CRS) (2010). *Securities and Exchange Commission Rule 151A and Annuities: Issues and Legislation*, CRS Report for Congress 7-7500. Washington, DC: CRS.

Financial Planning Coalition (2009). *Coalition Case Statement 2009-04.* Washington, DC: Financial Planning Coalition. www.cfp.net/downloads/Coalition_Case_Statement_2009-04.pdf

Hung, A. A., and J. K. Yoong (2013). 'Asking for Help: Survey and Experimental Evidence on Financial Advice and Behavior Change,' in O. S. Mitchell and K. Smetters, eds., *The Market for Retirement Financial Advice.* Oxford, UK: Oxford University Press.

—— N. Clancy, J. Dominitz, E. Talley, C. Berrebi, and F. Suvankulov (2008). *Investor and Industry Perspectives on Investment Advisers and Broker-Dealers.* Santa Monica, CA: RAND Institute for Civil Justice.

Infogroup (2010). *U.S. Investors & the Fiduciary Standard: A National Opinion Survey.* Papillion, NE: Infogroup. http://www.cfp.net/downloads/US_Investors_Opinion_Survey_2010-09-16.pdf

National Association of Insurance Commissioners (NAIC) (2005). *Life Insurance Disclosure Model Regulation*, MDL-580. Kansas City, MO: NAIC.

—— (2010). *Suitability in Annuity Transactions Model Regulation*, MDL-275. Kansas City, MO: NAIC.

Securities and Exchange Commission (SEC) (2011a). *Study on Enhancing Investment Adviser Examinations.* Washington, DC: SEC, pp. 3–4.

—— (2011b). *Study on Investment Advisers and Broker-Dealers.* Washington, DC: SEC.

Securities and Exchange Commission (SEC), North American Securities Administrators Association, and Financial Industry Regulatory Authority (2007). *Protecting Senior Investors: Report of Examinations of Securities Firms Providing 'Free Lunch' Sales Seminars.* Washington, DC: SEC.

Siegel & Gale LLC and Gelb Consulting Group (2005). *Results of Investor Focus Group Interviews About Proposed Brokerage Account Disclosures. Report to the Securities and Exchange Commission.* Washington, DC: SEC.

Turner, J. A., and D. M. Muir (2013). 'The Market for Financial Advisers,' in O. S. Mitchell and K. Smetters, eds., *The Market for Retirement Financial Advice.* Oxford, UK: Oxford University Press.

United States Government Accountability Office (GAO) (2007). *Securities and Exchange Commission: Steps Being Taken to Make Examination Program More Risk-Based and Transparent.* GAO-07-1053. Washington, DC: GAO.

—— (2009). *Insurance Reciprocity and Uniformity: NAIC and State Regulators Have Made Progress in Producer Licensing, Product Approval and Market Conduct Regulation, but Challenges Remain.* GAO-09-372. Washington, DC: GAO.

—— (2010a). Interviews by GAO staff and private communications with more than 30 organizations representing financial planners, the financial services industry, and consumer interests, and with federal and state financial regulatory agencies.

—— (2010b). Analysis of data provided at GAO's request by the Financial Industry Regulatory Authority from its Investment Adviser Registration Depository, which is maintained on behalf of the Securities and Exchange Commission. Personal communication.

—— (2010c). *Life Insurance Settlements: Regulatory Inconsistencies May Pose a Number of Challenges.* GAO-10-775. Washington, DC: GAO.

—— (2011). *Consumer Finance: Regulatory Coverage Generally Exists for Financial Planners, but Consumer Protection Issues Remain.* GAO-11-235. Washington, DC: GAO.

End Pages

The Pension Research Council

The Pension Research Council of the Wharton School at the University of Pennsylvania is committed to generating debate on key policy issues affecting pensions and other employee benefits. The Council sponsors interdisciplinary research on private and social retirement security and related benefit plans in the United States and around the world. It seeks to broaden understanding of these complex arrangements through basic research into their economic, social, legal, actuarial, and financial foundations. Members of the Advisory Board of the Council, appointed by the Dean of the Wharton School, are leaders in the employee benefits field, and they recognize the essential role of social security and other public-sector income maintenance programs while sharing a desire to strengthen private-sector approaches to economic security (for more information, see http://www.pensionresearchcouncil.org).

The Boettner Center for Pensions and Retirement Security

Founded at the Wharton School to support scholarly research, teaching, and outreach on global aging, retirement, and public and private pensions, the Center is named after Joseph E. Boettner. Funding to the University of Pennsylvania was provided through the generosity of the Boettner family whose intent was to spur financial well-being at older ages through work on how aging influences financial security and life satisfaction. The Center disseminates research and evaluation on challenges and opportunities associated with global aging and retirement, how to strengthen retirement income systems, saving and investment behavior of the young and the old, interactions between physical and mental health, and successful retirement (for more information, see http://www.pensionresearchcouncil.org/boettner/).

Executive Director

Olivia S. Mitchell, *International Foundation of Employee Benefit Plans Professor*, Department of Business Economics and Public Policy, The Wharton School, University of Pennsylvania.

Advisory Board

Gary W. Anderson, Austin, TX
David S. Blitzstein, United Food & Commercial Workers, Washington, DC
Robert L. Clark, College of Management, North Carolina State University, Raleigh, NC
Julia Coronado, BNP Paribas, New York, NY
Peter A. Fisher, Tapestry Networks, Waltham, MA
P. Brett Hammond, MSCI, New York, NY
Beth Hirschhorn, MetLife, New York, NY
Emily Kessler, Society of Actuaries, Schaumburg, IL
David I. Laibson, Department of Economics, Harvard University, Cambridge, MA
Annamaria Lusardi, School of Business, The George Washington University, Washington, DC
Jeannine Markoe Raymond, National Association of State Retirement Administrators, Washington, DC
Raimond Maurer, Finance Department, Goethe University, Frankfurt, Germany
Judith F. Mazo, Washington, DC
Alicia H. Munnell, School of Management, Boston College, Chestnut Hill, MA
Richard Prosten, Amalgamated Resources, Washington, DC
Anna M. Rappaport, Anna Rappaport Consulting, Chicago, IL
David P. Richardson, TIAA-CREF Institute, Charlotte, NC
Richard C. Shea, Covington & Burling LLP, Washington, DC
Kent Smetters, Department of Business Economics and Public Policy, The Wharton School, University of Pennsylvania, Philadelphia, PA
Nicholas S. Souleles, Finance Department, The Wharton School, University of Pennsylvania, Philadelphia, PA
Stephen P. Utkus, Vanguard, Malvern, PA
Jack L. VanDerhei, Employee Benefit Research Institute, Washington, DC
Mark Warshawsky, Towers Watson, Arlington, VA
Stephen P. Zeldes, Graduate School of Business, Columbia University, New York, NY

Senior Partners

Allianz SE
Federal Reserve Employee Benefits System
Financial Engines
William A. Frey
Investment Company Institute
Lincoln Financial Group
MetLife
Morgan Stanley Smith Barney
Mutual of America Life Insurance Company
New York Life—Mainstay
Pacific Investment Management Company (PIMCO)

Prudential
Retirement Made Simpler (FINRA)
Social Security Administration
State Street Global Advisors
T. Rowe Price
TIAA-CREF Institute
Towers Watson
The Vanguard Group

Institutional Members
International Foundation of Employee Benefit Plans
Ontario Pension Board
Society of Actuaries

Recent Pension Research Council Publications

Reshaping Retirement Security: Lessons from the Global Financial Crisis. Raimond Maurer, Olivia S. Mitchell, and Mark Warshawsky, eds. 2012. (ISBN 0-19-966069-7)
Financial Literacy. Olivia S. Mitchell and Annamaria Lusardi, eds. 2011. (ISBN 0-19-969681-9)
Securing Lifelong Retirement Income. Olivia S. Mitchell, John Piggott, and Noriyuki Takayama, eds. 2011. (ISBN 0-19-959484-9)
Reorienting Retirement Risk Management. Robert L. Clark and Olivia S. Mitchell, eds. 2010. (ISBN 0-19-959260-9)
Fundamentals of Private Pensions. Dan M. McGill, Kyle N. Brown, John J. Haley, Sylvester Schieber, and Mark J. Warshawsky. 9th Ed. 2010. (ISBN 0-19-954451-6)
The Future of Public Employees Retirement Systems. Olivia S. Mitchell and Gary Anderson, eds. 2009. (ISBN 0-19-957334-9)
Recalibrating Retirement Spending and Saving. John Ameriks and Olivia S. Mitchell, eds. 2008. (ISBN 0-19-954910-8)
Lessons from Pension Reform in the Americas. Stephen J. Kay and Tapen Sinha, eds. 2008. (ISBN 0-19-922680-6)
Redefining Retirement: How Will Boomers Fare? Brigitte Madrian, Olivia S. Mitchell, and Beth J. Soldo, eds. 2007. (ISBN 0-19-923077-3)
Restructuring Retirement Risks. David Blitzstein, Olivia S. Mitchell, and Steven P. Utkus, eds. 2006. (ISBN 0-19-920465-9)
Reinventing the Retirement Paradigm. Robert L. Clark and Olivia S. Mitchell, eds. 2005. (ISBN 0-19-928460-1)
Pension Design and Structure: New Lessons from Behavioral Finance. Olivia S. Mitchell and Steven P. Utkus, eds. 2004. (ISBN 0-19-927339-1)
The Pension Challenge: Risk Transfers and Retirement Income Security. Olivia S. Mitchell and Kent Smetters, eds. 2003. (ISBN 0-19-926691-3)

A History of Public Sector Pensions in the United States. Robert L. Clark, Lee A. Craig, and Jack W. Wilson, eds. 2003. (ISBN 0-8122-3714-5)

Benefits for the Workplace of the Future. Olivia S. Mitchell, David Blitzstein, Michael Gordon, and Judith Mazo, eds. 2003. (ISBN 0-8122-3708-0)

Innovations in Retirement Financing. Olivia S. Mitchell, Zvi Bodie, P. Brett Hammond, and Stephen Zeldes, eds. 2002. (ISBN 0-8122-3641-6)

To Retire or Not: Retirement Policy and Practice in Higher Education. Robert L. Clark and P. Brett Hammond, eds. 2001. (ISBN 0-8122-3572-X)

Pensions in the Public Sector. Olivia S. Mitchell and Edwin Hustead, eds. 2001. (ISBN 0-8122-3578-9)

The Role of Annuity Markets in Financing Retirement. Jeffrey Brown, Olivia S. Mitchell, James Poterba, and Mark Warshawsky. 2001. (ISBN 0-262-02509-4)

Forecasting Retirement Needs and Retirement Wealth. Olivia S. Mitchell, P. Brett Hammond, and Anna Rappaport, eds. 2000. (ISBN 0-8122-3529-0)

Prospects for Social Security Reform. Olivia S. Mitchell, Robert J. Myers, and Howard Young, eds. 1999. (ISBN 0-8122-3479-0)

Living with Defined Contribution Pensions: Remaking Responsibility for Retirement. Olivia S. Mitchell and Sylvester J. Schieber, eds. 1998. (ISBN 0-8122-3439-1)

Positioning Pensions for the Twenty-First Century. Michael S. Gordon, Olivia S. Mitchell, and Marc M. Twinney, eds. 1997. (ISBN 0-8122-3391-3)

Securing Employer-Based Pensions: An International Perspective. Zvi Bodie, Olivia S. Mitchell, and John A. Turner, eds. 1996. (ISBN 0-8122-3334-4)

Available from the Pension Research Council web site: http://www.pensionresearchcouncil.org/

Index

Bold entries refer to **figures** and **tables**

AARP survey 73
accounting theory paradigm 47, 48–51, 52–4, 55–6, 64, 65, 66
Accredited Financial Counselor 154
Advisers Act *see* Investment Advisers Act (1940)
Affordable Health Care Act 7
age
   annuity decision-making process 137
   asset allocation 89
   behavior change and financial advice 185, **186**, **187**, **188**, **190**, **198**, **200**, **202**, 203
   consumer finance protection 216
   credibility of observed relationships **167**, **168**, **169**, **170**, **172**
   mutual fund investors' use of financial advisers 251–3, **251**, **252**, 255, **257**, 261, **262**, 263, **264**, **265**
   Social Security benefits 71, 72, 77, 80, 85
   usefulness and importance of financial advice **236**, 243–4
A.M. Best 141
American College 19, 317
American Institute of Certified Public Accountants (AICPA) 19
American Life Panel (ALP)(RAND) 5, 157, 185, **186**, 193, 195, **196–7**
Ameriprise 28
anchoring 56, 58, 215
annual family income (AFI) 185, **186**, **187**, **188**, **190**, **198**, **200**, **202**
annuitization 4, 15, 26
annuity, inflation-indexed 56, 91
annuity decision-making process and guidance 125–48

active guidance **132**
adviser guidance 133
case studies 145–6
Chile 141–2, 143–4
competition, issuer selection and fee disclosure considerations 139–40
experience with guidance models 136–7
facilitated guidance 133
immediate annuity buyers 137–9
institutional adviser **132**, **134–5**
institutional facilitator **132**, **134–5**
institutional individual **132**, **134–5**
online direct to individual access 133
questions and concerns, handling of 140–1
quotes for $100, 000 deposit over one year **140**
retail purchase, institutional purchase and/or defined benefit (DB) payout **134**, **135**
single premium immediate annuities **138**
structural guidance 126, 129, 131, **132**, 135–6, 138, 144
suitability reviews 136
timeline from quotes to purchase 139
types of guidance or education provision provided by companies to employees **129**
United Kingdom 142–3
annuity puzzle 122
'arm's length' standard 32
asset allocation 4, 89–105
   dynamic modeling 97–100
   projected replacement rates 101–3
   replacement rates model 89–93

326 Index

asset allocation (*cont.*)
  target replacement rates 100–1
  see also retirement income targets and resources
asset-based fee 117, 239, 281
Assets Under Management (AUM) 16, 20
Australia 2
  Future of Financial Advice Committee 242
auto-enrollment techniques 119–20
auto-regressive process of order one (AR(1)) 97
Average Indexed Monthly Earnings (AIME) 101

Bachus, Spencer 295
balanced fund 120
bank-affiliated advisor 154
Bank of America Merrill Lynch 16
bank customer service specialist 154
bank representatives 77
behavioral paradigm 48–51, 56–9, 64, 65, 66
behavior change and financial advice 182–210
  advice presentation 194–5
  affirmative decision treatment 194, 195, 197, **200**, 202–3, **202**, 204–7, **205**, **206**
  age 185, **186**, **187**, **188**, **190**, **198**, **200**, **202**, 203
  American Life Panel (ALP) 185, **186**, 193, 195, **196–7**
  annual family income (AFI) 185, **186**, **187**, **188**, **190**, **198**, **200**, **202**
  best linear predictors (BLP) 185
  comparisons of means **201**
  control group 207
  default treatment group 194, **202**, 203–4, 207
  default versus optional advice 199–203
  defined contribution (DC) plans 183, 185, 186–9, **188**, **190**, **192**, 195, 197, **198**, **200**, **202**, 203

education 185, **186**, **187**, **188**, **190**, 192, **198**, **200**, **202**, 203
employment status **186**
ethnicity 185, **186**, **187**, **188**, **190**, **198**, **200**, **202**
experimental analyses 182
experimental design schematic **199**
experimental sample and summary statistics 195, **198**
financial literacy 185, **187**, 189–93, **192**, 195–8, **198**, **200**, 203, 204, **205**, **206**, 207, 208
401(k) plans 182, 185
gender 185, **186**, **187**, **188**, **190**, **198**, **200**
high-returns treatment 194
Individual Retirement Account (IRA) 183
intent-to-treat analysis **202**, 204, 206
linear probability (LP) model 185, 191, 197, **198**
low-returns treatment 194, **200**, **202**, 203
mandatory counselling 207
marital status **186**, **187**, **190**, **198**, **200**, **202**
motivation 208
multivariate regression framework 206
observational analyses 182
ordinary least squares regression **187**, 189, **190**, **192**, **200**, 201, **202**, **205**
portfolio allocations **188**, **190**, **192**, 204, 207
Portfolio Checkup Tool 194–5
portfolio checkup treatment 194
portfolio quality 204, **205**, **206**
propensity to seek advice 185–6, **187**, **200**
reverse causality 182, 191–3
rules treatment 194
self-selection 182, 185, 189–93, 195–8, **200**, 204, 207
solicited advice 184, 207
summary statistics **186**
unsolicited advice 184, 207
voluntary advice programs 208
see also portfolio 'mistakes'

Benjamin F. Edwards & Co. 25
Bernanke, B.S. 7
Bernard Madoff Investment
  Securities 277
best interest standard 276–7
  see also fiduciary duty/standard
Biggs, Andrew G. xv
bivariate estimates 165–6, 171
BMELV *see* Germany
Boettner Center for Pensions and
  Retirement Security 321
Boettner, Joseph E. 321
bonding 239
Borzi, Phyllis 293
Break-Even Analysis 78, **80**, 85
BrightScope Inc. 16–17
brochure (written disclosure
  statement) 22
broker-dealers 3, 35, 243, 307, **309**, **311**
  commission 239
  compensation and agency costs 241
  conflicts of interest 31
  fiduciary investment advisers 36
  financial information **297–8**
  financial planner regulation 312
  investment advisers as fiduciaries 32
  profit margins **280**
  regional 75, 76
  regulation harmonization of financial
    advisers 276, 277
  Securities and Exchange Commission
    (SEC) regulation 277–9, 281,
    282, 285, 286–8
Bromberg, Jason xv, 6, 54
budgeting paradigm 47, 48–51, 52–4,
  55–6, 64, 65, 66
Bureau of Labor Statistics 73
Business Roundtable v. SEC (2011) 289–91

Cackley, Alicia P. xv, 6, 54
Callan Investment Institute 130
Canada 154–5
captive agent 16
Casey, Kathleen L. 289–90
causality 158
  see also reverse causality

*Certain Broker-Dealers Deemed Not To Be
  Investment Advisers* proposed
  rule 282
certifications 39, 243
  see also professional certifications
Certified Financial Planner
  (CFP) 16–18, 154, 239, 314
  Board 17
  examination 243
Certified Investment Management
  Analyst 20
Certified Public Accountants
  (CPAs) 19, 25, 181–9
Chartered Financial Analyst (CFA) 18
Chartered Financial Analyst
  Institute 18
Chartered Financial Consultant
  (ChFC) 19, 314
Chartered Investment Counselor
  (CIC) 18
Chartered Life Underwriter
  (CLU) 19–20
Chevron v. NRDC (1984) 283
Chile 141–2, 143–4
  AFPs (private pension funds) 141–2
choice and information overload 215
churning 281
  reverse 20
Claim Now, Claim More Later 72
Claim and Suspend tactic 72
clients *see in particular* behaviour
  change; experienced adviser
  paradigm
coach (role) 155
coefficient of relative risk aversion
  (CRRA) 98–9
cognitive ability 231, **232**, 235
collaborators, investors as 255, 267
commission 26, 154, 220, 239, 312
  see also compensation; shrouded
  pricing
compensation 24–5, 54, **98**
  and agency costs 237–41, 242
  asset-based 280–1
  for retaining typical portfolio
    allocation **98**

compensation (*cont.*)
  special 279, 281, 283
competition 139–40
competitive bidding 139, 141–2, 143
competitive pricing 144
competitive quotes 135–6
compliance exams 36
computer models 37
confidence of investors 215, 219, 244, 263, **264**, **266**, 267
conflicts of interest 2, 30–5, 39
  annuity decision-making process 145
  consumer finance protection 217–19, 220–1
  fiduciary duty non-applicability 26–8
  fiduciary investment advisers 38
  individuals and financial advice issues 28–9
  investment advisers and fiduciaries 31–5
  planning paradigms and risk 54
  quality of advice provided to plan sponsors 29
  regulation of financial planners 310–13
  Securities and Exchange Commission (SEC) regulation 281, 288, 292
  usefulness and importance of financial advice 239, 242, 244
Consumer Federation of America 291
consumer finance protection 213–26
  age 216
  complexity of investment decisions 215
  conflicts of interest 217–19, 220–1
  customer characteristics **218**
  education 216, 217
  enhancement of financial advice market 219–21
  Europe 216–17
  financial capability of consumers 216, **218**
  financial investment problem 214
  financial literacy 216, 220
  gender 216
  Germany 216–17, 222, 224
  income 216
  mandatory disclosure 219–20
  risk management 222, **223**, 224
  self-interest 217–18
  systematic mistakes 215, **218**
  transparency 220, 221–4
  wealth 216
Consumer Financial Protection Bureau 213, 309
consumer protection authority 213
consumption smoothing 55–6, 58
contingent fees 220
Continuing Education 17, 18, 85, 315
contract 239
convenience features 112
counselor (role) 58, 59, 155
credentials and standards, clarification of (alternative approach to existing regulation) 317–18
crystallized intelligence 243–4

defined benefit (DB) plans 13
  annuity decision-making process 126–7, 128, 133, 139
  credibility of observed relationships **167**, **168**, **169**, **170**, **172**
  fiduciary investment advisers 34, 35, 36–7
  United Kingdom 142
  workplace advice 108–9, 115, 122
defined contribution (DC) plans 1
  annuity decision-making process 125, 126–7, 128, 130, 137, 143, 145
  behavior change and financial advice 183, 185, 186–9, **188**, **190**, **192**, 195, 197, **198**, **200**, **202**, 203
  credibility of observed relationships **167**, **168**, **169**, **170**, **172**
  fiduciary duty non-applicability 28
  fiduciary investment advisers 38
  mutual fund investors' use of financial advisers 249, 252–3, 262, **264**, **266**, 267

Social Security benefits 70, 73, 83
United Kingdom 142
workplace advice 107, 108, 120, 122–3
see also 401(k) plans
delaying retirement 95
delegators, investors as 255, 267
demographic factors 112–13, **114**, **117**, 235
Department of Labor (DOL) 2, 7, 38, 296
  annuity decision-making process 127
  compensation 24
  conflicts of interest 30
  fiduciary duty non-applicability 27–8
  Interpretive Bulletin 96–1, 109–10
  regulation harmonization of financial advisers 277
  Securities and Exchange Commission (SEC) regulation 291–3
  workplace advice 108, 110
derivatives markets 56
designations and titles 314
direct market channel 237, 260
disclosure 39, 242
  of advisory fees to individuals 21–2
  conflicts of interest 30–1
  consumer finance protection 219–20
  fiduciary investment advisers 32, 36, 38
  financial planner regulation 312
  forms (ADV forms) 22
  mortgage brokers 217
discretionary assets 26
discretionary management 115
disposition effect 221, 235
distribution option in plan 130
diversification (portfolio) 156, 160, 215, 220, 221, 250
  see also under-diversified *under* portfolio 'mistakes'
Dodd-Frank law 3, 296
  advisory fees charged to plan sponsors 24
  fiduciary duty non-applicability 28
  fiduciary investment advisers 36
  regulation harmonization of financial advisers 277

Securities and Exchange Commission (SEC) regulation 287, 288, 291, 294
Donovan v. Bierwirth (1982) 277
dual-registered advisers *see* 'hat-switching' problem
due diligence 112
dynamic modeling 97–100

Edelman Financial Services 24
education
  behavior change and financial advice 185, **186**, **187**, **188**, **190**, 192, **198**, **200**, **202**, 203
  consumer finance protection 216, 217
  credibility of observed relationships **167**, **168**, **169**, **170**, **172**
  mutual fund investors' use of financial advisers 255, **257**, **262**, 263, **264**, **265**
  usefulness and importance of financial advice 231, **232**, 235, **236**, 242–3, 244
  see also Continuing Education
Employee Benefit Research Institute xvi, 8
Employee Benefits Security Administration (EBSA) 30–1, 33, 35–8
Employee Retirement Income Security Act 1974 (ERISA) 2
  conflicts of interest 31
  investment advisers as fiduciaries 32–5
  managed accounts 115
  quality of advice provided to plan sponsors 29
  regulation harmonization of financial advisers 277
  Securities and Exchange Commission (SEC) regulation 291–2
  workplace advice 108, 109, 110
employee-stock ownership plan (ESOP) 124
employer-sponsored plans 259–61, 262

employment status 231, **257**
ethnicity
  behavior change and financial advice 185, **186**, **187**, **188**, **190**, **198**, **200**, **202**
  credibility of observed relationships **167**, **168**, **169**, **170**, **172**
Europe 216–17
  Financial Stability Board 213
European Commission: recast proposal for directive on markets in financial instruments (MiFID II) 213–14
evolution of workplace advice *see* workplace advice
Exchange Act 278–9, 286, 287
exclusive purpose rule 32
experienced adviser paradigm 48–51, 59–63, 64, 65, 66
  advisory deliverable changing faster than adviser training 63
  advisory standards, lack of and confusion 63
  client as center of planning process and adviser as trusted counselor 60
  client couples 61
  client engagement and reliance on iterative small steps 60
  clients seeing financial adviser as 'healer' 62
  clients unable to articulate basic facts about finances 61–2
  clients undergoing change 61
  information gaps confounding risk measurement 62
  investment risk management 64, 65
  longevity risk management 64, 65
  plan implementation as part of planning process 60
  planning strategy for when client has more than (or less than) enough 64, 66
  values clarification preceding goal-setting 59–60

face-to-face setting 216
facilitators (role) 58, 59, 60, **132**, **134–5**, 136, 146
Fanto, James 286
Federal Trade Commission (FTC) staff report on disclosure rules for mortgage brokers 217
fee-based advisers 21
fee-for-service model 239
fee-only adviser 21
fee-only planner 154
fees 20–5, 26, 140–1
  advisory 21–2, 23–4
  asset-based 117, 239, 281
  contingent 220
  disclosure considerations 21–2, 139–40
  hourly rates 23
  level fee model 37
  performance-based 21
  referral 25
  structures 39
  subscription 21
  tax deductible 22
  12b-1 26, 237–8
  wrap 26
  see also commission; compensation
fiduciary duty/standard 7, 39
  compensation and agency costs 239
  conflicts of interest 301–2
  extending coverage of (alternative approach to existing regulation) 317
  regulation of financial planners 310, **311**, 312–13
  Securities and Exchange Commission (SEC) regulation 294
  usefulness and importance of financial advice 241–2, 245
  see also regulation harmonization
fiduciary investment advisers, current rule making and reports on 35–8
financial advisers 15–20, 136, 160
  companies providing financial advice 15–16

duties 4
professional certifications 16–20
Social Security benefits 70, 73, **75**, 77
financial assets *see* wealth
Financial Engines 4, 15–16
  Plan Preview 116
  workplace advice 107–8, 110–11, 112–13, 114, 115–19
Financial Industry Regulatory Authority (FINRA) 3, 243, 296
  annuity decision-making process 127
  compensation and agency costs 239
  conflicts of interest 30, 31
  financial planner regulation 307, 308, **309**, 310–11, 312–13, 314, 316
  planning paradigms and risk 54
  professional certifications 17
  Securities and Exchange Commission (SEC) regulation 278, 279, 289, 293, 294, 295
financial literacy 161
  behavior change and financial advice 185, **187**, 189–93, **192**, 195–8, **198**, **200**, 203–4, **205–6**, 207–8
  consumer finance protection 216, 220
  mutual fund investors 250
  usefulness and importance of financial advice 231, 244
Financial Media Group (FMG) 74
financial planners 241, 276
Financial Planning Association (FPA) 282, 312
Financial Planning Association v. SEC (2007) 283–4
Financial Planning Coalition 309, 313, 315
financial planning software 14, 15
Financial Services Institute 316
Financial Stability Board (FSB) 213
Finke, Michael xv, 5
five-part test 291
fixed costs 231
fluid intelligence 243–4
Flynn, John T. 286
Form ADV *see* Uniform Application for Investment Adviser Registration

4 percent rule 91, 126
401(k) Forum (later mPower) 110
401(k) plans 13–14, 156
  advisory fees charged to plan sponsors 24
  age and financial advice 244
  annuity decision-making process 126
  asset allocation 92, 100, 102
  behavior change and financial advice 182, 185
  benefits from financial advice 234
  companies providing financial advice 15–16
  conflicts of interest 30
  dynamic modeling 97
  fiduciary duty non-applicability 26–8
  fiduciary investment advisers 32, 36, 38
  legal and regulatory issues, evolution of 29–30
  professional certifications 16–17
  retirement, delayed 95
  workplace advice 107–12, 114–15, 117, 119, 121–3
framing 56, 58, 78–82, **79**, 215
Free Loan strategy 71, 86
Frequently Asked Questions list 84

gambles 78, 85
Garland, Judge 283–4
Garrett, Scott 290
gender
  annuity decision-making process 137, 138
  consumer finance protection 216
  credibility of observed relationships **167**, **168**, **169**, **170**, **172**
  mutual fund investors' use of financial advisers **257**, **262**, **264**, **266**
  Social Security benefits 71
Germany 2, 154, 157, 160, 231, 233
  behavior change and financial advice 185
  consumer finance protection 216–17
  Department of Consumer Protection 222, 224

Germany (*cont.*)
  role of financial advice 250
Government Accountability Office (GAO) 6, 30, 35, 306, 307, 308, 314
Greenwald, Mathew xv–xvi, 4
Grundfest, Joseph 110
Guided Choice 16, 22
guidance *see in particular* annuity decision-making process and guidance

Hackenthal, Andreas xvi, 5, 143
  behaviour change and financial advice 183, 185, 191, 209
  impact of financial planners 154, 155, 157, 160, 161, 162
  importance of financial advice 229, 233, 250
'hat-switching' problem 3, 35, 37, 39, 312
health issues and Social Security benefits 79–80
Health and Retirement Study data 71, 93, 100, 101, **102**
hidden costs 215
Hogan, Paula xvi, 4
Holden, Sarah A. xvi, 6
holistic comprehensive planners 59
Hueler, Kelli xvi
Hueler Companies 125, 136, 137, 140
human capital 55–6, 59, 62
Hung, Angela A. xvi, 5, 35, 250, 275
  impact of financial planners 157, 161, 162, 163
  importance of financial advice 233, 239, 240, 241, 242
  regulating financial planners 312, 313

impact of financial planners 5–6, 153–78
  bivariate estimates 165–6, 171
  evaluation designs 153–63
    concepts measurement 154–6
    observed relationship credibility between consultation and outcome 157–63
    randomized field experiment to assess impact of consulting financial planner **159**
    result applicability to other settings 156–7
  instrumental variable approach 161–2
  multiple regression analysis 161
  national dataset analysis 163–74
    credibility of observed relationships 165–74
    generalizing to a population 164–5
    incremental effect of consulting a planner on number of different types of financial assets held **176**
    incremental effect of consulting a planner on proportion of total financial wealth held in stocks **175**
    incremental effect of consulting a planner on total financial wealth **174**
    logistic regression parameter estimates of first stage of propensity score analysis **172–3**
    ordinary least squares parameter estimates of number of asset categories **170**
    ordinary least squares parameter estimates of proportion stock equity **169**
    ordinary least squares parameter estimates of total financial wealth **168**
    Survey of Consumer Finances 2007 (SCF) 163–4
    weighted means for ordinary least squares regression covariates **167**
    weighted means and *t*-tests for financial outcome variables **166**
  non-experimental research design 159–61
  ordinary least squares regression 165–73
  outcome of interest 171
  population of interest 156–7
  propensity score approach 162–3, 165, 170–1, 175

randomized field experiment
(RFE) 158–9, 162, 175
reverse causation 160–1, 171
Survey of Consumer Finances 2007
(SCF) 163–4, 174
income
 annuity decision-making
 process 138, 139
 asset allocation 90
 Average Indexed Monthly Earnings
 (AIME) 101
 consumer finance protection 216
 credibility of observed
 relationships **167**, **168**, **169**,
 170, **172**
 gap calculator 140
 inflation-adjusted 82
 mutual fund investors' use of financial
 advisers 255, **257**, **264**, **265**
 usefulness and importance of
 financial advice 231, **232**, 235
 see also annual family income; lifetime
 income
Income Solutions 125, 129, 142
independent financial advisers 77, 154
Inderst, Roman xvii, 5, 143, 183, 250
 impact of financial planners 154, 157
 importance of financial advice 229,
 233, 242
India 238, 240
Individual Retirement Account
 (IRA) 14, 38
 age and financial advice 244
 annuity decision-making process 126,
 128–9, 131, 137, 145, 146
 asset allocation 100, 102
 behavior change and financial
 advice 183
 benefits from financial advice 235
 fiduciary duty non-applicability 26–8
 fiduciary investment advisers 34, 36–7
 legal and regulatory issues, evolution
 of 30
 mutual fund investors' use of
 financial advisers 249, 253, 263,
 264, **266**, 267

rollover alternative 130–1
Securities and Exchange Commission
(SEC) regulation 292
usefulness and importance of
financial advice **236**
individuals and financial advice
 issues 13–15, 25–9
 conflicts of interest 28–9
 marketing where fiduciary duty
 doesn't apply 26–8
 terminology 26
inertia 28, 121, 123, 215
inflation-indexed annuity 56, 91
initial public offering (IPO) 28
institutional advisers **132**, **134–5**
institutional individual **132**, **134–5**
instrumental variable approach 161–2
insurable risks 52
insurance agents 16, 307–8, **309**, **311**
 see also life insurance agents
insurance companies 16, 141
insurance, full 54
insurance laws **309**, 314
insurance products 311–13, **311**
Internal Revenue Code 126, 137
Internal Revenue Service IRS Form
 1099 22
Internet use *see* online access and advice
 for investors
Investment Adviser Association
 (IAA) 18
Investment Adviser Competency
 Exam 243
Investment Adviser Representatives
 (IARs) 3
investment advisers 276–7, 278–9, 285,
 309, **311**
 conflicts of interest 31–5
 see also Registered Investment Adviser
 (RIA) firms
Investment Advisers Act (1940) 276,
 278–9, 281–2, 284–5, 287–8,
 296, **309**
 fiduciary investment advisers 30–5, 36
 financial planner regulation 306,
 308, 310, 316

Investment Advisers Act (1940) (*cont.*)
  Securities and Exchange Commission (SEC) regulation 292, 294
Investment Company Act 278
Investment Company Institute (ICI) 27, 237
  Annual Mutual Fund Shareholder Tracking Survey 256, 259, 263
  household survey 250–1
  IRA Owners Survey (2011) 253
  Mutual Fund Shareholder Tracking Survey (2006) 263
Investment Funds Institute of Canada (IFIC) 154
investment horizon 215
investment risk 52, 64, 65, 109
Investor Protection Trust survey 25
issuer selection 139–40

Jones, Christopher L. xvii, 4

Laby, Arthur B. xvii, 6, 32
leaders, investors as 255, 267
legal and regulatory issues 6, 29–38
  conflicts of interest 30–5
  fiduciary investment advisers, current rule making and reports on 35–8
level fee model 37
levers 89, 93–4
Levitt, Arthur 288
Lieber, R. 2
life cycle paradigm 48–51, 54–6, 64, 65, 66
life insurance agents 75, 77
life planning 57, 63
lifetime annuity platform 4
lifetime income
  on a deferred basis 128
  inflation-adjusted 82
  and spending 55
lifetime standards of living 55
linear probability (LP) model 185, 191, 197, **198**
load (commission) 26
longevity risk management 64, 65

loss aversion 56, 78, 234
loyalty 32

Maloney Act 278, 294
managed accounts 115–19, **117, 118, 120, 121**
Mangla, I.S. 2
marital status
  behavior change and financial advice 186, 187, 190, 198, 200, 202
  credibility of observed relationships 167, 168, 169, 170, 172
  Social Security benefits 72, 85
market considerations 6
marketing and disclosure rules 308
matched-pair research design 162
Matthew Greenwald & Associates survey 74
Mayer, Robert N. xvii, 5
Mean Variance Optimization 47
Medicare program 7
Merrill Edge Advisory Center 21
Merrill Lynch 21, 22
  Global Wealth & Investment Management website 22
MetLife Securities Inc. 16
Miller, Frederick H. xvii, 4
Mitchell, Olivia S. xvii, 321
modern portfolio theory paradigm 47, 48–51, 52–4, 55–6, 64, 65, 66
Money Advice Service (United Kingdom) 143
Monte Carlo analysis/simulation 52–3, 111
Moody's 141
Morningstar Principia software 47
mortality risk 52
Motley Fool 223
Muir, Dana M. xviii, 4, 7, 54, 126, 153, 183
  importance of financial advice 229, 237
  regulating financial planners 305, 314
multiple source retirement plans 259, **260**
multivariate analysis 263–7
Munnell, Alicia H. xviii, 4, 71

mutual fund investors' use of financial
    advisers 249–71
  age 251–3, **251**, **252**, 255, **257**, 261,
    262, 263, **264**, **265**
  collaborators (investors) 255, 267
  confidence 263, **264**, **266**, 267
  defined contribution (DC)
    plans 249, 252–3, 262, **264**,
    266, 267
  delegators (investors) 255, 267
  demographic characteristics 255
  education 255, **257**, **262**, 263, **264**, **265**
  employer-sponsored plans 259–61, 262
  employment status **257**
  financial assets 255, **262**, 263, **264**,
    265, 267
  financial literacy 250
  gender **257**, **262**, **264**, **266**
  income 255, **257**, **264**, **265**
  Individual Retirement Account
    (IRA) 249, 253, 263, **264**, **266**, 267
  internet access and activity affecting
    investor decisions 263, **264**,
    266, 267
  investor/adviser split of decision-
    making **257–8**
  leaders (investors) 255, 267
  marital status **257**, **262**
  multiple source plans 259, **260**
  multivariate analysis 263–7
  ongoing advisory relationship
    status 254–6, **255**, **256**, 261–7,
    262, **265–6**
  outside-employer-sponsored
    plans 259, 261
  prior research 250
  probit regression model **264**
  reasons for seeking advice 253–4, **254**
  retirement status **257**
  risk 256, **258**, 263, **264**, **265–6**
  sources used by mutual fund
    investors 259–61, **259**, **260**
  trigger events 252–3, 267
  type of decision-maker **258**
mutual funds
  benefits from financial advice 237
  conflicts of interest 28
  quality of advice provided to plan
    sponsors 29
  usefulness and importance of
    financial advice 235–8, 242
  see also mutual fund investors' use of
    financial advisers

National Association of Insurance and
  Financial Advisors (NAIFA) 293,
  299
National Association of Insurance
  Commissioners (NAIC) 136
  model regulations on suitability
    standard for annuity
    transactions 311–12
  'Suitability in Annuity Transactions'
    model regulation 127
National Association of Securities
  Dealers (NASD) 278, 295, 316
National Institute on Aging (NIA) 104,
  208
National Longitudinal Survey of Youth
  (1979) 231
Netherlands 157, 162–3, 185
net worth *see* wealth
neuroscience theory 234
*New Foundation: Rebuilding Financial
  Supervision and Regulation* white
  paper 285
New Means Financial Planning 23
New York Stock Exchange (NYSE) 278
non-experimental research
  design 159–61
non-qualified assets 137

Obama Administration 285
online access and advice for
  investors 83–4, 111–12, **113–14**,
  137, 143, 263, **264**, **266–7**
opaque commissions *see* shrouded
  pricing
ordinary least squares regression
  behavior change and financial
    advice **187**, 189, **190**, **192**, **200**,
    201, **202**, **205**

ordinary least squares regression (*cont.*)
  credibility of observed relationships 165–6, 171
    asset categories (parameter estimates) **170**
    propensity score analysis **172–3**
    stock equity proportion (parameter estimates) **169**
    total financial wealth (parameter estimates) **168**
    weighted means of covariates **167**
Orlova, Natalia 89
outcomes-based approach 111, 160, 171
oversight board (alternative approach to existing regulation) 315–16

Paredes, Troy A. 289–90
pension consultant 16
Pension Protection Act 2006 (PPA) 2, 36, 37, 119–21, 184
Pension Research Council 321–4
  advisory board 322
  Boettner Center for Pensions and Retirement Security 321
  executive director 321
  institutional members 323
  recent publications 323–4
  senior partners 322–3
performance-based sales 220
performance measurement of financial advice 5–6
personal balance sheet 215
Personal Financial Specialist (PFS) 18–19, 314
planning paradigms 47–67
  adviser-client goal 48
  adviser-client relationship 50, 51
  adviser deliverable 51
  adviser questions (of clients) 50
  adviser role 51
  approach to risk 48–9
  behavioral paradigm 48–51, 56–9, 64, 65, 66
  experienced adviser paradigm 48–51, 59–63, 64, 65, 66
  key contributions 48
  language/framing importance 49
  life cycle paradigm 48–51, 54–6, 64, 65, 66
  model assumptions about clients 50
  risk capacity 49
  risk tolerance 49
  traditional or accounting/budgeting/modern portfolio theory paradigm 47, 48–51, 52–4, 55–6, 64, 66
  unit of analysis 48
  utility 48
planning strategy for when client has more than (or less than) enough 64, 66
plans *see in particular* defined benefit plans; defined contribution plans; 401(k) plans
Plan Sponsor Council of America survey 128
plan sponsors and financial advice issues 29
Ponzi scheme 277
population of interest 156–7
portfolio
  allocations 97–8, **188, 190, 192**, 204, 207
  all-stock 99
  checkup 194–5
  optimal 98–9, **99**
  risk 222
  typical– 98–9, **98, 99**
  see also modern portfolio theory paradigm; portfolio 'mistakes'
portfolio 'mistakes' 187–8, **190, 192**, 199, 200, **201**, 202
  systematic 215, **218**
  too aggressive **201, 205, 206**
  too conservative 200, **201, 205, 206**, 207
  under-diversified 200, **201, 205, 206**, 207
  zero equity **201, 205, 206**
Poser, Norman 286
pre-retirement salary required to maintain living standards **90**

President's Advisory Council on
    Financial Literacy (PACFL) 7
private pension funds 141–2
probit regression model **264**
Prochaska model 63
procrastination 215
professional certifications 16–20
    Certified Financial Planner
        (CFP) 16–18, 154, 239, 314
    Certified Investment Management
        Analyst 20
    Chartered Financial Analyst
        (CFA) 18
    Chartered Financial Consultant
        (ChFC) 19, 314
    Chartered Investment Counselor
        (CIC) 18
    Chartered Life Underwriter
        (CLU) 19–20
    Personal Financial Specialist
        (PFS) 18–19, 314
prohibition of specified actions
    (prohibited transactions) 30–1,
    39, 109
propensity score approach 162–3, 165,
    170–1, 175
propensity to seek advice 185–6,
    187, **200**
prospect theory 56
providers *see* broker-dealers; financial
    advisers; insurance agents;
    investment advisers
proxy access rule 290

Qualified Default Investment
    Alternatives (QDIAs) 119–21
quotation scenario 139

RAND 35
    Institute for Civil Justice 285
    see also American Life Panel
randomized field experiment
    (RFE) 158–9, 162, 175
Rappaport, Anna xviii, 4
Registered Investment Adviser (RIA)
    firms 2–3, 107, 243

regression analysis 161
    see also ordinary least squares
        regression
regulation of financial advisers 275–99
    financial information for broker-
        dealers **297–8**
    see also Securities and Exchange
        Commission (SEC) regulation
regulation of financial planners 305–19
    conflicts of interest 310–13
    credentials and standards,
        clarification of (alternative
        approach to existing
        regulation) 317–18
    existing regulation covering most
        financial planning
        services 308–10
    fiduciary standard of care 310, **311**, 317
    key statutes and regulations **309**
    marketing and disclosure rules 308
    oversight board (alternative approach
        to existing regulation) 315–16
    self-regulated organization
        (alternative approach to existing
        regulation) 316
    standards of care, differences in **311**
    suitability standard of care when
        recommending insurance
        products 311–13, **311**
    suitability standard of care when
        recommending security
        products 310–11, **311**
    titles and designations, consumer
        confusion about 313–14
    under broker-dealer laws 307
    under insurance agent laws 307–8
    under investment adviser laws 306–7
regulatory gap 305, 309
regulatory issues *see* legal and regulatory
    issues
replacement rates 89–93
    projected 93–4, 101–3
    Social Security 90–1, **91**
    target 93–4, 100–1, 103
Required Minimum Distributions
    (RMD) rule 126–7

Retirement Earnings Test 76
retirement income targets and
    resources 93–7
  asset allocation 95
  delaying retirement 95
  projected replacement rates 94
  reverse mortgage income 94–5
  spending, control of 95–7
  target replacement rates 94
RETIRE Project (Georgia State
    University) 90, 94, 100
return-return tradeoff 108
revenue sharing 29
reverse causality 160–1, 171
  behavior change and financial
    advice 182, 191–3
  Chile 141–2
reverse churning 20
reverse mortgage 97
  income 94–5
risk
  assessment 58
  asset allocation 93
  aversion 55, 57, 98, 99
  capacity 52–3, 56, 58
  explanation of *see* planning
    paradigms
  insurable 52
  investment 52, 64, 65, 109
  management 55, 59, 64, 65
    consumer finance protection 222,
    223, 224
  mutual fund investors' use of
    financial advisers 256, **258**, 263,
    264, 265–6
  retention 54
  -taking and workplace advice 108–9
  target 222
  tolerance 52–3, 55–6, 57–8, 215
riskless equities 95, 96–7
Roosevelt, Franklin D. 277–8
Roper, Barbara 293

S&P 500 index funds 215
safe-harbors 119–20
sales force channel 260

saving 78
  education on 83–5
savings rates
  implied 91–2
  required 91, **92**
Schapiro, Mary L. 289, 290
Schneider, Lisa xviii
Schwab 23–4, 28–9
  Private Client 28
Schwab, Charles 25
Scott, Jason S. xix, 4, 52
Securion 29
Securities Act (1933) 277
Securities and Exchange Act
    (1934) 229–30, 237, 276, 278,
    286, 289, **309**
Securities and Exchange Commission
    (SEC) 2, 3, 296
  companies providing financial
    advice 16
  compensation and agency
    costs 239–41
  conflicts of interest 31
  disclosure of advisory fees 22
  fees 21
  fiduciary duty non-applicability 26
  fiduciary investment advisers 33, 35,
    36–7
  financial planner regulation 306,
    307, 308, **309**, 310, 312–13,
    315, 316
  incentives and investment advice 238
  legal and regulatory issues 30
  market and regulatory
    considerations 6
  planning paradigms and risk 54
  registered investment advisers 314
  regulation harmonization of financial
    advisers 275, 276
  Special Study of the Securities
    Markets 294
  see also Securities and Exchange
    Commission (SEC) regulation
Securities and Exchange Commission
    (SEC) regulation 277–95
  Advisers Act rule 281–2

Business Roundtable v. SEC (2011) 289–91
congressional action 284–7
economic justification 289–91
Financial Planning Association v. SEC (2007) 283–4
historical development 277–81
retirement plan advisers 291–3
self-regulatory organization (SRO) for investment advisers 293–5
study on harmonization 287–8
securities laws **309**
securities products 310–11, **311**
securities regulators 314
securities salesmen 276
SEC v. Capital Gains Research Bureau Inc. (1963) 276, 292
SEC v. Tambone (2008) 277
self-interest 217–18
self-regulatory organizations (SROs) 278, 289, 293–5, 296, 307, 316
self-selection 182, 185, 189–93, 195–8, **200**, 204, 207
Senate Banking Committee 285
sentiment-driven flows 234–5
Series 7 examination 243
Sharpe, William 110–11
shrouded pricing 238, 240, 242, 244
Smart 401(k) 16
Smetters, Kent xix
Social Security Administration (SSA) 71–2, 77, 82, 86
Social Security Average Wage Index 101
Social Security benefits 4, 70–86, 101
 adviser input on timing of claiming **77**
 age 71, 72, 77, 80, 85
 annuity decision-making process 143, 144
 asset allocation 90
 Break-Even Analysis (adviser evaluation) 78, **80**, 85
 Claim Now, Claim More Later 72
 Claim and Suspend tactic 72
 defined contribution (DC) plans 70, 73, 83
 financial advice, importance of 73–4
 financial advisers 70, 73, 75–6, 77
 framing impact 78–82, **79**
 Free Loan strategy 71, 86
 gender 71
 health 79–80
 information, use of (adviser's) 82–5
 marital status 85
 methods and strategies for when to claim 78
 new emphasis on claiming strategies 71–2
 prevalence of Social Security conversations 76
 public understanding of benefit rules 72–3
 replacement rate 90–1, **91**
 retirement plan provider perspectives 83
 role of advisers in educating and advising clients **75**, 76
 saving, education on 83–5
 Social Security Administration (SSA) 71–2, 77, 82, 86
 Social Security Optimizer 84
 spousal 82
 training of representatives 84–5
 user-friendly content and presentation of online information 84
 wealth and dynamic modeling 98, 99
 when to claim in different scenarios **81**
 widows 72
Society of Actuaries, Fellow of (FSA) 20
socioeconomic controls and benefits from financial advice 235
Solis, Secretary 293
spending, control of 95–7
sponsor endorsement 112
Standard & Poor's 141
standard of care 35
structural equations 175
structural guidance *see* annuity decision-making process and guidance
suitability reviews 136

suitability standard 32, 239, 310–13, **311**
  see also regulation
SunAmerica Advisory Opinion
  (2001) 114–15
SunAmerica model 37
Survey of Consumer Finances 2007
  (SCF) 163–4, 174

target date investment fund 14, 120
target risk 222
tax complexity 230–1
tax-deferred retirement plans 2
tax-qualified assets 137
tax status, preferred 219
TD Ameritrade 22
technical expert (role) 155
titles and designations, consumer
  confusion about 313–14
TMF Money adviser 23
traditional or accounting paradigm 47,
  48–51, 52–4, 55–6, 64, 65, 66
training of representatives 84–5
transactional agent (role) 155
transaction costs 22, 221–2
transparency 220, 221–4
  see also disclosure
Treasury Department 213, 294
  revenue rulings 127
trigger events 252–3, 267
T. Rowe Price 23
trust 60, 217, 219
Tully Committee Report/Tully, Daniel
  P. 281
Turner, John A. xix, 4, 7, 54, 153, 183
  guidance in annuity decision-making
    process 126, 127
  importance of financial advice
    229, 237
  regulating financial planners 305, 314
12b-1 fees 237–8

Uniform Application for Investment
  Adviser Registration (Form
  ADV) 308
Uniform Securities Act 3
United Kingdom 2

annuity decision-making process and
  guidance 142–3
Financial Conduct Authority 213
Financial Services Authority
  (FSA) 241–2
Open Market Option (OMO) 143
Pensions Advisory Service
  (TPAS) 143
usefulness and importance of financial
  advice 229–45
age **236**, 243–4
benefits 233–5
calculated retirement needs **236**
certifications 243
cognitive ability 231, **232**, 235
compensation commission and
  agency costs 237–41, 242
conflicts of interest 239, 242, 244
education 231, **232**, 235, **236**,
  242–3, 244
employment status 231
fiduciary standard 241–2, 245
financial literacy 231, 244
financial planner regressions **236**
household characteristics **232**
household welfare
  improvement 230–3
incentives 235–8
income 231, **232**, 235
Individual Retirement Account
  (IRA) **236**
mutual funds 235–8, 242
potential regulatory
  alternatives 241–3
region **236**
retirement wealth **236**
self-esteem 231, **232**
shrouded pricing 238, 240, 242, 244
wealth (net worth) 231, **232**, 233,
  235, **236**

Vanguard 21–2

wealth 102–3
  annuity decision-making process 137
  consumer finance protection 216

levels by wealth deciles **96**
mutual fund investors' use of
    financial advisers 255, **262**, 263,
    264, **265**, 267
usefulness and importance of financial
    advice 231, **232**, 233, 235, **236**
Whitney, Richard 278
wirehouses 75
withdrawals, programmed or
    phased 141
workplace advice 107–24
    defined benefit (DB) plans 108–9,
        115, 122
    defined contribution (DC)
        plans 107, 108, 120, 122–3
    Financial Engines 107–8, 110–11,
        112–13, 114, 115–19
    401(k) plans 107–11, 112, 114–15,
        117, 119, 121, 122–3
    government regulators 107
    managed accounts 115–19
    new model 110–11
    online advice 111–14
    Pension Protection Act 2006
        (PPA) 119–21
    plan participants (employees) 107
    plan sponsors (employers) 107,
        109–10, 111–12
    Qualified Default Investment
        Alternatives (QDIAs) 119–21
    SunAmerica Advisory Opinion
        (2001) 114–15

Yoong, Joanne K. xix–xx, 5, 250, 275
    impact of financial planners 157,
        161, 162, 163
    mutual funds 233, 240
    regulating financial planners 312, 313

Zick, Cathleen D. xx, 5

CPSIA information can be obtained
at www.ICGtesting.com
Printed in the USA
LVOW10*2111140717
541149LV00004B/11/P

9 780199 683772